ISBN 978-1-332-87833-8
PIBN 10300762

For support please visit www.forgottenbooks.com

1 MONTH OF
FREE
READING

at

www.ForgottenBooks.com

By purchasing this book you are eligible for one month membership to ForgottenBooks.com, giving you unlimited access to our entire collection of over 700,000 titles via our web site and mobile apps.

To claim your free month visit:
www.forgottenbooks.com/free300762

English
Français
Deutsche
Italiano
Español
Português

www.forgottenbooks.com

Mythology Photography **Fiction**
Fishing Christianity **Art** Cooking
Essays Buddhism Freemasonry
Medicine **Biology** Music **Ancient**
Egypt Evolution Carpentry Physics
Dance Geology **Mathematics** Fitness
Shakespeare **Folklore** Yoga Marketing
Confidence Immortality Biographies
Poetry **Psychology** Witchcraft
Electronics Chemistry History **Law**
Accounting **Philosophy** Anthropology
Alchemy Drama Quantum Mechanics
Atheism Sexual Health **Ancient History**
Entrepreneurship Languages Sport
Paleontology Needlework Islam
Metaphysics Investment Archaeology
Parenting Statistics Criminology
Motivational

T. S. MILLER

Author and Educator, former Instructor in Cotton Classing A. & M.
College of Texas, now teacher in the Department of Cotton
Marketing in the same Institution—Author of "The American
Cotton System" and other works

DEDICATED
to
MY WIFE
Ida Bruce Miller
as a
TOKÉN ÓF LOVE AND AFFECTIÓŇ
and
For Her Valuable Assistance in
Compiling this Work

PREFACE

THIS VOLUME is written with a view of placing before the Student reliable data instructing him in the art of COTTON GRADING, and to acquaint him with the present System under which our American Crop is graded for the grower and consumer.

Our present system of handling cotton is a complex and expensive one; and while its development to the point we have it today is the result of practical experience through a series of years, it may be stated that its foundation began with the Cotton Buyers of Europe; and since the organization of the Cotton Exchanges both there and in America, their membership, and independent large Buyers, with the aid of Mill Rules and Rules of Mill Associations, have established the System now extant, of which this work treats. Knowing that imperfections exist in this System, business prudence would suggest that improvements should follow; but before they can be made, it is conceded that the present System must be understood.

This treatise is not exhaustive to the last degree, but covers the subject clearly and in such concise manner as can be compassed in one volume appropriately arranged as a Text-Book both for the Trade and our School System.

Reference is frequently made to the Cotton Exchanges, because they stand at the head of our present System of marketing cotton, by and through which we get our prices to buy and sell Cotton.

It is not the purpose of this work to endorse or condemn those Exchanges, or to exalt or condemn any System for buying and selling Cotton, but only to refer to the Exchanges as component parts of a certain System under which we operate, and to familiarize the Student with it.

The book is so divided into Chapters and Sections as to

lead from one subject to another by easy steps, and by such methods to gradually advance the Student in the knowledge of the subject.

Cotton calculations are so intimately connected with cotton transactions that it has been thought advisable to insert a number of problems of practical utility that come into the daily life of the Cotton Dealer. Every problem is original, and deals directly with some form of cotton transaction, especially those required in *averaging* prices and Grades, and translating foreign quotations to American values.

In mechanical construction, its pedagogical features have been designed for adaptability in giving instruction in this new course in the school room.

The data given is based upon an extensive research and the Author's practical experience of fifteen years service in the Trade, in connection with information given by men who have been or are now extensively engaged in some of the leading lines connected with the cotton industry, and whose ability to impart such information can not be questioned.

T. S. MILLER, SR.

Flat, Texas, June, 1915.

COTTON.

THE COTTON PLANT

THE DEVELOPMENT of the cotton plant to its present beautiful, symmetrical form, laden with one of Nature's most valued products known to mankind, is a study full of interest and wonder.

From its original type in the remote past, development and improvement have gone hand-in-hand with the achievements of the scientist and practical grower, whose efforts have given us the different types we now know.

Being semi-tropical in character, its habitat is confined to parts of the North and South Temperate Zones, where soil and climatic conditions are conducive to its most perfect growth. The tropics are well adapted for producing a vigorous plant, but insect depredation is too severe for its successful culture in that climate, except in Egypt and Southern India.

The fibers enfolding the seed of this plant constitute the cotton of commerce.

IMPORTANT FACTOR

AS A FACTOR in the daily life of the Southern Farmer, there is none more important to him than the culture and production of *Cotton*.

To its production he looks for his chief source of revenue, a bulwark to protect him in meeting the claims of his creditors who have indulged him.

It pays his taxes, buys his home, schools his children, builds the school house, erects the church, and gives to him financial strength. It improves the highways, builds the towns and cities, encourages manufacturing, stimulates the railroads, induces immigration, increases commercialism, emphasizes a New South and leads to a hoped-for higher civilization.

On it the Grower stands as his Gibraltar, and to it he looks for the future destiny on which he rests his faith.

History records no parallel in the growth of any agricultural commodity equal to the increase shown in the production of cotton in the South since its advent in the commercial world.

Its uses have broadened as production increased until it has belted the earth and covered the great Zones to which it is adapted.

Confined to a narrow limit on the southern border of the United States, restricted in its area of production in the Western World, this area still produces 75 per cent of the world's growth from which 66 2-3 per cent finds a market in other climes.

Having grown to be the largest producer of cotton in the world, the Southern cotton farmer enjoys a distinction not realized by any other engaged in any line of agricultural pursuit.

Having this advantage and distinction has inspired him for many years with the hope of being able to dictate the price for which his cotton should be sold; but when offering it for sale, he finds he is confronted with a System for marketing, the control of which rests entirely in the *hands of those who buy;* and since the dawn of cotton culture, the buying element has always been the dominant factor.

This purchasing element, headed by the Cotton Exchanges of the world, has established a System for buying through which every bale finds a Market. Connected with the Exchanges are found Spinners, Bankers, Exporters, Importers, Growers, Manufacturers and Speculators.

This System is founded on theory and practical experience.

Intelligence and an educated membership act through co-operative effort and understanding, guided and governed by prescribed Rules of procedure in all transactions.

The South's monopoly of increased cotton production has been followed with increased world consumption, and her millions of bales arising from the earth, magic like, annually gravitate into the hands of these purchasers as rapidly as the Trade will take them.

To this System the Grower looks with daily inquisitive anxiety for a price for his commodity that will reflect a financial credit for his labor. He lives in hope and works with enthusiasm.

The Foreign and Domestic Spinners familiarize themselves with the art of *Cotton Grading* for *self-protection;* every Exporter and Importer, for a *like purpose,* masters this art; the large and small Buyers alike, the world over, as a *prerequisite for success* in their business, learn the Grades of cotton. No Buyer dare enter the Market to purchase a single bale of cotton without equipping himself with a knowledge of the Grades of cotton. As an essential factor, it can not be avoided.

For more than a century Cotton Growers have thrown hundreds of millions of bales of cotton upon the Markets of the world, but for some cause have never seen the importance of learning the quality of the cotton they sell, and market it as freely today without that knowledge as if in full possession of it.

In the light of an acquired technical knowledge, this System takes the Grower's cotton; in the *darkness* of *indifference* the Grower surrenders the product of his labor.

For the Grower, the Dealer, the Cotton Student and the Youth in school, this volume is written.

To its pages they may refer with confidence that they will find information covering practically every point in connection with the Trade.

BOOK I.

COTTON CLASSING

A MANUAL FOR INSTRUCTION FOUNDED UPON STUDY AND EXPERIENCE.

A WOODEN SCREW PRESS.

A silent sentinel of the past, emphasizing man's original efforts to produce a commercial cotton bale, the form of which was exactly as that made today on the best improved gin Press, and a package equal in all respects. It has sent its hundreds of millions of bales, hugged with steel and covered with jute, to every nation and clime, receiving the welcome of the King and Peasant alike. Courtesy Lummus Gin Co., Columbus, Ga

SECTION I—COTTON CLASSIFICATION, GENERAL.

CAUSES FOR COTTON GRADES

1. Cotton ripens in a period of four months, more or less, according to the season, varying according to latitude within the cotton belt, usually beginning about August 1st, and ending with the first killing frost. The picking continues occasionally until March.

To say that cotton ripens in a period of four months, signifies that the time from the opening of the first bolls to the last, before the appearance of frost, may consume this stated time.

From the time of the opening of the first bolls, the cotton remains green and continues growing, unless interrupted by drouth or insect depredation, until stopped by attacks of cold sufficient to destroy vegetation. While some cotton is ripe and opening, on the same stalk may be seen young forms, blooms and small growing bolls approaching maturity.

2. The early maturing cotton gathered before any rain has fallen gives the better or high quality, while that remaining exposed to the vicissitudes of the weather has the stamp of inferiority indelibly placed upon it.

3. Winds, rain and sunshine so change the appearance of cotton while exposed to their influences in the fields as to originate a number of qualities of it. From these causes originates the necessity for designating each number or quality by a certain name, as "Class," "Type" or "Grade," as "Middling Class," a "good Type of cotton," or "High" or "Low" Grade, etc.

4. Weather influences affect the grade of cotton by causing discolorations, such as *"spots," "stains," "tinges"*

and *bleaching*. Cotton is stained by coloring matter from newly opened bolls, leaves, or squares, after recent rains, or as the result of the action of frost upon half and fully-matured bolls *before* opening; such discolorations are largely eliminated after exposure to the bleaching effects of sunshine for a few days, except frost discolorations, but the lustrous appearance of cotton, known as "bloom," which is seen before rainfall, will never be restored, though the cotton be left to bleach indefinitely in the sunlight.

5. All cotton bolls are enveloped in partial coverings of triangular-trifoliate forms, known as "squares," and when the bolls are ripe and burst, exposing the white, fluffy cotton protruding from the narrow limits of its former prison cell, the squares are dead and easily crumbled, and it is quite difficult to pick the cotton from the bolls without getting a portion or all of the dried, dead squares in small fragmentary particles into the cotton. When the leaves of the cotton plant die, from drouth, frost, or any cause, they are easily pulverized, and particles of these dead leaves often get into the cotton to a greater or less extent, governed by the care or carelessness of the picker. These leaf fragments, in addition to those of the squares, affect the quality of the cotton gathered by lowering its gradation.

6. Each pod or boll of cotton is composed of 3 to 5 parts, known as "locks;" each lock contains from 5 to 9 seed. These fiber-covered seed, composing the heavy part of the field cotton, naturally cause the locks to become pendant from the bolls, and finally fall to the ground by reason of their own weight. Sometimes the wind in its action on the hanging locks will cause them to become elongated to the extent of 6 to 8 inches, and frequently twists them about the adjacent limbs of the cotton plant as if wound there by hand. When so confined to the limbs, more or less dead leaves attach themselves to this cotton, and when carelessly gathered it is not infrequent that the stem and leaf follow the cotton into the picker's sack or basket. After frost, all the leaves of the cotton plant fall to the ground, and if the

growth has been generous and foliage excessive, the ground is covered with dead leaves. Cotton falling from the bolls to the ground finds lodgment among these leaves, to which its fibers adhere with tenacity. Rains beat dirt into such exposed cotton, and often pickers will gather it from the ground, exercising no care to separate the leaf, and cannot take away the dirt. Open bolls hanging near the earth become covered with dirt. Such character of cotton constitutes the Lower Grade quality.

7. Many ginneries are not sufficiently equipped with the necessary machinery for cleaning such trashy, dirty cotton, and quite often wet and damp cotton is presented to them for ginning, which can not be perfectly done; but the passage of dry cotton through the ginneries causes it to lose a large percentage of its foreign substance, and while all is not taken therefrom, the remainder is sawed into small fragments and exists as a factor to be considered in passing upon a sample for gradation.

8. Gin saws operating upon cotton that is damp, yet sufficiently dry to pass the ribs of the machine, will cut the fibers badly, and produce a class of cotton designated as *"gin cut."* Dry cotton will be "gin cut" if the machinery is run at too high speed.[1]

9. Fibers of damp cotton apparently have a great affinity one for another, and when much moisture exists in the cotton, it will be drawn by the gin saws through the gin ribs in unified quantities, exhibiting the appearance of tufts. Gin brushes taking the fibers from the saws can not separate these tufts, and they enter the baled cotton as taken from the saws. These tufts containing fibers of very uneven · short lengths are known by the cotton grader as *"naps"* or *"neps."* Twisted or stringy cotton results from damp cotton passing through the machinery.

10. Carelessness in operating gin machinery often leads to the accumulation of quantities of cotton in and about the

---

[1]This statement is questioned, as some authorities deny it.

bearings of the gin saws and brush shafts, also in any recess where loose cotton may accumulate. This slow, gradual accruement gives sufficient time for deposits of dust, dirt, small particles of trash, oil, etc., to become admixed with the cotton. If not removed by the operator, an excess portion of this accumulated inferior cotton will finally be thrown off to find lodgment in the bale being formed. Sometimes operators in taking away this deposit of dirt and cotton, will thoughtlessly throw it into the cotton, giving little heed as to what the results might be.

This character of cotton is entirely worthless, and impairs the value of the cotton with which it becomes mixed, if in sufficient quantity to be considered. It is recognized by the cotton trade as *"gin falls,"* and usually appears in lumps or "pockets." These "gin falls" are not as frequently found in cotton, however, as other contaminating substances that impair the quality of it.

SECTION II

GRADE NAMES, AS DEFINED BY COTTON EXCHANGES

To determine with some degree of accuracy any particular kind of cotton that may require the judgment of an operator, it is necessary that each class as described in the preceding should bear some name (or number) by which it may be easily known for purposes of identification and valuation, and to facilitate handling. They are divided into *Full, Half* and *Quarter Grades.* Classification can be well defined with the exception of the Quarter Grades.

TABLE I.

FULL GRADES

Fair	Low Middling
Middling Fair	Good Ordinary
Good Middling	Ordinary
Middling	Low Ordinary

Those grades falling midway between the "Full" Grades are known as "Half" Grades. The qualification distinguishing them is shown by the lesser amount of foreign substances contained in the cotton than that exhibited in the first Full Grade *below*. The grade name remains the same, but the adjective "Strict," precedes the name as a term applied for this Class of cotton. They are fairly well defined.

TABLE II

HALF GRADES

Strict Middling Fair	Strict Low Middling
Strict Good Middling	Strict Good Ordinary
Strict Middling	Strict Ordinary

In addition to the Full and Half Grades, there are others designated as "Quarter" Grades[2] and referred to as [3]"Fully" and "Barely." They come between the Full and Half Grade cottons. As with the "Stricts," the name for the primary Grade remains, with the words "Fully" and "Barely" prefixed. They are as follows:

TABLE III

QUARTER GRADES

Barely Middling Fair	Barely Middling
Fully Good Middling	Fully Low Middling
Barely Good Middling	Barely Low Middling
Fully Middling	Fully Good Ordinary

These Grades are measured by the excess of foreign substances contained in them compared with the next Half Grade *above,* or diminution of such substances in them,

---

[2]Recognized by the Trade as "splits" because of this Grade being a dividing line between Full and Half Grades.

[3]See page 46, "Fully" and "Barely."

compared with the next Half Grade *below*. These Grades are more difficult to define.

For convenience, the *Full, Half* and *Quarter* Grades[4] are arranged in tabular form for ready reference, and to show the relative position each occupies to its nearest approximate Grade, also its comparative value to Middling by reason of this position.

TABLE IV

FULL, HALF AND QUARTER GRADES[5]

FAIR		
STRICT MIDDLING FAIR	FAIR TYPES	
MIDDLING FAIR		
Barely Middling Fair		
STRICT GOOD MIDDLING		
Fully Good Middling		
GOOD MIDDLING		
Barely Good Middling		
STRICT MIDDLING		
Fully Middling	MIDDLING TYPES	
MIDDLING		
Barely Middling		
STRICT LOW MIDDLING		
Fully Low Middling		
LOW MIDDLING		
Barely Low Middling		
STRICT GOOD ORDINARY		
GOOD ORDINARY		
STRICT ORDINARY	ORDINARY TYPES	
ORDINARY		
LOW ORDINARY		

HIGHER GRADES — LOWER GRADES

---

[4] See Appendix.

[5] All the Grades, Fair to Good Ordinary, inclusive, constitute the N. Y. Cotton Exchange tenderable list for white cotton, as adopted September 11, 1912. The Grades, Ordinary, Strict Ordinary and Low Ordinary are recognized and accepted by the Trade. Barely Middling Fair is not in N. Y. list. It is rarely seen and a doubtful grade.

TINGES AND STAINS

The Tinges and Stains are qualifying terms, differentiating this character of cotton from lists of white Grades. Like the use of the words "Strict," "Fully" and "Barely," they are expressive of that particular Class of cotton carrying discolorations, more accurately defined by the use of these words.

The Tinges and Stains have reference to the shades of discoloration produced from stains received from the bolls and leaves after rainfalls, or from the action of frost on immature cotton in the bolls before they open.

A Tinge produced by such process, is the same in color and character as a Stain, but much lighter in its shade. A Stain may be so deep as to give the effect of having been dyed in a solution to produce a reddish brown color, referred to as "heavy Stain," or so light in appearance as to fade into a Tinge.

The shading of a Tinge to a heavier coloring carries it near to a Stain, and to determine when this coloring of a Tinge should end, and that of a Stain begin, has been and is a subject for contention as to when and where the line of demarcation should be drawn. Leading members of the Trade and Expert Classers affirm that this distinction can be made easily, while others equally high in the technical understanding of cotton classification, say that it is difficult to draw the dividing line.

Tinges and Stains are the same in character, if the fiber of the one is of equal length and strength as the other—differing only in the degree of color that qualifies them.

Rains beating upon cotton exposed to the soil, or on lower hanging limbs, will discolor the cotton to the color of the ground on which the cotton is grown—thus it is "blue," "smoky" or whatever color the soil imparts to it. It is not a Tinge or Stain, but is designated as "off color."

Tinges and Stains stand in a class to themselves, and are

recognized as distinct cottons from the other Grades. They are graded as the white cottons with respect to the foreign matter contained in them, with the extent of the coloring expressed by the word "tinge" or "stain" for more accurate description.

Instead of prefixing to the grade name of cotton, as in the case of "Strict," "Fully" or "Barely," these words, "Tinge" and "Stain," follow the Grade name.

In a relative way, *tinged cotton* implies a character of cotton better in quality than *stained,* and may be found as a qualifying consideration in Grades of cotton as high in class as Strict Good Middling; while *stained* cotton is not admissible to Grades higher than that expressed as Middling Stained.

NOTE.—The New York Cotton Exchange admits but one Grade of *Stained* to its Official List, and that is Middling Stained. The New Orleans Cotton Exchange recognizes one Grade of Stained cotton, and does not receive any cotton on its Contracts below Middling Stained, nor any of the Tinges below Low Middling. The New York Cotton Exchange admits to its list of Contract Cotton both *Tinges* and *Stains,* but not below Low Middling Tinged or Middling Stained, as follows:

TABLE V.

Strict Good Middling Tinged[6]	Strict Low Middling Tinged
Good Midding Tinged	Low Middling Tinged
Strict Midding Tinged	Middling Stained
Middling Tinged	

MEMORIZE GRADES

Having learned the causes for variable Classes of cotton of the same Type, and the different Grade names for these Classes, it is suggested that the student familiarize himself with them and *memorize the entire list,* before attempting to master the art of classification of cotton.

---

[6]New York Cotton Exchange classification, Const. & By-Laws, Ed. 1906, Sec. 93, p. 75, and Ed. 1910, p. 38.

The study should give a two-fold result: An accurate knowledge of the names of the different Grades, the relative position the one takes with the other, and the comparative value with reference to Middling of the adjacent Grades above and below.

NOTE.—The Grades Strict Good Middling, Good Middling, Strict Middling, Middling, Strict Low Middling, Low Middling, and Strict Good Ordinary, cover approximately 90 per cent of all the cotton handled in America.

Excluding the Grades Strict Good Middling and Strict Good Ordinary, the intervening ones will represent fully 75 per cent of the American cotton entering commercial channels annually, excepting the occurrence of unusual weather conditions, that occasionally inflict a greater or less damage to cotton exposed in the field.

SECTION III

GRADE CAUSES CONSIDERED

Early maturing cotton, gathered before being touched by rain or dew, gives the better or High Grade qualities, distinguished from other cottons with comparative ease.

Rain, dew, hail, and winds attacking cotton exposed in the fields greatly change its physical appearance and quality.

Depredating insects and worms in their ravages on the leaves and unopened bolls of cotton affect its fiber by weakening plant vitality, resulting in short or weak staple, or by direct attack on the unripe fruit, cut the immature fibers and cause discolorations.

These causes affecting cotton produce the *Stained, Tinged* and *Low Grades,* easily read by the Cotton Classer in the exercise of his technical skill.

There being no definite mechanical rule by which cotton can be classed, its quality is determined by the judgment of the individual, whose familiarity with some *Standard* mentally guides him in the execution of his work. If in doubt, he can refer to his Standard Types for comparison.

In passing on a sample of cotton for gradation, it can not
be said that it must be opened two, three or more times; it
can not be said that there must be three, four or five pieces
of large leaf, (say 1-4 inch in diameter) and ten, fifteen
or twenty specks of small leaf, to make it a certain Grade,
in addition to the motes, hulls, dirt, sand, etc.

All classers have a somewhat definite idea as to what constitutes a particular Grade of cotton, based upon what has
been taught them, or upon some Standard, and by practical experience have acquired the art of classification.

Some Classers become very confirmed in their judgment,
and unyielding in matters of controversy when their classification is questioned.

Absence of harmony in the Standards formerly established by the different Exchanges, and the similarity of
Grades that approach each other so nearly in quality, are
causes contributive to the diversity of opinions among
Classers of cotton.

It being rare that two Grades of cotton are identically
the same in every particular, then it follows that one Grade
approaches another so nearly in appearance as to be called
the same in character, and on these resemblances opinions
differ as to what definite Class of cotton the Grade should
be assigned; one saying it should be one thing, another,
confirmed in his opinion, says it should be something else.

In the main, there is a general agreement between *experienced* Cotton Classers as to what constitutes a specific
Grade of cotton, more particularly among those accustomed
to handling a certain character of cotton; as, for instance,
Classers familiar with and experienced in classing Texas
cottons, vary but little in their accustomed line of work,
nor are the discrepancies wide between them as Classers
of Texas cotton. Other Texas Classers, equally familiar
with the same kinds of cotton, if requested to classify North
Carolina or Georgia cotton, without referring to Type or
Sample, might find themselves somewhat at sea on first

attempt. Similarly, the Carolina or Georgia Classer would find his technical skill drawn into question in attempting to classify the Texas cottons upon his first observance of them, and until accustomed to their qualities and characteristics, as compared with the cottons with which he is familiar, would doubt his own ability to classify them, for a time at least.

Weather influences so change the appearance of cotton while exposed in the fields as to produce many qualities or Grades, and to *judge these Grades properly* and assign them in the list of gradation, is *the duty of the Classer*.

Owing to the fact that cotton can not be classed mathematically and mechanically correct, and in the absence of any rule defining gradation beyond that of standardization, it follows that expert Classers will sometimes differ in their results in passing judgment on certain samples of cotton, though acquainted with the Standard guiding their operations. Particularly will these differences arise in determining the Fully and Barely cottons, and occasionally differences will occur in comparison of the gradation for the Strict or Half Grades.

Classers not only differ with each other occasionally in *taking up lists of cotton*, but find by experience in looking over a list of samples the second time, that the results obtained do not exactly duplicate the first classification. The second effort may show a difference of only one or two Points,[7] or it may increase to four or five.

With the "Middling Base"[8] and a Standard for guidance, careful Classers can approximate almost to an exactness.

The fact that duplicate gradation may slightly vary in final out-turn as made by an expert Classer, does not justify the conclusion that the classification so made is incorrect, or not sufficient for practical Trade requirements.

---

[7]Treated further in Book II.
[8]See Middling, pp. 6, 28, 38.

All good Classers will raise or lower a Grade to place it properly in the list. If taking up cotton with the Quarter Grades[9] excluded from the list but *recognized* in the Grade, they will take, for illustration, a "full style Middling" for a Middling; the next "full style Middling," for a Strict Middling, and in this way "give and take," equalizing the gradation. They follow this procedure all the way through the list on all the Grades.

If they keep no record of each bale as to how they raised or lowered it in the first classification, and fail to raise and lower the same identical bales in the second gradation, the results will vary, yet the gradation will be as accurate as could be made in both instances so far as each sample is concerned, as measured in the examination. This is due to the fact that an experienced Classer knows every Grade will not be "clear cut" or *exact* in "style," and as the range in gradation must be recognized, he makes allowance for these divergences, as explained.

SUBSTANCES AFFECTING GRADATION

There being no mechanical means by which cotton can be graded, something, then, must guide the operator or inquirer in determining what makes Grades or Classes of cotton.

The Cotton Exchanges of the world in connection with the Trade, stipulates that cotton shall be graded as to its superficial appearances; which, interpreted, means that anything and everything in cotton that is not cotton, shall be considered in designating its Grade.

The Cotton Classer looks for *broken leaf, large* and *small; stems; broken seed; motes* (immature seed) ; *dirt; gin cuts; naps* and *discolorations*. These are the substances that enter into all Grades in small or large quantities—the smaller the quantity, the better the Grade.[10] As will be noted else-

9See Fully and Barely, Book I, p. 48.
10See Grades with brief descriptions, p. 27.

where, the *Staple* of the cotton in gradation is not an item for consideration, except under certain stipulations and requirements.[11]

It has been argued by some Classers that if in one pound of clean cotton the gin throws the fragments of one dead cotton leaf, the resulting gradation would be Good Middling; two leaves would give Strict Middling; three, Middling, and so forth.

While this illustration can not be used as a definite guide in making an exact classification, it illustrates nicely an idea of the comparative amount of leaf-trash that might be admitted as a proportion required to make the different Grades mentioned, and to that extent serve as a guide to the Classer.

Hurried Harvesting.—In their efforts to clear the fields of open cotton ready for the pickers, many Growers—practically all of them—in their rush to save it, will enter the fields soon after rains have fallen, or before the dews have gone, gather the cotton as rapidly as the hands can take it from the plants, regardless of the amount of moisture in it, and in this condition deliver it to the ginnery.

If an excessive amount of water is contained in the cotton it goes to the press in that condition, producing a "wet pack" bale.

The early picked cotton, damp with dew, is the first weighed into the wagon box or cotton bin, which, added to the dry cotton picked afterwards, makes the complete bale. Should the damp cotton pass through the ginnery in such condition, and appear on one side of the bale, the moisture will soon escape under favorable weather conditions, and the whole bale enters the Trade as a dry one, but evidence remains showing "wet ginning."

Gin saws acting on damp or wet cotton remove but little of its foreign substances, produce "gin cuts," and necessarily forms a Grade of comparatively "Low" cotton.

---

[11]See "Merit Values," p. 78.

MB—2

Cotton getting into the ginneries in a damp condition gives cause for serious objections by Buyers who must handle it, as such cotton is discounted in price from dry cotton when purchased.

Leaks in steam pipes and water pipes sometimes give an excess of water to a bale of cotton, subjecting it to Discounts.

To secure the best results in getting the highest qualities of cotton, none should be allowed to enter the ginneries before being thoroughly dried.

Leaf, stems and dirt are easily separated from dry cotton, but adhere with tenacity to damp fibers.

Bale Formation.—The tendency of the times is towards gin plants of four, six, and eight or more gin stands in each plant.

The "breasts" of all gin stands hold a quantity of cotton called a "roll."

After ginning the first bale of the season, this roll is held in the gin stand, going out only as a bale is formed.

When a gin stand gives up its roll in the formation of a bale, it receives another from the bale following, repeating the operation for each and every bale ginned throughout the season.

A gin roll going out falls on one side of the bale being formed, and if the roll of cotton be of a different quality from that passing through the machinery, the bale will have on its surfaces two different characters of cotton, and will be what is called a "two-sided" bale.

A ginnery operating several gin stands, will carry an equal number of rolls; the more rolls the greater the quantity of cotton to fall in the press on one side of the bale. If it be identical in all respects to the cotton received from the Grower's wagon, the bale will be of the same Class throughout, but if not, a "plate," represented by the roll cotton of more or less thickness, will appear on one side of the bale, creating the necessity for cutting the bale on both sides to determine this fact, when sampled for purchase.

Other factors may cause "two-sided" bales, as when part of a bale is gathered before, and part after rainfalls; or if the bale be made up from an area of 5, 6, 8 or more acres, a part of which cotton has bleached in the sun and received trash and dirt from the action of winds, and the other part made up from cotton recently opened.

The differences in appearance may be slight or more definitely marked.

Bales can be made uniform throughout if the seed cotton be "fed" carefully into the pneumatic elevators carrying it to the gin stands.

Assuming a Grower has a bale of seed cotton in his wagon bed, one half of which was gathered before, and one half after rain had fallen on it while exposed in the field, it is evident the bale made from the two cottons in the wagon bed will show two different qualities in the bale, or a "two-sided" bale.

This can be overcome by the Grower mixing his good and bad seed cotton before delivering to the elevator, by beginning at one end of the wagon box, at the top, and gradually "feeding" the cotton down to the bottom of the bed, continuing in this way until all the cotton is taken from the wagon and delivered to the elevator. Seed cotton composed of mixed lots of various pickings can be made entirely uniform in the bales if the above directions for delivery to the elevator be observed.

Let it be stated a Grower's bale of seed cotton is composed of one half picked before and one half after rainfall as stated, that the first half will produce Good Middling and the second half Middling, only, resulting in the Grower getting Middling prices for it, for, by the rules of the Cotton Exchanges and the practice of the Trade, the "low" side of the bale governs its sale and purchase. The Good Middling goes at Middling price, but if such seed cotton be delivered to the elevators equally mixed, the resulting bale will be Strict Middling in quality, for which the Grower will receive a premium over Middling.

Belt distributers as a part of a ginnery's equipment will greatly facilitate the mixing operation of the seed cotton before ginning.

The foregoing statement does not eliminate the idea that the "roll" from several gin stands may not be found composing a "plate" or thin layer of cotton on one side of the bale, as it is often possible to find such "rolls" of cotton differing in character from the bale in actual formation.

CUTTING AND DRAWING SAMPLES FROM A BALE

To draw a sample of cotton from a bale requires no special art after the operator has learned *how*, and knows the importance of correct sampling.

The sample should be large enough to give an index as to the character of cotton in the bale, and each sample adequately does this in the beginning of the season when the first cottons are gathered, before touched by rain; but as the season advances and rains and winds occur, the excess of damaged cottons that follow, often gives cause for two or more Grades of cotton appearing in the same bale under present gin methods. When such is the case, neither a large nor a small sample will give the true quality of the cotton in the bale, when, to proceed correctly, one should draw a sample from both sides of it.

The cut·should be semi-circular in form, made with a sharp knife, and deep enough to cut through at least an inch of cotton in depth. With the fingers digging into the opposite end of the cut from the Sampler, he should gradually work them under the cotton as he draws his hands towards himself, at the same time tearing it up until he has a sufficiently large sample loosened on *one side* of the cut. Beginning again in the cut at the opposite side from himself, he should draw the sample as he brings his hands forward. The cotton drawn should be a sample of about the same thickness all the way across the cut. Keep the sample intact, that is, do not draw small quantities repeatedly and attempt to make up a sample by combining them.

COTTON GRADING AT THE AGRICULTURAL AND MECHANICAL COLLEGE, COLLEGE STATION, TEXAS.

Note how samples are displayed and the U. S. Standard boxes opened ready for use when called into requisition. (Courtesy Prof. J. B. Bagley, Textile Department.)

If carefully drawn, the sample can be opened with ease and examined readily as to its imperfections; but if not, it will be a poor guide to the quality of cotton in the bale.

Before drawing the sample, after laying back the flap of cut bagging, the appearance of the cotton that lies immediately under the flap should be noted for any damage, stain, dirt or sand, and this surface cotton should be removed before drawing the sample, if any of these imperfections appear.

In detaching the sample, the operation can be performed often by the use of the steel hook used in handling the bales.

Drawn samples that are to be preserved should be rolled tightly and placed in bags, or securely wrapped in papers especially prepared for such purpose.

SECTION IV

WORKING TYPES

NOTE TO INSTRUCTORS.—The following explanation for students' class work are suggestive ideas only, inserted as a form of guide, and while thought to be practical and instructive, your ingenuity may be exercised in any way you think advisable to attain the desired results.

DISPLAYING SAMPLES FOR GRADATION WORK

Before attempting Gradation, a supply of samples covering the entire list of Commercial Grades should be had, or as near a full list as can be conveniently secured, for Gradation can not be taught without seeing the actual cotton. No description alone can acquaint the student.

In securing this list, additions must be made to the Government's nine Grades.

Above the Government's list[12] will be Strict Middling Fair and Fair, two Grades rarely seen in the Market, and difficult to obtain. If omitted from the list, classification work

---

[12]See p. 27, also p. 69.

will be interfered with but little. They can be fairly well explained by the use of Middling Fair as a parallel type for explanation.

The student should not only see the samples, but have an opportunity to hold them in his hands. The touch is very essential in determining the character of cotton as regards harshness or silky texture; to determine whether hard and wiry; course or fine; weak or strong staple; its admixture with such substances as dirt, sand, broken seed, motes, etc.

Written or printed descriptions alone cannot teach Gradation; neither can a knowledge of Gradation alone instruct the student in the theory and practice of buying, selling and handling cotton in all its details. A knowledge of all is absolutely essential to success. Practice and theory must be combined. A technical understanding is needed, but practical experience also is necessary.

CONCERNING GOVERNMENT STANDARDS

Below the scale of the Government's Standards, there are six Types of the Tinges,[13] viz:

Strict Good Middling Tinged
Good Middling Tinged
Strict Middling Tinged
Middling Tinged
Strict Low Middling Tinged·
Low Middling Tinged
Middling Stained.

These are important Grades and require classification.

The Types used in active practical work are termed "Working Types," in contradistinction to the Government's and other Types that are held for comparison, and remain undisturbed.

The Working Types can be used repeatedly, or until so

---

[13]Repeated here for convenience and emphasis.

deteriorated in character that they no longer express clearly the Grades intended.

Display.—Arrange the samples at commencement without formality of gradation. Make no attempt to designate Grades by position.

Endeavor to show the student, by such display, the little and great differences existing in the cotton before him. A visual examination of the cotton as it lies untouched will emphasize this fact well. Note the surface of the samples as they appear in rolls, or small masses of loose cotton.

The attention of every student should be drawn to this point, that all may note the similarity or dissimilarity existing in the cotton, that he may grasp the necessity for arranging them into some form for recognition by division into Classes or Grades.

While the samples are exhibited in this disorderly manner, do not allow them to be touched or handled until the explanation is fully made why they are so arranged.

The student having memorized the names of the Grades, let these names be now placed upon the blackboard, if not previously done.

From the list of samples displayed irregularly, let the instructor arrange some of them in the order of the names of the Grades, placing Middling Grade under Middling name, Strict Middling Grade under Strict Middling name, the other Full and Half Grades the same way, until all have been placed.

Use the samples just as they are, that is, do not attempt to open any of them for inspection, but lift and place them, each sample under its appropriate name as shown on the blackboard.

While performing this operation, call out the name of the Grade of the sample, explaining at the same time the conditions existing that cause the sample to be a Middling, Strict Middling, etc., as shown by its external appearance.

Having arranged all the samples on the table in regular

order, each under its right name on the board,[14] the instructor should now begin the operation of showing how to handle them for full inspection, by opening several times, that many facets may be seen.

In describing the Grades, reference may be had to full and brief description given (see pp. 26, 27, 28, 29), that the student may be enabled to review them at leisure for stamping the knowledge indelibly on his memory.

Gradation Work.—The student may now begin to handle the samples. If rolled, they should be carefully unrolled, and opened at several places. In separating, take a part in each hand, noting well the general appearance of each part as shown by such exposure, and mentally decide the Grade by this inspection.

It will be observed that the samples can easily be opened by layers, and on the surface of them the character of the cotton can be readily determined by its color, trash exhibited, etc., as previously described.

Do not tear the samples crosswise, that is, do not pull them in two.

If samples are abundant, the instructor may tear some of them crosswise in order to show the difficulty of classification by such procedure, and the inaccurate results obtained in that way for Grades, but not for Staple.

After using, the samples should be *rolled carefully and kept in a place of safety for future use.*

After oral explanations are given in defining gradation, the boxes containing the Government's Types should be open while practice work is in operation, then closed, to be opened only as circumstances may require, for confirmation in case of doubt.

Reference to the Government's Standards should be made

---

[14]The Government Types in the boxes can be used instead of the blackboard for guides in comparative gradation work, if preferable. Let the student place the Grades as he determines them in his judgment, beside the box, opened. He will know at a glance the result of his gradation.

as often as required, but no officious handling should be permitted.[15]

Light.—In making display of the samples, there is nothing more important in demonstrating their qualities to a class than the necessary light.

It can be received through windows at the side of the building, or through a proper opening overhead.

Side lights must be regulated with appropriate shades or curtains. The same should be said of light admitted through the roof.

If the light is too glaring, the shades should be partially lowered on the windows, or closed overhead.

Lights become variable as the sun's rays are obscured by clouds, or meet with no interference from them.

Bright sunlight should not be allowed to fall directly upon the samples, and if unavoidable, classification should not be attempted without moving the samples from such a light.

Exposure to sunlight will soon bleach all "creamy" cotton to whiteness and impair its natural appearance.

Do not attempt to grade cotton with a bright light falling directly upon it, nor face the light with sample in hand.

Grading cotton early in the morning with a reddish halo in the eastern sky, or trying to define its character late in the evening with a similar coloring in the western horizon, gives cause for an exaggeration of its Grade to fully a half more than it really is. Such lights are deceptive in their nature and approach very nearly artificial ones, which are valueless for classification purposes.

From light to shade and shade to light, as the passing of clouds during the day, are causes that produce varying

---

[15]In practice, the student should be required to make up lists of different Grades, as M., S. M., S. L. M., etc. Begin at the highest and go to the lowest Grades; from the lowest to highest Grades, or begin at M. and grade up or down from it, which he can do well after mastering the art. See p. 20.

ideas respecting gradation, and care should be exercised to allow for changeable lights.

While· classifying samples displayed near windows on that side of the room upon which the light proves too severe, the back should be placed to the light, with the body intervening between the light and sample—preferably the light should fall over the left shoulder while the cotton is being examined.

Classing cotton under a skylight in the roof requires that as much care be exercised in governing such light as that admitted by windows, which to a large extent is done by movable curtains, as previously stated.

Cotton is classed under three different lights—that from side windows, sky or overhead, and in the open air.

Open air classification possesses the same considerations as shown in both the former described lights, but the intensity or feebleness can not be governed as light admitted into a building, hence the Classer must govern himself.

In classing cotton in the bright sunlight, a better idea as to the real color of the cotton and its imperfections can be had by having the back turned to the light and the samples opened in the shade of the Classer holding the sample. To attempt to class cotton in sunlight reflected from white or gray earth or when snow is on the ground, renders the classification doubtful.

Alternately classing by window side light, or from overhead openings, or in the open air, conduces towards proficiency. A Classer familiar with window side light classification finds it difficult to grade cotton otherwise. The same results follow the experience of one conversant with overhead lights, while a Grader accustomed to open air work could not do satisfactory classing if confined to a room, no matter how the light be admitted.

Expert Classers whose duty requires them to examine cotton under different conditions, can, by practice, familiarize themselves so well with classification work that they can do good execution in any light, except artificial.

The old adage, "Practice makes perfect," applies forcibly in cotton gradation. Perfection can not be attained, but constancy and repetition lead near to it.

The penman does not hesitate to think how a letter is made before attempting the completion of a word; the telegraph operator does not stop to think how many dots or dashes are necessary to make a letter or build a word, but by practice, coupled with knowledge, the two execute the functions required of them intuitively.

The analogy is correctly drawn with reference to the Cotton Grader. He must acquire a knowledge of gradation, with which he becomes as familiar as the penman or operator. He must class intuitively. He cannot, in active work, stop to think how much or how many pieces of this or that are admissible in a sample of cotton to give it a certain Grade.

Usually the first impression in determining a Grade of cotton is the one that will hold.

Reverting to the sample a second or third time often results in confusion, doubt, and generally an error. This is not the rule, but an exception.

An experienced classer, familiar with a certain Standard, will call the Grade as fast as he can open the sample to be inspected.

PRACTICAL GRADATION WORK

With the immediately preceding explanation, let us again revert to the demonstration work.

The student may now disarrange the samples and place them as at first exhibited in disorder, then repeat the operation of the instructor, by placing the samples under the proper names.

If an error is made during the work, let it remain until all of the samples are placed. Should the operator not detect the mistake, and another student could, let the student call the attention of the class to it, and proceed to make the correction. Should no student notice the error, the instructor should do so, at the same time explaining how and why it is an error.

This disarranging and rearranging should be frequently repeated as a practice exercise leading to practical work.

Erase now all the grade names from the blackboard, and remove the Government's Types from view.

Each student with pencil and small tablet should commence the examination of the samples for gradation, as described, and write in the tablet the names of the Grades, as he determines them, and the number of each. After all have examined the types, a comparison of records can be made, one with another, and for correction, with the Standards on hand, or as called by the instructor.

Placing say 50 samples of different Grades upon the table, let them be numbered from 1 to 50, inclusive, by placing a small card, with a number on it, on each sample.

Students should take up and examine each sample, separately, placing the name of the Grade, as he determines it, opposite that number on his tablet, and continue this operation until he has classified the whole 50 samples. After all the students have completed the classification, the instructor should take the samples up, one by one, calling out the Grade of each as he proceeds. At the same time each student can check the calls as made by the instructor, and ascertain from them his nearness to accuracy, as measured by his own ability.

Such proceedings will enable each student to witness his progress in the work, and by frequent repetitions, finally achieve success.

Such exercises can be repeated over and over, until all the students classify with approximate accuracy.

Samples that have become impaired from repeated handling, and no longer represent the Grades intended, should be discarded and others representative of the Grades wanted, substituted.

CHAPTER II

SECTION V—COTTON CLASSIFICATION, SPECIFIC

SPECIFIC GRADATIONS

The student having learned the names of the Grades and what constitutes a Grade, to aid him in his work, the following arranged tabular forms will be found convenient.

Before attempting Gradation of cotton, he should know what to look for when inspecting a sample for that purpose.

For convenience the following tabular form is reversed from that given in Grade Descriptions (page 26) by commencing at the top of the scale and descending to the lowest Grade.

It will be noted in the column "Look for," that similar words, terms and expressions are repeated in several instances. The words indicating the character of impurities as appearing in the different Grades, must not be construed as an evidence that the Grades are similar, but as an evidence that they are alike only in an increasing scale of imperfections, and dissimilar to the extent of the *increased* amount of impurities.

Note the stated similarity between Strict Low Middling and Low Middling; Good Ordinary and Strict Ordinary, in *word descriptions*.

The class of impurities in Low Middling is about the same as in Strict Low Middling, but in an excess quantity. The same rule applies in the Ordinaries.

All the Grades, barring *dirt, sand, stain,* and *tinge,* are affected as indicated by the scarcity or abundance of foreign substances in them.

A Low Middling cotton could be brought to Middling if the excess of trash were removed, or even to Good Middling by further cleaning, if discolorations were absent and no gin cuts or other imperfections appeared.

In classing the Tinges and Stains, the same process must be gone through as for examination of the white cottons.

Look for the same imperfections in grading them as are looked for in grading the white cottons, but decide from the discolorations present as to where to assign them.

Deep coloring gives the Stains that are distinctly shown in the "Bolly Cottons" of West Texas and Oklahoma.[16].

TABLE VI

READY REFERENCE GRADE TABLE WITH BRIEF DESCRIPTIONS

NAME	LOOK FOR
FAIR[17]	Mature fiber, absence of all imperfections. Pure cotton, well ginned, fluffy, silky, lustrous. Color { Pale Cream / White
STRICT MIDDLING FAIR	Mature fiber, clean cotton, well ginned, fluffy, lustrous, silky. A speck may be seen occasionally. Color { Pale cream / White
MIDDLING FAIR[18]	Mature fiber, clean cotton, well ginned, fluffy, lustrous. Specks or motes barely perceptible. Color { Pale cream / White
STRICT GOOD MIDDLING[18]	Mature fiber. Well ginned, fluffy. Leaf specks, motes more prominent. Scarce. Color { Cream / White

[16]See "Bolly Cotton," Appendix.

[17]Fair and S. M. F. are two high Grades rarely seen, and are more technical than real for practical utility.

[18]Government Standard Types. (See Appendix.)

NAME	LOOK FOR

GOOD MIDDLING[18]
> Well ginned, less fluffy. Leaf pieces few, more prominent. Few motes. Good fiber.
>
> Color { Cream / White

STRICT MIDDLING[18]
> Well ginned, more leaf, motes. Good fiber, few naps.
>
> Color { Cream / White

MIDDLING[18]
> More leaf, seed fragments. Few naps, fair ginning. Reddish spots. slight, occasional, often missing.
>
> Color { Cream / White

STRICT LOW MIDDLING[18]
> Gin cuts observable, small and large leaf, broken seed, naps and Spots admissible, few.
>
> Color { White / Dingy

LOW MIDDLING[18]
> Gin cuts, small and large leaf. Motes, broken seed, naps, spots. Dirt perceptible.
>
> Color { White / Dingy

STRICT GOOD ORDINARY[18]
> Small and large leaf, motes, hulls, naps, dirt, spots, gin cuts.
>
> Color { White / Smoky / Dingy

GOOD ORDINARY[18]
> Large and small leaf, sticks, hulls, dirt, sand, naps, gin cuts, spots.
>
> Color { White / Smoky / Dingy

[18]Government Standard Types. (Appendix.)

NAME	LOOK FOR
STRICT ORDINARY	Grass, stems, sticks, whole and broken seed, pod particles, or scale, motes, gin cuts, naps, leaf, small and large, sand, dirt, stain, tinge, spots. Color { Smoky, Dingy, Blue, Reddish
ORDINARY **LOW ORDINARY** **INFERIOR**	The same imperfections as shown in all the Ordinary types, but in an increasing proportion in these.

[18]Government Standard Types.

MATCHING A LOOSE PIECE OF COTTON AGAINST THE GRADE BOX, DEPARTMENT OF AGRICULTURE, WASHINGTON, D. C.

Courtesy Dr. N. A. Cobb, Ag. Technologist, Bureau Plant Industry.

**A ROLLED SAMPLE BEING MATCHED TO DETERMINE ITS
GRADE BY COMPARISON WITH THE U. S.
GOVERNMENT STANDARDS.**

This completes this form of Gradation. (Courtesy Dr. N. A. Cobb, Ag.
Technologist, Bureau Plant Industry)

SEPARATE GRADE DESCRIPTIONS WITH THE ORDER REVERSED, ASCENDING FROM THE LOWEST TO THE HIGHEST GRADE.

Inferior

This class of cotton is made up of the odds and ends of the season. It carries an excess of dirt, fragments of cotton limbs, grass or weeds, broken bolls or burrs, broken and faulty seed, discolorations, gin cuts, naps, immature fibers, and tinges from the soil from which it has been taken, whether black, red, chocolate, gray or sandy lands, as most of such cotton is usually gathered from the ground, and is often damp from this exposure. As a nondescript cotton, it can not be exceeded. It is the lowest in the scale of cotton classification, and carries all the imperfections that can be introduced into any class, and is popularly derided as "Dog tail," as are some of the other kindred Low Grades.

As it is not recognized as a regular Grade, it enters the Market only by agreement of Buyer and Seller.

Being filled with foreign substances, the discount off the Middling[19] price is excessive, and is made more or less by guess. There is no rule to determine what it should be. As the Seller usually has no conception of the value of such cotton, which is not quoted in any official list, the Buyer must exercise his judgment for self-protection and fairness to the Grower. This character of cotton is not often seen, and is not wanted by the Trade, as it is unmerchantable.

Low Ordinary

This is the lowest Grade quoted publicly by the Trade. In its visual appearance it is but little removed from Infe-

[19]Middling is the basis price.

rior, as it is heavily loaded with impurities, but not to that excess harbored in its nearest congener below.

In its make-up, dinginess, loadings of stem, leaf, dirt, dust, fragments of seed, hulls, spots and stains, it has the general characteristics of Inferior, but as stated, a less percentage; and it is quite difficult to determine at all times where to assign such cotton.

While not recognized as "merchantable," it is quoted publicly by the Trade, and a value given to it.

It is penalized by discounting from Middling price varying from 440 to 575 points—or $22 to $28.75 per bale of 500 pounds.

These Discounts are discretionary, and may vary more or less as determined by the demand of the Trade for Low Grade cotton.

Ordinary

This is a hard Full Grade cotton. Its imperfections are many, and it rises but little above its companion, Low Ordinary. Its discolorations are a fraction less than Low Ordinary, but in general appearance its features are very similar. It carries dirt, leaf, gin cuts, naps, with its general color varying from a grayish hue to almost any shade that may have been imparted to it by the character of the soil from which grown, and the weather, before it was picked. ·

If from black land, the discoloration is bluish; if from red land, that shade of coloring emphasizes it.

While its imperfections are many, it does not contain them to that excess found in Low Ordinary, from which the dividing line is sometimes hard to distinguish, but more readily by comparison of the two Grades.

The Trade penalizes it heavily; anywhere from 320 to 375 Points, or $16 to $18.75 below the price of Middling cotton per 500 pound bale.

These Discounts are variable.

Strict Ordinary

This Grade, like the others preceding it, is a hard Grade of cotton.

Its external appearance, as shown by sample, bears great similarity to Ordinary. The prevailing characteristics of this cotton are significantly expressed as of the Ordinary Types; yet it shows to have less impurities than exhibited in its predecessors down the line. It shows leaf, dirt, dust or sand, discolorations, fragments of stem, seeds, hulls, and evidences of bad ginning by reason of its physical condition before passing through the gin, yet *less* motes, gin cuts, and imperfections than Ordinary.

It is a Half Grade cotton, but not quoted in the official list of merchantable cotton. This Grade is not recognized by some dealers in the Cotton Trade, and yet is so recognized by others. Showing less impurities than Ordinary, places it in the Half Grade column.

Its Discounts from Middling are not so excessive as Ordinary. No definite rule can be given to say what they should be, but as taken by the Trade, judgment would prescribe a less penalty than for Ordinary.

Good Ordinary

This is the lowest Grade of white cotton that can be applied on Contract in settlement of Future Sales on either the Liverpool, New York or New Orleans Cotton Exchange.

It is a Full Grade cotton, and regularly quoted in the merchantable list.

Its imperfections consist of some tinge or stain and not more than 1 per cent of dirt, sand or dust, also leaf particles, a sprinkle of motes, seed fragments, and occasional gin cuts. These extraneous substances and shades of coloring are less in evidence than in Strict Ordinary. Like the Lower Grades preceding it in the Ordinary Types, a large per cent of this cotton is picked up from the soil and off the limbs of the cotton plant, and its shading of tinge is pronounced, according to the character of the land from which it is gathered.

Its Type should be studied closely, as it is a Full Grade and bears a distinction which should be remembered in classifying it.

While recognized as the lowest Grade in white cotton by the Cotton Exchanges mentioned, it is not an absolutely white cotton; for it may carry spots and discolorations more or less marked, although less than its adjacent Half Grade below it, and yet not a Tinge or Stain as those terms are used.

Good Ordinary receives less penalty as a Discount from the Middling base than any of the Ordinary cottons described preceding it, for the reason of its carrying less contaminating substances.

These Discounts run anywhere from 150 to 300 points off Middling—$7.50 to $15 per bale, governed by the Market in which it is offered and the demands of the Trade for such a Class of cotton.

Discounts are heavy when the supply is abundant and the demand light; but if these conditions are reversed, they are not so excessive.

Strict Good Ordinary

This, as the name implies, is a half grade above Good Ordinary; the same peculiarities that typify Good Ordinary are the measuring conditions that describe this Grade, except that the impurities and discolorations are not so pronounced. More white cotton is plainly shown with less spots, Tinges or Stains, and fewer motes, naps, broken seed and leaf particles, than in Good Ordinary.

This is the best style of the Ordinary cottons, and while not a Full Grade, yet if the Classer can determine fairly well the Good Ordinary Grade, he can distinguish pretty clearly the difference between it and Strict Good Ordinary.

It is midway between Low Middling and Good Ordinary. It must exhibit characteristics better than the latter Grade, and not so good as the former.

It is most usually found, as the other Ordinaries are, at the end of the season, having received its peculiarities from exposure to unfavorable weather conditions, and contamination with substances that produce inferiority.

This completes the list of Ordinary cottons. They constitute the list of *very Low Grades, and are the most difficult to classify of all the white cottons.*

While known as white cottons, they all divulge evidences of coloring, yet the coloring is not so pronounced as to give such proof of general discoloration as is seen in the Tinges and Stains.

It must be remembered that the coloring disappears gradually as the Grades become classified in a higher order; that is, where discoloration or dinginess appears excessive in the very Low Grade, as in Inferior or Low Ordinary, it is distinctively and markedly less in Strict Good Ordinary.

While the Ordinaries are classed as the other Grades, by their general appearance as to dirt, leaf, stem and color, the *touch* is another factor to help guide the Classer in establishing gradation.

Classing a sample of cotton in the hand, or pressing it between the hands will give emphasis to the character of the loadings by the feeling of the excessive amount of substances contained therein. Whole and broken seed, broken bolls, sticks and dirt are readily distinguished in this way. Opening the sample exposes them largely to the eye, but the hand can give a good idea as to the excess or diminution of such materials in the cotton.

A sample carrying a percentage of dirt or sand is more readily distinguished by its weight (if in excess), or by the hand, than by the eye.

Both touch and sight are essential as guides to good judgment in classing cotton.

As the Strict Grades are not quoted in any of the daily reports, no definite Discount can be given as to what should come off for Strict Good Ordinary Suffice it to say it will be less than for Good Ordinary, conditions being equal.

The Trade Discount varies from 140 to 200 points off Middling—$7.00 to $10.00 per bale. Trade requirements, location and conditions of the Market are contributory factors.

Low Middling

A Full Grade Cotton, superior in all its qualifying considerations to Strict Good Ordinary, but like that Grade, a little color is admissible, in irregular quantities, yet not to such extent as to give it a *tinged* or *stained* appearance. Particles of broken seed, leaf and motes may be seen.

The leaf may appear in large or small fragments with a minimum quantity of other things that go to destroy cleanliness and create imperfections, as some gin cuts and naps are barely perceptible. Its percentage of loadings must of necessity be less than Strict Good Ordinary, evidencing a better quality of cotton in all respects.

From a clearcut sample of it, the student should impress upon his memory its peculiar features and superficial appearances, with the view of establishing it indelibly in his mind.

The student acquainting himself with the Full Grades can, with a greater degree of accuracy, familiarize himself with the intervening Half Grades, and can more readily approach a nearness to perfection in cotton grading.

It should be remembered, however, that a perfect classification can not be made, but an approximation to it is quite possible.

Should this Grade be well ginned, but exhibit too much trash, too much color, its gradation would fall to Strict Good Ordinary.

This Grade is distinctive in character, and like all Full Grades, may be of such good quality as to almost reach the Half Grade above; or so poor as to fall almost to the Half Grade below, when "Fully" and "Barely" apply.

As the Grades get better in the ascending scale below Middling, the Discounts become less and less.

Low Middling, being a good style of Low Grade cotton below Middling, is subjected to a small but variable Discount compared with the Grades beneath it.

Its Discounts range from 50 to 125 points off Middling, amounting to $2.50 to $6.25 per bale.

Strict Low Middling

This Half Grade above Low Middling possesses the qualities of that Grade to a lesser degree, but shows in its general characteristics less of these imperfections or colorings, more especially exhibited in spots, and may have a faded, dingy blue appearance, as indicated by weather markings.

The carelessness of the pickers is clearly stamped in this Grade, but not so marked as in Low Middling. To the touch it does not reveal the excessive loadings of hulls, broken and faulty seed, motes, etc., that its lower Full Grade neighbor carries. Evidences show much more white cotton, still the distinguishing marks of Low Grade are clearly evident in a modified expression.

It may be well ginned, devoid of all discolorations, naps, gin cuts, free from motes and remnants of seed, but if heavily sprinkled with much leaf in a finely powdered form, as if injected with a pepper box, such disqualifying substances stamp it with the Strict Low Middling class. Off color, as in other Grades, lowers its value.

Falling so close to Middling, its Discount in value is very slight, ranging anywhere from 25 to 37 1-2 Points—$1.25 to $1.87 1-2 per bale, most usually around 5-16 of a cent, or 31 1-4 Points.

Middling

This Grade has a double signification. It is the starting point from which all other Grades are measured, also the *base* from which all other Grades are valued, whether deliverable "on spot" or against a sale for Future delivery on some Cotton Exchange.

It can be classed as Middling White, Middling Tinged, Middling Stained, or Middling Off Color.

NOTE.—Reference to it here will be as a white cotton.

Middling cotton being the Basis Grade and the one receiving the Basis Value in all the Markets of the World, should be well studied for the permanent mental impression it may make.

Too much care can not be bestowed upon it to become familiar with its Class, neither should the fact be lost sight of that the quality of cotton considered Middling in one Market is not always Middling in another, because of varying standards having existed.

Middling in America is not the same type called Middling in Europe—to distinguish which the Trade quotes Middling Liverpool, Bremen or Havre class, Middling New York or New Orleans class.

Middling[20] is a wide departure from the Ordinary Types, as it may or may not show a slight evidence of weather exposure, but no evidence of having been taken from the soil.

By reason of good ginning (having been picked dry), it will come in the Middling Class, even though slight spots may appear; but they must be hardly perceptible.

An occasional mote or seed fragment may be seen, but not in excess, and leaf trash is permissible if not too finely powdered. Its general characteristics are white cotton "good color," either white or "creamy," both of which are

---

[20]See Appendix.

taken for "good color." A dingy appearance, tinge or stain would discard it from the Middling white cotton.

Like all Full and Half Grades, this class of cotton does not present to the eye the same superficial appearance in each and every sample, for the reason that damp cotton passing through the ginnery, though almost free from leaf, motes or other substances, can not be classed as Middling because of *gin cutting* and its nappy condition; it can not be taken for Middling though carefully picked and well ginned, if discoloration is in excess, or too many spots of color; but the gradation of the amount of leaf, or fragmentary particles that might appear to affect the Grade, as to render the cotton a "hard type of Middling," a "clear cut type," or a "Full style of Middling," sometimes in the parlance of the Trade, expressed as "Middling shy" or "Middling full," indicate that the Type of Middling may vary from a definite Standard, and while one sample is "off" in style, another is "full;" yet both would be taken for Middling.

This variability in range is found in all the cotton Grades, regardless whether Full or Half.

Middling is the beacon to which all other Grades point. Every Grade is classed with reference to Middling, as being superior or inferior to it, respecting superficial qualifications shown in the cotton.

Briefly, Middling cotton is white, practically free from gin cuts, naps, yet some motes or pieces of cotton seed may be seen, with pieces of large leaf, say 1-8 to 1-4 inch in diameter, but scant in quantity.

Middling usually shows the colors of the Higher Grades, but the excess of impurities confines it to its designated position.

As it is the "Basis Grade," there is neither any Discount taken from, nor any Premium added to it, but the calculations for all other Grades are made with reference to Middling—except when cotton is handled at an average price or on even-running Types.[21]

---

[21]See p. 89, "Even Running Cotton."

On all Contracts having Middling cotton as the basis, it has the distinction of being the Grade securing the exact price indicated in the Contract. All other Grades bear a relationship thereto, and their values are measured by it.

Quotations in Markets where cotton for Future delivery is traded in are for *Middling Upland*.

Strict Middling

This is another Half Grade in the ascending scale, being a little better than Middling in its general appearance as regards the amount of leaf trash or similar imperfections it may have. It is a cotton of good color, well ginned, bearing a great resemblance to Good Middling in this respect, but its excess of small particles of broken leaf, of which its impurities consist mostly, confine it to the Half Grade cotton. Such cotton, if more heavily loaded with similar particles of trash, would fall to the Middling Grade; if lighter it would be advanced to Good Middling.

Abnormal weather conditions are not apparent in this cotton; the hands of careful pickers bespeak for it great consideration, and its Class is regarded as one of the higher type Grades.

Its quality being superior to Middling puts it in the class of cottons receiving *premium* values, which sometimes range from 12 1-2 to 31 1-4 points "on" Middling, that is, these values would be added to the price of Middling, equal to 62 1-2 cents to $1.56 1-4 per bale of 500 pounds weight, but the usual variance is 12 1-2 to 25 points on Middling, expressed as: 1-8 to 1-4 "on."

When a great scarcity of High Grades exists, the Premium may be so abnormal, relative to Trade values as to reach in such cases, 5-16 or 3-8 of a cent, although the latter figure would be exceptional.

Good Middling

This is a Full Grade of the "Higher Grade" cottons.

It has good color, creamy or white tint, well ginned, free

from gin cuts or naps, and its "bloom" or lustrous appearance gives it that distinctive character found only in the High Grades.

Leaf trash, sparsely exhibited, but not too finely powdered, is clearly shown. A faulty small seed may occasionally be seen or felt, but not in quantities. The cotton is soft, fluffy and almost free from impurities except those admissible as stated in the foregoing description. Any excess of trash would shade this Grade to a lower Class, while reducing the quantity of trash, other qualifications being equal, would advance the Grade to Strict Good Middling or perhaps only to Fully Good Middling.

These shadings are hard to distinguish until the student has familiarized himself well with the Good Middling Type. Having once learned it, the impression remains with the Classer, more especially if actively engaged in the classification work. It should be remembered, as stated, that variations can and do constantly occur in the Grade. No absolute line can be drawn as to where it should be, as all good Classers allow latitude for variation from a fixed point.

Its qualifications are very well defined in a general way, and what would be accepted by one Classer as Good Middling, another would perhaps take it to be Barely Good Middling; yet should he select a Type considered as Good Middling, the first Classer would accept, but possibly call it "good style," etc.

By reference to the 12 samples of Good Middling in the Good Middling box, U. S. Standards, it will be seen no two are exactly alike, yet all are so nearly similar as to be received and passed upon as Good Middling. These twelve samples are used to show the range of Grade allowable on this style of cotton, and the same is done with all the other eight Grades bearing the stamp of standardization by the Government.

This, like all other Grades above Middling, commands a Premium—25 to 62 1-2 points on Middling—$1.25 to

$3.12 1-2 on each bale of 500 pounds weight. These Premiums are variable, conforming to the location and the condition of the Trade. The usual Premiums given by the Trade are 3-8 to 1-2 cent a pound "on" Middling.

Strict Good Middling

Like Good Middling, this Grade is a good type of High Grade cotton. A pure white or cream tint, exhibiting all the good qualities set out in the description of Good Middling, but owing to a less amount of leaf and specks of any other substance than shown in Good Middling, its position is advanced to a Half Grade above.

The lustre of Strict Good Middling is as marked as it is in Middling Fair or Fair, with its superficial appearance indicating the same qualities; yet the greater number of imperfections in it restrict it to its class.

Pressure between the hands finds no broken or faulty seed. Its brightness is a self-evident proof of its good qualities, as a result of careful picking and good ginning.

That it has been gathered dry and passed through the gin in the same condition, is indicated by the absence of any gin cuts or naps.

Its Premium value ranges anywhere from 60 to 80 points on Middling, as conditions may warrant—$3 to $4 a bale.

Many Buyers at interior country points make no allowance for Strict Good Middling above Good Middling—taking both Grades at same price, due to its scarcity there, but large Dealers make allowances for its value, more especially when it can be received in sufficient quantities to admit of assembling it into even-running Grades for special delivery on Contracts demanding this Type of cotton.

Middling Fair

A Full Grade, high type cotton.

It is beautiful in color, white or slightly creamy, well ginned, with its specks of leaf particles perceptibly less than shown in Strict Good Middling.

Its similarity of color to Strict Good Middling or Strict Middling Fair is very striking. The difference of gradation must be looked for in the excess or diminution of leaf that may appear. Leaf trash is the principal element to be detected in the gradation of the very High Grades, although an occasional mote or small piece of seed may be seen. As these substances appear in diminished quantities, the Grade becomes higher; reversing, the gradation is lowered as they increase.

No gin cuts or naps admissible.

Its Premium value is largely increased over Strict Good Middling in some of the Markets. On New York Cotton Exchange Contracts it is 50 points to 130 points on Middling. Trade requirements do not at all times harmonize with these Premiums, but when lots of 50 or 100 bales can be assembled they bring this Premium.

Strict Middling Fair[22]

In this type a strong resemblance is seen to that expressed in Middling Fair, but differing from it only in foreign materials shown to be less, superficially. The same coloring for High Grade cotton exists, with perhaps shadings from cream to white or white to cream, or distinctly one or the other, clearly marked. This Type is said to have "bloom" or "sheen;" that is, its shading in the light would seem to indicate a silky appearance or lustrous effect, and a distinctiveness peculiarly its own.

Its resemblance to Fair above or Middling Fair below in the scale of gradation is so close that it is difficult at times to determine whether it should be called the one or the other, and this can be done only by deciding as to whether there are more or less imperfections. On these points the skill of the Classer will be taxed to separate the one from the other. Should any doubt arise as to what Grade to place upon it, this doubt to some extent can be removed by

---

[22]Not in U. S. Gov. Standard.

comparison with the samples of the three Grades of Fair cotton.

It is an admitted fact that the Higher Grades can be classed with greater accuracy than the Lower ones, yet those at the top of the list puzzle even the expert at times to know exactly where to place them; referring here to Middling Fair, Strict Middling Fair and Fair.

The Premium for Strict Middling Fair in the New York Cotton Exchange official list is about 20 points on Middling Fair or 150 points on Middling—$7.50 per bale.

This, like the other Premiums, is movable, its variation changing as the seasons, conditions or circumstances may demand.

Fair

This is the highest Grade of cotton to which **any** name is attached, and by reason of this position, must of necessity be as near all pure cotton as human agency can secure.

Its ginning is perfect, the color as that described for Middling Fair and Strict Middling Fair.

Every requisite that can be demanded for a perfect cotton is reached in this Grade.

It is bright, clean, fluffy, lustrous, and while a creamy white may appear, a pure white might be stated as preferable in approximating perfection.

This Grade, if free from all foreign substances, and carrying the other qualifications, can be distinguished from its fellows in the Fair list with certainty; but if the slightest imperfections appear scattered through the cotton, then its gradation becomes questionable, creating in the mind of the Classer some doubt as to where to assign it—whether it shall retain its position of supremacy, or be dropped to Strict Middling Fair.

These discretions might seem of little moment; yet, if the Fair Grade can be distinguished definitely, its Premium usually is $1.25 a bale above Strict Middling Fair.

The Premium for this Grade is the highest of all by

reason of its character and position. Like the Premiums for all the Higher Grades, contingencies make them variable.

The usual Premium is 175[23] points on Middling, or $8.75 per bale.

NOTE.—These Grades, as defined, constitute the official list of cotton as established by the Cotton Exchanges, with the addition of those recognized by the Trade, namely: Ordinary, Strict Ordinary and Low Ordinary.[24]

It will be found by practical tests that in making up the entire list of Full, Half and Quarter grades, the difference in the visual appearance in the named Grades is so slight as to make it quite difficult to establish the line of demarcation between them; that is, to determine, for illustration, the difference between a clear cut Middling and a Fully Middling or any proximate Grades.

In listing out cotton even-running, the necessity for this distinction as to the *names* of the Grades will be immaterial.

TINGES AND STAINS, SPECIFIC GRADATION

Strict Good Middling Tinged[25]

Classify this Grade as if it were a Strict Good Middling. The same characteristics that govern in that Grade of white cotton obtain in its tinged parallel type.

The student should make himself familiar with that Grade, then to classify one of similar character, but "off grade" in color, will not be so difficult.

In classifying this Grade, as well as all the others having tinge or stain, first establish the Grade as directed for white cotton with reference to limitations of its foreign substances shown upon and through the cotton, then attach the term "tinge" or "stain" as the colorings would indicate. The *tinge* may be general throughout the sample as if all the fibers therein were tinged, or may appear deeper in

[23]New York Cotton Exchange Revision, Nov. 15, 1911.
[24]See Foot Note, p. 6.
[25]New York Cotton Exchange gradation. Const. and By-Laws, Contract, p. 75, Ed 1906, page 38, Ed. 1910.

some parts than others, as if clouded. If the deeper shadings fade into whiteness, with white cotton conspicuous, then the cotton should be classed as "spotted" and taken from the tinged list.

The tinge, appearing as a discoloration resulting from exposure to freezing weather on the bolls before opening, gives a reddish hue or cast to the cotton, which is termed a "tinge;" if the tinge is excessive it is called a "stain."

To determine a Tinge, look for slight redness well diffused throughout the cotton.[26]

The judgment of the Classer must determine this; he must decide as to how far he can go with a *Tinge* before encroaching upon a *Stain*. This is important, as Trade custom has placed a ban of heavier Discount upon Stains than Tinges. If the reddish coloring is heavy, call it *Stain;* if light, call it *Tinge*. The coloring may assume a reddish yellow cast, or reddish brown, as seen in "Bolly cotton," or "Bollies."[27]

Strict Good Middling Tinged had a premium of 43 points on Middling, or $2.15 per bale, as given by the Revision Committee of the New York Cotton Exchange in November, 1911. This premium is subject to change.

Good Middling Tinged

Classify as to its white prototype.

Classifying tinged cotton gives practical experience to the Grader in offering a wider range of Grades for examination. Examine this style of cotton first, as to its Grade in white cotton; second, determine as to *tinge* or *stain*, and so pronounce it. (Read explanation under Strict Good Middling Tinged.)

In valuation, it is given the Middling base—no Premiums or Discounts reckoned—a point to be remembered in classification of this cotton.

---

[26]See page 46, Bolly Cotton. (Also Appendix.)
[27]Page 7, Tinges and Stains.

TABLE VII

Strict Good Middling Tinged Strict Low Middling Tinged
Strict Middling Tinged   Low Middling Tinged
Middling Tinged

These remaining four Grades of Tinges complete the official list of that kind of cotton as established by the New York Cotton Exchange.

Grade them as stated for gradation of white cotton, and determine the *tinge* as previously directed.

The Trade Discounts are very indefinite. The New York Cotton Exchange Discounts are not constant. The Discounts increase as the Grades descend in quality, but not at an even ratio. They are stated as follows[28] to show the idea:

Strict Middling Tinged_____$ .15 off
Middling Tinged _____ .30 "
Strict Low Middling Tinged_____ .80 "
Low Middling Tinged_____ 1.90 '

Middling Stained

This is the only Grade of stained cotton recognized as official in the tenderable list on the New York Cotton Exchange.

Classify it as required for Middling white cotton, determining the coloring as to tinge or stain. If the coloring is deep, pronounce it Stain. It may be light or heavy Stain.[29]

The New York Cotton Exchange Discount for this Grade usually is 90 cents off, but abnormal conditions, when occurring, may and do increase it.

------

[28]Revision of classification Sept. 15, 1912, New York Exchange, and means per hundred pounds.

[29]See p. 8 for Grades of stained cotton, New Orleans and New York.

Fully and Barely

These Quarter Grades have been purposely omitted from the descriptions of the cotton Grades given, as it was not thought necessary to describe them, because the Classer should remember that they fall between the Full and Half Grades.

Any Grade of cotton pronounced as "full style" or "shy" in character, would be recognized as "Fully" or "Barely."

A Middling bale of cotton, almost good enough in physical qualifications to reach Strict Middling, or so inferior in quality as to fall near the Strict Low Middling Grade, would be construed as Fully or Barely Middling.

Dealers operating in Spot Cotton usually make allowances for Quarter Grades, or "splits," as they are sometimes termed, and give and receive value for value. That is, a Classer taking up a list of cotton will allow a *shy* Middling to be taken as a clear-cut Middling, and will at the same time accept a *full* style Middling for a Middling, reasoning that any deficiency in one sample of cotton can be offset in another sample, if the superior qualities of the first counterbalance the deficiency of the second, and the weights of the two bales be equal or nearly so.

The practice is almost universal for cotton manufacturers, in their demands for Mill requirements, to accept cotton on such terms—taking it as "even-running,"[30] as their Rules state.

Bolly Cotton

This peculiar class of cotton had its origin on the Plains of Texas and similar altitudes in Oklahoma. Situated as it is near the extreme northern limit of the Cotton Belt, and because of the altitude there—two conditions that militate against the successful growth of cotton—the planting season is necessarily retarded on account of the late frosts,

[30]See p. 89, "Even-Running Cotton."

while the growing period is abridged because of the early advent of cold weather. These physical conditions have resulted in the production of cotton of unusual appearance and varying degrees of immature quality, which has received the name of "Bolly Cotton."

Cotton fibers confined in the bolls before opening contain a greater or less percentage of moisture, and are white; but soon dry after exposure to the atmosphere, and if opened before touched by frost or extreme cold weather, the whiteness is permanent. The nearer the fibers approach maturity, the greater is their tensile strength. Another special quality imparted to cotton by frost is a reddish discoloration, not caused by any other known agency in Nature affecting the plant. If the fibers are fully matured the discoloration is slight. The greater the immaturity of the bolls when unopened, the heavier the stain.

All Bolly Cotton is tinged or stained.[31] It is not gathered as other cottons, but instead, the *unopened bolls* are taken from the stalks, passed through specially made machinery equipped for receiving and bursting them, taking the fibers therefrom and passing it on to presses for baling, as done with white cotton.

Cotton treated in this way is practically free from trash, smooth and soft, and if the fibers are mature, it is a valuable cotton; but if loaded with weak staple, broken fibers, pod remnants and heavily stained, its classification is extremely low. Frequently some cotton in the stated area will open and catch leaf trash, some falling to the ground and becoming mixed with dirt and other trash. This, if gathered and mixed with frost-bitten Bolly Cotton opened by machinery, lowers the Grade still more. Once familiar with its characteristics, Bolly Cotton is easily distinguished from other Tinges and Stains recognized by the Trade. It is not a tenderable cotton on any Cotton Exchange Con-

---

[31]See Appendix. Bolly Cotton, p. 49.

tracts, nor is it quoted by the Trade as merchantable. Its valuation is purely arbitrary, governed by its qualities and the demand of the Trade, with differences always at a Discount from the Middling price.

Gin stands not equipped with "Hullers" cut unopened bolls when they pass over the saws, and fill the ginned cotton with an excess of fragmentary particles, called *Scale*, which give to it a low grade and reduce its value.

Off Colors, Etc.

Previous mention has been made of Tinges and Stains as being cottons "off in color," and so they are, but as it quite often happens that at the latter end of the cotton season, Low Grade cottons appear on the Market showing distinct and peculiar discolorations different from the Tinges and Stains, to which no name nor Class has been given, except in general terms, such as "Low Grades," "Off Grades," "Blues," "Reds," "Sandies," "Dusties," etc.

Cotton gathered late in the season from black land areas, a large percentage of which has been taken from the ground on which it had fallen, has imparted to it a distinct blueness not found elsewhere, and so indelibly stamped as to defy the rays of the sun to bleach it.

Such character of cotton is referred to in the parlance of the Trade as "Blue Cotton" or "Blues." The causes that give to it the discolorations of blueness from black or dark land, are the same that produce "Reds" or "Greys" from red or grey soil. The Greys resemble Light Blues so closely as to be termed Light Blues, usually.

Blues and Reds do not always have perished Staple, although weak Staple is characteristic of them.

While being difficult to grade, it is also quite puzzling many times to determine just what values to place on them, and the new beginner should be given advisory precaution not to buy such cotton until after submitting samples to experienced Dealers, or to those making a specialty of handling Low Grades, Off Colors, &c.; even then there is some hazard attendant on their sale and purchase owing to want of agreement sometimes between Buyer and Seller as to the actual qualities of the cotton.

The Trade usually quotes so much "off" for Tinges and Stains, and more recently it has quoted the Discounts for Blues, Spotted, etc.

It would be a comparatively easy matter to determine with some degree of accuracy the Grade of Blues or any of the "off colors," were their Discounts equalized with the Half and Quarter Grades, but as they are not in mathematical harmony with them, they are defined as to value and not to Grade.

For illustration let it be stated that S. L. M. is 31¼ off, M. and Blues quoted the same, then M. Blues would have the same value as S. L. M., and would be quoted "M. Blue with S. L. M. value," or "S. L. M."

Were S. L. M. quoted at 5/16 off, Blues 50 off and L. M. 100 off, it is evident the Blues fall midway between M. and L. M., and as they are subjected to a heavier Discount than S. L. M., they can not be quoted for that Grade of cotton in any way, nor so low as L. M. because of their lighter quality.*

"Sandies" and "Dusties" constitute a Low Grade of cotton found occasionally in the Market. Cottons gathered damp, containing an excess of sand or dirt, afterwards dried before passing through the ginnery, have the dirt or sand so diffused throughout the cotton as to receive the names of "Dusty" or "Sandy." They are penalized with a varying Discount if containing more than one per cent of sand or dirt.

---

*See "Difference Sheets," p. 156. App. 437.

Sea Island Cotton

Sea Island Cotton has certain special features not found in any other cotton, which mark it as one of the best cottons grown for special purposes. It is more specially referred to as Staple Cotton, and may be classed as the prince of cottons.

Its fibers are soft, silky, strong, and range in length from 1 1-2 to 2 inches; generally about 1 5-8 inches.

The condition of the weather at gathering time is a factor influencing its quality, causing a variation in its color and body, which variations are largely overcome at gathering time in the care exercised by the Growers who specialize in the production of the best quality.

Sea Island Cotton is not classed as are the long or short staple Uplands referred to as Middling, Strict Middling, etc., but designated with reference to the locality where grown, with such adjective prefixes as, *Fancy, Choice, Fine,* etc.

The quotations are:

TABLE VIII

Fancy Floridas
Fancy Georgias
Extra Choice Floridas
Extra Choice Georgias
Choice Floridas
Choice Georgias

Extra Fine Floridas and
  Georgias
Fine Floridas and Georgias
Medium Fine
Common or Dogs

While the Sea Islands have been sold by grade names, as *Choice, Extra Choice,* etc., such a plan has been found unsatisfactory because these qualifying terms have reference to the color only, a distinctive consideration that should not be overlooked. These appellations do not give the characteristics as to the length and strength of the staple, two of the most important features this Type of cotton possesses.

It is the prevailing custom now with Exporters and Dealers to sell on Types, guaranteeing the cotton on delivery to be the same in quality as that shown by the Types submitted.[32]

Bender Cotton—"Benders"

Soil and location possess influences that affect cotton and produce different qualities, resulting in giving us the character of cotton previously mentioned as the "Uplands," "Gulf Types," "Texas" and "Oklahoma" varieties, and the Sea Islands.

There grows in the State of Arkansas a variety of cotton valuable for its physical qualities of length and strength of staple that give to it extra merit.

It is a medium between the long and short staple varieties, and in the Market has a distinctive valuation compared with other cottons grown in that territory.

It attains its best qualities from the river bottom soils, producing from them a strong staple with heavy and good body, pulling frequently full 1 1-8 inch. Enjoying such a habitat, environed in the river bottoms and *bends* of the river, such cotton has been designated as "From the bends," "River bend cotton," "Bender Cotton" or "Benders." In quoting such cottons, the Trade places them on the market as "Benders," and those familiar with their classification and qualities, readily know what character of cotton is quoted when such a name is given.

The author has been unable to get the true history and origin of this specific class of cotton. Evidences seem to indicate its origin to be from the alluvial soils of the river lands in Arkansas, in which silt and certain chemical ma-

_____

[32]See "Mill Buying—Northern," in Book III, p. 241.

terials exist that are peculiarly well adapted for the growth of this particular cotton.

While peculiarly adapted to the alluvial river soils of Arkansas, "Benders" of equal quality are found growing in the Mississippi valley of Louisiana, and is quoted occasionally from Missspipi River soils in the State of Mississippi, and it is not unusual to find them appearing in the Market from West Tennessee.

Linters

Linters constitute that character of cotton secured by regirining the cotton seed. This is done at the Cotton Seed Oil Mills, to better prepare the seed for grinding before admission to the machinery used for that purpose, and to secure the excess of lint remaining attached to the seed.

Linters are not classed as other cotton in respect to their qualities, but are pressed and baled as other square bales. Being secured exclusively by the Oil Mills, they are never sold on the open Markets; but instead, are offered by themselves to a class of purchasers who make a specialty of dealing in such cottons.

As a staple cotton, they have no value, and are never referred to as Middling, Strict Middling, etc., as to Class.

Ginning fibers from seed containing dirt, or when the seed are hot and damp, gives a lower grade of Linters than if taken from clean, dry seed, producing in this way two or three Grades or qualities, as A, B, C, etc.[33]

Due to the nature of the seed, that from Sea' Island cotton is never re-ginned, but only those seed termed "fuzzy" are passed through the machines.

The amount of Linters obtained from a ton of seed varies from 35 to 50 pounds, and sometimes reaches 80 or more if the seed have not been closely ginned at first ginning.

---

[33]Many mills make but one quality of Linters and refer to them as "Linters" only; no attempt being made to classify them in any way.

They are not tenderable on any of the Cotton Exchange Contracts, hence are not classed with other commercial cottons.

SECTION VI—COTTON DAMAGE

LOOSE

"Loose Cotton," as defined by the Trade, is not a cotton of any definite character, nor has it any grade name signifying its quality beyond that given to it as "Loose." Under the American System of handling cotton, samples are drawn from the bales for the purpose of obtaining the quality of cotton contained in them, which after being drawn are never returned to the bale from which they were taken, therefore become at once surplus to the purchaser of the bales.

Buying cotton in promiscuous lots containing a diversity of Grades causes the accumulation of many qualities of it in the hands of the purchaser, and when the drawn samples are received in sufficient quantities for the purpose, they are pressed into a bale and become at once a part of the "City Crop."

Estimating the average cotton crop of the South to be 14,000,000 bales, from each of which approximately 12 ounces of cotton are taken as a sample, the "City Crop" from such a source equals a total of 296,000 bales as a result of our Sampling System.

Often a bale of cotton is cut on both sides for the purpose of getting samples therefrom, and in this way the amount of cotton taken is virtually double that generally drawn. Should the bale exhibit evidences of containing cotton of different qualities, it is not unusual for it to receive cuts in many places, from each of which samples are taken, varying in weight from a few ounces to a pound or more, which materially adds to the thousands of bales of "Loose."

It is a prevailing custom in all spot markets and also the rule of the Cotton Exchanges to weigh all cotton before sampling, such proceeding giving full weight to the seller at the time for his bale.

Drawing samples from a bale usually leaves a small quantity of "Loose" clinging to the edges of the cut, giving it a ragged appearance, and this is an inviting source for fire, to remove which the cotton yard man, warehouse manager, or compress employees closely pick all such cotton therefrom, and in this manner greatly increase the quantities of "Loose."

"City Crop" is the proper name given to that character of cotton made into bales from accumulated samples taken from other bales as described in the preceding.

The Discount from Middling value is not constant. It is governed principally by the quality of cotton in the bales, as to whether it is made from high, low grade, or mixed sampled cotton of many Grades.

"Loose" is not tenderable on any Cotton Exchange Contract.

DAMAGED COTTON

"Cotton Damage," as recognized by the Trade, has reference to damage affecting the cotton fibers, and not to the bagging covering the bale.

Bleached or rotten bagging gives evidence of weather exposure, and is the first indication of possible damage to the cotton. Bagging may be bleached, yet no damage exist to the cotton wrapped in it.

Damaged cotton is found underneath all rotten bagging, retaining the color of the soil on which the bale has lain, unless the damage has existed for some time; in the latter case the cotton may be almost black from mildew, or reddish brown from the continued exposure.

Cotton in contact with the ground, or on open platforms, soon damages after getting wet, if the bales are not turned to allow the damp part to dry. Damage results quicker to cotton lying upon the ground than to that resting on cotton platforms.

A bale of cotton standing on end has its fibers pressed closely together where it touches the ground or floor, rendering it more ready to accept moisture by reason of the capillary attraction induced through such compression, and when once begun, wet cotton fibers willingly give up a part of their moisture to others in touch with them, causing the dampness to grow and spread within the bale until the damage corresponds with the area dampened.

Wet cotton soon mildews, and is hard to dry when in such a condition, consequently should be taken from the bale at once, or increased damage follows. Wet cotton underneath or inside of a bale dries so slowly that the whole damp mass soon decays and mats into a lump, at the same time affecting, to a greater or less extent, other cotton touching it.

Cotton fibers have a great affinity for moisture, and the longer they remain damp or wet, the greater the possibility for damage. Every time a bale of cotton gets wet, it should be turned and dried if possible.

Subsequent wettings increase the possibility for damage, a fact that emphasizes the necessity for drying the bale after each wetting. Cotton will resist moisture and damage a long time if it be dried after receipt of water.

A rain of one day or several hours on cotton will not result in damage if it can be dried soon afterward, but if compressed while damp, or confined in closed cars and shipped any great distance in this condition, damage will accrue.

Compressed cotton damages quicker than the gin bale, because of the close contact of the fibers under heavy compression. Cotton always begins to damage first under the hoops, or where compression is greatest.

COUNTRY DAMAGE

Country damage, as known in the Trade, has a two-fold meaning: First, a bleached and soiled bagging without any real damage to the cotton; second, the bale covering not only shows weather exposure, but actual damage exists with the cotton.

Apparent damage is recognized as "country damage" because of the fact that the bales of cotton have bagging that is bleached or soiled, giving evidence that the cotton has been ginned for some time, and for the assumed damage, the Trade often penalizes the bale by discounting the current price. When demand for cotton is good, showing a tendency to advance in price, the Discount may not be applied; but if cotton be offered freely on a declining Market, advantage is taken of the apparent damage, with a penalty inflicted on the seller by reducing the price.

A careful inspection of the bale will easily confirm the apparent damage or want of any.

Actual damage to the cotton is indicated by the appearance of the bagging, as it shows to be soiled, discolored or rotten. Where the bales have been resting upon red lands, the bagging shows the colorings of such soils; if on black or dark ground, the bagging indicates such shades.

If actual or other damage is suspected, a close examination of the cotton should be made by picking tufts of lint from the bale and looking for moisture and rotten cotton. Every place on the bale exhibiting any evidence of damage should be carefully inspected.

A recent damage is known by the dampness of the cotton, and the strength of the fibers having been destroyed; but if the damage has existed for some weeks or months, the cotton will show to be darkened by mildew or will form compact mats or lumps of a reddish brown color with a total destruction of the fibers. These mats may be wet or dried. If the latter, the examiner should dig deeper into the bale, removing the dried mass and any damp cotton underneath it, until the good or undamaged cotton is reached.

Such examinations are guides in determining the extent of damage; but if the damage is extensive, the actual amount can only be determined by removing one or more, and sometimes all of the bands. As much as 100, 200 and in some instances 300 pounds of damaged cotton have been taken from a single bale by reason of long exposure to damaging sources.*

It is not unusual for farmers to allow cotton bales to lie on the ground on one side or stand on end for days and weeks, turning them occasionally to prevent damage, so that when offered for sale, they appear externally as if in good condition; yet a close examination will reveal an actual damage existing. This damage arises when the damp exterior of the bale is allowed to dry but not long enough to dry all the wet cotton; hence damp cotton under the dry still exists, and being concealed, remains to cause further damage, unknown to the owner.

Holders of cotton frequently resort to the practice of placing the bales on poles or skids to prevent their coming in contact with the soil underneath, believing the plan a good one to prevent the occurrence of damage; but if not utilized in an efficient way, poles prove factors or agencies of destruction to cotton placed on them. The ends of poles extending beyond the edge of the cotton bale will receive rain, which is easily conducted along the poles under the bale, coming in direct contact with fibers under greatest compression, where evaporation is slow, and moisture is rapidly absorbed, leading to early damage. Subsequent rains add more moisture, and so conduce to further damage.

Poles or skids placed under bales should not protrude beyond the edge of them if the bales are standing on end; but, if used at all for this purpose, the ends of the poles should be trimmed slanting *from* the bales, that any water

---

*See Pickings, p. 64.

falling on the poles may run away *from*, and not under the bales.

Bales resting upon their sides, with poles underneath, should be turned after all rainfalls, that careful examinations may be made by drawing tufts of cotton from them which may reveal moisture or damage.

Where a bale of cotton shows a small damage on one side, it is usual to adjust it for sale and purchase by agreement between Seller and Buyer, and while the transaction may be satisfactory to both parties, yet such a form of adjustment does not in every instance establish the amount of damage.

The records are many showing satisfactory adjustments by agreement between dealers for an estimated damage, yet when the bands are taken from the bale, the real damage shows to be much in excess of that agreed upon. As stated, external damage may appear slight, but a careful examination sometimes shows that the moisture has not only damaged the exterior of the bale, but has penetrated deeper, and in some instances has gone entirely through the bale.

Cotton having once received moisture will absorb it again with greater rapidity.

Where moisture has penetrated deep into the bale, with dry cotton covering the surface, the examiner should be so familiar with such cotton as to lead him further into its examination. Buried cotton in a bale saturated with moisture, will retain the moisture for a long and indefinite time, often carrying so much that water can be squeezed from it.

Dealers, classers and examiners should familiarize themselves thoroughly with the preceding for personal protection. A knowledge of this will be an asset in every transaction.

TRANSPORTATION DAMAGE

This occurs from carelessness or hurried action of the transportation companies.

If damaged cotton pass the inspection of the examiners,

compressed and loaded into closed cars or vessels in this condition, the damage will not only be retained, but the probabilities for its increase are manifold, to be revealed on examination at destination.

The transportation company will be held liable, because its bill of lading will show that the cotton was received in good condition, and delivered in bad condition.

"Country damage" cotton passing inspectors will retain the damage to destination, resulting in a claim against the transportation company, if the damage be not discovered and removed before final delivery.

Cotton received dry on a compress or railway platform, compressed in that condition and shipped without any rain falling on it while in transit, will be delivered at destination as received at point of origin.

Cotton received dry, having had rain upon it before compression, compressed damp, loaded into closed cars in this condition, will damage in transit, and if for export, the damage will increase.

Cotton in good condition, loaded into leaky cars, receiving rain through the leaks during transmission, will not damage in transit, provided the shipment is not longer than two or three weeks reaching destination, and no claim will follow if the cotton is unloaded and dried before inspection and compression. The cotton unloaded wet does not signify it is damaged. Inspection should be refused until the cotton dries, as inexperienced examiners might report damage when only wet. Wet cotton is not always damaged cotton.

Damp or wet cotton will absorb moisture with greater rapidity than dry cotton, and for this reason should not be loaded into any car or vessel in such a condition that no evaporation can take place.

Cotton placed upon wharves of river fronts or sea landings takes up moisture rapidly by reason of its nearness to the water's edge, and such are undesirable points to land damp cotton.

Let it be remembered that compressed cotton will absorb moisture more rapidly than the loose gin bale; and, when a compressed bale carrying an excess of moisture is loaded into the hull of a sea-going vessel, it is at the water's edge or beneath it; confined where steam may have access to it; so closely packed by the seaman's screw that practically every avenue for the escape of moisture is closed, further increasing the possibilities for a greater damage.

While cotton can be shipped with greater ease than any other agricultural commodity grown, yet too much care can not be exercised in its protection while in transit.

PICKINGS

Cotton exposed to weather influences as described in "Damaged Cotton,"[34] is more or less affected, showing first on the exterior of the bale, and afterwards deeper in it, as damage increases from continued exposure, resulting in finally destroying half or more of the bale.

Damaged cotton not being acceptable to the Trade as a commercial commodity, necessity demands that it be "conditioned" before acceptance by the Buyer. To do this often requires that all bands be removed, bagging stripped off, and wet or damaged cotton taken away, leaving the remainder to be again wrapped as the original bale, with new bagging.

A peculiar feature shown in damaged cotton is the reddish brown appearance it acquires after long exposure, which colored cotton must be removed from the bale before assurance can be given that it has been properly prepared for sale.

It is practically impossible to take the entire damaged portion away without getting some of the good, mixed with the bad, cotton; which fact causes the "pickings" to show different qualities of it.

[34]See Damaged Cotton, p. 57.

Owing to carelessness or willful negligence practiced by growers in not properly protecting their cotton at home or storing it in some public warehouse, it is left to suffer the penalties inflicted by weather exposure, for which the farmer pays in damaged cotton when he offers it for sale, and often the penalty proves excessive.

To prepare such cotton for market, "Pickeries" have been established in several of the Southern market centers where thousands of bales are treated annually, while large quantities of "pickings" are gathered at the compresses from damaged cotton that accumulates there, along with other cotton. Experience has shown that moisture lingers a long time in a bale of cotton after once getting in it, and to preserve the integrity of the bale, all wet cotton must be removed. For this purpose "pickeries" and compresses prepare platforms for displaying damaged, wet cotton to sunlight and air for drying it thoroughly, after which hand pickers separate the different qualities of pickings into different lots, putting the best cotton to itself, the next best to itself, etc., until the whole is assorted and again rebaled for market into bales containing the separated qualities of cotton.

Recently inventors have given to us the combing gin that has proven itself to be of great service in re-ginning "Loose" and "Pickings" in preparing them for a better commercial value.

Separating the better Grades from the medium or inferior ones, ana passing them through combing gins or cards in separate divisions, adds greatly to the value of the cotton by increasing its gradation, but the operation reduces its staple value by breaking or cutting a large per cent of the fibers.

Damaged cotton is a fruitful source for the origination of thousands of claims against transportation companies whose agents sign bills of lading stating that the cotton received is in good condition at the time of acceptance for shipment, but followed with claims for damage after reaching destination.

No doubt the large number of claims, amounting to hundreds of thousands of dollars, is caused in part by the inability of the transportation agents to discover the damaged cotton when received, and the absence of any proper or correct guide to tell them how to determine damaged cotton.

No records are extant giving fully the loss inflicted upon the South by reason of the carelessness of the Growers in not protecting their cotton from weather exposure; but it is safe to say that it will run into millions of dollars annually, more or less, according to the character of the weather obtaining during the season for gathering, and the time immediately following it.

The Trade, knowing the approximate loss from the cotton crop caused through sampling and weather damage, estimates its percentage, and deduct for it in making quotations for purchase. This charge falls, of course, upon the Grower.

"Pickings" are not tenderable on any Cotton Exchange Contract, nor quoted at any price by the Trade, hence no quotations are given for their purchase.

No definite Discount is made for them from the Middling price.

COTTON FIBERS

Cotton fibers are long hollow tubes, possessing transverse joints at irregular intervals, and when these tubes are deprived of moisture, they appear flattened and more or less curled. The twists in ripe or mature fibers are more prominent than those shown in immature ones and give to good cotton the quality of buoyancy, known in trade parlance as "body." Such fibers have the greater tensile strength and give to commercial cottons their best value for fabrication into yarns or cloths, and are the most eagerly sought by thread manufacturers, especially if they show to be of the requisite length.

When twisted fibers are brought into contact with each

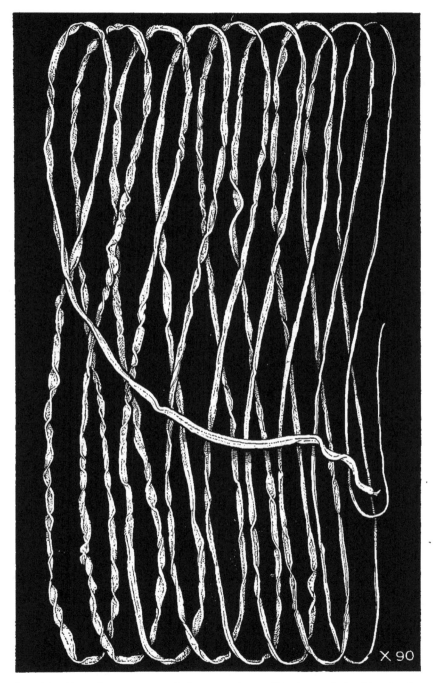

Complete fiber of cotton magnified ninety times   The base of the fiber is shown in front, and is the most massive portion   The front end or tip of the fiber is shown at the right and is very much finer   Observe that the fiber has a special form of attachment to the seed. If the fiber is ripe and the seed cotton is dry when ginned, other, the microscope shows that they cling together and twist about each other with remarkable tenacity, which is a valuable feature for giving strength to a thread when many fibers are wound together to make it.

Immature fibers do not exhibit that buoyancy shown in the mature ones. They do not show so much curl or twist, and when drawn out are not so inclined to assume their former curled shape, hence a lack of buoyancy or good body.

Immature and weakened fibers possess qualities in common; the one may be weak from insufficient growth, the other from decay brought on by exposure.

Cotton exposed to weather conditions alternating frequently from wet to dry, soon suffers impairment or destruction of the vitality of its fibers, and the same result follows if the cotton be stored, but a longer time is required to bring about this result.

The humidity of the atmosphere rarely remains the same for 36 hours, and each and every change is quickly recorded by the altered weight of the cotton, due to the fact of the fibers taking up moisture or giving it off as conditions vary. This repeated change of the humidity and dryness of the cotton fiber will finally destroy its tensile strength, though protected from weather influences by ample shelter. The cotton on the outside of the bale is the first to show the attacks of time and exposure, and its fibers are the first to become impaired. Fibers buried deep in the bale remain vital indefinitely.

---

each fiber tends to break away at the base Note that throughout the greater part of its length the fiber tapers regularly. Here and there the fiber is twisted first one way, then another. This feature is known under the descriptive name of spirality. It is a mistake, however, to regard the fiber as a continuous spiral. An examination will show that for two or three turns the fiber is twisted to the right and this twist is followed by a reverse twist of about equal length. These pairs of twists may be seen throughout the middle portion of the fiber. They are less pronounced near the base and for a long distance below the tip. The fiber shown is of such a size that if uncoiled and straightened out it would measure nearly ten feet in length. It should be borne in mind that this drawing has been made with the very greatest care and that it represents the facts faithfully Only the attitude of the fiber is abnormal In order to get all into the compass of one of the pages of this publication it was necessary to coil the fiber. A cotton fiber would never normally assume such a form. Copied by consent and courtesy Dr. N A. Cobb, Washington, D. C.

The fiber being a natural product of the seed, continues to receive strength from it after the seed cotton is gathered and stored. Tests made to determine this fact have demonstrated that the storing of seed cotton in a dry place for several weeks caused the fibers to become a rich cream yellow by taking up oil from the seed, and at the same time increased the tensile strength.[35]

SECTION VII

STANDARDS

To guide the student in cotton classification, samples of cotton showing the different Grades should be placed before him.

These Types should conform as nearly as possible to what the name of the *Grade* implies, and for that purpose those Grades selected by the Agricultural Department of the United States known as Government Standards[36] will be referred to, with exceptions noted.

These Types, having been made by expert Classers, give by actual representation what is termed a Grade or Half Grade of cotton as definitely, perhaps, as it can be done.

The Grades known as the Government's Official list are made up of five Full and four Half Grades, with the name of each on the box.

---

[35]This was verified by a practical test made in Texas by the author in 1882.

[36]See U. S. Government Standards, Appendix.

TABLE IX

They are designated as

Middling Fair	Strict Low Middling
Strict Good Middling	Low Middling
Good Middling	Strict Good Ordinary
Strict Middling	Good Ordinary
Middling	

In establishing these Full and Half Grades, the Government conceived the whole range of gradation to be sufficiently covered for all practical purposes in marketing the American cotton crops.

The boxes contain 12 samples of each Grade, showing the range of variation of each Type.

Each sample in the box is representative of the Grade therein.

It will be noticed that no two samples in each box are alike, yet they approach each other so nearly as to be called the same Grade, and furnish a corroboration of the statement that cotton can not be *exactly* graded.

If one of the twelve samples is taken as a definite type of that Grade, then the eleven other samples are similarities.

If the one selected as a *true* type of that Grade be held as the ideal one, it would be a difficult task to find another *similar in every respect*, hence the necessity, for practical purposes, of approximating as near to an ideal as consistent with the requirements of the Trade, and skilled ability can perform.

The Government Standards are representatives of the Grades named, and should not be disturbed or handled as "working types," but for practical purposes, samples to be classed should be graded by comparison with them.

Matching samples is not grading cotton, but where the gradation is based on superficial characteristics, it can be

GRADING COTTON, DEPARTMENT OF AGRICULTURE,
WASHINGTON, D. C.

A general view of the classification room with the working Types
on the tables and sets being made up to match the Standards   Note
the reception of light from overhead and back of the graders through
side windows   Courtesy Dr N A Cobb, Ag Technologist, Bureau
Plant Industry.

fairly well done by comparison; and is the only way it can be accomplished by the use of any Standard, where the Types are not to be molested.

By the use of Standards, the bulk of our cotton crops are measured and pass into the channels of Trade sufficiently standardized for practical purposes and for commercial valuation.

By means of Standards, the experienced Classer can grade cotton to so near an exactness as to determine its value within 25 cents, or even 10 cents, on a bale. This, interpreted, means that the original Classer will receive the same gradation from the one to whom the cotton is consigned as that made by himself, because of the fact that both are familiar with and use the same Standards.

If both Classers are inexperienced, or one experienced and the other not, or one operating under one Standard and the other a different one, or one unscrupulously and wilfully violates the ethics of the fraternity in falsely classifying, contention and friction follow.

It might be urged that if A, the consignor, sells to B, the consignee, a bale of cotton, and both assert its Grade to be Strict Middling, this fact would tend to disprove the statement that classification is not an exact science.

While agreements exist in this instance, it should be remembered that numbers of other bales are classed Strict Middling, no one of which would be identical to the one in question. This gives evidence that variance from a definite Type is admissible, and obtains constantly in the open Market.

The starting point for Grade and valuation, as accepted by the Trade, is the Middling Grade, as previously stated, and this practice obtains now in passing upon samples of the Government's Types, as required for classification of cotton under any Standard.

Custom has held to the Middling Type, despite efforts to place it upon some other Grade.

All the Cotton Exchanges, in establishing the different Grades of cotton to be recognized by them as exhibiting the character of cotton they would accept in settlement of all transactions made by its members, or members with non-members, refer to these different Grades as their "Standards," signifying by this that differences of opinion by its members, or controversies arising over the classification of any cotton handled by them, could and must be settled by having the cotton in controversy harmonize with the samples provided by the Exchange.

These Standards serve the further purpose of providing Types of cotton for the Exchange members in their dealings in Spot Cotton, and as guides for Classers in passing upon samples submitted to them for classification.

These Standards were made to cover all the Grades handled by the Exchange, and included the entire range of Grades mentioned in Section I and II, except as otherwise stated.

These lists are called the *"Official Lists."*

The *Official Lists* are made up each season by some of the Exchanges and are retained for the year; others do not make any change in their Standards, if the character of the cotton for the new season shows no marked difference from that of the previous one, but if the appearance of the cotton for the new season shows such distinction as to merit a change, Standards are made of the new cottons and serve as guides for the ensuing year.

Every crop grown is not always a counterpart of the other. One season the crop is said to be "creamy," another "white," another "dingy" or faintly "smoky," (but not the dinginess caused by the effects of weather), and while not *perfectly white* it would be received as cotton of "good color."

These peculiarities do not change gradation.

The Exchanges usually place six samples of each Grade in a box, which are carefully preserved as reference Types for the Classers and the membership. These are rarely disturbed, but for practical purposes, six other samples, similar in all respects, are made up, called "working types," and are as often used for reference as occasion requires.

The samples are approximately 6 ounces in weight.

There are Cotton Exchanges at New York, New Orleans, Houston, Galveston, Waco, Dallas, Little Rock, Memphis, Natchez, Selma, Mobile, Savannah, Augusta, Atlanta, Shreveport, Norfolk, Charleston, Vicksburg, St. Louis, and Portsmouth.[37]

All of these Exchanges at one time or another had their established Standards. Some maintain them yet, others do not. Some renew them annually if conditions warrant it, as stated.

In establishing their Standards, some of the Cotton Exchanges made them to conform to the character of the cotton grown locally; others so broadened their basis as to recognize the leading characteristics of all cottons dealt in through their membership, while others were governed, to some extent, by the Standards of Foreign Exchanges through whom their transactions were made, notably Savannah, Ga., which has practically the Liverpool Standards, because it is primarily an Export Market.

The discrepancy existing in the Standards of Savannah and Augusta (Ga.) is clearly marked; Augusta Middling being higher than Savannah Middling. In fact it is higher than most other American markets.

While a divergence exists in the Standardizing of cotton, the Middling Type may, and often does, remain the same with many Exchanges, the dissimilarity resting with the relative Grades.

The Standards of New York and New Orleans are nearly similar on the white cottons, but the difference between these Markets and those of some of the other Cotton Exchanges is clearly defined.

[37]See page 98.

The Middling of Charleston is widely at variance with that Grade at Norfolk. The difference in Standards between Houston and Galveston is so slight as to be scarcely distinguishable.

The Standards of Liverpool compared with those of New York or New Orleans do not harmonize in all the Grades.

Liverpool, Bremen and Havre have the same Standards.

The Standards of all the Exchanges are prepared in a similar manner, the Grades being determined by the superficial appearance of the cotton with reference to the *leaf, trash, motes, hulls, dirt*, etc., as described under "COTTON CLASSIFICATION SPECIFIC,"[38] with no regard being had for other factors that affect its qualities, such as the length and strength of the *Staple*, which are elements of important consideration in determining Merit Values[39] by those buying for *Spinners*.

In determining the Grades as type samples for their Standards, experienced Classers, appointed as a committee, supervise their selection.

Cotton of the Carolinas does not conform in all respects to that grown in Georgia or Mississippi. Uplands do not have the same "body" as Staple or Gulf Cottons. Cotton from Texas and Oklahoma stands in a separate class from that of the States mentioned, which fact gave cause for the creation of different Standards, and an equal cause for the origination of controversies, by reason of the want of harmony in cottons of similar grade names.

Under such conditions, a Middling in Texas could not be a Middling in South Carolina, Alabama, Mississippi or Georgia. The same rule would apply for the relative Grades.

PRIVATE STANDARDS

Some Dealers who operate largely in Spot Cottons have, for their convenience and for trade purposes, established

---

[38]See p. 26.
[39]See "Merit, or Spinnable Values," p. 77.

their own *private Marks* to distinguish the qualities of cottons handled by them, preferring to call the different Grades by some name or Mark, other than Middling, Strict Middling, etc., as SOL, MOT, 555, or BADE, TIME, or any markings desired.

Such markings are known as "Class Marks," each of which represents a certain Grade of cotton.

Those who have operated under such proceedings for a number of years have established a business upon them, and find it quite convenient, for private and personal reasons, to maintain their own Standards.

Both Buyers and Sellers being conversant with them, controversies are less frequent in their' trade relationships.

TABLE X

STANDARDS COMPARED[40]

The Government Classification compares with Liverpool as follows:

UNITED STATES			LIVERPOOL
Middling Fair	equal to		Middling Fair
Strict Good Middling	"	"	Barely Middling Fair
Good Middling	"	"	Fully Good Middling
Strict Middling	"	"	Good Middling
Middling	"	"	Fully Middling
Strict Low Middling	"	"	Middling

Low Middling
Strict Good Ordinary } No comparisons can be made owing to inequality of Low Grades.
Good Ordinary

[41]NOTE.—At a conference of American and European Cotton Exchange representatives, held in Liverpool in June, 1913, the Liverpool Cotton Exchange agreed to widen the difference between their Lower Grades,

---

[40]As given to the author by Sec. Hester of the New Orleans Cotton Exchange.

[41]See Farmers' Bulletin 591, U. S. Department of Agriculture, p. 12.

to become effective September 1, 1914, in order to conform nearer to the United States Standards. There is more color in Fully Low Middling to Ordinary, inclusive, in the Liverpool than in the United States Standards. Fully Low Middling (Liverpool) has one type in the twelve tinged, while the whole exhibits a grayer cast than the U. S. Standards. Liverpool Fully Good Ordinary and Good Ordinary show several types of "off color." The use of the European word "Fully" corresponds to the American "Strict."

The comparison of United States Standards with Bremen and Havre are not given, because the Standards of those Exchanges are the same as Liverpool.

The American Standard Classification is that adopted by the New York Cotton Exchange, and also by the Cotton Manufacturers' Association of North and South Carolina, and not compared here to Liverpool, as it is thought these organizations will adopt that of the Government at a near future date.

The revised Liverpool Standards, compared to the U. S. Standards, are as follows:

UNITED STATES			LIVERPOOL
Middling Fair	equal to		Middling Fair
Strict Good Middling	"	"	Fully Good Middling
Good Middling	"	"	Good Middling
Strict Middling	"	"	Fully Middling
Middling	"	"	Middling
Strict Low Middling	"	"	Fully Low Middling
Low Middling	"	"	Low Middling (grayer)
Strict Good Ordinary	"	"	Good Ordinary (off color)
Good Ordinary	"	"	Ordinary

CHAPTER III

MERIT OR SPINNABLE VALUES.

SECTION VIII—STAPLING COTTON

GRADE VALUES

Cotton has a commercial value as measured by its Grades.

Grades are determined as set forth in Section 2, by describing the means for classing them.

Grade Values are those employed in the Trade between Merchants[42] and Cotton Buyers who make no deliveries to the Mills.

A Grade Value represents the cotton fully with respect to its cleanliness and discolorations, but irrespective of its Staple.

Determining the length and strength of the cotton fibers by physical tests is called Stapling.

The Staple of cotton represents its length of fibers, but not the strength of them, and it may be short or long, coarse or fine, rough or silky, hard or soft, but to express its physical qualities fully, the *strength* or *weakness* of the fibers should also be considered.

Staple Values are those given to the cotton as determined by the length and strength of its fibers, as required for spinning demands.

. These values modify the *Grade Values* by adding to or taking from them an indefinite percentage.

Staple Values increase in a relative way, by greater differences than those determined by superficial gradation.

Cotton showing a 1 1-4 inch *staple* has a greater value than 1 1-8 inch, by approximately 150 to 250 points, while a

---

[42]Referring to Dealers who handle cotton as merchandise.

difference between Middling and Strict Middling, or Strict Middling and Good Middling as to *Grade,* would probably not be more than 12 1-2 or 25 points, only in exceptional cases.

Each increase of 1-8 inch in Staple length adds practically 250 points, or 2 1-2 cents a pound on cotton of High Grade.

This increase is not constant. A superabundance of Staple Cotton on the Market, with an inactive demand, may reduce such a Premium.

Staples are just as susceptible to market fluctuations as short fiber cottons. Contingencies govern in the one as in the other.

Staple Cotton is classed as other cotton respecting its Grade, as Middling, Strict Middling, etc., then its Staple Value is ascertained by an examination of its fibers for length and strength.

There is no Standard for stapling cotton. Frequent disagreements between operators dealing in Staple Cotton give evidence that none has been established. What one operator would call 1 1-8 Staple, another might call "1 1-8 full," another "shy 1 1-8," or "Liverpool 1 1-8," etc.

These discrepancies evidently arise from different methods in "pulling" the fiber, the Classers depending on their judgment as to what constitutes 1 1-8 or 1 3-16-inch in length, as reflected from their memory, or possibly, from the fact that one Classer may draw fibers of 1 1-8-inch from a sample, while another may draw a staple measuring actually 1 3-16-inch from another sample from the same bale.

All Mills using Staple (long fiber) Cotton do not require the same lengths. Some have machinery suited to spinning 1 1-8 to 1 3-16-inch Staple, and could not use 1 3-8 or 1 7-16-inch without expensive change in machinery or the introduction of new equipment. Some are equipped to use a wider range of lengths and a greater variety of Grades.

Mills operating upon short Staple Cotton are more specific in their demands for supplies.

Selling cotton to Mills in which all their demands are fulfilled is called selling cotton on its *Merits*.

A Merit Value is two-fold: a value placed upon its *Grade*, and another on its *Staple*.

The average Grade used by American Mills is about Strict Middling; and 1 1-16-inch Staple[43] as a minimum length in the production of the better grade of light fabrics.

The following table will give a good idea of the comparative values of different Grades of cotton in connection with the Staple varieties.

These prices are subject to the contingencies of the Market, and the relative values are not permanent.

TABLE XI

STAPLE COTTON MARKET QUOTATIONS[44]

GRADE	Length (Inch) 1 1-2	Length (Inch) 1 7-16	Length (Inch) 1 3-8	Length (Inch) 1 5-16	Length (Inch) 1 1-4	Length (Inch) 1 3-16	Length (Inch) 1 1-8
	Cts.	Cts.	Cts.	Cts.	Cts.	Cts.	Cts.
G. Mid.	20	19	17¼	16	15	13½	12¼
St. Mid.	18	17	16	15	14	13	12¼
Middling	15½	15¼	15	14	13½	12¼	12
St. L. Mid.	Dem'nd	good					
Low Mid.	Prices	advanci	ng slow	ly			

An inspection of this table shows some remarkable difference in Staple Cotton, and the high values placed on the extreme lengths of good Grades.

It will be noted that on 1 1-8-inch staple, a difference of 1-2 cent a pound between Middling and Good Middling is

---

[43]This has reference to Short Staple Cotton.

[44]From a quotation of Staple Cotton in one of the prominent Southern markets, January, 1908, inserted for explanation.

shown, equivalent to $2.50 a bale, while the quotation shows the difference between Middling and Good Middling, 1 1-2-*inch staple* to be 4 1-2 cents a pound, equivalent to $22.50 a bale.

The strength of the fiber is an important matter to be considered in classing for Staple. A perished or weak fiber in a High Grade cotton would so weigh against its usefulness as to impair its value as a Staple Cotton altogether.

A Staple Cotton of 1 1-8 or 1 1-4-inch, of good strength, merits a higher consideration than cotton showing 1 3-8 or 1 1-2-inch, if its fibers are immature.

Members of the Trade and Spinners differ as to what is termed "weak staple." What might be considered by one as "good staple," another would call "weak." These disputes evidently arise from the fact that a very strong fiber is required to produce a certain fabric in the one case, while in the other, the article to be produced does not require that extreme tensile strength.

Cottons of different Types possess different inherent qualities of strength. In one Class the strength is a feature of great distinction, while in another it is not so marked, yet in both the fibers may show maturity.

The Upland Cottons of Mississippi show preferential distinction over the same Class of Georgia Upland cotton, while those of Georgia have merits above those of the Carolinas. The Mississippi Upland Cotton has a better Staple than that grown in Georgia, and Georgia's Type of Upland is superior to the Short Staple of the Carolinas' Upland.

A good Staple of cotton with well-matured fibers has a better "body" than imperfect fibers. A cotton of good "body," when compressed in the hand, will quickly resume its former size after being released from pressure. Immature or "dead staple," when subjected to compression, does not show that buoyancy when released.

The Mississippi Uplands are credited with having a better Staple and "body" than any of the cottons east of the

Mississippi river, with the exception of Louisiana, the Piedmont[45] section of South Carolina, Georgia and the Alabama canebrakes.

The cottons of Texas and Oklahoma stand in a class to themselves. They occupy a position relatively between the Staples (long lint) and the Uplands east of the Mississippi river. The cottons grown in the deep, black soils of Texas have a better Staple than those grown on the clayey or sandy soils, and while not classed as Staple Cotton, they are sold on their merits in addition to their gradation, if for Mill delivery. Their fibers are said to be hard and wiry.

The Staple Cottons grown in the lower part of Mississippi possess great merit, and almost equal Sea Island in the length and strength of their fibers.

The Staple Cottons, both the Gulf Types and the Sea Islands, are the highest Types grown.

The finest Staples are found in South Carolina, Georgia and Florida.

STAPLING

Pulling for Staple.—Light is an essential factor in determining Grades, but is not so necessary for *Stapling.* Any light in which the fibers can be clearly seen suffices for the work.

Stapling being an entirely different process from that of classification, it must be performed in a different manner.

Gradation for the moment is lost sight of, and the sample manipulated differently for a distinct purpose.

Tear the sample in two by force, by slowly pulling it, and note the extended fibers protruding from each part. From one part draw some of these extended fibers. Between thumb and fingers of each hand, with fibers held tightly, repeatedly draw these fibers until they show an approximate evenness of length.

---

[45]See Appendix. The Piedmont cottons have exceptional values, and are especially quoted to the Trade for their exceptional qualities of fiber, length and strength.

After making one test, make several others from the same sample, the average of which will constitute the Staple for the length.

Press a small bunch of these test fibers flatly between thumb and finger, hold them tightly; make a test for strength by attempting to break them.

The judgment of the individual must determine the tensile strength of the fibers as proven by the tests described.

A few fibers can be gathered at random over the sample and tested for length and strength as prescribed.

In getting the length of Staple, the beginner should make sufficient measurement of the fiber to familiarize himself with lengths that make an inch, or more, in length.

Guess work should not be tolerated until practice can give the results wanted.

Controversies arise often because those pulling for Staple are unable to determine what constitutes an inch in length —depending too much on guess-work, and not enough on measurements.

There is an art in pulling for Staple that must be acquired before success can be assured.

With thumb and fingers slightly moistened, the fibers can be better handled.

At the time of drawing the fibers, slightly roll them between thumb and fingers, but not enough to put them in a twist. Keep the fibers parallel and on tension. Lapping the fibers back upon each other each time a draw is made will facilitate the process and give greater accuracy.[46]

NOTE.—Demonstration by the instructor will render this explanation quite clear, yet the fact should be made known that it is much more difficult to Staple cotton than to acquire the art of classification. Dealers operating extensively employ skilled operators for Stapling, whose experience has especially qualified them for such work. Staplers operate individually, that is, each has his own way for pulling staple.

---

[46]See "Spinnable Values," p. 78, for further information.

Showing position of the hands when pulling for Staple

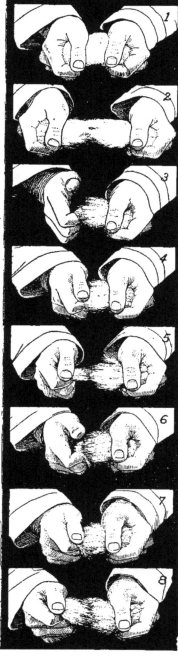

1   Grasping the first lot of cotton to begin the pull   Make the pull *slowly*   If too fast many fibers are broken   Hold close to the ear and listen at the tearing sound produced when drawing or making the first pull, caused by the fibers breaking or dragging upon themselves   This is the "drag"

2   Showing sample when first pulled in two

3   One-half the sample dropped and a beginning made for getting the length of fibers on the remnant left in the right hand

4.   Showing position of the grasp

5   Taking away the loose extended fibers.

6   Loose short fibers stripped out.

7   Repeating the operation as shown at 4.

8   Pull made the same as at 1, with longer or longest fibers of the sample drawn out and held in the left hand

By taking the bunch of fibers in the left hand and lapping them back on those in the right, and drawing them again, as shown at 2, the Stapler can soon arrive at the average length

There is no definite number of times to repeat the laps or pulls, but they should be repeated until the desired result is obtained

While this picture gives an idea how to begin to ascertain the Staple of cotton, it should be remembered it is not given as a stiff-legged rule   Each Stapler generally has a peculiar way of his own for getting the length and strength of cotton fibers

If the Stapler will turn this picture upside down, he can very well see or imagine his own hands doing the work.

Courtesy Dr. N. A Cobb, Technologist Bureau Plant Industry, Agricultural Dep't., Washington, D C

Squaring ·or evening up the right
hand end of the "pull."

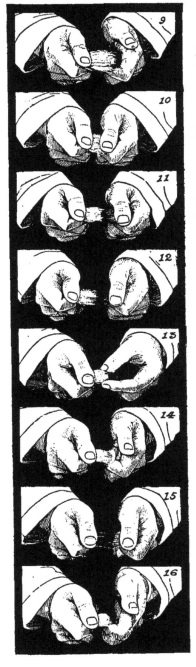

9 Beginning to make a grasp for another pull. Fibers should be held tightly in the left hand.

10 Position of the hands before making the pull.

11. Showing the fibers drawn after the pull is made The few fibers in the left hand are discarded.

12. Taking away the loose extended fibers

13 Compressing the fibers latterally at their ends to prevent their flaring out too much.

14. A repetition of 12.

15 Four single fibers drawn parallel to each other, each showing a different degree of tension.

16 Repeating the operation as shown at 9, with the right hand end of the fibers showing to be nearly even in length, or "squared," and the whole bunch ready to be pulled to square the other end of them.

Squaring the left hand end of the
"pull."

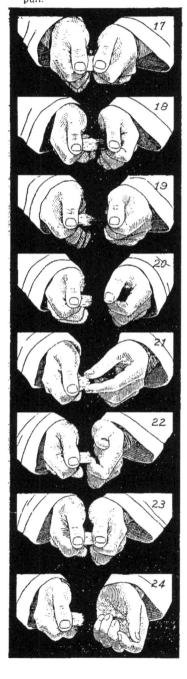

17   Smoothing out the fibers by stroking
them between thumb and finger.

18   Pulling out the loose extended fibers

19 and 20   A continuation of the process
shown at 18.

21.   Repeating the operation shown at 13

22.   Smoothing out the "pull"

23   Continuatnig the same towards showing final results

24   The process completed, with the bunch
of fibers showing the Staple of the cotton,
and ready to be measured if desired

These illustrations are given as a guide to
offer the student to aid him in the process of
Stapling cotton, but he should not think the
positions shown by the hands are the only
ones to be taken in executing the work   Many
others, similarly applied, are equally as effective, for no two Staplers, as previously
stated, practice the same methods   These
shown here explain nicely how the work can
be done

It should be remembered in Stapling cotton
that it is not necessary to draw out all the
short fibers to get at the Staple

PROJECTION METHOD.

Under the accustomed practice of stapling cotton, no definite results can be had as to the exact length of the cotton fibers drawn, the Trade seemingly satisfied to accept present day methods for practical purposes, which give approximations only, yet so near an exactness as to satisfy Mill requirements.

The Trade is not so directly concerned in knowing the exact length of cotton fibers as are the Mills, and so long as they assume a willingness to accept what the Trade gives to them, the latter make no effort, nor manifests any desire, to change the adopted methods for stapling cotton.

The Trade and the Mills are familiar with the finger and thumb method of "pulling for Staple," and both know that approximate, average lengths result only, yet neither manifest any apparent concern to devise something that will give greater accuracy in fiber measurements, although controversies often arise by reason of disagreements over the diversity of opinions between the Mills and the Trade as to the length of Staple cotton sold and purchased.

Knowing this fact, and since the United States Department of Agriculture has taken an active interest in the subject of marketing cotton, it has devised a method for measuring the length of cotton fibers exactly, defined as the *Projection Method.**

In making tests by this method, the fibers to be measured are placed between two pieces of glass, so clamped together as to confine the fibers rigidly in position; these pieces are then inserted into a projection lantern and the shadows of the fibers displayed upon a screen, which operation magnifies them to about twenty diameters, the screen being covered with transparent paper suitable for tracing purposes.

---

*To Dr. N. A. Cobb, Technologist, Bureau Plant Industry, Dept. of Agriculture, Washington, D. C., credit is due no doubt for the origination of the Projection Method of measuring the length of cotton fibre exactly.

PROJECTING COTTON FIBERS ON A SCREEN.

Being exhibited this way, the fibers can be traced with a pencil on the paper (as the work is being done by the gentleman shown in the picture), and the lines measured then or at some subsequent time.

A specially devised wheel has been perfected for making the required measurements. It is so arranged that any number of revolutions are recorded upon a dial in direct connection with it, each revolution equalling a certain length in linear measurement.

As no two fibers can be found easily that measure the same in length, a definite number can be taken of uneven ones, say 20, 30, 50 or 100, from which number an average can be made, and in this way, get a practical result. Care must be exercised to see that fibers of all lengths are placed in the apparatus for measurement on the screen.

The operator measures by rolling the little wheel along on the lines, taking care to follow all their crooks and meanderings with exactness. Were the fibers made straight and held in that position between the two pieces of glass, the magnifying apparatus would display the fibers in like manner on the screen and make the measurement of them quite easy.

EVEN-RUNNING COTTON

Mill Requirements.—Having considered *gradation* and *stapling,* the subject of combining the two is now appropriate and opportune.

The final destination of all cotton is the Mill.

Mills are restrictive in their demands, and state definitely what they want when buying.

Mills equipped for the manufacture of specific lines of fabrics or yarns must have a definite character of cotton from which to produce them, hence not all Mills can or do use the same Class of cotton.

This gives requisition from them for a variety of cotton. No two Mills use the same kind of cotton, unless engaged in making similar fabrics.

Unless Mills produce a variety of manufactured articles the demands from them for raw material are narrowed to a close range, which is confined to both Class and Staple.

One will use Middling, another Strict Middling, another Good Middling, or perhaps one may confine itself to Low Middling or to the Ordinaries.

A Mill using Middling or any other one Grade designates its wants by demanding *"even-running"* Middling or whatever the Grade is. To say that it will use "Shy Middlings" or "Full Middlings" is equivalent to expressing a willingness to accept the required Grades with slight variations from their true Type.

Some Mills are so restrictive in their demands for supplies that they practically exclude everything not exactly as ordered; others will accept a variation of one-Quarter or one-Half Grade above and below that demanded.

Mills accepting shades of variations from the Grade wanted usually require the number accepted below to be offset by a similar number above.

Let it be stated, by illustration, that a Mill accepting a list of 500 bales of cotton, if 100 bales are accepted as running 1-4 or 1-2 Grade below, 100 bales will be demanded as running 1-4 or 1-2 above that ordered.[47]

Mills specifying even-running cotton prescribe the length of Staple also, in most instances.

------

[47]If more latitude is allowable than 1-4 Grade, on or off, this should be understood and agreed upon when the order is given and received.

Purchases made by the mills of New England are under Rules prescribed by the "New England Terms for Buying and Selling American Cotton." (Sea Island excepted), and allow a variation of "5% half a grade below the grade specified, if offset by an equal number of bales of half a grade above that specified."

The mills of North and South Carolina buy under terms specified in their "Carolina Mill Rules," and if bought even running grades, "10% of the shipment may be one-half grade below the grade specified, if offset by an equal number of bales one-half a grade above the grade specified."

Their terms usually being, "Middling, even-running,"[48], or any other Grade and Staple usually seen, as 1 inch, or 1 1-16, 1 1-8, 1 1-4, etc., as conditions and requirements may warrant.

Spinnable values are measured in two ways: First, by the gradation and fiber tests; second, by the amount of waste, such as motes, leaf, sand, etc., which are factors governing the purchase for Mills, so far as the physical qualities are concerned.[49]

AVERAGING GRADES AND VALUES

An "average" list of cotton expresses the mean quality and value of it, and may be a high or low average.

An average list does not always express an *even-running* one, while an even-running list should be an average one.

An average list can be composed of many Grades; there can be several Grades of one Class and few of another, or vice versa.

To average a list it is necessary that the Middling Price be known as the base, and the Differences[50] between the Grades relative to Middling must also be known.

Average lists may take in all Low Grade Cotton, or all High Grade Cotton, and the average prove to be above or below the Middling Value. When the average shows to be above Middling, it is said to be so many "Points 'on' Middling" or if it is below, so many "Points 'off' Middling."

To facilitate business in making calculations for getting the value of a list of cotton, especially a large one, it is often convenient to make an average of the list.

Operators in the Trade handling all Grades of cotton deal with one another on average lists basis terms, or make

---

[48]See "Merit Values," p. 77.

[49]See Mill Buying, Southern, p. 246.

[50]See Appendix, Revision Committee.

a lump sale of the whole, calling such "hog round sales;" but when dealing with the Mills, even-running Grades are usually specified.

Dealers requiring High Grade Cottons will not use an average list unless it be stated that nothing *below* a certain Grade shall be admitted, and the same thing obtains with those handling only Low Grades, the instructions requiring that nothing *above* a certain Grade is wanted and accepted, unless concession in price is given on the High Grade to reduce it to the value of the Grade demanded.

SECTION IX

DIFFERENCES IN GRADES

The expressions "differences in grades," "differences in value," are terms used in a relative way which one often hears from those interested in the Cotton Trade. The expressions are well used, most applicable, and can be readily understood when tabulated forms are presented for clearness and to aid the memory.

To find the average of any list of cotton, it is necessary that the value of the relative Higher and Lower Grades be known; they having a value of their own, as so much "on" or "off" the price of Middling. These "on's" and "off's," having a different price, are referred to as *Differences*.

Recognizing Middling as the basis, the Cotton Exchanges and the Trade establish the relative Grades. For illustration, say Middling is 10 cents a pound, and showing the "Full" and "Half" Grades, the following table will exhibit relative and comparative values:

TABLE XII

Grade—	Price.	Price.	Price.
Good Middling	10¼	10⅜	10½
Strict Middling	10⅛	10 3/16	10¼
Middling (Basis)	10	10	10
Strict Low Middling	9⅞	9⅜	9¼
Low Middling	9½	9	8½

The five Grades shown are sufficient to explain the *differences* in *Grades* and the three different prices shown will illustrate the idea of *difference* in value.

In the first price column the difference in value for Strict Middling above Middling is 1-8 "up;" for Good Middling, 1-4 "up;" the difference in the second price column for Strict Middling above Middling is 3-16 "up;" for Good Middling, 3-8 "up;" while in the third price column the difference for Strict Middling above Middling is 1-4 "up;" for Good Middling, 1-2 "up." In the first price column the price "off" Middling for Strict Low Middling is 1-8, in the second column 5-8, in the third column, 3-4, leaving the remaining fractional values respectively, 7-8, 3-8, 1-4.

In the first, second and third columns, the discounts for Low Middling are respectively 1-2, 1, and 1 1-2, equal to 50, 100 and 150 points, leaving the Low Middling values 9 1-2, 9, and 8 1-2 cents.

The Discounts of 1-2 and 1 1-2 for Low Middling are exceptional both ways. The first rarely ever applies, and the second is equally out of line. Both are used here for explanation only, to illustrate how the Trade makes these Discounts. They vary with the season and the demands of the Trade.

This Grade is usually subjected to a Discount ranging somewhere from 3-4 to 1 1-4 cents off. Conditions must be very abnormal to make them so slight as 1-2, or so excessive as 1 1-2.

The Differences applied by the Trade are not always in agreement with those promulgated by either the New York or New Orleans Cotton Exchanges.

The Differences applying as made by the New York Cotton Exchange for delivery of cotton on Contracts are *fixed* for either three or nine months,[51] while those for New Orleans Cotton Exchange follow more closely those established by the Trade, but not always in harmony with it. They are altered once a month, or oftener if thought advisable, by one or more members of the Spot Quotation Committee.

The expressed Differences in the preceding are those established by the Trade and Cotton Exchanges, generally referred to as arbitrary, frequently without having any regard to the spinnable value of this particular Grade of cotton, but when influenced by panic, or little demand, heavy Discounts apply.

They are the ones used in the Trade, and the talent is familiar with them.

Grades of cotton are distinguished by the greater or less percentage of waste carried in them, in connection with their discolorations, as previously shown.

Each Grade carrying a certain or probable amount of waste can have it determined by the Mills.

Determining this waste tells its spinnable value to that extent.

Spinnable Values are not in line with the Differences established by the Trade.

The Premiums and penalties prescribed by the Trade and Cotton Exchanges are determined by the arbitrary Differences assessed for the relative Grades, and are measured to the Mills the same way.

The arbitrary Differences are made upon the assumption that the more waste, the more Discount; the more trash, the more waste. This applies to the operation of the Mills also,

---

[51]See Const. and By-Laws New York and New Orleans Cotton Exchanges.

but comparatively, the results do not show the same Differences.

Practical tests have been made by many Mills and technical colleges in their textile departments, to show the actual waste and spinnable Differences existing between the different Grades.

The Clemson Agricultural College, of Clemson College, South Carolina, made tests to determine the amount of waste in the following Grades, with the results as shown:

Strict Good Middling	11.5 %	Low Middling	14.75%
Good Middling	12 %	Strict Good Ordinary	
Strict Middling	12.5 %	nary	16.00%
Middling	13 %	Good Ordinary	17.5 %
Strict Low Middling	13.75%	Ordinary	18.75%

As stated, the higher the percentage of waste, the lower the Grade of cotton.

The tests made demonstrated the fact that the same amount of waste did not prove constant in the same Grades[52]

This can arise from two causes: (1) The same Grade of cotton does not carry the same quantity of trash, and (2) gin saws running at a high speed cut or break more fibers than if running at a normal rate, producing a larger number of short fibers, which are thrown out when passing through the carding machinery, or dislodged as waste, when the fibers are being paralleled in other machines.

---

[52]Clipping from Bulletin Clemson College, 1912. The variation in waste ranges from 4 per cent to 10 per cent in M. F.; 5 per cent to 12 per cent in G. M.; 6 per cent to 13 1-2 per cent in M.; 6 per cent to 15 per cent in L. M.; 8 per cent to 17 per cent in G. O.; 9 per cent to 18 1-2 per cent in O. (Bulletin 4, Cotton Classing, J. G. Coman, Clemson College, October, 1913.) Tests made by the Department of Agriculture. Washington, corroborate pretty closely the foregoing, further emphasizing an inconstant variation of the same Grade in Mill waste.

The percentage of waste given excludes the weight of the bagging and ties.

Reference to the statement of results obtained by Clemson College shows a difference of only one-half of one per cent. between the Full and Half Grades *above* Middling, while the differences on the *Lower* Grades widen as the gradation is reduced.

Note that Middling has a waste of 13 per cent., Strict Low Middling, 13.75 per cent. A 13 per cent. waste is equal to 65 pounds on a 500-pound bale of cotton. Deducting 22 pounds for bagging and ties, leaves 43 pounds of actual waste in a Middling bale. A similar calculation shows a loss of 46 3-4 pounds in a Strict Low Middling, and a difference of 3 3-4 pounds only between these two Grades. The other Grades, lower, have a slightly increased percentage of loss.

The spinnable Difference for the Higher Grades, as shown, is only 2 1-2 pounds to the 500-pound bale, equivalent to the 1-2 of 1 per cent. indicated.

With a difference of 2 1-2 pounds between the Full Higher Grades, one-half such amount would represent the "Stricts," and one-fourth the "Quarter" Grades.

Tabulating, the following will make clear the comparative usual Trade Differences with those designated as spinnable:

TABLE XIII[53]

Grade Name—	(Cents)	Trade Dif. (Points)	Spin. Dif. (Percentage)
Good Middling	⅜ "on"	=37½=	1% "on"
Strict Middling	¼ "on"	=25	=½ of 1% "on"
Middling	Base	00	00
Strict Low Midd	5/16 "off"	=31¼=	¾% "off"
Low Middling	⅞ "off"	=87½=	¾% "off"
Strict Good Ord	1½ "off"	= 125=	3% "off"
Good Ordinary	2¼ "off"	– 225=	4½% "off"
Ordinary	3 "off"	= 300=	5¾% "off"

Extending this Table to get the values of the Points and percentages expressed will show more fully the comparative differences on the bale in Dollars and Cents.

TABLE XIV

Grade Name—	Trade Dif. (Points)	Trade Dif. (Cts. on or off bale)	Spin. Dif. (Per cent)	Spin. Dif. (Cts. on or off bale)
Good Middling[54]	37½=	1.87½ "on"	1 "on"=	.50 "on"
Strict Middling	25 =	1.25 "on"	½ "on"=	.25 "on"
Middling	00	00	00	00
Strict Low Middling	31¼=	1.56¼ "off"	¾ "off"=	.37½ "off"
Low Middling	87½=	4.37½ "off"	1¾ "off"=	.87½ "off"
Strict Good Ordinary	125 =	5.75 "off"	3 "off"=	1.50 "off"
Good Ordinary	225 =	11.25 "off"	4½ "off"=	2.25 "off"
Ordinary	300 =	15.00 "off"	5¾ "off"=	2.87½ "off"

NOTE.—While the tests made by the Clemson A. & M. College were on a particular lot of cotton, and are not representative of an exact percentage, yet they corroborate very closely tests made by others for similar purposes.

---

[53]Calculated on basis of definite percentage figures given in Table XIV.

[54]These stated *trade differences* are not constant. They vary as conditions warrant.

Comparing the Trade Differences with those indicated as spinnable would seem to show with emphasis that there is no necessity for the multiplicity of Cotton Grades now extant, but as the Trade holds to its established custom, and spinnable differences are not applied in spot transactions, there is no getting away from its mandates now.

Under the United States Cotton Futures Act, recently passed by Congress, nine Spot Markets are designated by the Secretary of Agriculture as those taken for determining the Differences between Grades relative to Middling. They are Augusta, Ga.; Boston, Mass.; Dallas, Texas; Houston, Texas; Little Rock, Ark.; Memphis, Tenn.; Montgomery, Ala.; Norfolk, Va.; Savannah, Ga.

Quotations for Middling Cotton and the Differences for other Grades, are received daily from these nine Spot Markets by both the New York and New Orleans Cotton Exchanges, and upon the average of the quotations received, the commercial Differences for each Grade is made for the day by the Exchanges.

The use of the commercial Differences established as above indicated is compulsory in the settlement of Future Contracts only.

Twelve Spot Markets have been designated by the Secretary of Agriculture as bona fide Spot Markets. Quotations as to the value of Middling and the relative Grades are received each day by wire from these Spot Markets by the Secretary of Agriculture.

BOOK II.

ARITHMETIC OF COTTON.

Beginning with a Review of the Elemental Principles of Arithmetic entering into the Commercial Cotton business, and extended through an elucidation of some problems that Professionals may find of interest to review.

CHAPTER I

SECTION 1—DEFINITIONS—ARITHMETICAL PROBLEMS.

ARITHMETICAL SIGNS

For addition, the plus sign . . . . . $+$
For subtraction, the minus sign . . . $-$
For multiplication, the sign . . . . . $\times$
For division, the sign . . . . $\div$
For equal, or equality . . . . $=$

In connection with these signs and supplementary to them, many expressions and abbreviations peculiar to the Cotton Trade will be introduced. For the sake of brevity, they will enter largely into the statements and solutions of the problems in this volume.

The student should familiarize himself with them, as their need becomes more apparent as the study advances.

ABBREVIATIONS

B/L...Bill of Lading
B/C...Bales of Cotton
M/B...Middling Basis
B/M...Basis Middling[1]
C. I. F. ....Cash, Insurance and Freight
F.O.B or fob...Free on board
Cwt...Hundred weight
Lbs. .... Pounds
Point..................One hundredth (1/100) of a cent=$.0001

---

[1] M/B and B/M mean the same.

TERMS

Arbitrators, Arbitration.—Arbitrators are parties designated by two or more in controversy as mediators to amicably adjust their differences regarding the character of cotton delivered on Contract.

Arbitration—The hearing of a cause and determining it for parties in controversy by a person or persons chosen for the purpose.

Arbitration Committees of both the New York and New Orleans Cotton Exchanges are to "hear and decide such matters as may be referred to" them with reference to disputes arising among members, respecting "transactions in spot, future Contracts and free on board cotton."

Each member of the committee shall be entitled to a fee of $5.00 for each case arbitrated, to be paid by the party losing in the controversy. An appeal may be taken before the Board of Appeals.

This Committee has the settlement of all claims coming before it, except those in which the question of classification is involved. Matters determined by it are those directly concerning the delivery of cotton on Exchange Contracts.

Dealers handling spot cotton often settle their own controversies by the selection of their own *Arbitrators*, through mutual agreement, and such determination in the matter is final; such *Arbitrators* are not amenable to any Cotton Exchange.

Bear, Bears.—Those who sell "short" desire the Market to decline, and exert efforts to that end, which efforts are supposed to press or *bear down* the price; hence the term "bear." While its real meaning expresses verb action, the word has been paraphrased into a noun signification, and those operating on the "short side," are designated as "Bears" (animals) invading the Market.

Broker, Brokerage.—Dealers buying and selling, as agents, and known as *Exchange, Insurance, Produce, Stock* and *Cotton Brokers.*

Cotton Brokers are referred to as members of the Cotton Exchange who act in the capacity of agents for buying and selling Cotton Contracts. No one can act as Broker on the Cotton Exchanges except the members composing it. Brokers of the New Orleans Cotton Exchanges make a minimum charge of $7.50 for buying, and the same amount for selling, each 100 bales; that is, $15.00 commission for the "round transaction." New York Brokers charge $10.00 and $20.00, respectively.

This commission applies on business done for those who are not members of the Exchanges, or, in other words, "outside business."

A commission of half this sum is charged by one member for his services as Broker for another member. Under the Rules there seems to be no free trading by Brokers for themselves or customers.

The *brokerage* is the commission for the sale or purchase of 100 B/C *Contracts*, and no less.

Some members deal exclusively in Future Contracts, others handle both Spot and Future business. The *brokerage* is based on percentage. Brokers may have agents.

Bull, Bulls.—A class of Dealers whose operations are exactly opposite to those of a "Bear." A Dealer possessing Spot Cotton, or Contracts, which he has bought at a satisfactory price, wishes an advance, and exerts his influence to secure it, which action is to lift up (bull) the price, hence the term "Bull."

Those operating on the bull side—those trying to advance the price of cotton, are called "Bulls." These expressions are framed from the same sources as those applying to Bears, but have an opposite meaning.

Bulls make money on an *advancing* Market, and lose it on *declines.* Bears *profit* by *declines,* and lose on *advances.*

Bulls often buy cotton with the view of advancing the Market by bidding it up, for the purpose of getting a higher level on which to sell. A market advanced by such procedure is termed a "manipulated Market."

Bulls carrying the Market to as high a point as desired or deemed consistent, reverse their efforts and *sell* on the advance. The moment they sell, they become Bears.

Not all advances are manipulated ones, but the Trade reacts one way or the other to them.

Briefly, Bulls are those who want and try to make the Market *advance;* Bears are those who want and try to make the market *decline.*

Code, Cipher Code, Cotton Code.—The frequent transmission of telegrams or cablegrams in connection with the Cotton Trade is an item of no small expense, and to resort to this means of transmitting intelligence concerning cotton transactions requires the use of a Code as an economic measure.

There are several in use, among which may be mentioned Meyer's and Shepperson's, as the most prominent and universally used. Private Codes are used by the talent who operate on an extensive scale, in addition to the others.

Codes are small books, generally of size suitable for the pocket. They contain long lists of words and phrases alphabetically arranged, similar to a dictionary in construction.

To each word a distinctive phrase is given, and a phrase may have an extensive meaning.

To illustrate, let us use the following words for explanation:

Abate—Market 1/8 down.
Abater—Market 3/16 down.
Abating—Market 1/4 down.
About—Reduce your limit one-eighth.
Destroy—Market 1/8 up.
Destroyer—Market 3/16 up.

Destroying—Market 1/4 up.

Ender—Better feeling in market, 10 points up.

Control—Report all sales on last limit at once.

Controler—Don't buy until further orders.

Emzine—Mills buying freely, demand good, movement falling off.

Enquire—What is best price fob here, basis Middling, on 100 bales?

Famine—Offer you 10 1/8, usual differences fob your station, immediate acceptance.

From the foregoing let us put out a "wire" (telegram) in Code and note the convenience and economy of it:

TELEGRAM

New Orleans, La., October 12, 1915.

To Smith & Jones, Decatur, Ala.

Control controller.

STUART BROS. COT. CO.

This wire of only two words will go at minimum rate; it gives full advice for the moment. The operator sending it does not understand its meaning, nor can he betray any information connected with it.

From the few words given with their meanings, it will be seen that the Code as a means of giving out limits, advice, and Market information of a private nature, is exceedingly valuable, beyond its economic consideration.

The Code, with its long list of words, practically covers everything connected with the Trade; but to be of value, both parties must have books of similar Code words. That is, if one has "Shepperson," the other must have it in the same edition.

In the preceding "wire" it is supposed that Smith and Jones represent the New Orleans Cotton Company, and were buying on limits.

In cablegrams (telegrams across the ocean) the Code is indispensable between Dealers in America and those in foreign countries. Owing to the heavy expense of sending messages across the water, necessity has devised the Code, and through its instrumentality International Cotton Trade has received benefits that could never have been gained otherwise, and by its usefulness the Markets of the world are placed within easy reach.

"C. N. D'S." (COMMERCIAL NEWS DEPARTMENT)

To give the Market to all parties in the South where cotton is bought and sold, and to all commercial centers, requires that the most economical method, consistent with full efficiency, be used.

The Commercial News Department (referred to as the C. N. D. Department, or briefly, "C. N. D's"), in transmitting reports of the Boards of Trade, Stock and Cotton Exchanges, uses a Code of its own, and when reports are made, they are followed with the time of day the report was taken.

These reports are sent directly from the large Cotton Exchanges and translated for all who care to take and pay for them. The charges are usually so much a month to patrons.

In quoting cotton, the report from Liverpool is first posted, then New York and New Orleans follow.

The first reports are the Opening Calls, followed every few minutes with the varying quotations; then the Noon Call, with varying fluctuations, until the "Close" or Closing Call. These quotations are all for Futures. After the "Close," the *Receipts* at the leading Ports, and the *Spot price* for Liverpool, New York and New Orleans are given. Sometimes the price for Spots is given for Galveston, Houston, Memphis, Augusta, Savannah, Bremen and Havre, more especially for the leading daily papers.

This Code is different from the regular Cotton Code, and

is used especially for the transmission of Market Reports.

In quoting the months, one letter for each month usually expresses it, preceded by the name of the Market from which it comes, and followed by the time of day.

The telegraph operator translates the Code for the Trade, hence it is not so material whether the Trade is acquainted with it or not, he usually writing: "Jan. 13, 12-13, Feb. 13, 14-15," etc., for the market price.

The months given in the C. N. D. Code are as follows:

QUOTED MONTHS

F	Jan.	July	N
G	Feb.	Aug.	Q
H	Mch.	Sept.	U
J	Apr.	Oct.	V
K	May	Nov.	X
M	June	Dec.	Z

The Opening Cotton Market would be expressed something like this in the Code:

N. Y. open V 13.15-16 X 13.17-18 Z 13.21-22 F 13.16-17 10 a. m., etc.

N. O. open U 13.12-13 V 13.14-15 X 13.17-18 Z 13.19-20 F 13.22-23 9:10 a. m.

Similar reports are made for the Noon Call and the Close, at which time the Spot Market is given for New York and New Orleans.

The Liverpool Market is 5 hours ahead of New York and 6 hours ahead of New Orleans. New York opens at 10 a. m., while New Orleans follows an hour later, opening at 9:05 a. m. for the transaction of business.

Port receipts and the tone of the Market usually accompany the Close and Spot quotations.

Contracts, Agreements.—An understanding or agreement between two or more parties to perform certain stipulated acts. With reference to dealings in cotton, they may be two-fold: They may refer to deals between individuals or corporations who execute Contracts to sell and deliver, buy and receive cotton, one from another; or they may have reference to Cotton Exchange Contracts which are dealt in as commodities, and while its stipulation prescribes the delivery or receipt of cotton on them, yet they may be settled as stated in Future Sales.[2]

Contracts of the latter character are made between individuals or corporations and members of some Cotton Exchange, or between members.

Discounts.—(1) The difference between the prices of Spots and Futures. If the price of Spot Cotton in New York is 9.65 March, and the quotation for May cotton is 9.33, the *Discount* for the May Option under March Spots is 32 Points. (2) Middling being the basis, the Grades under it are inferior in quality with a corresponding depreciation in value, which values of the Lower Grades are *Discounts* off the basic price. (3) Cotton Merchants selling cotton for future delivery in some instances protect the sales by buying Futures for the same number of bales.

Were Anderson and Smith to sell 5,000 bales of cotton in August, to be delivered in September, October and November at 10 cents at the ship's side in New Orleans, and if at the time of this sale August cotton is worth 9.80 as the publicly quoted price (the sale being effected at 20 Points on August), and they buy Octobers at 9.50 as a Hedge, they get them at 50 Points *Discount* from the price for Spots.

Factors, Cotton Factors.—Those interested in the Cotton Trade who do not buy cotton direct, but instead, receive and sell for others, who consign cotton to them. As Commission Merchants they make a charge for their services based on a small percentage of the amount of business handled.[3]. Factors engaged in handling cotton exclusively, are known as *Cotton Factors*. *Factorage*, commission allowed.

---

[2]See Future Sales, Book IV, pp. 316, 332.
[3]See p. 279.

Flat Cotton.—The original bale of cotton as it comes from the press before compressing. Transportation companies prefer, for economic reasons, to handle cotton in compressed form, compressing it at their expense, if not otherwise instructed. Conditions sometimes require that cotton be shipped "flat" (without compressing), and if so, the words, "To be shipped flat," or "Ship flat," must appear on the face of the Bill of Lading.

Futures, Future Sales.—Contracting to sell cotton to be delivered at some future time. The phrase is applied to deals originating with the Cotton Exchanges, and has direct reference to *Contracts* dealt in by them. They are dealt in as one would deal in Stocks, Bonds, Notes, Mortgages, etc., with the exception that Contracts bought or sold through the Cotton Exchanges are often settled for by the terms expressed; transferred from one to another, or canceled by offset.[4]

Sales or purchases of Contracts for future delivery are made only by the New York and New Orleans Cotton Exchanges, but independent of, and outside of these Exchanges, a large volume of spot business is done annually between Spinners and Cotton Merchants, who bind themselves to a Contract which implies *future delivery* of cotton, and they are not subject to any control beyond the terms of their specific agreements.

Spinners purchasing from Merchants direct, will not do so, unless the Merchant be financially strong or gives assurance the Contract is hedged.[5]

Hedge, Hedging.—To protect one's purchase or sale of cotton; to accomplish this, one resorts to the New Orleans or New York Cotton Exchange, securing from a member of one or the other a Contract for some designated future month, calling for the same number of bales as the number of spot bales on hand, or in a contemplated purchase.

---

[4]See Del. Spot Cot. p. 318.
[5]See Mill Buying, p. 241 et seq.

MB—5

A Contract bought in one Month may be *hedged* by disposing of it and taking some other forward month. One to offset the other, must be of like character and equivalent value, that is to say, if the first Contract bought stipulates 100 bales of May cotton, the same may be *hedged,* and possibly a profit gained, by settling for that month and taking 100 bales of July; were a loss to occur on May, an equal gain should accrue on the July sale. This form of hedging, would come under *Speculation,*[6] but a similar procedure in protecting spot cotton is often resorted to in spot transactions as a business practice.

The student may infer from the statements given explanatory of the Hedge[7], that the process of hedging is quite a simple and easy one, which as a matter of fact may be so recognized, but it will be recalled that each original Contract purchased cost at least $100 as a Margin; that the exchanging from one month to another cost $100 if the Market has declined; that a decline of 17 points (if Dealer is not well rated), will call for an additional $100, and a subsequent decline of a similar number of points, calls for a remargin of like amount.

For the protection of spot cotton, the payment of these sums for hedging facilities is not objectionable, if parities were undisturbed; but those who handle spot cotton and try to protect themselves against loss by resorting to the Hedge, find that disparities so often confront them as to practically defeat the purpose for which the Hedge was intended; and for this reason a large percentage of small Merchants throw their cotton upon the Market as fast as purchased, to avoid losses resulting from declines that may appear at any moment, and never use the Hedge.

Invoice.—A bill or statement that describes in detail the shipment of cotton; generally sent through the mail by the

---

[6]See Speculation, p. 328.
[7]See Selling Hedge, p. 323.

local Bank attached to the Draft and B/L, and usually precedes the arrival of the cotton. It gives the date, the number and weight of each bale, total weight, sometimes the classification, and full value when payment is requested before the arrival of the cotton at destination. Invoices are sent direct from Shipper to Consignee if no Draft is drawn against the cotton. Some Dealers prefer forwarding the Invoice direct to Consignee with their letters of advice. If a Draft is made to cover the value of the shipment, it is sent under separate cover by the Bank.

Long.—Long cotton signifies the amount of actual cotton one has in his immediate possession. If Jones has 100 B/C on hand, he is "long" 100 bales.

Margins.—(1) Payments required to protect a Broker for the purchase or sale of a Contract, or to maintain them after purchase or sale. The usual Margin is $1.00 a bale, but often is as high as $5.00 a bale, when fluctations are frequent and wide.

Both parties to a Contract have a right under the Rules to call for a *Margin.* (2) The difference between the price paid and that received *for cotton.* If cotton be bought for 8½ cents and sold for 8, the *marginal* difference is ½ cent loss; if it is bought for 8 cents and sold for 8½, the gain is ½ cent *Margin.* (3) The difference between the price of Spot Cotton and that of Futures.

Market Closes.—The last figures posted on the Boards in the Cotton Exchanges for the day's quotations, referred to as the *"Closing Calls,"* or more often as "The Close."

Market Opens.—The first figures that are chalked (put on the blackboard) in the Cotton Exchanges at the beginning of the day's business, and referred to as the *"Opening Calls."*

Parity, Equal Values.—If Middling cotton is quoted in New Orleans at 9.80 for spots, and 30 points are necessary as a freight charge to put it in New York, 30 added to 9.80 would give 10.10 as a *parity* value for spot cotton in New York.

If March cotton is quoted at 9.75, and May futures at 9.60, the *parity* difference is 15 points.

If March cotton is quoted at 9.75 in that month, and Middling Spots registered at 9.85 for the same time, the parity difference between the two is 10 points.

Premiums.—(1) The profit offered by a Buyer to a Seller as an inducement to secure a lot of cotton. If the basis price is 10 cents in the open Market, and a cotton Merchant has 500 bales for sale, a Buyer might offer a Premium of 1/8 or 3/16 to secure the list, if it is shown to be practically near what the Buyer desired. (2) The Grades of cotton ranging in quality above Middling, and known as *Premium* Grades, whose values are termed *Premium* Values.

Reclamations.—Claims made for shortage in weights, class, or deviation in the cotton from the samples submitted. Should a consignee pay full value on receipt of the Invoice and B/L for a shipment of cotton, and find, after weighing at destination, that it is short 100 pounds, it is clear he has paid for 100 pounds too much. In such a case he would *reclaim* from the shipper the value of the 100 pounds. Likewise, when the classification on the outturn shows not to be as high as stated in the Invoice, or when the cotton is bought on sample and shows on arrival not to come up fully in class to it, then in both instances *reclamations* would be made on the Seller for the value of the differences in class and variation from type samples on which the cotton was sold.

Shipments of cotton into foreign ports have *reclamations* drawn against them if over-tared with an excess of wrapping weight, short weight of cotton or variation of types submitted.

Scalpers.—Those who mediate between primary Buyers and Sellers, and act in capacity of both Buyer and Seller. They may or may not be recognized as *regular Dealers*.

Short, Short Cotton, Shorts.—These terms imply that the Seller has sold cotton before getting it in his possession, and he is "short" the amount of cotton sold; when received for delivery, he has acquired his "Short Cotton;" those operating on the "Short Side," speaking collectively, are called "Shorts."

Short Sellers make money on *declines* in the Market, and lose on *advances*. If no rise or fall in price, no gain or loss results.

Short sales can be made in real or Future Cotton, with gains or losses occurring on Future Cotton the same as on spot sales.

Short Sellers sometimes find the Market does not decline as expected, but instead, remains practically steady or advances. In the former case they make no gains; in the latter they suffer a loss.

Seeing the Market advancing, Shorts often rush in to buy, and in so doing advance the Markets against themselves and suffer self-imposed losses.[8]

Spot Cotton, Spots.—Denote about the same thing as "long" cotton; in the preceding, Jones is "long" 100 bales; that is, he has 100 bales of actual cotton in his possession, expressed in the vernacular of the Trade as "Spot Cotton," or 100 bales of "Spots."

Shippers Order, Notify.—These words must be on the face of a B/L where the Shipper desires to draw through his local bank for the full or part value of his cotton before it reaches destination. If so worded, the Shipper has a legal advantage, and the bank a protection.

The local bank taking care of a shipment operates through some bank at or near destination, to which the cotton is billed. On receipt of the Documents[9] the receiving bank notifies the transportation company, and also the consignee, both of whom are put on notice—the first, not to deliver the cotton to consignee until the payment of the Draft; the second, that a Draft is drawn on him for the whole or part

---

[8]See "Short Selling Spot Cotton," p. 273.
[9]"Shipping Documents," Book III, p. 280.

of the cotton in the shipment. When the Draft is paid the B/L for the cotton will be surrendered, and then consignee can receive the cotton from the railway company.

This is the usual procedure for American domestic shipments. Those destined for foreign markets are handled in a similar manner, except that Time Drafts are usually sold to some American Bank which makes a specialty of handling such accounts, on receipt of all Documents properly indorsed and authenticated.[10]

Where cotton Merchants, or Factors, as consignees, are known to be men of undoubted financial ability, it is accepted as a general practice, by local banks, to give the Shipper full credit for the face of his Draft; but if the consignee be practically unknown or of doubted ability to meet the Draft on presentation, it is taken by the local bank for collection only.

A Market showing rapid and wide fluctuations downward necessarily leads banks to exercise caution in payment of Drafts drawn on consignments, unless the consignee has given instruction to draw for a definite sum, and is financially able to protect the Draft himself.

If J. H. Hicks ships 50 B/C from Talladega, Ala., valued at $2,500, to W. D. Thompson & Co., New Orleans, drawing through his local bank for this amount, the Talladega bank would give Mr. Hicks credit for this sum the same as if he had deposited that much cash, if the bank recognizes Thompson & Co. as trustworthy for this amount; otherwise the Draft would go to New Orleans for collection.

Splits.—Those types of cotton that can not be classed as clear-cut Half Grades (Stricts), and known to the Trade as *Quarter Grades,*[11] designated by the Cotton Exchanges as "Fully" and "Barely."[12]

A good style of Low-Middling, not sufficient in character

---

[10]See p. 280.
[11]The U. S. Standards do not recognize the Quarter Grades.
[12]See Appendix.

to be classed as Strict Low Middling, would be known as Fully Low Middling.

Straddles or *Spreads.*—These terms mean the purchase and sale of one month against another. One desiring to "Straddle" the Market, may *buy* a July in New Orleans and *sell* the same month in New York, or sell in New York and buy the same month in Liverpool.

COMMON AND DECIMAL FRACTIONS.

NOTE.—Believing it advantageous to the student to be familiar with the Common and Decimal fractions before attempting to master the art of Cotton Grading, and assuming he is grounded in the rudiments of them before taking up this work, the details of their operation will not be given.

SECTION II

COTTON QUOTATIONS AND PROBLEMS.

TABLE XV

NEW ORLEANS SPOTS

New Orleans, May 13 (1913).—The Spot Market closed steady, 1-8 up, sales 930 bales; stock, 68,503 bales. Quotations:

	Today.	Yesterday.	Last Year.
Low Ordinary	8 15/16	8 13/16	8 3/8
Ordinary	9 3/4	9 5/8	9 3/16
Good Ordinary	11 3/8	11 1/4	10 5/8
Low Middling	11 7/8	11 3/4	11 5/16
Middling	12 5/16	12 3/16	11 15/16
Good Middling	12 11/16	12 9/16	12 1/2
Middling Fair	13 5/16	13 3/16	13

NEW ORLEANS FUTURES

The following are the opening and closing quotations on the New Orleans Cotton Exchange, compared with the close of yesterday. Tone steady:

May 13, (1913).

	Open.	Close.	Yes. Close.
May	12.31	12.24-25	12.25b
June	12.10-12	12.06-08	12.10-12
July	12.07a[13]	12.02-03	12.06-07
August	11.66-67	11.62-63	11.66-67
September	11.33-35	11.27-39	11.32-34
October	11.21-22	11.15-16	11.20-21
November	11.20-22	11.15-17	11.20-22
December	11.20-21	11.14-15	11.20-21
January	11.23b[13]	11.18-19	11.23-25

[13]Prices (a) asked, and (b) bid.

February	11.20-22	11.15-17	11.20-22
March	11.31-33	11.25-26	11.28

In their communications, and in giving out the Markets, Dealers use divided decimal terms, with the use of the period for a separating point in the fraction.

In making calculations ascertaining the value of cotton, a limit was placed on the use of the Decimal to the *fourth place* by the New York and the New Orleans Cotton Exchanges, prescribing that all cotton dealt in by them shall be calculated in cents and Decimal Fractions of a cent, observing that no Decimal Fraction less than one-hundredth (1-100) of a cent a pound be allowed.

A Cent being 1/100 of a dollar, and a Point being 1/100 of a cent multiplies the fraction to 1/100 of 1/100, equaling one-ten thousandth (1/10,000) of a dollar, expressed decimally, $.0001, reducing in this way the Decimal Fraction to the fourth place.

This one-ten thousandth ($.0001) of a dollar has given rise to the introduction of this Fraction, designated as a "Point," and it will have a conspicuous place in this work.

To readily understand the relative value of the Point in comparison with the Dollar and Cent, the following Table is given:

TABLE XVI

TABLE OF POINTS

1 Point equals .0001 of a Dollar
2 Points equal .0002 of a Dollar
3 Points equal .0003 of a Dollar
4 Points equal .0004 of a Dollar
5 Points equal .0005 of a Dollar
6 Points equal .0006 of a Dollar
7 Points equal .0007 of a Dollar
8 Points equal .0008 of a Dollar
9 Points equal .0009 of a Dollar
10 Points equal .0010 of a Dollar= 1/10 Cent
20 Points equal .0020 of a Dollar= 1/5 Cent
25 Points equal .0025 of a Dollar= 1/4 Cent
50 Points equal .0050 of a Dollar= 1/2 Cent
75 Points equal .0075 of a Dollar= 3/4 Cent
100 Points equal .0100 of a Dollar= 1 Cent
250 Points equal .0250 of a Dollar= 2 1/2 Cents
300 Points equal .0300 of a Dollar= 3 Cents
500 Points equal .0500 of a Dollar= 5 Cents
1000 Points equal .1000 of a Dollar=10 Cents

For convenience the Points are generally expressed in concrete numbers, as 2 Points, 3 Points, 6¼ Points, instead of the long Decimal showing equivalent values.

Where Cents are connected with the Points, the Decimal notation is usually disregarded as indicating the value of the Fraction, and instead the dot is placed so as to divide the Fraction, the reading of which calls into use both the Cents and Points.

Take the following Decimals:

.1002 of a Dollar
.0601 " "   "
.1220 " "   "
.0278 " "   "
.1525 " "   "
.1875 " "   "
.0500 " "   "

For convenience of expression and to indicate the position of the Point relative to the Cent, the following statement of the same Decimals is given and the manner of reading as indicated.

Ten Cents and 2 Points, 10.02, is read ten naught two.

Six Cents and 1 Point, 6.01, is read six naught one.

Twelve Cents and 20 Points, 12.20, is read twelve twenty.

Two Cents and 78 Points, 2.78, is read two seventy-eight.

Fifteen Cents and 25 Points, 15.25, is read fifteen and a quarter.

Eighteen Cents and 75 Points, 18.75, is read eighteen and three-fourths.

Five Cents and no Points, 5.00, is read five cents.

The dot separating the numbers should not confuse the student in making his calculations. It should be remembered that all Fractions involving the Point carry the Decimal to the fourth place, and the Decimal point considered in pointing off the result as recognized in all computations, according to the rules of arithmetic.

·For more readily understanding the comparative value of the Common with the Decimal Fraction, both which find daily use in the Cotton Trade and Cotton computations, the Table illustrating the same follows:

TABLE XVII

COMMON FRACTIONS WITH DECIMAL EQUIVALENTS OF A DOLLAR

```
                        1/32= .03125 of a Dollar
                1/16= 2/32= .0625   "  "     "
                        3/32= .09375 "  "     "
          1/8=2/16= 4/32= .125    "  "     "
                        5/32= .15625 "  "     "
                3/16= 6/32= .1875   "  "     "
                        7/32= .21875 "  "     "
      1/4=2/8=4/16= 8/32= .250    "  "     "
                        9/32= .28125 "  "     "
              5/16=10/32= .3125   "  "     "
                       11/32= .34375 "  "     "
          3/8=6/16=12/32= .375    "  "     "
                       13/32= .40625 "  "     "
              7/16=14/32= .4375   "  "     "
                       15/32= .46875 "  "     "
  1/2=2/4=4/8=8/16=16/32= .500    "  "     "
                       17/32= .53125 "  "     "
              9/16=18/32= .5625   "  "     "
                       19/32= .59375 "  "     "
              5/8=10/16=20/32= .625    "  "     "
                       21/32= .65625 "  "     "
             11/16=22/32= .6875   "  "     "
                       23/32= .71875 "  "     "
      3/4=6/8=12/16=24/32= .750    "  "     "
                       25/32= .78125 "  "     "
             13/16=26/32= .8125   "  "     "
                       27/32= .84375 "  "     "
      7/8=14/16=28/32= .875    "  "     "
                       29/32= .90625 "  "     "
             15/16=30/32= .9375   "  "     "
                       31/32= .96875 "  "     "
  1=2/2=4/4=8/8=16/16=32/32=1.000    "  "     "
```

Retaining the tabular form of Decimals for convenient reference, the same are compared with the Common Fractions for equivalent value, and extended to show the value of the Point in connection with both Fractions of same value.

TABLE XVIII

DECIMAL FRACTIONS WITH EQUIVALENT VALUES IN COMPARISON WITH DOLLARS, CENTS AND POINTS.

.0006¼ of a Dollar= 1/16 of a Cent= 6¼ Points
.0012½ of a Dollar= 1/8 of a Cent=12½ Points
.0018¾ of a Dollar= 3/16 of a Cent=18¾ Points
.0025 of a Dollar= 1/4 of a Cent=25   Points
.0031¼ of a Dollar= 5/16 of a Cent=31¼ Points
.0037½ of a Dollar= 3/8 of a Cent=37½ Points
.0043¾ of a Dollar= 7/16 of a Cent=43¾ Points
.0050 of a Dollar= 1/2 of a Cent=50   Points
.0056¼ of a Dollar= 9/16 of a Cent=56¼ Points
.0062½ of a Dollar= 5/8 of a Cent=62½ Points
.0068¾ of a Dollar=11/16 of a Cent=68¾ Points
.0075 of a Dollar= 3/4 of a Cent=75   Points
.0081¼ of a Dollar=13/16 of a Cent=81¼ Points
.0087½ of a Dollar= 7/8 of a Cent=87½ Points
.0093¾ of a Dollar=15/16 of a Cent=93¾ Points
.0100 of a Dollar= 1   Cent=100 Points

EXAMPLES INVOLVING THE USE OF THE CENT—DECIMAL EQUIVALENT $.01=100 POINTS.

NOTE.—Should any difficulty arise in making calculations for cotton, the quotations for which are connected with Common Fractions, let the student apply the corresponding Decimal for same value, as shown in the preceding Tables. The result will be the same.

Problems for cotton calculations in which the whole cent, ½, ¼, ⅛, 1/16 and 1/32 part are used, fall under the observation, annually, of the Southern cotton Grower, and are made without reference to Grade.

RULE.—*For a single bale, multiply the weight by price; two or more bales of different qualities, add the weights of the separate qualities, and multiply them by the price.*

Add the values of the different lots to find the total value of all.

PROBLEMS.

Ex. 1. A sells 1 B/C weighing 520 pounds at 10c a pound. What amount of money did he receive?

—Ans. $52.00.

Ex. 2. Two B/C weighing 516 and 534 lbs. respectively, were sold for 9c a pound. What was their value?

—Ans. $94.50.

Ex. 3. Tom Adams was offered 9c a pound for his 6 B/C, which he sold 30 days afterward for 10c a pound, but which lost in weight 30 lbs. The original weights were 560, 586, 522, 518, 530 and 494 lbs., respectively. Did he gain or lose by holding his cotton 30 days, and how much?

—Ans. Gained $29.10

Ex. 4. John Anderson sold 2 B/C weighing, each, 535 and 515 lbs., at 11c; 3 B/C weighing, each, 521, 485 and 514 lbs., at 10c. He owed for ginning $15, and 10c a bale for weighing. How much did he receive for the cotton, and what amount did he have left after paying the charges?

—Ans. Total received, $267.50; net received, $252.00.

Ex. 5. Frank Kelly refused an offer of 10c for 4 B/C, which he sold 2 months later at 9c a lb., on which charges for insurance, 35c a bale, and yardage, 20c a bale, had accumulated, and lost 10 lbs. in weight. The weights at first were 2010 lbs. What was his loss?

—Ans. $23.20.

Ex. 6. A farmer was offered 10c a lb. for 21 B/C weighing 11,340 lbs., with no expenses deducted. He sold 4 months later for 11c a lb. The charges were, insurance, 30c; weighing, 10c, and delivering, 10c a bale. The cotton gained 60 lbs. in weight. What was his gain?

—Ans. $109.50.

Ex. 7. Jones & Brown, ginners, having refused 9c a lb. for 40 B/C, sold 5 months later for 10c a lb. The original weights were 20,960 lbs., on which there was a gain of 140 lbs. in final sale. The charges were: Insurance, 60c; sampling, 10c; commission, 15c a bale. What did they gain by holding?

—Ans. $189.60.

Ex. 8. What would be Jones & Brown's loss if they refused 10c a lb., hold 5 months, sell for 9c a lb., and lose 140 lbs. in weight, with charges and original weights same as in Ex. 7?

—Ans. $256.20.

Ex. 9. Fred Smith is offered 11c a lb. for 4 B/C; 10c a lb. for 5 B/C; 9c a lb. for 6 B/C; 8c a lb. for 10 B/C, or 9c a lb. average for the entire lot. Cotton averages 500 lbs. per bale. Should he accept the latter price, and what the loss?

—Ans. No. Loss $15.00.

EXAMPLES INVOLVING THE USE OF THE HALF CENT—DECIMAL EQUIVALENT $.005=50 POINTS.

NOTE.—By reference to Tables XVI and XVIII, it will be observed that ¼ Cent is represented as .0050 of a Dollar, which in value is the same as $.005 shown in the caption.

Ex. 1. Three B/C weighing, respectively, 520, 535 and 485 lbs., were sold for 10 1-2c a lb.; 2 B/C, weighing 510 and 525, at 9 1-2c a lb. What was the total value?

—Ans. $260.02½.

Ex. 2. A Grower sold his 7 B/C, which had been exposed to the weather for several months, for 11½c if not damaged, but on delivery, they showed to be badly injured. It was agreed to take nothing off in weight, but reduce the price ½c a lb. The cotton weighed 3,650 lbs. What was realized from the sale?

—Ans. $401.50.

Ex. 3. What was the Grower's loss for weather or "country damage" on his cotton in Ex. 2?

—Ans. $18.25.

Ex. 4. A man sold 5 B/C weighing 2,640 lbs. at 9½c, for which he was offered the week previous 8½c a lb. How much was his gain by holding 1 week?

—Ans. $26.40.

Ex. 5. In a competitive bid for a list of 15 B/C, two Buyers ran the price from 9c to 9½c a lb. What did the Seller realize on the sale, the total weight being 7,815 lbs.?

—Ans. $742.42½.

Ex. 6. A Buyer bought 50 B/C at an average of 7½c, which he sold 6 months afterwards at 9½c a lb. His expenses were $1.50 a bale. What was his gain, the cotton weighing 26,000 lbs.

—Ans. $445.00.

Ex. 7. A Farmer having 6 B/C, sold 2 for 8c; 2 months later, 2 for 8½c; 3 months after this he sold 2 for 9½c. The first two weighed 1,125 lbs., the second two 990 lbs., and the last two 1,105 lbs. What was the amount realized?

—Ans. $279.12½.

Ex. 8. Will Smith sold 12 B/C for 7½c per lb. He paid his landlord ¼ for rent, and ¾ of the ginning, which was $3.00 a bale. What did the cotton bring him after paying the expenses for ginning and rent? Weight of the 12 bales was 6,190.

—Ans. $321.18¾.

Ex. 9. John Hamlin sold his entire crop of cotton in the spring at 10½c a lb., to be delivered as gathered in the fall. He made 12 bales that weighed 6,240 pounds. At delivery time he could have sold 5 bales for 12c; 3 bales for 11½c; 2 bales for 10c and 2 bales for 9½c a lb. Did he gain or lose by his trade, and how much? The bales averaged 520 lbs.

—Ans. Lost $39.00.

EXAMPLES INVOLVING THE USE OF THE QUARTER CENT—
DECIMAL EQUIVALENT $.0025=25 POINTS.

NOTE.—Remember that four Decimals must be used when the Point is brought into requisition.

Ex. 1. Tom Brown sold 5 B/C weighing 2,580 lbs. at 8¼c. What was their value?

—Ans. $212.85.

REMARKS.—The 8 Cents are expressed thus—$.08. The 25 Points, as shown above, thus·$.0025. Eight Cents and 25 Points, thus $.0825. Multiplying the weight by this Decimal will give the total value.

Ex. 2. Two B/C weighing 1,030 lbs., were sold for 9¾c and one bale of 495 lbs. weight for 10¼c. Find the total value.

—Ans. $151.16¼.

Ex. 3. A Buyer bought a list of 30 B/C over the telephone for which he paid 9¼c, thinking it would average Middling. On inspection after receipt, he found it would bring 9½c. What was his gain if the cotton weighed 15,480 lbs.?

—Ans. $38.70.

Ex. 4. Henry Jones took 1,500 lbs. of seed cotton to the gin for which he was offered 3¼c per lb. Proof showed it "thirded itself" in passing through the ginnery. The cost for ginning was $3.00. He sold the bale at 10¼c per lb., and the seed at the rate of $16 per ton. What was his gain or loss by having the cotton ginned?

—Ans. Gain $7.50.

Ex. 5. Would Jones have gained anything had he sold the cotton for 9¾c a lb. and the seed at $12 per ton?

—Ans. Gain $3.00.

Ex. 6. A Farmer had a bale of damp cotton ginned, causing the lint to show "gin cuts" and "naps;" had it been ginned dry it would have brought 10½c but owing to imperfect ginning, it sold for 10¼c, and 10 lbs. were deducted for dampness. The original weight was 560 lbs.

How much loss to this man for having his cotton ginned damp?

—Ans. Loss $2.42½.

Ex. 7. A Grower offered 3 B/C for sale weighing 516, 522 and 532 lbs., for which he was offered 9¼c, gin weights, or 9½c and have the cotton re-weighed at the public scales; he sold on gin weights. What was his gain or loss? The re-weights were 506, 519 and 530 lbs.

—Ans. Loss $2.50.

Ex. 8. Tom Sanders found the market down ¼ (25 Points) when he offered his 4 B/C for sale, which weighed 2,620 lbs. What was his loss by the decline if he sold for 9¼c?

—Ans. Loss $6.55.

Ex. 9. Mr. Henderson offered to take 10c a lb. for his 5 B/C and deduct 30 lbs. for damage. The Buyer made a counter offer of 9¾c with no deduction in weights. The cotton weighed, without deduction, 2,580 lbs.. Mr. Henderson accepted the Buyer's offer. Did he gain or lose?

—Ans. Lost $3.45.

Ex. 10. A Tenant rented 40 acres of land at $3.00 an acre, on which he produced 10 B/C weighing 5,390 lbs. He sold the cotton at 8¼c and paid for ginning $32.34. Would he have gained or lost in the transaction had he rented to pay ¼ of the cotton, if he and the landlord had paid, each for his own ginning?

—Ans. Gained $16.92 to pay ¼ rent.

EXAMPLES INVOLVING THE USE OF THE ONE-EIGHTH CENT. DECIMAL EQUIVALENT $.00125=12½ POINTS.

Ex. 1. A man sold 1 B/C, 560 lbs., for 9⅛c per lb. What amount of money did he get?

—Ans. $51.10.

NOTE.—By reference to Table XVIII, it will be noted that ⅛ of a Cent is, Decimally, .0012½ of a Dollar, or to make a pure Decimal, it will be $.00125. Nine Cents equals $.09, then 9⅛ Cents equals $.09125, which if multiplied by the weight, gives the total value.

Ex.   2.   Find the value of 1,600 lbs. seed cotton at 3⅛c a lb.

—Ans. $50.00.

Ex.   3.   Mr. Smith sold 8 B/C for 11¼c, after refusing 11⅛c by the first Bidder.   What did he gain by selling to the second Buyer?   The cotton weighed 4,120 lbs.

—Ans. $5.15.

Ex.   4.   Mr. Anderson sold 1 B/C, 512 lbs., at 9½c a lb., 1 bale, 520 lbs., at 9¼c, and 1 bale, 560 lbs., at 9⅛c. How much money did he get for all?

—Ans. $147.84.

Ex.   5.   Jones & Adams bought 50 B/C weighing 25,500 lbs., on which they made a profit of ⅛c.   What was their gain on the whole?

—Ans. $31.87½.

Ex.   6.   John Knox, having 900 lbs. of seed cotton, bought 600 lbs. more to make a bale.   He paid 3⅛c for the 600 lbs.   Including the weight of the bagging and ties, the cotton "thirded itself" when ginned.   The bale was sold for 10⅛c per lb. and the seed at $20 per ton.   What did Mr. Knox gain on the seed cotton bought?

—Ans. $5.50.

Ex.   7.   Henry Brown sold 1 B/C, 520 lbs., at 6⅝c per lb.   What was its value?

—Ans. $34.45.

Ex.   8.   In a sale of 10 B/C, 3 weighed 1,616 lbs. and brought 10⅛c; 4 weighed 2,120 lbs. and brought 9⅞c; 3 weighed 1,560 lbs. and sold for 9⅛c.   What was their total value?

—Ans. $515.32.

Ex.   9.   Three B/C are worth $161⅜; 2 bales $102⅛; 5 bales $252⅜.   What is their total value?

—Ans. $515.87½.

NOTE.—See value of ⅞ in Tables XVII and XVIII, and add as in simple addition.

EXAMPLES INVOLVING THE USE OF THE ONE-SIXTEENTH CENT.
DECIMAL EQUIVALENT $.000625=6¼ POINTS.

Note.—The following Problems, like the preceding, are solved under Rule 1:

Ex. 1. Find the value of 1 B/C, 534 lbs., at 7 1/16c.
—Ans. $37.71 3-8.

Ex. 2. One B/C, 544 lbs., sold for 9 1/16c; another of 528 lbs. for 8 1/16c. What was the value of both?
—Ans. $91.87.

Ex. 3. A Grower refused 8½c a lb. for his cotton, but sold it the following day for 1/16c less. His 10 bales weighed 5,160 lbs. What did he lose by not selling the first day.
—Ans. $3.22½.

Ex. 4. Mr. James had 4 B/C of 4 different Grades. One bale, 544 lbs., 9 1/16c; 1 bale, 540 lbs., 9c; 1 bale, 640 lbs., 8 15/16c; 1 bale, 528 lbs., 8⅞c. What was the total value?
—Ans. $201.96.

Ex. 5. Three B/C weighing 516, 524 and 520 lbs., were sold for 8 3/16c; 2 B/C, 519 and 541 lbs., for 8 1/16c. What was their total value?
—Ans. $213.18¾.

Ex. 6. A list of 100 B/C, high grade, sold for 3/16 above the market quotation. The weights being 52,480 lbs., what was the gain in Premium value?
—Ans. $98.40.

Ex. 7. A Cotton Buyer classing 40 B/C after sunset, found on inspection of the cotton in a good light, that he had made an error, and offered the Seller 1/16 to release him from the trade. The Seller accepted. The cotton weighed 20,480 pounds. What did the error cost the Buyer?
—Ans. $12.80.

Note.—One-sixteenth of a Cent is .0006¼ of a Dollar. Multiply the weight by this Decimal of a dollar, or divide the total weight by 16 and point off 4 Decimals in the answer. The result will be the value of the cotton at 1/16c.

Ex. 8. A Buyer received a limit (price) of 10½c a lb. B/M (See Abbreviations), on which to buy cotton. He sold "short" 100 bales on it. The market declined 25 Points during the day. On his limit he bought 40 bales, 20,320 lbs., at 10 7/16c; 28 bales, 14,560 lbs., at 10⅜c; 32 bales, 16,160 lbs., at 10¼c. What did the Buyer gain on the day's business?

—Ans. $71.30.

Ex. 9. A Farmer rented 50 acres of land "on halves," from which he gathered 20 B/C, averaging 500 lbs. per bale, which he sold at 10 3/16c. The landlord gave his half of the seed to the tenant for hauling 10 bales to the gin and to Market. The ginner charged 60c per cwt. for ginning, which he gave, in addition to the payment of $3.00 for the seed in each bale of seed cotton. The Farmer sold 17 bales of seed, put 1,500 lbs. of seed cotton in each bale, and hired 14 bales picked at 70c per cwt. What amount of money did he get for his part of the crop and hauling for the landlord?

—Ans. $404.37½.

Explanation—

Twenty bales of 500 lbs. each=20×500=10,000 lbs.

10,000 lbs. at 10 3/16c...=$1,018.75

Received $3 a bale for 17 bales 17×3=value of
seed ....=   51.00

Receipts for cotton and seed.........................=$1,069.75

    Paid for ginning... $ 9.00

    Paid ½ of cotton to landlord........................... $509.37½

    Paid for picking 14 B/C at 70c....................

    1,500 lbs. at 70c=$10.50.................................

    14 bales=14×$10.50......................................   =$147.00

    Total Paid $665.37½

    $1,069.75—$665.37½=$404.37½   Ans.

Ex. 10. August Wilhof sold 4 B/C, weighing 1,584 lbs., on Wednesday, to be delivered the following Saturday, at 11 5/16c all around. On the way to the market the cotton accidentally caught fire. Repacking it a week later, the cotton lost in weight 512 lbs.; the ginner charged $1.00 a bale for re-wrapping, and the Market had declined ½c. What did Mr. Wilhof lose by the accident?

—Ans. $66.28.

EXAMPLES INVOLVING THE USE OF THE ONE-THIRTY-SECOND CENT—DECIMAL EQUIVALENT $.0003125=3⅛ POINTS.

Ex. 1. What is the value of 1 B/c, 512 lbs., at 8 1/32c per lb.?

—Ans. $41.12.

NOTE.—This Fraction is an exceptional one in the Trade; that is, it is not used so extensively as the others in the preceding. In order to know the position of the Decimal Point, if the full Fraction is used, seven figures must be counted off from the right towards the left in the product.

Ex. 2. I was offered by one Buyer for my 6 B/C, 12¼c by another 1/32c better. I sold to the latter. My cotton weighed 3,072 lbs. What was the total amount realized, and what did I gain by selling to the last Buyer?

Ans.—Total $377.28; gain 96c.

Ex. 3. Johnson & Smith bought 20,560 lbs. of cotton at 9 1/32c and sold it for 9¼c. What was their gain?

—Ans. $44.97½.

NOTE.—Refer to Table XVII, which shows 1/32 of a Dollar to be .03125 Decimally, and for a Cent, 1/100 of that amount, which equals $.0003125.

The value of the Fraction ¼ converted to thirty-seconds, equals 8/32. From the 8/32 (¼) subtract the 1/32.

$$8/32=\$.0025000$$
$$1/32=\$.0003125$$
$$7/32=\$.0021875$$

Multiply the weight, 20,560 lbs., by $.0021875, which equals $44.97¼.

Ex. 4. I sold 3 B/C, 526, 497 and 545 lbs., respectively, for 8 15/16c. I lost 1/32 in weights. What did I get for the cotton?

—Ans. $135.76.

Ex.   5.   A Buyer bought 50 B/C for 10 7/32 average, held it 2 months and sold for 10 23/32c. His expenses were: insurance 40c, weighing 10c and drayage 10c a bale. The cotton weighed 25,600 lbs. What was his gain or loss?

—Ans. Gain $98.00.

Ex.   6.   A Farmer sold 35 B/C for 8½c a lb. to be delivered in 5 days, during which time the Market declined 5/32c. The Buyer offered $40 to the Farmer to cancel the sale. The cotton weighed 18,550 lbs. What would the Buyer have saved or lost had the Farmer accepted the $40?

—Ans. Saved $11.01 9/16.

Ex.   7.   Eldred Miller was offered 10.37½ for 8 B/C by one Buyer and 10 12/32 by another. Which offered the best price and what would he have gained or lost by selling to the first Buyer?

—Ans. Neither. Nothing.

Ex.   8.   Thompson & Brown shipped 100 B/C to New Orleans, of which the out-turn showed a loss equal to 1/32 in price. The cotton weighed 52,800 lbs. What was the money loss?

—Ans. $16.50.

Ex.   9.   Edgar Clark shipped 60 B/C to Savannah, which lost 2 2/3 lbs. average to the bale, and 3/32 valuation in classification. He paid for 30,592 lbs. at 8 3/5c, and sold it delivered in Savannah at 9 9/32c. The freight rate was 30c per cwt., and commission $1.00 per bale. What was the gain or loss on the shipment?

—Ans. Gain $13.25 1/5.

Ex.   10.   Two Buyers in discussing the average of a list of 100 bales, disagreed. One said it was worth on the Market 9⅜c, the other argued that it was worth 3⅛ Points better, and he would give that Premium for it. What is the difference in value between the two Buyers? The cotton weighed 48,000 lbs.

—Ans. $15.00.

CHAPTER II.

SECTION III.

BASIC COTTON CALCULATIONS.

Under this heading a starting point is assumed, from which the beginning for calculations is made, and the abbreviations expressive of the terms[14] will be frequently used.

As the student advances in the subject of the cotton question, he will find it convenient to observe the Terms and Abreviations used by the Trade in solving cotton problems by rapid calculations.

In figuring cotton on basis classification, it is necessary to know the Base and the Grades relative to it, also the Letters, Figures and Characters representing those Grades.

Having learned in Chapter I the value of the Cent, Half, Quarter and Eighth cents, etc., in connection with the value of the Point, in making cotton calculations, the following Problems to be solved are stated on the assumption that the student is conversant with those values, meaning and application, and is now prepared to accept shorter methods for getting definite and average results.

For clearness, the Grades are again given with corresponding Numbers, Letters and Characters, to which the student's attention is called, with the request that he familiarize himself with them, as they will frequently appear in stating Problems.

The Cotton Exchange now recognizes 23 Grades of cotton, including the Tinges and Stains and Half and Quarter subdivisions.

It is immaterial the number of Grades to be considered, for the *principle* for calculating them is the same.

---

[14]See "Terms," p. 88.

For practical purposes in making calculations covering a variety of Grades, the New York official list is quoted, less the Quarter Grades, with Characters, Numbers and Initials representing them, preceding and following the Grade name.

TABLE XIX.

Character and Number	Grade Name.	Initials
a	Fair	F.
b	Strict Middling Fair	S.M.F.
c	Middling Fair	M.F.
d	Strict Good Middling	S.G.M
1	Good Middling	G.M.
2	Strict Middling	S.M.
3	MIDDLING (Basis)	M.
4	Strict Low Middling	S.L.M.
5	Low Middling	L.M.
6	Strict Good Ordinary	S.G.O.
7	Good Ordinary	G.O.
8	Strict Low Ordinary[15]	S.L.O.
9	Low Ordinary[15]	L.O.
d-t	Strict Good Middling Tinged	S.G.M.T.
1-t	Good Middling Tinged (Middling value)	G.M.T.
2-t	Strict Middling Tinged	S.M.T.
3-t	Middling Tinged	M.T.
4-t	Strict Low Middling Tinged	S.L.M.T.
5-t	Low Middling Tinged	L.M.T.
3-S	Middling Stained	M.S.

Members of the Trade do not all use the same symbols to indicate the Grades. Some use Letters, some Numbers, some Characters of their own devising for their special private use, but all are used for brevity in gradation work, correspondence, making calculations, etc.

---

[15]These Grades are not in the New York official list, and Fully and Barely are left out.

All Grades better in quality than Middling receive a *Premium*—better price—while those inferior in gradation are penalized at a *Discount*—less price. The Premiums are so much "on" the Middling price; the Discounts so much "off" the Middling price.[16]

Good Middling Tinged (G.M.T.) is recognized of equal value with Middling.

There being no definite difference to be taken off or added for Tinges and Stains by the Trade, beyond what may be arbitrarily applied, calculations involving the operation to find their values will be stated in the Problems showing such kinds of cotton.

The Cotton Exchanges assess a variable Discount on all the Tinges and Stains except the Grade S.G.M.T., which is given a small Premium above Middling.

Cotton quotations being often given in halves, quarters, eighths, sixteenths etc., are easily converted into Points by calculation, or by reverting to the Table of Points, or Table XVIII.

TO FIND THE TOTAL VALUE OF COTTON WHEN DIFFERENT
PRICES FOR DIFFERENT GRADES ARE GIVEN.

Where the Price of each Grade is known, with its corresponding weight, it is an easy matter to ascertain its value— by multiplying the price by the weight. If several weights, the value of each will be calculated separately, and the sum of the separate values will make the total value.

The *Rule* applying for the preceding Examples will be found applicable for the solution of the following Problems:

NOTE.—To accelerate the work it is frequently easier to perform the multiplication by multiplying the weight by the price.

———

[16]See " Discount and Premiums," pp. 108 and 112; also Specific Gradation, p. 45.

PROBLEMS.

Ex.   1.   Find the value of 1 M. B/C, 520 lbs., at 10c.
—Ans. $52.00.

Ex.   2.   In the sale of 2 B/C, one classed M., the other S. M., the basis price was 10c with ¼ on for S. M.   The M. weighed 500 lbs. and the S. M. 520 lbs.   What was their value?
—Ans. $103.30.

Ex.   3.   Jones sold 3 B/C; 1 M., 548 lbs., at 10c; 1 S. L. M., 520 lbs., at 9¾c; 1 L. M., 580 lbs., at 9c a lb.   What was their value?
—Ans. $157.70.

Ex.   4.   What is the difference in value between 4 B/C, 2,640 lbs., at 8¼c and 8 5/16c a lb.?
—Ans. $1.65.

Ex.   5.   Find the value of 7 G. M. B/C, .3,620 lbs., at 10½c; 5 S. M., 2,600 lbs., at 10¼c; 4 M., 2,250 lbs., at 10c; 3 S. L. M., 1,650 lbs., at 9¾c and 1 L. M., 560 lbs., at 9c.
—Ans. $1,082.87 1-2.

Ex.   6.   In a controversy over the gradation of 2 B/C one Buyer said one was a S. M. and the other a G. M. The second Buyer classed them as 2 S. M.   The cotton was sold to the first buyer who allowed a ¼ on S. M. for G. M.   What did the Seller gain by selling to the first Buyer?   The weight of the S. M. was 560 lbs., the other 580 lbs.
—Ans. $1.45.

NOTE.—It makes no difference what the basis price in this Problem— the gain of ¼ was on 1 bale only.

Ex.   7.   The differences expressed by the Cotton Exchanges for relative Grades do not always harmonize with those demanded by the Trade.   Will Eddins had 12 bales of L. M. cotton, which was quoted at ¾ off M.   When he sold, the Buyer deducted 1¼ off as a Trade Discount.   What was the difference in value between the Trade and Exchange Discounts? The cotton weighed 6,480 lbs.

—Ans. $32.40.

Ex. 8. A Grower knowing the price of cotton to be 8½c M/B, took 15 bales to Market, but on arrival found the price had declined 12 Points. The cotton weighed 7,860 lbs. What was his loss on the decline?

—Ans. 9.43+

Ex. 9. Suppose the Market had gone up 20 points, what would have been the price per lb., and what would the Grower in Example 8 have gained?

—Ans. 8.70c.
Gain $15.72.

Ex. 10. Find the value of 2 G. M. B/C, 1,160 lbs., at 9.87½c; 3 S. M., 1,648 lbs., at $9.62½c; 5 M., 2,824 lbs., 9⅜c and 2 L. M., 1,000 lbs., at 8⅝c.

—Ans. $624.17.

NOTE.—The 87½ and 62½ equal ⅞ and ⅝ respectively. The Fractions then are ⅞, ⅝, ⅜ and ⅝. These can easily be converted into Points. (See Tables XVII and XVIII) and annexed to the Cents to complete the Decimal, which can be used as a multiplier instead of the Mixed Fraction.

Ex. 11. What can I get for 5 B/C, the weights being 522, 518, 547, 560 and 503 lbs., if the price is 7 2/5c?

—Ans. $196.10.

NOTE.—One-fifth of a Cent equals 20 Points (see Table XVI); 2/5 equals 40 Points. Decimally, then the price is 7.40c.

Ex. 12. Find the value of 20 B/C at 11¾c. Weight 9,900 lbs. —Ans. $1,163.25.

NOTE.—Convert the ¾ into Points.

Ex. 13. In the sale of 80 B/C, 41,280 lbs., the basis price was raised by competition from 9.60 to 3/10 of a Cent better. What was the sale price and what was the gain over the basis value?

—Ans. Sale price 9.90c.
Gain, $123.84.

NOTE.—The price 9.60, means 9 Cents and 60 Points. Expressed Decimally it is .0960 of a Dollar. Ten Points (see Table XVI) are expressed as .0010 of a Dollar. Thirty Points equals 3x10 Points equals $.0030, or 3/10 of a Cent.

The 9.60 decimally is	$.0960
The 3/10 is, decimally	.0030
The price, then, is	$.0990=9.90c.

Ex. 14. A Cotton Merchant bought 100 B/C after nightfall by telephone; the Market came in 15 Points up the following morning. What was his gain on each 500-lb. bale?

—Ans. 75c.

Ex. 15. If this lot of cotton averaged 520 lbs. to the bale, what was the Merchant's gain on the entire lot?

—Ans. $78.00.

Ex. 16. M. cotton being worth 7⅝c, what can I get for 1 G. M. T., 560 lbs., and 1 G. O., 540 lbs., with 250 off for G. O.?

—Ans. $70.37½

Statement: G. M. T. has M. value;

7⅝c	=.07625 Dollar
250 Points off	= .0250 Dollar
Difference	=.05125 Dollar
.05125 Dollar =5⅛ Cents.	
540 lbs.×5⅛=value G. O.=27.67½	
560 lbs. ×7⅝	=42.70
Total	$70.37½

CHAPTER III.

SECTION IV (Continued).

TO FIND THE AVERAGE PRICE WHEN THE PRICE AND WEIGHTS OF THE BALES ARE DIFFERENT WITH BOTH WEIGHTS AND GRADES GIVEN.

In calculating large lists of cotton, time is saved by getting the *average* price, and multiplying it by the total weights to ascertain the total value.

FIRST PROCESS.

In getting the average under this Process, the weights of the different Grades, and the prices for those Grades must be known.

The averages secured under it are absolutely correct, but owing to the amount of mathematical work involved, and the slowness of operation in computing extended lists of cotton, the Trade does not utilize it for every-day practical purposes.

(Introduced for the purpose of showing Problems solved with accuracy, in comparison with other practical methods in daily use, whose results are close approximations to it.)

RULE 2.—*Arrange the bales, grades, weights and prices in columns; placing bales under bales, grades under grades, weights under weights, prices under prices. Find the value of the different grades separately, by multiplying the weight of each grade by its price, and placing the amount opposite its grade, which will form a column for the values of the different grades. Add these values, divide the sum by the total number of pounds; the quotient will be the average price.*

NOTE.—When the M. price only is given, with the statement that so many sixteenths, eighths or quarters are added as Premiums for the Higher Grades and similar relative differences or Discounts off for the Lower ones, find the value of each Grade by adding the Premiums for the Higher Grades to the M. price and deducting the Discounts for the Lower ones.

After ascertaining the Grade price, proceed as stated in the Rule.

When the totals of all the values show Dollars and Cents, reduce them to Cents by multiplying by 100, the number of Cents in a Dollar, and divide this Product, as stated, by the total number of pounds; the answer will be the average price in Cents and fractions of a cent.

PROBLEMS.

Ex. 1. Let it be required to average the following list of cotton: 8 G. M., 7 S. M., 5 M., 3 S. L. M. and 2 L. M. Basis 10c; $\frac{1}{4}$ "on" for S. M. and $\frac{1}{2}$ "on" for G. M., with $\frac{1}{4}$ "off" for S. L. M., and $\frac{3}{4}$ "off" for L. M., with the weights shown in explanation.

—Ans. 10.14+c.

EXPLANATION.—We must, from the Problem, get the price of each Grade. M. is the basis, and is 10c a lb. From the statement, S. M. is $\frac{1}{4}$ on M., and G. M. $\frac{1}{4}$ on that, or $\frac{1}{2}$ on M. Then for the Lower Grades $\frac{1}{4}$ and $\frac{3}{4}$ off respectively, for S. L. M. and L. M.

From this quotation let us arrange the Problem according to the Rule, in tabular form.

G. M. $10\frac{1}{2}$, ($\frac{1}{2}$ "on" makes $10\frac{1}{2}$)
S. M. $10\frac{1}{4}$, ($\frac{1}{4}$ "on" makes $10\frac{1}{4}$)
M. 10 (Basis)
S. L. M. $9\frac{3}{4}$, ($\frac{1}{4}$ "off" leaves $9\frac{3}{4}$)
L. M. $9\frac{1}{4}$, ($\frac{3}{4}$ "off" leaves $9\frac{1}{4}$)

Continuing further:—

Grades.	Price	Weights.	Value.
8 G. M.	$10\frac{1}{2}$	× 4160 lbs.	=$ 436.80
7 S. M.	$10\frac{1}{4}$	× 3612 lbs.	= 370.23
5 M.	10	× 2510 lbs.	= 251.00
3 S. L. M.	$9\frac{3}{4}$	× 1620 lbs.	= 157.85
2 L. M.	$9\frac{1}{4}$	× 1000 lbs.	= 92.50
		12902	$1308.48

1308.48×100c=130848 Cents.

130848÷12902=10.14+Cents=average price.

NOTE.—The number of bales in this Problem are not reckoned—only the weights of them.

Ex. 2.   Average this list:
2 G. M. 1120 lbs. at 8c.
1 S. M. 560 lbs. at 7¾c.
2 M. 1000 lbs. at 7½c.

—Ans. 7.76+c.

Ex. 3.   What should I pay as an average price for the following list?
2 G. M. 980 at 9c.
3 M. 1610 at 8 ½c.
4 S. L. M. 2180 at 7¾c.
2 L. M. 1050 at 7c.

—Ans.   8.03+c.

Ex. 4.   As an all-round price, what should a Buyer pay for 15 B/C at 8c B/M ;.1-4 up (on) for S. M., and 1-2 up for G. M.; ¼ down (off) for S. L. M. and 100 down for L. M. Three G. M., 1610; four S. M., 2012; one M., 503; five S. L. M., 2490, and two L. M., 1015 lbs. respectively?

—Ans.   7.95+c.

NOTE.—To the M. base, add the Premiums; from it take the Discounts, as stated in Statement, Problem 1. "One hundred down" means 100 points or 1 Cent deducted from the M. price.

Ex. 5.   C is offered 10.30 for 1 S. M., 536 lbs., and 10.05 for 1 M., 520 lbs., or 10.15 as an average price.   He sold for 10.15; did he lose or gain by accepting the average price and how much?

—Ans.   Lost 28 4/10c.

Ex. 6.   Find the cost of 1 G. M. B/C, 496 lbs., at 10¼c, and 2 M. bales, 512 and 528 lbs., at 9.80. What will be the total value and what is the average price?

—Ans.   Total value $152.76.
Average price 9.94+c.

Ex. 7.   Average 3 S. G. M., 1,640 lbs.; 2 S. M., 1,080 lbs.; 2 S. L. M., 992 lbs.; 1 L. M., 576 lbs.; 2 S. G. O., 1,120 lbs.;

B/M 5c, 5-8 on for S. G. M., 1-2 on for G. M., 1-4 on for S. M., 3-8 off for S. L. M., 125 off for L. M. and 200 off for S. G. O.

—Ans. 4.62+c.

Ex. 8. Average the following list on a 9c basis: 1 M. F., 150 up, 520 lbs.; 2 S. G. M., 100 up, 1,040 lbs.; 3 S. M., 3-8 up, 1,560 lbs.; 8 M., 4,160 lbs.; 5 S. L. M., 3-8 down, 2,600 lbs.; 1 L. M., 100 down, 520 lbs.; 2 S. G. O., 200 down, 1,040 lbs.; 10 S. M. T., 10 down, 5,200 lbs.; 9 S. L. M. T., 75 down, 4,680 lbs.; 7 L. M. T., 125 down, 3,640 lbs.; 2 M. S., 50 down, 1,040 lbs.

—Ans. 8.60½c.

Getting the average under this Process is of no material benefit to a Dealer, beyond the fact he can establish it accurately, as the value of the quantity of each Grade, and the total value of all is secured before the average can be found.

The Dealer knows the total value before knowing the average.

SECOND PROCESS—TO FIND THE AVERAGE PRICE WHEN THE NUMBER OF BALES AND CLASS OF EACH ARE GIVEN BUT NOT THE WEIGHTS.

The following rule describes one of the short methods of finding the average price where the weights of the bales are unknown.

The average thus found is not absolutely correct, but approximates accuracy very closely.

RULE 3.—*Assume the whole number of bales as so many pounds; multiply the number of bales in the different classes by the Grade prices of the respective classes; add the products and divide by the whole number of bales. The quotient will be the average price, very nearly.*

Let it be required to find the average price of the following 25 B/C.

Ex. 1.   Six S. G. M., 10.75c; 5 S. M., 10¼c; 4 M., 10c; 6 S. L. M., 9 11/16c; 4 L. M., 9⅛c.

—Ans.   10.01½c.

EXPLANATION.—Following the Rule we make the tabular statement, with the number of bales representing pounds, to be multiplied by the price of each pound.

$$
\begin{aligned}
\text{S. G. M.} \quad & 6 \times 1075 && = 64.50 \\
\text{G. M.} \\
\text{S. M.} \quad & 5 \times 10.25 && = 51.25 \\
\text{M.} \quad & 4 \times 10.00 && = 40.00 \\
\text{S. L. M.} \quad & 6 \times 9.6875^{17} && = 58.1250 \\
\text{L. M.} \quad & 4 \times 9.125 && = 36.50 \\
\hline
25 \qquad && = 250.375 \div 25 = 10.01\tfrac{1}{2}
\end{aligned}
$$

The approximate average made as detailed in the preceding Problem is upon the hypothesis that if 1 lb. of S. G. M. cotton is worth 10¾c, 6 lbs. would equal 6 times that value; 5 lbs. S. M. at 10¼c a lb., equal 5 times the value of 1 lb., etc.   Reasoning by analogy, if 25 lbs. are worth two Dollars, fifty and three-eighths Cents ($2.50⅜, see Statement in Problem above), 1 lb. is worth 1/25 of that amount, which equals 10.01½ Cents.

This average price is not exact, because of a difference in the weights of the bales of cotton.   Were all the bales of the same weight, the average would prove absolutely correct.

While the weights of the bales are not shown in the Problem, the numbers representing them, are indicative of that many pounds for that Grade, which, as seen, are variable, hence a cause for inaccuracy.

This process of averaging is sufficiently near correctness to be of practical value in the cotton Trade, although as stated, it is used but little.

Ex. 2.   On a 10c basis, I bought 10 B/C, with the Differences of ¼ and ½ up for S. M. and G. M., and 5/16 and 1 Cent down for S. L. M. and L. M.   I classed it out as 3 G.

[17]See Table XVII—11/16=.6875, ½=.125.

MB—6

M., 1 S. M., 5 M., and 1 S. L. M. The Buyer for whom I bought showed his out-turn to be 2 G. M., 2 S. M., 3 M., 1 S. L. M. and 2 L. M. What amount of *Reclamation* did he claim from me? Total weight 5,000 lbs.

—Ans. $11.25.

NOTE.—Tabulate each classification as shown in Explanation for Ex. 1, subtracting the lesser from the greater amount.

Ex. 3.   Thompson & Hendrix shipped 50 B/C from Jackson, Miss., to Jones & Brown, New Orleans, which was sold on a 11c basis f. o. b. Jackson, with the weights and Grades guaranteed by the Shippers, who classed it as 2 S. G. M., 5 G. M., 7 S. M., 10 M., 15 S. L. M., 6 L. M., 3 S. G. O. and 2 G. M. T. The Differences to apply were 5/16, ½ and ¾ on for S. M., G. M., and S. G. M. respectively, with 5/16, ¾ and 1½ off for S. L. M., L. M., S. G. O.; G. M. T., M. value. Thompson & Hendrix drew for the full value of their cotton on the B/L and Draft, which the local bank paid on Invoice weights, 26,500 lbs., at Jackson. The returns showed 26,-180 lbs. weight at New Orleans, and the classification of Jones & Brown to be 1 S. G. M., 5 G. M., 5 S. M., 11 M., 16 S. L. M., 7 L. M., 4 S. G. O. and 1 G. M. T. What will be *reclaimed* by Jones & Brown for over-classification and short weight?

—Ans. $55.66+

The disagreement in classification shown in examples 2 and 3 is of frequent occurrence in the Trade, and emphasizes the necessity for a uniform Standard and familiarity with it by all parties concerned.

NOTE.—It may be stated that over- or under-classification is resorted to by both Buyer and Seller for pecuniary purposes sometimes, but it is easily detected and the aggressor usually gets punished in the end. Such practices are exceptions, and not indorsed by the Trade.

Ex. 4.   A Street Buyer bought from wagons during the day 13 B/C at 9.80c; 3 at 10⅜c; 6 at 9.42½c; 2 at 8.60c. What was the average price paid?

—Ans. 9.68c nearly.

Ex. 5. A Grower was offered 8.85 for his 35 B/C at Macon, Ga., but thinking the offer too small, shipped the cotton to a Commission Merchant at New Orleans. The cotton was held 4 months and sold for 10c a lb. If Freight was 55c a cwt., charges $1.00 a bale, the first month, and 30c a bale each subsequent month, not reckoning any interest on the money, what was gained or lost by consigning this cotton? The cotton weighed 18,720 lbs.

—Ans. Gained $45.82.

Ex. 6. A Cotton Buyer bought from farmers' wagons 100 B/C which cost him an average of 22 Points on Middling; but when he sold it he found his second classification to run 25 on Middling. What was his gain by re-classing? The cotton weighed 51,860 lbs.

—Ans. $15.55 4/5.

NOTE.—Cotton Buyers in buying cotton in small quantities from Growers, occasionally find their own classification at time of sale to be at variance with that at time of purchase. This can be accounted for by reason of the fact that at time of purchase, smaller samples were drawn, or possibly they were viewed in a different light.

Ex. 7. A list of 140 B/C was offered for sale. Three Buyers, A, B and C, bid on it. The Market was 12¼c basis. A had 12 5/16, with ¼ and ⅜ up; 5/16, ⅞ and 150 down; B had 12¼ with ¼ and ½ up; 5/16, 100 and 150 down, with a discretion of 1/16 if needed, and C had 12¼ with the Market Differences which were ¼ and ⅜ up; 5/16, ⅞ and 125 down, but being an Exporter, figured Liverpool Class on the purchase, which averaged ⅛ on American Class, except L. M. and S. G. O. The Grades were 30 G. M., 40 S. M., 45 M., 12 S. L. M., 10 L. M., 3 S. G. O. What was the average price of each and to whom should the cotton be sold?

—Ans. Sell to C.
A's average 12.34c.
B's average 12.36c.
C's average 12.40c.

Statement: B had a quarter (¼) basis with a "discretion" of 1/16,
which he used; A had a 5/16 basis; C had a ¼ basis, but in order to
get the cotton, bid, and figured Liverpool Class on all Grades except
L. M. and S. G. O.

For the grades shown there were for

	A.	B.	C.
G. M.	12 11/16	12 13/16	12 3/4
S. M.	12 9/16	12 9/16	12 5/8
M.	12 5/16	12 5/16	12 3/8
S. L. M.	12	12	12 1/16
L. M.	11 7/16	11 5/16	11 3/8
S. G. O.	10 13/16	10 13/16	11

By reverting to Table 2, the Decimal Fraction equivalent to the
Common Fraction should be *annexed* to the Cent price, and the Rule
followed in making the necessary multiplications.

The prices stated for B and C are their final bids, after B added
his discretion of 1/16 and C had figured his Liverpool Class.

A's prices converted to Decimals, for calculation with the number
of bales, follow. Let the Student calculate the others from this one.

$$
\begin{array}{rcl}
\text{No.} & & \\
\text{Bales.} \quad \text{Price.} & & \text{Value} \\
30 \times 12.6875 & = \$ & 3.806250 \\
40 \times 12.5625 & = & 5.025000 \\
45 \times 12.3125 & = & 5.540625 \\
12 \times 12. & = & 1.440000 \\
10 \times 11.4375 & = & 1.143750 \\
3 \times 10.8125 & = & .324375 \\
\hline
140 & & \$17.280000
\end{array}
$$

$17.28 ÷ 140 = $.1234 + = 12.34c = A's average price.

NOTE.—The Statement that B "had a quarter basis" is a Trade expression, and is used to indicate the M. price, exclusive of the 12c.
Instead of saying "12¼ basis," or "7⅝ basis," or "9½ basis," it
is common to hear Dealers say "I had a quarter today," "I had 5-8
last night" or "The best I can get is a half;" the inference being pre-
sumed that all know the Cent price.

Sometimes to secure a list of good cotton, or to get what is wanted,
large Buyers will allow a small Premium to be added to the Market
price or to the "limit" their representatives have, which Premium is
called a *"Discretion."*

Ex. 8.   I bought a list of 10 bales of hard cotton in No-
vember.   There were 3 S. G. O., 2 M. T., 1 M. spotted, 2. G.
O., 2 M. S.   Basis 8½c.   The Discounts were S. G. O., 150;

M. T., 30; M., Spotted, 35; G. O., 250; M. S., 90. What was the average price?

—Ans. 7.27 1-2c.

Ex. 9. If the weights of the bales taken in order named are 1620, 1130, 1180, 1090 and 522 lbs., what is the value of the cotton in Ex. 8?

—Ans. $403.18.

Ex. 10. Under this Process, average Ex. 3 given under Process I.

—Ans. 8.04+c

NOTE.—It will be seen that the average under this Process gives about 1 Point more than shown under Process I, which is correct.

THIRD PROCESS.— TO FIND THE AVERAGE PRICE WITH NUMBER AND CLASS, BUT NOT WEIGHTS OF EACH BALE GIVEN.

This is known as the sixteenth, or 6¼ Point Process.

To make cotton calculations involving its use, quotations must be in sixteenths or multiples of sixteenths.

Averages are ascertained under this Process as in the preceding one, without the use of weights, and the result is a close approximation.

For practical purposes, among all Buyers, this Process is used almost universally, as it is brief, easily learned, and very convenient for those buying and selling in lots, after making the classification.

After making the average, the weight of the entire lot is multiplied by the average price to obtain the total amount.

Consignees in giving account-sales of cotton received by them as purchasers or Factors, do not always use this method in showing the result of the sale, but instead, multiply the total weight of each Grade by the price of that Grade, and from the sum of the totals, deduct the amount of the Charges, remitting the balance.

The result of this Process is practically the same as that obtained under Process II.

In performing the operation under this Process, it is more convenient to understand and represent the different Grades by characters, letters, numbers or initials. (See page 118.)

To obtain the average under the 6¼ Point method, let us be governed by the following:

RULE 4.—(1). *Designate the Grades by their character representations, as a, b, c; 1, 2, 3, etc.; opposite each Grade place the number of bales of that Grade; multiply these numbers by the number of sixteenths the class shows to be above or below Middling value; add the products of the sixteenths above and below Middling, separately; subtract the lesser from the greater amount, multiply the remainder by 6¼, divide the product by the number of bales; the quotient will be the number of Points to be added to, or subtracted from, the Middling price.*

(2.) *If the excess is above, add the Points to; if below, subtract from the Middling price, the result will be the average price, nearly.*

Ex. 1. Find the average of 1 M., 2 S. L. M., 5 L. M.; M. B. 10c, ¼ off for S. L. M., ¾ off for L. M.

—Ans. 9.54 1/6c.

NOTE.—It should be remembered in calculating averages under this Rule, the Middling Grade is *passed*—that is, it does not enter into the computation of the Problem further than being added to the number of bales to be averaged.

The arrangement of the form 'and the Rule should be memorized, after which, the familiarity of the operation will become quite easy.

Arrange the work in this way:

Grades.	Bales.	Price	Sixteenths. (Bales.)	Sixteenths.
(M) 3	1	10		
(S. L. M.) 4	2	9¾	4×2=	8
(L. M.) 5	3	9¼	12×3=	36
Added= 6			=16	=44

Explanation: The 3, 4, and 5 represent the Grades; ¼ off=4/16, represented as 4; ¾ off equal 12/16, shown as 12. There are 2 bales of S. L. M. The 2 (bales) is multiplied by the 4 (sixteenths)=8 six-teenths; 3 (bales) multiplied by 12 (sixteenths)=36 sixteenths. Add-ing the sixteenths=44 sixteenths. 6¼ Points =1/16. Multiplying the 44 by 6¼ Points, gets the total number of Points in 44 sixteenths, which, divided by the number of bales (6) gives the number of Points to be taken from the Middling price, the remainder of which equals the average price.

It will be noticed the S. L. M. price is 9¾ and the L. M. 9¼ Cents. The M. price is 10c, ¼ off leaves 9¾; the ¼ is the amount "off;" it is the amount used—the 4/16 reckoned. The numerator of the Fraction 4, is the *figure* used. From the M. price down to L. M. is ¾ off, ¾=12/16, of which the 12 only is used.

Explanation:

(Sixteenths)		(Points)		
44	×	6 1/4	=275	Points
(Points)		(Bales)		
275	÷	6	= 45 5/6	Points
M. Price	=	10c	=1000	Points

The Grades S. L. M. and L. M. are *under* M., hence the 45 5/6 Points must be subtracted from the 1000 Points   45 5/6 Points

954 1/6 Points

954 1/6 Points=   9.54 1/6c Answer

Now, work the Problem as it would be solved by a Dealer who knows, to begin with, that the numerator of the Fractions 1/4 and 3/4, when reduced to sixteenths, are 4 and 12, and there are 2 bales of the 4- and 3 of the 12-sixteenths. Note the few figures to get the average.

$$2\times 4=8$$
$$3\times12=36+8=44$$
$$44\times 6\,1/4 \quad =275\div6=45\,5/6$$
$$10c—45\,5/6 \quad =9.54\,1/6.$$

Ex. 2.   Work the same Problem by Rule 3.

Explanation :

$$1 \text{ bale } 10c \quad = \quad 10c$$
$$2 \text{ bales } 9\ 3/4c = 9.75c$$
$$3 \text{ bales } 9\ 1/4c = 9.25c$$
$$10c \times 1 = 10.00$$
$$9.75c \times 2 = 19.50$$
$$9.25c \times 3 = 27.75$$

$$6 \quad 57.25$$
$$57.25 \div 6 = \quad 9.54\ 1/6c$$

NOTE.—In the following Problems the names of the Grades[18] are represented by letters or figures, unless specifically stated otherwise.

Ex. 3.   On a basis of 7 1/2c, what will be the average of 2 G. M., 1 S. M., 2 M., ¼ and ½ up for Strict and Good Middling?

—Ans. 7 3/4c.

Explanation :

Grades	Bales	Sixteenths	Sixteenths[19]
1	2	×8=	16
2	1	×4=	4
	2	(Pass)	

Sum =20 sixteenths

20 × 6 1/4 = 125 Points.
125 ÷ 5 (No. bales) = 25 Points.

The Gardes other than M. are *above*, and must be added to the M. price.

M. price is		$.0750
Plus,	Points	.0025

Equaling (7 3/4) =   .0775, or 7.75c

Ex. 4.   Average the following list:

Two G. M., 5 S. M., 5 M., 2 S. L. M. and 1 L. M. Basis 8½c. Premiums ⅜ and ½, with Discounts ½ and ¾.

—Ans. 8.57 1/2c.

NOTE.—There are two Grades above and two below M., hence in the Problem there must be additions and subtractions in the solution, as follows :

---

[18]See list Grade names, p. 132.

[19]See Table XII, p. 93, for numerators of the sixteenth fractions.

Explanation:

Class (Grades)	Bales		Sixteenths		Sixteenths
1	2	×	8=		16
2	5	×	6=	'	30
					—
	5 Pass				
					46 up
4	2	×	8=		16
5	1	×	12=		12
					—
					28 down

46 ups—28 downs =18 ups.

18×6 1/4=112 1/2 Points.

112 1/2÷15=7 1/2 Points to be added to the M. price.

M. price	$.0850
Plus, Points	.0007 1/2
	———
Average Price	$.0857 1/2=8.57 1/2c.

Ex. 5. What should I pay for a list of cotton as an average price, in which there are 1 G. M., 8 S. M., 10 M., 22 S. L. M., 25 L. M., 10 S. G. O., 5 S. L. M. T. and 19 G. O., on an 8½ basis, with 5/16 and 9/16 up; 6/16, 100, 150, 8/16 and 300 off respectively, in the order named?

—Ans. 7.45+c.

Statement:

Class	Bales.	Sixteenths.	Sixteenths.
1	1	× 9=	9
2	8	× 5=	40
			—
			49 up
3	10 (Pass)		
4	22	× 6=132	
5	25	×16=400	
6	10	×24=240	
7	19	×48=912	
4-t	5	× 8= 40	
	——		——
	100	Total	1724 down

NOTE.—The Grades L. M. 100, S. G. O. 150, and G. O. 300 Points off, are represented as 16, 24 and 48, respectively. As 100=16/16, it is given as 16; 16/16=100, 8/16=50, thus 16/16+8/16=24/16=150, given as 24; if 150=24/16, 300 will = twice 24/16=48/16, given as 48. Again, 100=16/16, 300=3×16/16=48/16.

Ex. 6. What would be the price of G. M. cotton at 17/32 "on," if the M. base is 10 3/8?

—Ans. 10.90 5/8c.

NOTE.—Refer to Table 2; convert the 3/8 and 17/32 to Decimals for 32nds, and add the Decimals. Remember it takes four figures (Decimals) to make Points. The M. price, 10 3/8=10c and 37 1/2 Points, = 10.37 1/2 or 10.375. 17/32c=53 1/8 Points = .53125c Decimally, then to 37 1/2 Points add 53 1/8 Points = 90 5/8 Points = 10.90 5/8c.

Cotton Buyers often speak of G. M. as "goods," S. M. as "stricts," S. L. M. as "strict lows," L. M. as "lows," or G. M. as "ones," S. M. as "twos," M. as "threes," S. L. M. as "fours," L. M. as "fives," S. G. O. as "sixes," G. O. as "sevens," S. L. O. as "eights" and L. O. as "nines."

These expressions are not universal, even in the State of Texas, but prevail over the State to a large extent.

Trade formalities are more or less localized, and what might be termed a "three" for M. in one locality, might be expressed as "one" or some other number for this Grade elsewhere.

The Grades from S. G. M. to G. O. practically cover the entire list, and from G. M. to S. G. O. probably takes in 75% of the marketable cotton of the South, and these Grades find expression in most cotton calculations.

Ex. 7. A gentleman sold three 2's, four 4's and five 6's at 8 7/8 M. B.; the differences being 5/16 up and 5/16 and 1 1/4 down. What is the average price?

Ans. 8.32+c.

Ex. 8. Solve Ex. 7 by Rule II, the weights of S. M. being 1632, S. L. M. 2208, and the S. G. O. 3120 lbs.

—Ans. 8.29 nearly.

Ex. 9. Solve it by Rule III.

—Ans. 8.32+c.

Ex. 10. Find the average of 10 "Goods," 5 "Stricts," 5 "Strict Lows," four 5-t's and one 3-s. Premiums 1/8 and 1/4 for "Stricts" and "Goods." Discounts 3/16 for "Strict Lows," 93 3/4 for 5-t's and 56 1/4 for M. S. B/M 7c.

—Ans. 6.91½c.

Statement and solution:

1	10	× 4	=40
2	5	× 2	=10
			—
			50 up

3	0 (Pass)		
4	5	× 3=15	
5-t	4	×15=60	
3-s	1	× 9= 9	
	—	—	
	25 bales	84 down	

84—50=34; 34×6 1/4=212.5 Points.
212.5÷25=8.5 Points= 8 1/2.
M. price, 7c   =$.0700
Less 8 1/2 Points   = .0008 1/2
                       ———————
Difference, average, is $.0691 1/2=6.91 1/2c

Ex. 11. A number of Farmers having 200 B/C stored in a cotton yard, thinking the Market satisfactory, offered the lot for sale to the highest Bidder, who bought it at 8c M/B. The Premiums were 5/16, 1/2 and 3/4 up; the Discounts for the Lower Grades were 5/16 and 3/4. In this lot were 5 "St. Goods," 55 "Goods," 102 "Stricts," 30 M's and 8 "Strict Lows." What was the average price received?

—Ans. 8.30+c.

Statement:

	M/B 8c.		
d	5	×12=?	
1	55	× 8=	
2	102	× 5	—up
3	30 (Pass)		
4	8	× 5	?—down

Ex. 12.   How Many Points did this cotton run on Middling?   —Ans. 30+.

Ex. 13.   If the open Market was 7 7/8c, what was the gain to the Farmers by selling in bulk for 8c M/B, and the cotton weighed 102,000 lbs.?

—Ans. $127.50.

Ex. 14.   A number of Farmers sold for themselves 4,000 B/C, in Atlanta, Ga., at a Premium of 5/16 above the Market.   For S. M., G. M. and S. G. M., the Premiums were 3/8, 9/16 and 100; for S. L. M., L. M. and S. G. O., the Discounts were 5/16, 7/8 and 150 respectively.   M. price was 10 1/4c.   The cotton weighed 1,960,000 lbs.   There were 50 S. G. M., 870 G. M., 1,520 S. M., 1,260 M., 205 S. L. M., 70 L. M., and 25 S. G. O.   What was the average price, the gain on each bale, and what the whole gain to the Farmers from this co-operative sale?

—Ans.   Average 10.80c nearly.
Gain on each bale, $1.53 1/8.
Gain to Farmers, $6,125.00.

Statement:

M/B 10 9/16 Cts.

d	50	×16= ?
1	870	× 9=
2	1520	× 6= —up
3	1260	(Pass)
4	205	× 5=
5	70	×14 ?
6	25	× 24= —down

NOTE.—The market price is 10.25; the gain in class is 23.66+ Points, which, added to 10.25, equals 10.4866+ Cts., the average price on 10 1/4 basis.   The market being 10 1/4, and a Premium of 5/16 (31 1/4 Points) offered to secure the list, equals 10.25+31 1/4= 10.56 1/4, or 10 9/16 as the *basis* for this sale.   Now, 10.56 1/4 being the basis, and the gain in class being 23.66+ Points, added to the basis, equals 10.799+ or 10.80 (nearly), as the average price.

It is not usual to secure such Premiums as this even on a large list of cotton, but as the list shows to be largely high grade, with a small percentage of "hard" cotton, exceptional values were obtained.

REMARKS.—For practice in securing averages under the 6 1/4 Point method, it is suggested that the Student go over the Problems under Rules II and III, solving them by Rule IV.

It should be noted that the results obtained under Rule III are the same as those secured under Rule IV; which, as stated, are close approximations, and are practically operative for business purposes.

FOURTH PROCESS—PROBLEMS SOLVED AS THE $6\frac{1}{4}$ POINT
METHOD WITH THE 1/16 CENT ELIMINATED.

Cotton is sometimes quoted to the Trade as so many Points on or off Middling, but not in relative proportion of 1/16, 1/8, or 1/4 up or down for the Higher or Lower Grades.

When the "ups" or "downs" do not conform to the differences of 1/2, 1/4 or some multiple of them, the 6 1/4 Point method will not apply in determining averages without involving in the computation the use of Fractions, which would render the calculation cumbersome and somewhat complex.

Cotton delivered on New York or New Orleans Cotton Exchange Contracts seldom coincides with the 1/16 or 1/8 Differences as quoted generally to the Trade, but the averages can be obtained by making use of the Point differences, just as indicated for the relative Grades, and on the same principle as that utilized in the 6 1/4 Point method.

PROBLEMS.

Ex. 1. A delivered 100 B/C at the warehouse in New York on his July Contract on the 20th of that month. There were 5 G. M., 20 S. M., 38 M., 10 S. L. M., 12 L. M. 5 S. G. O., 1 G. M. T., 8 S. L. M. T. and 1 M. S. The *fixed differences* at the time were, respectively, 46 and 24 on; 35, 80, 140, 0, 80 and 90 off. M/B; 10.40. What was the average price of his delivery?   Ans. 10.197 Cts.

Explanation:

Grade Names.	No. Bales.	Points Up.		
G. M.	5	×46		=230
S. M.	20	×24		=480
M.	38	(Pass)		
		Points Down.	Total Pts. Up.	=710
S. L. M.	10	× 35= 350		
L. M.	12	× 80= 960		
S. G. O.	5	×140= 700		
G. M. T.	1	(Pass)		
S. L. M. T.	8	× 80= 640		
M. S.	1	× 90= 90		

100 Total Points down 2740
Less "ups"   710

Total net Points down 2030

2030 Points÷100 (bales)=20.3 Points.
Basis, 10.40, less 20.3=10.197 Cts. average.

PROOF.—This can be verified by the following tabular statement as exemplified under Second Process, by *adding* the Premiums to, and *deducting* the Discounts from, the M. price, and executing the work as indicated.

Grade.	Price.	No.	Bales.	Totals.
1	10.86	×	5=	54.30
2	10.64	×	20=	212.80
3	10.40	×	38=	395.20
4	10.05	×	10—	100.50
5	9.60	×	12=	115.20
6	9.00	×	5=	45.00
1-t	10.40	×	1—	10.40
4-t	9.60	×	8—	76.80
3-s	9.50	×	1—	9.50

         100   1019.70c

1019.70÷100=10.197c average.

NOTE.—It should be remembered that the number of bales represent that number of pounds of each Grade, and if 1 pound is worth 10.86c, 5 pounds are worth 5 times as much, or 54.3c. The same reasoning applies for any number of pounds.

The formula for getting the average is similar to finding it under process Three. The differences are stated in Points, the excess being divided by the whole number of bales, which is added to, or taken from the M. Price as stated.

RULE.—*Arrange the bales in consecutive order from the highest to the lowest Grade. Multiply each Grade by the number of Points it shows to be above or below Middling. Add the Points above and below Middling separately, subtracting the lesser from the greater amount. Divide the remainder by the whole number of bales; the quotient will be the number of Points to be added to, or taken from, the basis price. The result will be the average.*

Ex. 2. On a purchase of two lists of cotton, I secured in the first lot, 3 S. G. M., 20 G. M. and 2 S. M.; in the second lot 22 L. M., 1 G. O., 1 L. M. T. and 1 M. S. I sold it for 11.10 basis, with 72, 47 and 26 Points on; and 90, 215, 190 and 85 off, respectively, for the Premiums and Discounts. What was the average price obtained?

—Ans. 10.84+c.

Ex. 3. In August I sold 100 bales of New York Decembers at 10.36. I delivered this cotton on the 10th day of December. I had 12 S. G. M., 23 G. M., 41 S. M., 20 M. and 4 S. L. M. At the time of sale the differences were, in the order named, 24, 46 and 70 Points on, with 35 off. The Revision Committee in November made the differences 32, 50 and 80 on, with 37 off. What was my gain on delivering by reason of the action of this Committee, and what was the average[20] price?

—Ans. Gain $26.60.
Average 10.687+c

[20]No insurance, warehouse charges nor any expense reckoned in this problem.

Some members of the Trade, in putting out their *Difference Sheets*, say their Discounts for off colors are so many Points "off white," meaning that the Discounts must be taken from the Grades of white cotton of similar name, that is, if, Tinges are 25 Points "off white," then S. L. M. T. would be discounted 25 Points off of S. L. M. and not 25 Points off M., to get which the Discount off white would be added to the Discount off M. for that Grade.

Let it be stated that S. L. M. is 37½ Points off M., and Tinges are 25 Points "off white," then adding the two Discounts equal the total Discount to be taken from M., or 62½ Points off M. gives the value of S. L. M. T.

The following Problem will show clearly the meaning of the Discounts "off" and "off white," in a comparative way.

Ex. 4.   A Dealer bought 25 B/C at 10c basis M., grading as follows: 3 M., 2 S. L. M., 2 L. M., 5 S. L. M. T., 3 L. M. T., 4 S. L. M Blues, 6 M. S.   Discounts 35 and 90 Points off for S. L. M. and L. M., respectively.

Tinges 25, Stains 35 and Blues 50 off white.   What was the average price?   —Ans.   9.42c.

(Off White.)

Explanation:

Grade.	Bales.	Points.	Points.
M.	3		
S. L. M.	2 × 35=		70
L. M.	2 × 90=		180
S. L. M. T.	5 × 60=		300
L. M. T.	3 ×115=		345
S. L. M. Blue	4 × 85=		340
M. S.	6 × 35=		210
	25		1445

1445÷25=   58.

10cts—58 Points =   —Ans.   9.42cts.

(Off.)

Explanation:

Grade	Bales	Points	Points
M.	3		
S. L. M.	2 ×	35=	70
L. M.	2 ×	90=	180
S. L. M. T.	5 ×	25=	125
L. M. T.	3 ×	25=	75
St. L. M. Blue	4 ×	50=	200
M. S.	6 ×	35=	210
	25		860

860÷25= 34

10cts—34 Points=   —Ans. 9.66cts.

It will be noted that calculating the same list of cotton as a certain number of Points "off" and "off white," make a difference of 24 Points, or $1.20 on each bale of 500 pounds weight.

CHAPTER IV.

SECTION V—FREIGHTS.

In all cotton transactions connected with transportation, the subject of Freight Rates enters as a factor, of which cognizance must be taken in calculating prices for payment on cotton.

Domestic Freights Rates may appropriately be placed under two heads.

INTRA-STATE OR LOCAL RATES.
INTER-STATE OR THROUGH RATES.

INTRA-STATE RATES are those applying within the boundaries of the State, which, usually being governed by a State Railway Commission establishing them, are said to be *permanent,* that is, they remain as established by the Commission, until changed by it.

INTER-STATE RATES are those applying between one State and another. Freight originating in one State and transmitted to another have rates established covering the shipments to destination, and are termed *Domestic Through Rates.* Such Rates are established by the Interstate Commerce Commission and come under its jurisdiction, yet while exercising its authority the Commission does not deprive the railroads under the law from making their own Interstate Rates, which they generally do, but are subject to revision and control by the Commission[21].

———

[21]Railway companies having lines extending into and through several States, establish their own Rates, but are subject to revision by the Interstate Commerce Commission, as stated.

OCEAN FREIGHT RATES.

MARITIME FREIGHT RATES are those instituted by Maritime Transportation Companies covering the charges for transmitting Freights across the ocean to Foreign Ports.

They are governed in some instances by associate or corporate agreement and are never constant in application, fluctuating often during the season.

Competition occasionally enters as a factor affecting the Rate to be applied, and has a material effect in determining the schedules of charges, more especially when contentions arise between competing lines for tonnage.

Active bidding for Freights often results in reducing the charges, at which time Exporters have an opportunity for securing advantages for future shipments not otherwise obtained.

Those periods of the year when Freight Rates are at their lowest points are seized upon by Exporters as opportune times for booking their contemplated shipments for certain designated future months when cotton will be moving freely.

Rates are influenced as stated, also to some degree, by the relative supply of freight room and quantity of cotton to be exported.

A proposed export shipment of 10,000 bales of cotton would not secure or merit the same rate as one of 75,000 to 100,000 bales.

Steamship Rates quoted in their circulars or through newspapers for the solicitation of business, are not those agreed upon by individual agreement, neither are private terms reported regularly to the public.

Rates applying between the Southern Ports and the Northern and Eastern cities are constant year in and year out.[22]

---

[22]For schedule of Rates from Southern Ports to Foreign Markets, see Appendix.

Freights being essential in price making to the cotton Shipper, the following Problems are introduced for explanation:

PROBLEMS.

Ex. 1. Engle & Hart, Galveston, Texas sold 500 B/C to a Fall River, Mass., Mill, at 12.80 for even-running Middling delivered, 90-days shipment. Assuming the order is filled in Dallas, Texas, what price can be paid for it there if Freight to Galveston is 51c and ocean Rate to Fall River is 35c per hundred lbs., with a Profit of 50c a bale calculated in the selling price?

—Ans. 11.84c.

Explanation:

Delivered Price		12.80
Railway Rate	=51 Points	
Ocean Rate	=35 Points	
Profit[23]	=10 Points	
Total expense		.96
		11.84

Ex. 2. Williams & Orms at New Orleans paid 9.85 "all round" for a list of 200 B/C at Meridian Miss. Assuming that they figured a profit of 40c a bale, the local railway haul 32, and ocean Rate of 36 to New Bedford, Mass., with Wharfage at 2 Points, what was the delivered selling price?

—Ans. 10.63c.

Explanation:

Paid in Meridian		9.85c
Profit 40c	= 8 Points	
Railway Rate	=32 Points	
Ocean Rate	=36 Points	
Wharfage	= 2 Points	
78 Points		.78
		10.63c

[23]Fifty cents per bale equals 10c per hundred pounds, equals 10 Points per pound.

Ex. 3. White & Sansom at Dallas, Texas, sold 300 bales of 1 1-8 even-running Strict Middling cotton to a ·Providence, R. I. Mill in June for September and October delivery at 50 Points on October which was quoted at 11.60, with New York Cotton Exchange Differences to apply on delivery, which for S. M. was 24 Points on. What could this firm pay for this cotton in Terrell, Greenville and Cooper, Texas, if charges were, Freight to Galveston 51, Wharfage 2, Ocean Freight 35, Insurance 8, Profit and Office Expenses 10 Points?

—Ans. 11.28c.

Explanation :

New York October Futures		11.60
Points on October	50	
Premium for S. M.	24	
Total Points to be added		.74
Delivered price		12.34
Freight, R. R.	51	
Freight, Ocean	35	
Wharfage	2	
Insurance	8	
Profit and Expense	10	
Total offset		1.06
Could pay		11.28

Were competition not too close, this firm would offer for S. M. cotton at the places mentioned, 11.25c. The usual practice is to buy it M/B and from the large quantity of mixed Grades bought, the specific ones are selected and separated at concentration points, from which places they will be forwarded to the Mills.

Ex. 4. Johnson & Wells at Oklahoma City, Oklahoma, sold 500 B/C for Liverpool at 30 Points on August-September, which was quoted at 7.20d. What could be paid for this cotton at "common point" territory stations in that State if the rail haul to New Orleans is 52, and

Ocean transportation 57 Points, Tare 6 per cent, Insurance 1 per cent, with further charges of ¼ per cent Brokerage, ½ per cent Exchange, ½ per cent Interest, 1 per cent Agents' Commission, less weight of Franchise[24] and Patches,[25] 2 per cent.

—Ans.   12.80c.

Explanation:		Pence	
Aug.-Sep. Liverpool		7.20	
Points on future months		.30	
Invoice C. I. F. & 6%		7.50	
In American money, 7.50d			=15.00c
Less 6% Tare			= .90
Price C. I. F.			=14.10
Less inland and ocean Freight			= 1.09
Price C. & I.			=13.01
Less Insurance at 1% (13.01+10%)			= .13
			12.88

Charges:			
Brokerage	1/4%		
Exchange	1/2%		
Interest	1/2%		
Com.	1 %		
Total	2 1/4%		
13.01 less 2 1/4%		=.2925	
Cost for bagging		=.0500	
Total		.3425	
Less wt. of Franchise, 2% of 13.01		=.2602	
Net charges		=.0823	
Net landing price			12.8800
Less net charges			.0823
			12.7977

Net price can pay f. o. b. in Oklahoma 12.80c.

---

[24]See Franchise, p. 252.
[25]Patches 5 lbs. per bale=1%.

Not all Merchants calculate in such great detail the method of getting a base for payment of cotton in their respective territory.

In this calculation it will be noted no profit was estimated, the presumption being that the Merchant expected to make it by buying for as much less than 12.80 as competition would allow, and also from the patches put on the bales at the compress, a further gain was contemplated.

After a Contract sale is effected and the price calculated for local payment, further gains accrue if the Market be a declining one, as the policy with the talent is to "follow the Market."

Profits may be realized from the result of the application of the 6% Tare, as the following assumed transaction will show:

Ex. 5. A firm in Atlanta, Ga., is offered 6 1-2 pence for cotton delivered in Manchester, England. To get at the price it can pay the farmer, the firm deducts the following items that must be taken into account:

The 6 1-2 pence	=13.00c
Tare, 6%	=78 Points
Inland Freight	=34 "
Ocean Freight	=56 "
Insurance	=10
Expense	=12
Profit	=10
Total	= 2.00

Price to be paid to the farmer =11.00

The statement shows 10 Points—50c a bale—was figured as a profit in making the calculation to be paid the farmer.

The 6% Tare equals 78 Points. The usual weight for bagging and ties is 22 lbs., equivalent to 4.4% on a standard weight bale of 500 lbs.; 4.4% of 13c equals 57 Points; the difference is 21 Points the Buyer gets as an additional profit to the 50c already calculated, less some deductions.

A standard bale is 500 lbs., 6% of which is 30 lbs. The export Buyer deducts 30 lbs. from the farmer's bale, because Foreign Trade exacts it, to cover the weight of the wrapping, and as shown, gets too much of the farmer's cotton in figuring the net weight of his bale.

In order that the Exporter may not lose, he puts on 8 lbs. of Tare in the form of patches,[26] for which he pays, say, 32c, and the Freight and Expense on it at $1.12 per hundred pounds is 9c, making the cost for patches 41c, which he sells at $1.17 (9 pounds at 13c) leaving a profit of 76c; in this transaction, he has the 10-Point profit, 50c a bale as shown in the outset, and 76c on the patches besides, which he holds if competition does not force him to relinquish a part or all of it, which it often does.

Ex. 6. An Exporter in Waco, Texas, found the total charges for delivering cotton in Bremen to be 13.6% including his profit of 40c a bale. What would be the price he could pay at Texas interior points, gross weight, for the farmers' cotton, if the Bremen price was 13.60?

Ans. 11.75c.

Ex. 7. A firm in Savannah, during the month of July, 1912, contracted with a Steamship Company for exportation of 100,000 bales[27] of cotton to be shipped the following September, October, November and December to Bremen, at a rate of 35c per hundred pounds. During the shipping months, the rates ranged in their respective order, 57c, 56c, 56c and 55c. If 25,000 bales moved each month, what did this firm save or make, by contracting its shipments ahead?

—Ans. $105,000.00.

Ex. 8. Birdwell & Scott, Little Rock, Ark., contracted 75,000 bales of cotton for export to Liverpool, in July at 40c, for shipment in September to December, inclusive.

---

[26]See "Patches," Book III., p. 268.

[27]In this and the following Problems, where weights of the bales are not given, it is assumed that they average 500 lbs. each; five hundred pounds being the weight of a standard bale.

After shipping 14,000 bales in September and 36,000 in October, they sold the Freight for 25,000 bales to a Yazoo, Miss. firm at 54c, of which 16,800 were shipped in November and 8,200 in December. The whole was shipped in Birdwell & Scott's name. The rates effective in the four fall months were 65c, 64.7c, 66c and 67c. What was the net gain to the shippers and what they did lose on the sale of Freight.

—Ans. Net gain $79,460.00.
—Loss $11,310.00.

Ex. 9. An Exporter engaged Freight transportation for 50,000 bales of cotton at 45c; after shipping 30,000 bales, he sold the remaining Freight on 20,000 at 58c, Freight having advanced to this point. What did he gain by selling this Freight?

—Ans. $13,000.00.

Ex. 10. A Steamship Company during July quoted their rates for September, October and November at 50c, 52c and 55c respectively. An Exporter contracted with their Agent for shipment of 50,000 bales during these months at 50c. In September the Company reduced its rate to 40c, in October it was further reduced to 35c and in November raised to 44c. The Exporter shipped 10,000 bales in September, 5,000 in October and 35,000 in November. What did he lose by contracting ahead on this shipment?

—Ans. $19,250.00.

Ex. 11. A Cotton firm in New Orleans contracted with a Steamship Company's Broker in July for shipment of 26,000 bales of cotton to Havre at 45c. In September 3,000 bales were shipped; in October, 2,000; in November, 9,000; and in December, 12,000. The quoted rates effective for those months were 50c, 53, 44c, and 40c, respectively. What did this Firm gain or lose by this Contract?

—Ans. Lost $1,900.00.

It may be stated that it takes practically 2c per pound to cover all expenses attached as a charge for Export Cotton.

Contingencies that arise, as reduced Freight Rates, lessened Interest Charges, Discounts on Exchange, Cheaper Rents and Clerical help, are factors that can reduce this expense.

Exporters contracting cotton for future shipment in the summer when Freight Rates are generally cheaper, must assume some risk, as Ocean Rates fluctuate, and may be lower at shipping time than when contracted.

It should be remembered that if one Exporter books his contemplated shipments ahead, at the same time many others may do the same thing, and if one has a profit of say, 25c per hundred pounds on Freight, active competition among Shippers for Export may cause a loss of it all.

It must not be assumed because of the fact that an Exporter has a profit of one dollar or more in a fortunate Freight Contract, as appears between the difference of Contract price and that obtaining later in the season, that this fact alone gives the profit.

The profit must be made in the buying.

For illustration, let it be stated that a firm in Jackson, Miss., has contracted shipment for 60,000 B/C at 40c in July. During the fall months Rates range in the order, 52c, 57c, 55c, and 61c out of New Orleans. The Shipper has a difference for a profit of 12c to 21c per hundred pounds, or 60c to $1.05 per bale.

If in September cotton is bought in Jackson at 12c M/B, based on a 52c Ocean Freight Rate, the Shipper would have a profit of 60c a bale to his competitor's nothing, and would be in position to reap a rich harvest. But had this competitor contracted cotton at 40c., the same as the first Buyer, then both would be on an equal footing for competitive bidding, or by acting in harmony, both could retain a handsome profit.

CHAPTER V.

SECTION VI—EXCHANGE.

CHECKS AND DRAFTS.

Payments liquidating claims for cotton often involve the use of large sums of money, to avoid the handling of which, the use of *Checks* and *Drafts* are employed.

Orders drawn on banks, individuals, firms or corporations, for immediate payment of money are called *checks*.

Checks are generally used in the payment of *local claims*. They state the date, place, amount, and the name of the bank or firm to make the payment.

A written order to an individual, firm or bank for the payment of money is called a *Draft*, and usually on some *distant point*.

A Draft for immediate payment, is termed a *Sight Draft*.

If its payment is directed at some future time, it is designated a *Time Draft*.

Drafts made by one bank upon another, are sometimes called *Bills of Exchange*.

When a Draft does not sell for its face value the Exchange is made at a *Discount*.

When it commands face value, its Exchange is made at *Par*.

When a Draft is sold for more than face value, the Exchange is made at a *Premium*.

Drafts written at one place to be paid at another are drawn to be paid at the other place.

A person *draws* upon another, when *he writes* the Draft to be paid.

Drafts drawn for payment in any country having the same currency, are called Domestic Drafts, and the Exchange is *Domestic Exchange* in .contradistinction from Drafts drawn for Foreign Account.

Drafts are sometimes not paid when presented, but are *accepted* to be paid in a certain number of days. In such cases the word *"accepted"* is written across the face of the Bill, usually in red ink, with the signature of the *acceptor*, date, and place of payment, if desired.

Drafts are similar to Checks in Showing the *amount, date, place of the maker, the one to whom the money is to be paid,* and the *name of the remitter.*

There are. always three parties to transactions in Ex-·change. The *Drawer,* or person making and signing the Draft; the *Drawee,* or person to whom the Draft is ad·dressed; the *payee,* or person to be paid.

The Payee may be the one to whom the money is to be paid.

NOTE.—For example, a person in Memphis, Tenn., wishing $1000 paid to himself in New York, may put $1000 (if Exchange is at Par) in a Memphis Bank, have the Memphis Bank write a Check (Draft) on some designated New York Bank for $1000, and with this Draft ın his possession, he presents it to the New York Bank on arrival there, which Bank will pay him the $1000 desired.

Exchange is a convenient method adopted by our banking institutions for payment of sums of money for a party in one place, to a party in another place, without actually transmitting the cash. The risk and trouble of sending the money is thus avoided each time a Draft is made.

The *Rate of Exchange* is· a certain Rate per cent. calculated on the face of the Draft to determine the cost for getting the Exchange value and charge for transmission.

The *Course of Exchange* refers to the price paid at one place for a "bill of Exchange" on another. This price or rate is variable, fluctuating as the demand for Exchange fluctuates.

Bills of Exchange are Drafts drawn by one bank upon another in a different place.

Under the United States Banking System,[28] it is usual for banks to place a portion of their funds as credits in other banks. By so doing, greater facilities are offered for the payment of money at distant points through the instrumentality of the Draft.

Banks receiving these credits are termed *Correspondents of the Bank,* or *Reserve Agents.*

If a Bank in Waco, Texas, has deposits amounting to $500,000, a part of them may be placed in banks in Houston, Galveston, St. Louis, Chicago, and New York.

Let it be stated that the Houston bank has $25,000 of this money; a Galveston bank $25,000; a St. Louis bank $50,000; a Chicago bank $75,000, and a New York bank $100,000, making a total with these Reserve Agents of $275,000, and leaving with the Waco bank a deposit of $225,000. Of this amount, smaller deposits may be placed with other banks in Texas, or perhaps with banks in Memphis, Altanta, Philadelphia, Cincinnati, Denver, and San Francisco.

Parties in Waco desiring to pay certain sums of money in any of the cities mentioned, buy Drafts from the Waco bank payable by some bank in the city designated. The purchaser who receives the Draft, transmits it by mail to the one to whom it is payable, who in turn, upon its receipt, presents it to the bank on which it is drawn and receives the money or takes credit for it.

Should a person in Waco wish to pay a claim in Little Rock, Ark., he would buy a Draft on St. Louis, Chicago or New York from the Waco bank, remit this Draft (called Exchange), say, on St. Louis, to the Little Rock payee (creditor—claimant), who upon its receipt gives the Waco person full credit for it, as he can have the Draft cashed at face value at his bank in Little Rock.

---

[28]Recent enactment of new laws has created a new financial or banking system for the United States. The meaning of the above statements is not impaired by reason of such fact.

Every bank in Little Rock no doubt has deposits in St. Louis similar to the Waco bank, hence can cash the Waco Draft on St. Louis at Par.

Buying and selling Drafts is called *Buying and Selling Exchange.*

Calculations respecting Exchange between one place and another involve the principles of percentage.

Outside of banking channels, individuals, firms and corporations sometimes place money in other places for credits and utlize the principles of Exchange in the transaction of their business.

DOMESTIC EXCHANGE.

Domestic exchange has reference to the issuance of Drafts in the country where they are drawn. Drafts drawn in one place in the United States, to be paid at some other place in the same country, are Domestic Drafts.

Charges for Bills of Exchange, or Drafts, vary as the demand for them increases or diminishes, requiring calculations to determine the value of the fluctuations, which are shown in the following:

PROBLEMS.

Ex. 1.   A wishes to remit $500 to New York in payment of a Margin on 500 B/C. The Exchange being 1-4% Premium, what is the cost of this Draft?

—Ans. $501.25.

NOTE.—A wishes to send $500 to New York, and wants a bank to send it for him. The bank knowing the rate to be ¼ of 1%, agrees to send the money for $501.25. A then pays the bank $501.25; the bank writes a Draft for $500, hands it to A, who encloses it in an envelope and sends it by mail to the man he owes in NewYork. The bank keeps the $1.25, it being the amount it charges for giving the sender the privilege of Exchange; that is, the home bank will *Exchange* $500 from itself to some one else in New York, and issue the accommodation for $1.25.

The bank is safe, because it receives from the sender in this instance $501.25 in cash before it issues the Draft for the $500.

The statement is, that Exchange between the two places is "¼ of 1%."

Explanation:

(1)   One Cent is $.0100 (4 Decimals)

¼ of 1 Cent is .0025=2½ Mills.

The bank charge is 2½ Mills on the Dollar=25c on $100, and 5 times that on $500=$1.25.

(2)   The Exchange being at Premium, it is added to $1.00 and =$1.0025.

$1.0025×500=$501.25.

REMARKS.—It will be noted that the ¼%, expressed Decimally, necessitates the use of 4 Decimals. The usual practice is to divide the sum to be paid by 4 and point off 4 Decimals in the quotient.

Example : $500.00÷4=$1.2500.

Ex. 2.   A Cotton Merchant in Macon, Ga., wishes to remit $1200 on account in payment on a cotton claim, to New Orleans.   What will be the cost of the Draft at 1-8% Premium?

—Ans. $1,201.50.

SUGGESTION.—Solve as the preceding Example, No. 1.

As the Rate is a certain per cent. on or off the Dollar, the Dollar can be used as a base on which to make a Rule.

TO FIND THE COST OF A DRAFT.

(a)   *For Sight Drafts.*

RULE—Add to 1 Dollar the rate of Exchange, if at Premium; subtract from 1 Dollar if at Discount; multiply the sum or remainder by the face value of the Draft; the result will be its cost, including Exchange.

NOTE.—As Sight Drafts are generally used in payment of Domestic Cotton, a time consideration does not enter into any calculation in determining their value or cost of Exchange.

Ex. 3.   Tom Anderson bought 50 B/C in Ft. Smith, Ark., amounting to $2,580, for which he gave a Sight Draft on

New York. Exchange being 3-4% Premium, what was the face value of the Draft, and what did the bank charge for making the Exchange?

—Ans. Face $2,599.35.
Exchange $19.35.

NOTE.—It is usual for purchasers of cotton, buying from interior points, to pay the Exchange on the money, unless otherwise stated.

Ex. 4.   A Commission Merchant at Savannah, Ga., sold 60 B/C for $3,650. After deducting his Commission of 2 1-2% and Exchange at 1-8% Premium, what amount was remitted in the Draft to the owner at Milledgeville?

—Ans. $3,554.30.

Ex. 5.   A Cotton Buyer locating at Ennis, Texas, to buy cotton for the season, drew a Draft on a Chicago bank for $10,000; Exchange being at a Premium of 3-4%, what did the Ennis bank pay for this Draft?

—Ans. $9,925.00.

Ex. 6.   An Agent was allowed a Commission of 1% to buy cotton. After purchasing 100 bales, valued at $5,750, he wished to make a Draft on "his house" at Philadelphia, sufficient in amount to cover his Commission, and Exchange at ¼% Premium. What was the face of the Draft?

—Ans. $5,822.02.

Ex. 7.   A Merchant in Charleston bought 200 B/C from a Dealer in Columbia, after business hours, by telephone, for which he offered f. o. b. Columbia 9 3-8c all round and pay the Exchange, or 9 13-32c, and the Dealer pay the Exchange. The Dealer accepted the latter proposition.

The Exchange was ¼% Premium. The cotton weighed 104,000 lbs. Did he gain or lose, and how much?

—-Ans. Gained $8.05.

(b) For Time Drafts.

Time drafts are more particularly utilized in the payment of *Export Cotton.*

A Bill not paid at Sight, but drawn to mature at a stated time after Sight, (date) presents a mixed question of Exchange and Bank Discount.[29]

Solving Problems involving the use of the two, require the use of the Rules necessary for the solution of each, but into the one computation, the two must be combined.

Three Days of Grace are still permissible in some of the States.

Bank Discount is Simple Interest on the face of the Note or Draft for the time to elapse from date of discount until maturity, therefore it is Simple Interest on the face of the Note or Draft paid in Advance.

The *Proceeds* of a Note, Draft or Account, is the amount left after deducting the Bank Discount.

TO FIND THE COST OF DRAFTS PAYABLE AFTER SIGHT.

RULE.—Find the Proceeds of One Dollar at Bank Discount for the stated time, at the Rate prescribed, or the Legal Rate, if no Rate is expressed; to this add the Rate of Exchange if at a Premium, or subtract if at a Discount; multiply the result by the face of the Draft.

PROBLEMS.

Ex. 1.   A Buyer in Selma, Ala., bought 100 B/C valued at $5,000 for which he presented a Draft on New York, payable in 60 days, with 6% Interest. Exchange being ¾% Premium, what amount did the Selma bank allow as a cash credit for the Buyer?

—Ans. $4,985.00.

---

[29]Banks will not buy Drafts and pay cash for them unless they know the party on whom they are drawn is financially responsible. Not all banks deal in Exchange.

MB—7

Explanation:

The Interest (Bank Discount) on $1 for 63 days	=$.0105
The Premium of Exchange on $1 at ¾%	= .0075
The difference is	.0030

As the face of the Draft is $5,000, the bank will deduct 3/10 of 1%, $15, leaving $4,985 to the Buyer's credit.

This is a brief, clear way to obtain the result quickly. The Interest must be calculated before attempting to formulate the statement.

By the Rule.—Interest on

$1 for 63 days	=$.0105
$1 —.0105	= .9895
.9895+$.0075 (Premium)	= .9970
$.9970×$5,000=$4,985.00	

We may again state the Problem as follows, for clearness of conception:

Find the Simple Interest on $5,000 for 60 days, plus 3 days of Grace, at 6%, which

	=$52.50
The Premium of Exchange	= 37.50
Difference between Interest and Exchange	= 15.00

to be deducted directly from the face of the Draft. $5,000—$15=$4,985.

The Bank Discount on $5,000 being $52.50, deducted from $5,000 leaves the *Proceeds*,

	=$4947.50
To which add the Exchange	= 37.50
Cost of Draft	=$4985.00

Ex. 2. I sold 360 B/C for $21,200; accepted a 90-day Draft on New York at 6% Interest, on which the Exchange was 1-8% Discount. What did my home bank pay me for it?

—Ans. $20,844.90.

Ex. 3. A Texarkana Firm gave a 30-day Draft for $45,620 in payment for a list of cotton. With Interest at 6% and Exchange at 1 1-2% Discount, what would be the value of this Draft in Texarkana, with no Days of Grace?

—Ans. $44,707.60.

Ex. 4. H. Kempner & Co., Galveston, Tex., sold a list of 212 B/C at 11c, it being 1-8 above quotation. The cotton gained 4 Points in class and 460 lbs. in weight. It was held 3 months, on which were charges of $1.00 per bale the first month, and 23c a bale each month thereafter. The cotton averaged 510 lbs. to the bale. What was the amount of the S/D after deducting the Charges, Exchange at 1-4% Premium, and what was the gain in class, weight and quotation?

—Ans. Amount of S/D $11,554.72.

Gain in Class $43.24.

Gain in weight $50.60.

Gain in quotation $135.15.

Ex. 5. A Dealer in Atlanta, Ga., sold 500 B/C, valued at $25,890, to Huggins & Co., Norfolk, Va., on whom he made a Draft 60 D/S at 6% Interest and Exchange 1-8% Premium; they were to pay the Exchange as agreed upon. The Dealer found 2 days after the cotton was moving and he had cashed the Draft at the local bank, that Huggins & Co. had failed, and could not receive the shipment. He immediately diverted it to Wilson Cotton Co., Savannah, Ga., to whom he had to sell for 1-16 less, and pay the Exchange at the Rate of 1-4% Premium on a Sight Draft. What was his loss or gain by reason of the failure of the Norfolk Firm?

—Ans. Gained $45.64+

NOTE.—The failure of Huggins & Co. voided the Draft on them to the apparent loss of the bank cashing it for the Dealer previously, but as the shipment was immediately sold to another, the Dealer accepted the surrender of the original Draft and issued a second one on Savannah, protecting both himself and the bank.

In such instances, where a B/L is properly indorsed with the notation "Shipper's Order, Notify," on its face, the bank and Shipper are both protected.

INDIRECT EXCHANGE.

Owing to the difference of the Rates of Exchange between any two places, and the frequent variation of them, it is often advantageous for one wishing to make payment of any sum on some other place to draw through one, two or more intermediate points.

By this process of *Circular Exchange* the Rate is sometimes cheapened.

Exchange of this character is called *Indirect, Circular* or *Arbitration of Exchange.*

For explanation we submit the following

PROBLEMS.

Ex. 1. A Galveston Dealer sold $60,000 worth of even-running cotton to a Providence, R. I., Mill, f. o. b. destination. Having to pay the Exchange, he sought the cheapest way. To New York the Exchange was 1-2% Premium; to New Orleans 1/4%; New Orleans to New York 1/4% Discount. What was the amount of his Draft drawn indirectly through New Orleans, and what did he save by not drawing directly on New York?

—Ans. $59,999.62 1-2.
Saved $300.37 1-2.

Explanation:
(1) $60,000=value of purchase
      $ 1.005=amount of $1 on New York at 1/2% Premium
      $60,000×$1.005=$60,300=value of Draft to be drawn to net
         $60,000 in Galveston
      $1.0025=1/4% Premium on $1 on New Orleans
      $60,000×$1.0025=$60,150=value of S/D on N. O.
      $1.00—1/4% (0025) =$.9975
      $60,150×$.9975=$59,999.62½

         Cost Direct Exchange   =$60,300.00
         Cost Indirect Exchange   =$59,999.62½
                                        _____
         Amount saved $300.37½

(2)   By making the following equations, the Problem is simplified:
      $60,000 in N. Y.=What in Galveston?   =$60,300.00 Direct
      $1.00½ in Galveston=$1.00 in N. Y.   =$59,999.62½ Indirect
      $1.00¼ in Galveston=$1.00 in N. O.
      $ .99¾ in N. O.   =$1.00 in N. Y., then
      $60,000×$1.00½
      $60,000×$1.00¼×$.99¾
                                            _____
         Subtracting, leaves gain, $300.37½

Ex. 2. A Shreveport Firm bought for a New Bedford Mill, a list of cotton amounting to $16,530. Exchange on Boston being 1-4% Premium, he could, by drawing indirectly through New Orleans and Havana, Cuba, secure Exchange on New Orleans at 1-8% Premium; from New Orleans to Havana 1-8% Discount; from Havana to Bos· to 1-4% Discount. What was the cost of the Draft each way, and what was the gain by Circular Exchange?

—Ans. Cost Direct $16,571.32+
Cost Indirect $16,488.65+

Gain $82.67+

FOREIGN EXCHANGE.

People of one nation doing business with those of another, must have some basic value on which to place their financial transactions.

This basis is the unit value established by the Mint of a country as its Monetary Standard.

In Foreign Exchange it is necessary to find the value of money of one country in terms of unit value of the other.

The established value of the coin or Standard of value of one country when expressed in the coin or standard of another is called *Parity of Exchange.*

This value, determined by the Director of the Mint, is the *Intrinsic Par of Exchange,* while the market values of such coins dealt in by the banks showing slight variations are termed *Commercial Par of Exchange.*

REMARK.—By virtue of an Act of Congress, August 27, 1894, the Director of the Mint proclaimed "the values of foreign coins to be values of such coins in terms of the money of account of the United States, to be followed in estimating the value of all foreign merchandise exported to the United States during the quarter beginning July 1, 1913, expressed in any such metallic currencies."

Copying from United States Treasury Department Circular No. 1, under date of July 1, 1913, the subjoined Table No. XX is given for reference in estimating moneys of foreign account:

TABLE NO. XX.

VALUE OF FOREIGN COINS.

Country	Standard	Monetary Unit	Value in terms of U. S. Gold Dollar
Austria-Hungary	Gold	Crown	$0.203
Belgium	Gold	Franc	.193
British Possessions	Gold	Dollar	1.000
China[30]	Silver	Tael[31]	.713
Denmark	Gold	Crown	.268
Finland	Gold	Mark	.193
France	Gold and Silver	Franc	.193
German Empire	Gold	Mark	.238
Great Britain	Gold	Pound Sterling	4.866½
Italy	Gold	Lira	.193
Japan	Gold	Yen	.498
Mexico	Gold	Peso	.498
Netherlands	Gold	Florin	.402
Persia	Gold and Silver	Kran	.1704
Portugal	Gold	Milreis	1.080
Russia	Gold	Ruble	.515
Spain	Gold	Peseta	.193
Norway and Sweden	Gold	Crown	.268
Switzerland	Gold	Franc	.193
Turkey	Gold	Piaster	.044

These are the countries to which most of our cotton is exported, and the principal ones on which Exchange must be calculated.

Knowing the United States value of the "Monetary Unit" of any country, it is an easy matter to convert one into the other.

The unit values here given are those established by the Director of the Mint of the United States at Par value. Based upon the Gold Standard, they are permanent.

Bankers handling Bills of Exchange, or Customers

---

[30]Canton.

[31]The value of the Tael is different in each of its National territorial divisions. In Amoy it is $.715; Chefoo $.683; Hankow $.669 and Nankin $.707.

Drafts, on other countries, make a charge for buying and selling them. These Rates of Exchange vary more or less daily.

The varying Rates are termed *Commercial Exchange,* and may be higher, equal to, or lower than the Par of Exchange.

Calculations connected with Exchange are computed on quoted values, recognized as Commercial Exchange.

Exchange on England, Ireland and Scotland is computed in Pounds, Shillings and Pence, and the Drafts are generally drawn payable through London.

Exchange on France is calculated in moneys of that country, being computed in Francs and Centimes, with Drafts drawn payable through Paris. Drafts covering the payment of cotton destined for France are often drawn through London.

Exchange on Germany is converted into Marks and Pfennigs, and Drafts for payment of cotton shipped there are drawn through Berlin, Vienna or Hamburg. Often Drafts issued for payment of cotton exported to Germany are payable through London.

ENGLISH EXCHANGE.[32]

The English coinage consists of Pounds (£), Shillings (s) and Pence (d).

1 Pound (£)=$4.8665 (Monetary Unit)

20 Shillings (s)=1 Pound.

12 Pence (d)=1 Shilling.

$1.00=4s, 1d.

TO CONVERT ENGLISH COINAGE INTO U. S. VALUES.

RULE.—(1) *Multiply the face of the Draft in £'s by the stated Exchange Rate in Dollars and Cents.*

(2) *Reduce Shillings and Pence to a Decimal of a £ before multiplying. The answer will be in Dollars and Cents.*

---

[32]Bills of Exchange for foreign accounts are generally drawn now in duplicate, instead of the old triplicate form. Some Dealers use only a single Draft. See Bill of Exchange, page 153.

PROBLEMS.

Ex. 1.   I sold a list of cotton for which the Buyer gave me a Draft on London for 500£ at Par.   What was its value in Dollars and Cents?

—Ans. $2,433.25.

Note.—By Table No. XX, a £ Sterling is quoted at $4.8665, then 500£ would be 500×$4.8665, which would equal $2,433.25.

Ex. 2.   What could I get in U. S. money for £500 worth of cotton at an Exchange Rate of $4.85½?

—Ans. $2,427.50.

Ex. 3.   How much could a Buyer realize on a shipment of cotton from New Orleans, in U. S. money for a Bill on London for £219, 10s., 6d., with Exchange at $4.87?

—Ans. $1,069.08+

Explanation:

Multiply the 10s. by 12, as 12d. equals 1s., which gives 120d., to which add the 6d., making 10s. and 6d. equal 126d.   Reducing £1 to Pence, equals 240d.   Now, with these two numbers, form the Common Fraction 126/240; annexing naughts to the 126, and dividing by the 240, according to the Rule for division of Decimals, gives .525 of a £, which annexing to the £, gives the statement £219.525, which, multiplied by $4.87, gives $1,069.08 for the answer.

Ex. 4.   An Augusta Exporter received a Draft for £830, 16s. for a list of cotton.   Exchange on London at the time being at the Rate of $4.85 7-8, what was its value in Federal money?

—Ans. $4,036.65

Ex. 5.   Allen & Jude sold to a Manchester Firm, 3,000 B/C, for which they received a Draft, 90 days Sight at 6% Interest, with Exchange at the Rate of $4.86 1-8, what did the bank pay in U. S. money for the Foreign Exchange, if the Draft was for £43,199, 15s., 3d?

—Ans. $206,749.77+.

CONVERTING U. S. TO ENGLISH COINAGE.

Ex. 6. An Austin Firm sold 500 B/C, amounting to $32,500, to an English Buyer. For what amount of English money should the Draft read for 60-day paper at $4.80 7-8?

—Ans. £6,758, 10s., 8d.

In converting United States money to Pounds, Shillings and Pence, the operation is exactly the reverse of that performed in Examples 1 to 5, inclusive, under Exchange on England.

RULE.—Divide the amount of money in Dollars and Cents by the Sterling Exchange Rate for £1; the result will be Pounds and Decimals of a Pound. Multiply the Decimal by 20, (20 Shillings make a £), which will give Shillings and Decimals of a Shilling. Multiply the Decimal of a Shilling by 12; (12 Pence make a Shilling), the answer will be Pence and Decimals thereof.

Ex. 7. I sold a list of cotton for $6,699.80, payable in 60 days at 6%. I accepted a Draft on London with Exchange at $4.82, but did not cash it until 5 days later, when I sold it for $4.82 7-8. What did I gain on it, and what was the amount of the Draft?

—Ans. Gain $12.16.

Amount £1390.

FRENCH EXCHANGE.

The French coinage consists of the Franc and Centime.
1 Franc (Fr.)=$.193 (Monetary Unit).
100 Centimes (C.)= 1 Franc.
$1.00=5.18 Fr.

TO CONVERT FRENCH COINAGE INTO UNITED STATES VALUES.

RULE.—Divide the stated number of Francs and Centimes (Centimes expressed as Decimals of a Franc), by the quoted Rate; the answer will be in Dollars and Cents.

PROBLEMS.

Ex. 1. A sold 120 B/C to an Exporter for Havre, who gave him a Draft on Paris for 38,700 Fr. What amount of U. S. money did he get? Exchange at 5.16.[33].

—Ans. $7,500.00.

Explanation:

$$38,700 \div 5.16 — 7,500$$
$$\$1 \times 7,500 — \$7,500$$

Ex. 2. A 90-day Draft on Paris, for the payment of 208 B/C was given to a Buyer at McGregor, Texas, amounting to 53,300 Fr. With Exchange at 5.20, what did the First National Bank there pay for the Draft in U. S. money?

—Ans. $10,250.00.

Ex. 3. Angus & Southworth, Waco, Texas, sold 500 B/C to Nedervelt & Stromberg for Berne, Switzerland, for which a Draft on London was given, amounting to 167,375 Fr. What was the amount of Federal money received for it if sold at an Exchange Rate of 5.16¼.[34]

—Ans. $32,421.30.

TO CONVERT U. S. MONEY TO FRENCH COINAGE.

RULE.—Multiply the amount of Dollars and Cents by the Rate. The product will be in Francs and Centimes.

Ex. 4. I received $10,250 for the sale of 208 B/C. The payment was made with a Draft on Paris at the Exchange Rate of 5.20. What was the face of the Draft in French coinage?

—Ans. 53,300 Fr.

Ex. 5. Jones & Hoyt sold $7,500 worth of cotton for Shipment to Havre, and received a Draft drawn through

---

[33]The Exchange Rate, 5.16, 5.18½, etc., mean 5.16 and 5.18½ Francs to one Dollar.

[34]The Franc in Switzerland has the same value as in France. See Table XX, Value of Coins.

Havre for its equivalent in Francs at the Exchange Rate of 5.16. What was the value of the Draft in Dollars and Cents?

—Ans. 38,700 Fr.

CONVERTING ENGLISH COINAGE TO UNITED STATES MONEY.

For practical purposes and ready reference, the following Tables and explanations will prove valuable in converting English to United States money. By the use of the Tables the process of finding these values is much shortened.

Most English Exchange Rates are combined with Common Fractions, which, when converted to decimal forms, make the computations easier in multiplying the numbers.

The Fractions quoted usually being in eighths, quarters, &c., their decimal values are given in the following:

TABLE NO. XXI.

Decimal values of a Cent used in connection with the Pound (Sterling) Rate:

$\frac{1}{8}$ Cent=.0013
$\frac{1}{4}$ Cent=.0025
$\frac{3}{8}$ Cent=.0038
$\frac{1}{2}$ Cent=.0050
$\frac{5}{8}$ Cent=.0063
$\frac{3}{4}$ Cent=.0075
$\frac{7}{8}$ Cent=.0088

Let any Rate be stated, as 4.80\frac{1}{8}$, 4.82\frac{1}{4}$, 4.83\frac{3}{8}$ or 4.84\frac{1}{2}$ as representing the £ Sterling, the same values may be given decimally, as, $4.8013, $4.8225, $4.8338 and $4.845.

It will be noted that the decimal of a Cent is to

the fourth place, and must be applied in that way to get accurate results.

The quoted Rate, $4.80⅛, expressed in decimal form, as $4.8013, is found as follows:

One Pound (Sterling) =$4.80
⅛ Cent   = .0013
_____
Then $4.80⅛   =$4.8013

In similar manner the decimal values can be determined for any Rate.

TABLE NO. XXII.

Showing the decimal value of Shillings and Pence compared to a Pound Sterling:

Shillings.
1=.05 of a £
2=.10 " " "
3=.15 " " "
4=.20 " " "
5=.25 " " "
6=.30 " " "
7=.35 " " "
8=.40 " " "
9=.45 " " "
10=.50 " " "
11=.55 " " "
12=.60 " " "
13=.65 " " "
14=.70 " " "
15=.75 " " "
16=.80 " " "
17=.85 " ' "
18=.90 " " "
19=.95 " " "
20= 1

Pence.
1=.004 of a £
2=.009 " " "
3=.013 " " "
4=.017 " " " .
5=.021 " " "
6=.025 " " "
7=.030 " " "
8=.034 " " "
9=.038 " " "
10=.042 " " "
11=.046 " " "
12=.05 ==1 Shilling

Ex. 1. Mike Thomas sold 100 B/C to Covert & Co., Liverpool, for which he accepted a Draft on London for £932 12s. 10d.

What was its value in U. S. money at an Exchange Rate of $4.82½?

—Ans. $4,500.00.

STATEMENT.—Shillings and Pence must be converted to a Decimal of a £. The operation is as follows:

£932 =£932.000
12s.=   .60   (See Table—Shillings)
10d.=   .042 (See Table—Pence)

Val. with decimal=£932.642
Multiplied by Rate   4.825   ($4.82½=$4.825)

4663 210
18652 84
746113 6
3730568

Answer $4,499.997 650=$4,500.00

NOTE.—Get the Decimal values of Shillings and Pence from the Table and add them as shown in the above statement.

By use of these Tables comparative values for any Rate of Shillings and Pence Exchange is easily obtained.

The Rule for calculating English money applies here, as in the preceding examples.

GERMAN EXCHANGE.

THE GERMAN COINAGE consists of the Marks[35] and Pfennigs of the minor pieces.

1 Mark   (M)   =.238c (Monetary Unit)
100 Pfennigs (P)   = 1 Mark
$1.00   = 4 M.

[35]Exchange is quoted for 4 Marks to 1 United States Dollar.

TO CONVERT GERMAN COINAGE INTO U. S. VALUES.

RULE.—Multiply the face of the Bill in Marks and Pfennigs (Pfennigs as Decimals) by the Exchange Rate, and divide the product by 4; the answer will be in Dollars and Cents.

PROBLEMS.

Ex. 1.   Bond & Ellis sold 360 B/C to Weil & Newberg, for which they received a 60 day Draft, at 6%, on Berlin for 99,310.35 M.   At an Exchange Rate of 94¼, what would the bank pay for it in U. S. money?[36]

—Ans. $23,400.00.

Explanation:

$$99,310.35 \times 94\tfrac{1}{4}c = 93,600.00c$$
$$93,600c \div 4 = 23,400 \text{ Dollars}$$

Ex. 2.   A Draft for 38,266.13 M. was given for a shipment of cotton to Munich.   With Exchange at 94⅛, what would be its value in U. S. money?

—Ans. $9,004.50.

TO CONVERT U. S. COINAGE TO GERMAN VALUES.

RULE.—Divide the amount of money in Dollars and Cents by the Rate of Exchange; multiply the quotient by 4; the answer will be in Marks and Pfennigs.   (Pfennigs expressed as Decimals of a Mark.)

The quotations 94 1/16, 94⅛, 95½, etc., mean that 94 1/16c or 94⅛c will buy 4 Marks of German money.

Ex. 3.   Williams & Edwards sold 500 B/C, even-running Strict Middling, to Newberg & Schulte for Export to Trieste, Austria, for 11⅜c.   The bales averaged 516 lbs.   With Exchange on Berlin at 93¾, what was the amount of the Draft in German money?

—Ans. 125,216.00 M.

---

[36]The Ex. Rate of 94 1/4 is supposed to be for 60-day paper at the 6% Rate.

Explanation :

516 lbs. ✕ 500	=258,000 lbs.=Total weight
11 3/8c ✕ 258,000	=$29,347.50 =Value U. S.
29,347.50÷94 3/4c	=31,304
31,304 ✕ 4	=125,216.00 Marks

Ex. 4.   A shipment of cotton valued at $23,400 was paid for with a Draft on Berlin with Exchange at 94¼. What was its value in Marks and Pfennigs?

—Ans.   99,310.35 M.

OTHER FOREIGN COUNTRIES TO WHOM WE EXPORT COTTON.

The countries named in the subjoined list have a coinage whose *Monetary Units* are in subdivisions of 100 parts, making it quite easy for calculations involving those fractional parts.

The values stated are those established by the Director of the Mint of our Government, as compared with a Dollar.

TABLE NO. XXIII.

BELGIUM.

[Francs and Centimes.]

1 Franc (Fr.)	—19.3c
100 Centimes (Ce.)	—1 Franc
$1.00	=5.18 Francs

ITALY.

[Lire and Centesimi.]

1 Lira (L.)	=19.3c
100 Centesimi (Ci.)	=1 Lira
$1.00	=5.18 Lire

GREECE.

[Drachmas and Lepta.]

1 Drachma (Dr.)	=19.3c.
100 Lepta (Le.)	=1 Drachma
$1.00	=5.18 Drachmas

SPAIN.

[Pesetas and Centimos.]

1 Peseta (P.)	=19.3c
100 Centimos (C.)	=1 Peseta
$1.00	=5.18 Pesetas

SWITZERLAND.

[Francs and Centimes.]

1 Franc (Fr.)	=19.3c
100 Centimes (Ce.)	=1 Franc
$1.00	=5.18 Francs

AUSTRIA-HUNGARY.

[Crowns and Hellers.]

1 Crown (Cr.)	=20.3c
100 Hellers (H.)	=1 Crown or Krone
$1.00	=4.93 Crowns

NORWAY.

[Crowns (Krone) and Ore.]

1 Crown (Cr.)	=26.8c
100 Ore (O.)	=1 Crown
$1.00	=3.73 Crowns

SWEDEN.

[Crowns and Ore.]

1 Crown (Cr.)	=26.8c
100 Ore (O.)	=1 Crown
$1.00	=3.73 Crowns

DENMARK.

[Crowns and Ore.]

1 Crown (Cr.)	=26.8c
100 Ore (O.)	=1 Crown
$1.00	=3.73 Crowns

RUSSIA.

[Rubles and Kopecks.]

1 Ruble (Ru.)	=51c
100 Kopecks (Ko.)	=1 Ruble
$1.00	=1.96 Rubles

MEXICO.

[Peso and Centavos.]

1 Peso (Po.)	=50c
100 Centavos (Cv.)	=1 Peso
$1.00	=2 Pesos

JAPAN.

[Yen and Sen.]

1 Yen (Y.)	=50c
100 Sen (S.)	=1 Yen
$1.00	=2 Yens

All countries having a *Monetary Unit* of 19.3c, can have their coinage converted into terms of United States values by following the Rule for conversion of French monies.

PROBLEMS.

Ex. 1. Crespi & Co., Waco, Texas, sold 500 B/C, valued at $35,000 for Export to Milan, Italy, for which they received a 60-day Draft at 6% on Genoa at an Exchange Rate of 5.24¼. What was the face of the Draft in Lire and Centesimi? —Ans. 183,487.5 L.[37]

---

[37]The Centesimi are expressed as a Decimal of the Lire.

Ex. 2.   An Exporter at Savannah sold 1200 B/C for Export to Barcelona, Spain, valued at $62,400.   The cotton went out in 4 shipments of 300 bales each, but the payment of the whole was in one Draft, drawn on Madrid at the Rate of 5.25 for 60-day "spinners paper." What was the face of the Draft in Pesetas and Centimos?

—Ans.   327,600 P.

NOTE.—If 1 Dollar is worth 5.25 Pesetas, or Francs, or Drachmas, or Lire, 5 1/4 times the number of Dollars, equal that number of Pesetas. Francs, etc.

Drafts for Export cotton read usually at 60 or 90 days time, with Interest generally at 6%

Banks buying these Drafts, customarily pay an Exchange Rate to cover the Interest and other incidental charges, which Rate varies from the Par Rate.

Let it be stated that a Draft for $550 at 60 days, 6% Interest, is drawn on Paris, in Francs and Centimes.   The Rate of Exchange is, say $\frac{1}{4}$% Premium; Par of Exchange 5.18; Commercial Rate 5.24$\frac{1}{2}$.

Interest on $550, 60 days		=$5.50
Premium of Exchange		= 1.38
Total		· =$6.88
Commercial Rate	= 5.24$\frac{1}{2}$ Francs	
Intrinsic Rate (Par)	= 5.18 Francs	
Difference	= .06$\frac{1}{2}$ Francs or 6$\frac{1}{2}$ Centimes	
$550×6$\frac{1}{2}$ (C.)	=35.75 Francs	
35.75 Fr.	=$6.90	

The payment of a Commercial Rate above an Intrinsic one, as shown, will cover the Interest and Premium of Exchange.

OTHER EXCHANGE RATES.

Smaller Exchange Rates are required, as the value of the Monetary Unit increases. The Crown (Krone) of Austria-Hungary has a basic Intrinsic American valuation of 20.3c. One Cent above the Franc, Lira, Drachma, etc., therefore, its Exchange Rate is smaller.

The Rate at Intrinsic Par is 4.93; that is, 4.93 Crowns, equal $1.00 in value. In commercial transactions this Rate varies.

Follow the Rule for determining French, Italian, etc., Exchange in getting comparative values.

RULE.—To know the number of Crowns in $1,000, multiply the Dollars by the Exchange Rate, 4.93; to know the number of Dollars in a given number of Crowns and Hellers, divide them by 4.93.

PROBLEMS.

Ex. 1. Johnson & Wilde sold 800 B/C at $60 a bale net, for shipment to Vienna. The Draft was for 90 days at 6%. What was its value in Kronen (plural of Krone) and Hellers at an Exchange Rate of 4.97½?

—Ans. 238,800Cr.

Explanation:

$60 × 800   =$48,000
$48,000 × 4.975 =238,800 Cr.

Ex. 2. Johnson & Wilde sold 800 B/C, for which they received a 90-day Draft on Vienna at 6% for 238,800 Crowns. What was its value in Dollars and Cents at an Exchange Rate of 4.97½?

—Ans. $48,000.

Explanation:

238,800 ÷ 4.97½ $48,000

The same plan of operation in determining comparative values for France, Austria-Hungary, etc., will serve for Norway, Sweden, Denmark, Japan, Mexico and Russia.

The Rates of Exchange applying for the Scandinavian Peninsula are the same for each country in it, all having the same designated currency.

Norway (Krone)=26.8c
Sweden (Crown)
Denmark (Crown)

Its Rate at Intrinsic Par is 3.73; that is, 3.73 Crowns equal $1.00 in value.

TABLE NO. XXIV.

Comparative values of the minor coinage of the following countries, as compared to $1, Cents and fractions thereof, U. S. Mint valuation:

United States. Cents. $.01	Germany. Pfennigs. $ 00238	France. Centimes. $ 00193	England. Pence. $.0202
1 ($ or c)38	4.20 (M or Pfgs.)38	5 18 (F. or Cen)38	0.50
2	8.40	10.36	1.00
3	12.60	15.54	1.50
4	16.81	20 73	2.00
5	21.01	25.91	2.43
5⅛	21.53	26.55	2.54
5¼	22.06	27.20	2.59
5⅜	22.58	27.85	2.66
5½	23.11	28.50	2.73
5⅝	23.63	29.14	2.78
5¾	24.16	29.79	2.84
5⅞	24.68	30.44	2.91
6	25.21	31.08	2.97
6⅛	25.73	31.74	3.03
6¼	26.26	32.38	3.09
6⅜	26.79	33.03	3.15
6½	27.31	33.68	3.21
6⅝	27.84	34.33	3.28
6¾	28.36	34.97	3.34
6⅞	28.89	35.62	3.40
7	29.41	36.27	3.47
7⅛	29.94	36.92	3.53
7¼	30.46	37.56	3.59
7⅜	30.99	38.21	3.65
7½	31.51	38.86	3.71
7⅝	32.04	39.50	3.77
7¾	32.55	40.15	3.83
7⅞	33.09	40.80	3.89
8	33.61	41.45	3.96
8⅛	34.14	42.10	4.02
8¼	34.66	42.75	4.08
8⅜	35.19	43.39	4.14
8½	35.71	44.04	4.20
8⅝	36.24	44.69	4.26
8¾	36 76	45.34	4.32
8⅞	37.29	45.98	4.39

38This Table can be read: One Dollar=4 20 Marks and 5.18 Francs, or One Cent=4 20 Pfgs. and 5.18 Centimes

United States. Cents $.01	Germany. Pfennigs. $.00238	France. Centimes. $.00193	England. Pence. $.0202
9 ($ or c.)	37.82 (M. or Pfgs.)	46.63 (F. or Cen.)	4.45
9⅛	38.34	47.28	4.51
9¼	38.87	47.92	4.58
9⅜	39.39	48.57	4.64
9½	39.91	49.22	4.70
9⅝	40.44	49.87	4.76
9¾	40.96	50.51	4.82
9⅞	41.49	51.16	4.88
10	42.02	51.81	4.95
10⅛	42.54	52.46	5.01
10¼	43.07	53.11	5.07
10⅜	43.59	53.76	5.13
10½	44.11	54.40	5.19
10⅝	44.64	55.05	5.26
10¾	45.17	55.70	5.32
10⅞	45.69	56.35	5.38
11	46.22	56.99	5.44
11⅛	46.74	57.64	5.50
11¼	47.26	58.29	5.56
11⅜	47.79	58.94	5.62
11½	48.32	59.59	5.68
11⅝	48.84	60.23	5.75
11¾	49.37	60.88	5.81
11⅞	49.89	61.53	5.87
12	50.42	62.17	5.94
12⅛	50.94	62.82	6.00
12¼	51.47	63.47	6.06
12⅜	51.99	64.11	6.12
12½	52.52	64.76	6.18
12⅝	53.05	65.41	6.24
12¾	53.57	66.06	6.31
12⅞	54.09	66.70	6.38
13	54.62	67.35	6.44
13⅛	55.15	68.00	6.50
13¼	55.67	68.65	6.56
13⅜	56.19	69.30	6.62
13½	56.72	69.95	6.68
13⅝	57.25	70.59	6.74
13¾	57.77	71.24	6.80
13⅞	58.29	71.89	6.86
14	58.82	72.54	6.93
14⅛	59.35	73.18	6.99
14¼	59.87	73.83	7.05
14⅜	60.39	74.48	7.11
14½	60.92	75.13	7.18
14⅝	61.45	75.77	7.24
14¾	61.97	76.42	7.30
14⅞	62.50	77.07	7.36
15	63.03	77.72	7.42
15⅛	63.55	78.37	7.49
15¼	64.07	79.02	7.55
15⅜	64.60	79.66	7.61
15½	65.12	80.31	7.67
15⅝	65.65	80.96	7.73
15¾	66.17	81.60	7.80
15⅞	66.69	82.25	7.86
16	67.23	82.90	7.92
16⅛	67.75	83.55	7.98
16¼	68.28	84.20	8.04
16⅜	68.80	84.84	8.11
16½	69.33	85.49	8.17
16⅝	69.85	86.14	8.23
16¾	70.38	86.79	8.29
16⅞	70.90	87.44	8.35
17	71.43	88.08	8.42

The Monetary Units having subdivisions of 100's are figured as *percentages*, the same as Cents and Dollars.

The expressions 50 Francs, 10 Centimes; 50 Crowns, 10

Hellers; 50 Lire, 10 Centesimi; 50 Drachmas, 10 Lepta; 50 Pesetas, 10 Centesimos; 50 Crowns, 10 Ore; 50 Pesos, 10 Centavos; 50 Yen, 10 Sen; can be and are written as 50.10 Francs, 50.10 Crowns, 50.10 Lire, etc. The customary fractional denominations are stated as the Decimal part of the Monetary Unit.

BANKERS DEALINGS.

But few banks, comparatively speaking, buy and sell Drafts for payment of Export cotton, and those who do, determine the Rate of Exchange applying between any two countries, or use a quoted Rate.

The daily press usually gives the current Rates, and Dealers Exporting cotton know these Rates before accepting the Draft in payment for the cotton; if not, they can readily ascertain them through their banks.

Knowing the value of a Draft on any foreign commercial center, in Dollars and Cents, the Rate of Exchange, Freight Charges, Tare, and all incidentals attached to the movement of the cotton and the price on the Foreign Market, one can readily figure a base for local purchases, as previously shown.

Bankers being exclusive factors dealing in Exchange, that province falls within their line of business, and through them the Trade is enabled to move cotton at all times, and by the banks have its interests protected.

FOREIGN EXCHANGE QUOTATIONS.

Bremen and Havre issue Cotton Quotations in Millimeters for Staple, and Pfennigs and Francs for valuation. Liverpool quotes in Inches for Staple, and Pence for valuation, based on the avoirdupois Pound weight.

Bremen and Havre conform to the Metric System for weights, quoting in Kilograms or Kilos (pronounced Keeloz).

Bremen quotes, Spot Terms, ½ Ko. per Pfennig. Havre prices are quoted in Francs for 50 Kilos.

A Kilo equals 2.20507 lbs. (See Table XXVIII), or for practical usage 2.205 lbs., one-half of which is 1.1025 lbs. The French Quotation being for 50 Ko. is 100 times that weight, or 110.25 lbs.

The German and French Markets publicly quote their cotton valuations, as do the Exchanges of America, but their weights, measurements and values must be translated into ours to become intelligible to us.

Foreign Buyers sometimes make firm offers for cotton in American Quotations, but when not so made, the American Vendor is left to make his own translation of their terms.

It should be remembered that the Quotations issued to the public are not those always obtained in actual transactions. The Foreign Trade, as well as our Domestic Operators, will sometimes pay more than the quoted prices, when a sale and purchase is said to be made "above the Market;" conversely, if the transaction is made at less than quotation, it is made "under the Market."

As stated, three factors must be considered in converting Foreign to Domestic values, namely: Weights, Measurements and Prices.

The theory of conversion should be understood, while the operation to be performed mathematically may be done by Rule.

In connection with the three factors mentioned, the *Rate of Exchange* is a component part to be reckoned in computations determining comparative values.

Let it be stated that Bremen quotes Middling at 48 Pfennigs; that the current Rate of Exchange applying is 93¾, (93¾c for 4 Marks), what would be the value of the German Quotation in Cents?

Analyzing, and observing the preceding Tables for Foreign weights and Money values, we determine the value of 48 P. in c., as follows:

48 Pfgs.=½ Ko.
96 Pfgs.=1 Ko.
1 Ko. =2.205 lbs.
100 lbs. =45.35 Ko.

If 1 Ko. is worth 96 Pfgs. 45.35 Ko. is worth 45.35 times 96 Pfgs.
96×45.35=4353.6 Pfgs. per 100 lbs., or 43.53 Pfgs. per 1 lb.
43.53×93¾ (Ex.) =40.8093c.
40.8093c÷4 (4 M. to 1 Dollar) =10.20c per lb.

Computations for finding the French values are made in a similar manner to those required for getting the German prices, ascertaining first the value of 5 Francs at the Rate of Exchange.

Referring to Table XXIV, it will be noted that 47.79 P. equal 58.94C., or 48 P. would about equal 59 C. An Exchange Rate of 5.24¾ on France, practically equals one of 93¾ on Germany.[39] A Rate of 5.24¾ equals 19.06c (see Table XXVI), as the value of one Franc; 5 Francs equal 95.3c—5 times 19.06c. With this statement we are prepared to make a solution of a Problem.

If Havre quotes Middling at 59 F., what is its equivalent value per lb. in Cents with Exchange 5.24¾?

NOTE.—For convenience we can call the 59 Francs, 59 Centimes—1 Centime=1/100 of a Franc.

59 Ce. =½ Ko.
118 Ce. =1 Ko.
100 Ko. =45.35 lbs.
118×45.35=5351.3 Ce. per 100 lbs., or 53.51 Ce. per 1 lb.
53.51×95.3c   50.995

50.995÷5 (5 F. to 1 Dollar)=10.199c per lb., or practically 10.20c, which is parity with the German Quotation of 48 Pfennigs.

For abbreviating the process of finding equivalent values of Foreign Quotations, the following Tables are added for the German and French Markets. No Table is given for Liverpool, as the Trade takes the English Quotations at half the American, that is to say, if Liverpool quotes M. cotton at 6½d., the American Trade accepts 13c as a parity value to it.

---

[39]This is a Commercial Exchange Rate and not one of Intrinsic value.

These Tables will be found convenient for converting German and French monies to U. S. Mint values, or vice versa.

RULE.—*To find the value of U. S. money in Marks and Pfennigs, or Francs and Centimes, multiply the amount of U. S. money by the value of 1 Mark or Franc at the Exchange Rate.*

To find the value of Marks and Francs in U. S. money, divide the Dollars and Cents by the Exchange Rate for 1 Mark or Franc.

TABLE NO. XXV.

SHOWING THE VALUE OF ONE MARK AT DIFFERENT RATES OF EXCHANGE.

NOTE.—This Table virtually covers all the Rates, (with some exceptions) that ordinarily apply in Germanic Cotton Transactions.

Exchange Rate for 4 Marks.	Value of Mark at Ex. Rate.	Exchange Rate for 4 Marks.	Value of Mark at Ex. Rate.
93	23.25c	94 1/4	23.56c
93 1/16	23.26c	94 5/16	23.58c
93 1/8	23.28c	94 3/8	23.59c
93 3/16	23.30c	94 7/16	23.61c
93 1/4	23.31c	94 1/2	23.62c
93 5/16	23.33c	94 9/16	23.64c
93 3/8	23.34c	94 5/8	23.65c
93 7/16	23.36c	94 11/16	23.67c
93 1/2	23.38c	94 3/4	23.69c
93 9/16	23.39c	94 13/16	23.70c
93 5/8	23.40c	94 7/8	23.72c
93 11/16	23.42c	94 15/16	23.73c
93 3/4	23.44c	95	23.75c
93 13/16	23.45c	95 1/16	23.76c
93 7/8	23.47c	95 1/8	23.78c
93 15/16	23.48c	95 3/16	23.79c
94	23.50c	95 1/4	23.81c
94 1/16	23.52c	95 5/16	23.83c
94 1/8	23.53c	95 3/8	23.84c
94 3/16	23.55c	95 7/16	23.86c

Exchange Rate for 4 Marks.	Value of Mark at Ex. Rate.	Exchange Rate for 4 Marks.	Value of Mark at Ex. Rate.
95 1/2	23.87c	96 5/16	24.08c
95 9/16	23.89c	96 3/8	24.09c
95 5/8	23.90c	96 7/16	24.11c
95 11/16	23.92c	96 1/2	24.12c
95 3/4	23.94c	96 9/16	24.14c
95 13/16	23.95c	96 5/8	24.16c
95 7/8	23.97c	96 11/16	24.17c
95 15/16	23.98c	96 3/4	24.19c
96	24.00c	96 13/16	24.20c
96 1/16	24.01c	96 7/8	24.22c
96 1/8	24.03c	96 15/16	24.23c
96 3/16	24.04c	97	24.25c
96 1/4	24.06c	97 1/16	24.27c

TABLE XXVI.

SHOWING THE VALUE OF ONE FRANC AT DIFFERENT RATES OF EXCHANGE.

Note.—The Cent valuation for 1 Franc has been carried to the fifth Decimal place for greater accuracy. In practice, four Decimals are ordinarily used, due regard being had for the ending number.

Exchange Rate in Francs	Value of Franc at Rate	Exchange Rate in Francs	Value of Franc at Rate
5.17	19.342c	5.19	19.268c
5.17⅛	19.338c	5.19⅛	19.263c
5.17¼	19.333c	5.19¼	19.259c
5.17⅜	19.328c	5.19⅜	19.254c
5.17½	19.324c	5.19½	19.249c
5.17⅝	19.319c	5.19⅝	19.245c
5.17¾	19.314c	5.19¾	19.240c
5.17⅞	19.310c	5.19⅞	19.235c
5.18	19.305c	5.20	19.231c
5.18⅛	19.300c	5.20⅛	19.226c
5.18¼	19.294c	5.20¼	19.222c
5.18⅜	19.291c	5.20⅜	19.217c
5.18½	19.286c	5.20½	19.212c
5.18⅝	19.282c	5.20⅝	19.208c
5.18¾	19.277c	5.20¾	19.203c
5.18⅞	19.272c	5.20⅞	19.199c

Exchange Rate in Francs	Value of Franc at Rate	Exchange Rate in Francs	Value of Franc at Rate
5.21	19.194c	5.24⅝	19.061c
5.21⅛	19.190c	5.24¾	19.057c
5.21¼	19.185c	5.24⅞	19.053c
5.21⅜	19.180c	5.25	19.048c
5.21½	19.175c	5.25⅛	19.043c
5.21⅝	19.171c	5.25¼	19.039c
5.21¾	19.166c	5.25⅜	19.034c
5.21⅞	19.162c	5.25½	19.029c
5.22	19.157c	5.25⅝	19.025c
5.22⅛	19.153c	5.25¾	19.020c
5.22¼	19.148c	5.25⅞	19.016c
5.22⅜	19.143c	5.26	19.011c
5.22½	19.139c	5.26⅛	19.007c
5.22⅝	19.134c	5.26¼	19.002c
5.22¾	19.130c	5.26⅜	18.998c
5.22⅞	19.125c	5.26½	18.993c
5.23	19.120c	5.26⅝	18.989c
5.23⅛	19.116c	5.26¾	18.985c
5.23¼	19.111c	5.26⅞	18.981c
5.23⅜	19.107c	5.27	18.975c
5.23½	19.102c	5.27⅛	18.971c
5.23⅝	19.098c	5.27¼	18.966c
5.23¾	19.093c	5.27⅜	18.962c
5.23⅞	19.088c	5.27½	18.957c
5.24	19.084c	5.27⅝	18.953c
5.24⅛	19.079c	5.27¾	18.948c
5.24¼	19.075c	5.27⅞	18.944c
5.24⅜	19.070c	5.28	18.939c
5.24½	19.066c	5.28⅛	18.935c

In making computations for equalizing Foreign values with ours, observe the following:

RULE.—Multiply the German Quotation by the value of the Mark, at the designated Rate of Exchange; divide the product by 1.1025 (lbs.)—equal to ½ Kilo.

Multiply the French Quotation by the value of a Franc, at the designated Rate of Exchange; divide the product by 110.25 (lbs.)—equal to 50 Kilos. The answer to both calculations will be in Cents per pound.

If Bremen quotes M. at 48 Pfennigs, what would be its value in Cents at an Exchange Rate of 93¾? (Calculate by the Table.)   —Ans.   10.20c.

NOTE.—Find the value of 1 Mark by referring to the Exchange Rate, which is 23.44c.

Explanation:

$$23.44 \times 48 = 11.2512c$$
$$11.2512 \div 1.1025 = 10.20c \text{ a pound}$$

If the Havre Bourse (Exchange) quotes cotton 59 F. for M., what is its value in Cents per pound at an Exchange Rate of 5.24¾, calculated by the Table?

Explanation:
5.24¾ Exchange = 19.06c per 1 Franc (By the Table.)
$$59 \times 19.06 = 1124.54c.$$
$$1124.54 - 110.25 = 10.199c \text{ or } 10.20c \text{ a pound.}$$

American valuation figured here, represents the net F. O. B. values in Europe, from which Tare, Insurance and all the incidental Expenses must be deducted to obtain a basis price on this side.

PROBLEMS.

Ex. 1.   Bremen quotes M. cotton at 62¼; what is its value in Cents at an Exchange Rate of 93, 93½, 94 and 94⅛?

—Ans.   13.13c, 13.20c, 13.28c, 13.28c.

Ex. 2.   If I am offered 30 American Points on Bremen Marches at 64, what will be its spot value there at 94 1/16 Exchange?

—Ans.   13.95c.

Ex. 3.   What can I pay B/M in Atlanta for the cotton in Ex. 2, with Tare 5%, Freight 90, Insurance 10, Profit 8 and Expenses 12 Points?

—Ans.   12.05c.

Ex. 4.   The Havre Market for M. was 65½; what is that per lb. in Cents with Exchange at 5.23½?

—Ans.   11.35c.

Ex. 5.   If the Freight between Havre and Houston is 58c, what is the price at the latter place, if Havre quotes M. Spots at 75, Sight Exchange at 5.25?

—Ans.   12.38c.

From the preceding it will be noted Foreign Exchange can be quoted in two ways, namely: for illustration, 94¼c for 4 Marks, or 23.56c per 1 Mark for German accounts. For French moneys, 5.24⅜ Francs for $1.00, or 19.07c per 1 Franc at same Rate.

Bear in mind that Rates of Exchange refer to *Commercial Transactions*, and not to intrinsic Par Value, as established by the U. S. Director of the Mint.

Port charges are not the same in all American Ports, neither are they in harmony in Foreign ones, but must be considered in figuring prices to be paid for cotton on this side. Such charges are obtainable from Foreign Buyers and Domestic Exporters.

Tables and calculations for Foreign Exchange on other countries, as Scandinavia, Italy, Switzerland, Spain, etc., are not given because transactions for Cotton exported to them are generally settled for with Exchange on London, Paris, Bremen, Hamburg, etc., London being the great commercial center for the adjustment of the greater percentage of European or Asiatic accounts.

SECTION VII.

AMERICAN, GERMAN AND FRENCH WEIGHTS, AND METRIC MEASUREMENTS.

The standard of weights for most all the European countries is based on the Metric system, and calculations are made in Kilograms; for convenience and brevity, generally expressed as Kilos.

Lengths for cotton Staple are in Millimeters, and length and strength are qualifying considerations in determining values, but not exclusive of other factors that go to make up the Grades.

Millimeters in quotations for Staple Values are abbreviated thūs—m/m.

A Meter being about 39.37 inches, a m/m equals 1000th

part of it, equal to .03937 inch, and for practical purposes may be expressed as .04 inch.

To determine the length of cotton Staple measuring, say 28 m/m, by multiplying by .04 would equal 1.12 inches, an approximation close to accuracy.

Quotations for Staple Cotton are given as definite lengths, and those intermediate; as 28 m/m; 28/30 m/m; 29 m/m; 29/30 m/m; 30 m/m; 30/32 m/m, and so forth.

The expression "28/30," means 28 to 30 m/m in length; that is for cotton measuring 1.12 to 1.20 inches, equal to about 1 1/8 to 1 1/5 inches.

TABLE NO. XXVII.

To detremine readily the length of the m/m as compared to an Inch and its fractional parts, the following comparative tabular statement is given:

Inch.		Milli-meter.	Inch.		Milli-meter.
7/16	equals	11.11	1 1/4	equals	31.74
1/2	"	12.70	1 5/16	"	33.33
9/16	"	14.28	1 3/8	"	34.92
5/8	"	15.87	1 7/16	"	36.50
11/16	"	17.46	1 1/2	"	38.09
3/4	"	19.05	1 9/16	"	39.68
13/16	"	20.63	1 5/8	"	41.26
7/8	"	22.22	1 11/16	"	42.85
15/16	"	23.81	1 3/4	"	44.44
1		25.39	1 13/16	"	46.02
1 1/16	"	26.98	1 7/8	"	47.61
1 1/8	"	28.57	1 15/16	"	49.20
1 3/16	"	30.15	2		50.79

Milli-meter.		Inch.	Milli-meter.		Inch.
16	equals	.63	31	equals	1.22
17	"	.67	32	"	1.26
18	"	.71	33	"	1.30
19		.75	34		1.34
20		.79	35		1.38
21		.83	36		1.42
22		.87	37		1.46
23		.91	38		1.50
24		.95	39		1.54
25		.98	40		1.58
26		1.02	41		1.62
27		1.06	42		1.66
28		1.10	43		1.70
29		1.14	44		1.74
30		1.18	45		1.77

TABLE NO. XXVIII.

AMERICAN-GERMAN WEIGHTS.

Kilos to 2 Decimals.   100 lbs.=45.35 Kilos.

Lbs.	Kilos.	Lbs.	Kilos.	Lbs.	Kilos.
1	0.45	70	31.74	4,000	1,814.00
2	0.90	80	36.28	5,000	2,267.50
3	1.36	90	40.81	6,000	2,721.00
4	1.81	100	45.35	7,000	3,174.50
5	2.26	150	68.02	8,000	3,628.00
6	2.72	200	90.70	9,000	4,081.50
7	3.17	300	136.05	10,000	4,535.00
8	3.62	400	181.40	20,000	9,070.00
9	4.08	500	226.75	30,000	13,605.00
10	4.53	600	272.10	40,000	18,140.00
15	6.80	700	317.45	50,000	22,675.00
20	9.07	800	362.80	60,000	27,210.00
30	13.60	900	408.15	70,000	31,745.00
40	18.14	1,000	453.50	80,000	36,280.00
50	22.67	2,000	907.00	90,000	40,815.00
60	27.21	3,000	1,360.50	100,000	45,350.00

TABLE NO. XXIX.

GERMAN-AMERICAN WEIGHTS.

Lbs. to 2 Decimals.　45.35 Kilos=100 lbs.

Kilos.	Lbs.	Kilos.	Lbs.	Kilos.	Lbs.
¼	0.55	50	110.25	3,000	6,615.21
½	1.10	60	132.30	4,000	8,820.29
¾	1.65	70	154.35	5,000	11,025.36
1	2.20	80	176.40	6,000	13,230.43
2	4.41	90	198.46	7,000	15,435.50
3	6.61	100	220.51	8,000	17,640.57
4	8.82	150	330.76	9,000	19,845.64
5	11.02	200	441.01	10,000	22,050.72
6	13.23	300	661.52	20,000	44,101.43
7	15.43	400	882.03	30,000	66,152.15
8	17.64	500	1,102.54	40,000	88,202.87
9	19.84	600	1,323.04	50,000	110,253.58
10	22.05	700	1,543.55	60,000	132,304.30
15	33.07	800	1,764.06	70,000	154,355.02
20	44.10	900	1,984.56	80,000	176,405.73
30	66.15	1,000	2,205.07	90,000	198,456.45
40	88.20	2,000	4,410.14	100,000	220,507.17

PROBLEMS.

Ex. 1.　A man sold one B/C weighing 522 lbs.; what is its weight in Kilos?

—Ans.　234.9 Kilos.

Explanation:
(1)　1 lb. (Table)=.45 Kilos.
　　　522 lbs. =522×.45 =234.9 Kilos. (Ans.)
(2)　By the Table　2 lbs.=　.90 Kilos.
　　　　　　　　　20 lbs.=　9.07 Kilos
　　　　　　　　500 lbs.=226.75 Kilos.
　　　　　　　　　————　　————
　　　　　　　　522 lbs.=236.72 Kilos.

The difference is caused by carrying the relative value of the Kilo to the pound to only 2 Decimal places. The true Decimal to 4 places is .4535+; .4535×522=236.72+Kilos.

Ex. 2.   What is the equivalent weight in Kilos of 5 B/C weighing respectively, 510, 532, 496, 501, 566 lbs.?   Give results by the Table.

—Ans.   1,181.36 Kilos.

Ex. 3.   Bought from a German 13 B/C which weighed 3482 Kilos at 9.80 cents a pound.   What was the value of the cotton?

—Ans. $752.44×

NOTE.—Get weights in lbs. from Table, and multiply by the price.

Ex. 4.   A Buyer offered 1 Mark per Kilo for 3 B/C weighing 685 Kilos.   What was the value in U. S. money?

—Ans. $163.03.

Explanation:

$$685 \times 1 \text{ M.} = 685\text{M.}$$
$$685 \times \$.238 = \$163.03 \quad \text{Ans.}$$

Ex. 5.   What is the price per pound in U. S. money in Example 4?

—Ans.   10.80c nearly.

Explanation:

600 Kilos	1,323.04	lbs.
80 Kilos	176.40	lbs.
5 Kilos	11.02	lbs.
685 Kilos	1,510.46	lbs.

If 1,510.46 lbs. cost $163.03, 1 lb. will cost 1/1,510.46 of $163.03, which equals $163.03÷1,510.46 lbs., equals 10.80c, nearly.

Ex. 6.   I sold a list of cotton weighing 1,260 Kilos, which I classed 28 m/m Staple, at 110 Pfennigs per Kilo; the outturn from this shipment showed the cotton to Staple 30 m/m; what did I gain in Dollars and Cents by this latter gradation if each m/m of extra length was equivalent to 10 Pfennigs?

—Ans. $59,976.

MB—8

Explanation :

    1,260 Kilos ×110 Pfennigs =138,600 Pfgs.

    138,600×$.00238=$329.868,=28 m/m.

    Gain on each m/m=10 Pfgs.

    Out-turn showed gain of 2 m/m, then—

    10×2 Pfgs. =20 Pfgs.

    110 Pfgs. +20 Pfgs. =130 Pfgs.

    1,260 Kilos ×130=163,800 Pfgs.

    163,800×$.00238=$389.844, 30 m/m.

        Value at 30 m/m=389.844

        Value at 28 m/m=329.868

        Gain   =$59.976 Ans.

NOTE.—A Mark=23.8 Cents; a Pfennig is 1/100 of a Mark, therefore =$.00238.

Ex. 7.   Prove otherwise Ex. 6 is correct.

Explanation :

1,000	Kilos	2,205.07	lbs.
200	Kilos	441.61	lbs.
60	Kilos	132.30	lbs.
1,260	Kilos	2,778.38	lbs.

$389.844÷2,778.38 lbs. = cost 1 lb., 30 m/m=$.1403+.

329.868÷2,778.38 lbs. = cost 1 lb., 28 m/m=$.1187+.

$.1403—$.1187=$.0216=gain on 1 lb.

2,778.38 lbs. × $.0216=$60.013 Ans.[40]

Ex. 8.   What will be the value in Francs for 150 B/C weighing 231.28 Kilos each, at 1 Mark per Kilo?

    —Ans. 42,780.8 Fr.

Ex. 9.   Adams & Smith, Houston, Texas, shipped 1,000 B/C to Mitsui & Co., Osaka, Japan; the Invoice Weights were 235,820 Kilos; this cotton was sold for an average of 10⅞ cents per pound f. o. b. Houston; the Draft was drawn through a New York bank for U. S. money; it drew on Mitsui & Co. in Yen; find the face of the Draft in Yen.

    —Ans. 113,554.21 Yen.

NOTE.—Consult Tables XX and XXVII in solving Problems 8 and 9 above.

---

[40]The slight difference in the two answers is caused by not extending the Decimals beyond 2 places.

REVIEW PROBLEMS.

I.

	Find the value of—					Answer.
1.	10 B/C averaging 516 lbs. at	9		Cents per lb.		$ 464.40
2.	13 B/C averaging 533 lbs. at	10 1/2		Cents per lb.		$ 727.55
3.	22 B/C averaging 498 lbs. at	11 1/4		Cents per lb.		$1232.55
4.	19 B/C averaging 519 lbs. at	12 3/4		Cents per lb.		$1257.28
5.	48 B/C averaging 542 lbs. at	13 1/8		Cents per lb.		$3414.60
6.	36 B/C averaging 500 lbs. at	14 7/8		Cents per lb.		$2677.50
7.	60 B/C averaging 490 lbs. at	15 7/16		Cents per lb.		$4538.63
8.	53 B/C averaging 539 lbs. at	15 3/16		Cents per lb.		$4338.61
9.	27 B/C averaging 507 lbs. at	12 1/32		Cents per lb.		$1646.96
10.	81 B/C averaging 535 lbs. at	14 9/32		Cents per lb.		$6188.78

II.

Find the value of the following—

	Price.	$9\frac{5}{8}$c	$9\frac{3}{8}$c	9c	$8\frac{3}{4}$c	$8\frac{1}{4}$c	$7\frac{1}{2}$c	
	Avg. Wt.	G.M.	S.M.	M.	S.L.M.	L.M.	S.G.O.	Answer.
11.	520 lbs.	5	6	10	4	2	1	$1317.55
12.	548 lbs.	8	12	16	5	3	4	$2367.36
13.	492 lbs.	18	25	31	20	14	7	$5065.76
14.	535 lbs.	12	14	24		3	1	$2648.25
15.	500 lbs.	10	20	30	2	4	6	$3246.25

	Price	11c	$10\frac{3}{4}$c	$10\frac{1}{2}$c	10c	$9\frac{1}{2}$c	$8\frac{3}{4}$c	
16.	502 lbs.	25	38	42	17		5	$6718.02
17.	489 lbs.	5	19	27	33	9		$4685.84
18.	550 lbs.	13	40	41	39	8	2	$8178.50
19.	530 lbs.	14	18	20	18	14	12	$5170.15
20.	561 lbs.	23	19	24	11	3	8	$5148.58

III.

Find the average of the following, with Differences as stated—

	Dif.........½ on	¼ on		¼ off	¾ off	1½ off	
	B/M	G.M.	S.M.	M.	S.L.M.	L.M.	S.G.O.	Answer.
21.	9c	1120[41]	2180	2560		1480	3150	8.55c
22.	9½c	560	1030		2002	490	1515	9.03c
23.	9¾c	2611	4753	5382	6809	3195	2097	9.56c
24.	8½c	560	1130	486	2540	490	1110	8.17c
25.	12c		2612	1585		1005		11.98c
26.	13¼c	1624		1390	520	610		13.30c
27.	7⅜c	488	3160	1002	560	585		7.45c
28.	10⅝c	1639	509	499	1010	484	1522	10.28c
29.	11¼c	4197	6338	5381	3294	2621	573	11.25c
30.	14½c	7377	8502	2055	3088	4806	998	14.50c

IV.

Find the average of the following, with Differences, as stated—

		⅝ up	⅜ up	¼ up		5/16 down	¾ down	
	B/M	S.G.M.	G.M.	S.M.	M.	S.L.M.	L.M.	Answer.
31.	11c	4	10	21	32	46	17	10.88c
32.	10½c	1	19	69	81	57	15	10.48c
33.	10⅜c		75	98	109	72	93	10.29c
34.	10¾c	10	14	12	18	22	31	10.60c
35.	9½c	25	59	75	99	3	1	9.71c
36.	8c			251	486	582	600	7.71c
37.	7½c	8	15		66		95	7.17c
38.	12c		100	316	361	399	501	11.77c
39.	12½c	2	2	4	8	6	9	12.32c
40.	13c	13	28	65	66	44		13.10c

---

[41] These figures refer to pounds.

V.

Find the average of the following, with Differences as stated—

	5/16 on	3/16 on		5/16 off	100 off	50 off	
B/M	G.M.	S.M.	M.	S.L.M.	S.G.O.	S.L.M.T.	Ans.
41. 7¾c	3	6	18	20	10	2	7.50c
42. 9½c		4		14	36	16	8.45c
43. 8 1/16c	20	26	50	2	13	5	8.02c
44. 10c	1	9	7	19	10		9.70c
45. 10 9/16c	60		100	23	41	9	10.42c
46. 12¾c	40	50	89	11	8	2	12.80c
47. 13½c	1	1	1	1	1	1	13.28c
48. 14c	29	37	53		18	13	13.94c
49. 14⅞c	73	80	15	12		27	14.97c
50. 15c	2	6	6	3	1		14.99c

VI.

Find the average of the following, with Differences as stated—

	52 on	26 on		84 off	156 off	82 off	
B/M	G.M.	S.M.	M.	L.M.	S.G.O.	S.L.M.T.	Ans.
51. 7c	6	18	23	19	10	2	6.67c
52. 7⅜c	3	12	14	9	8	5	7.49c
53. 8¾c	10	25	38	33	19	7	8.36c
54. 9 3/16c	24	46	53	10	6	1	9.23c
55. 10⅝c		28	43	29	16	10	10.23c
56. 11 7/16c	31	68	84		12	4	11.50c
57. 12 13/16c	15	26		20	10	12	12.48c
58. 13 15/16c	36		59	40	23	6	13.60c
59. 14c	51	71	50	13	15	13	14.00c
60. 15½c	29	47	63	20	4		15.53c

VII.

What can be paid M/B for Domestic Cotton, on any Foreign Price, with the following Points considered as Railway and Ocean Freight, Insurance, Expenses, Profit and Tare?

	F.P.	Ry Frt.	O. Frt	Ins.	Exp.	Profit	Tare	Ans.
61.	8.30c	62	46	2	6	10		7.04c
62.	8.80c	42	70	3	5	8	6	7.46c
63.	9.10c	50	65	$3\frac{1}{2}$	$5\frac{1}{2}$	8		7.78c
64.	10.00c	65	40	$4\frac{1}{2}$	7	$10\frac{1}{2}$		8.73c
65.	10.50c		72	$2\frac{3}{4}$	4	$9\frac{1}{4}$		9.62c
66.	11.25c	62	45	5	3	10		10.00c
67.	11.90c	58	50	$4\frac{3}{4}$	$5\frac{3}{4}$	$10\frac{1}{2}$	6	10.55c
68.	12.10c	40	58	4	6	7	6	10.89c
69.	12.65c	45	64	$3\frac{3}{4}$	$6\frac{3}{4}$	$7\frac{1}{2}$	6	11.32c
70.	13.05c	56	68	$3\frac{3}{4}$	$4\frac{3}{4}$	$8\frac{1}{2}$	6	11.58c

VIII.

ENGLISH EXCHANGE.

Find the value of   Answer.

71.	$510.00 Exchange Rate $4.87\frac{1}{2}$	£104 12s. 3d.
72.	$780.15 Exchange Rate 4.85	£160 17s. 1d.
73.	$1,091.25 Exchange Rate $4.86\frac{1}{2}$	£224 6s 1d.
74.	$6,842.35 Exchange Rate 4.85	£1,410 15s. 10d.
75.	$15,963.95 Exchange Rate 4.84	£3,298 6s. 9d.

76.	£ 54 5s. 10d. Exchange Rate 4.80	$260.60
77.	£ 119 16s. 2d. Exchange Rate $4.80\frac{7}{8}$	$576.13
78.	£ 943 11d. Exchange Rate $4.82\frac{3}{4}$	$4,552.55
79.	£ 1865 18s. 9d. Exchange Rate $4.83\frac{5}{8}$	$9,024.14
80.	£19917 6s. 5d. Exchange Rate 4.85	$96,599.01

IX.

FRENCH EXCHANGE.

Find the value of—			Answer.
81.	$615.10	Exchange Rate 5.10	3,137.01 Fr.
82.	$1,840.65	Exchange Rate 5.12½	9,433.33 Fr.
83.	$5,908.35	Exchange Rate 5.13⅞	30,361.53 Fr.
84.	$9,984.90	Exchange Rate 5.15	51,422.24 Fr.
85.	$18,550.20	Exchange Rate 5.16¼	95,765.41 Fr.
86.	863.55 Fr.	Exchange Rate 5.16⅞	$167.08
87.	1,488.35 Fr.	Exchange Rate 5.17⁴²	$287.88
88.	5,690.00 Fr.	Exchange Rate 5.18¼⁴²	1,098.19
89.	15,772.75 Fr.	Exchange Rate 5.19⁴²	$3,039.06
90.	185,999.60 Fr.	Exchange Rate. 5.20⁴²	35.769.17

X.

GERMAN EXCHANGE.

Find the value of			Answer.
91.	$50.00	Exchange Rate 93	215.05 M.
92.	$193.65	Exchange Rate 94⅛	822.95 M.
93.	$5,642.10	Exchange Rate 95	23,756.21 M.
94.	$10,338.85	Exchange Rate 96½	42,855.32 M.
95.	$516,973.50	Exchange Rate 97	2,131,849.46 M.
96.	110.05 M.	Exchange Rate 93½	$25.73
97.	3,264.10 M.	Exchange Rate 94⅞	$774.20
98.	8,505.90 M.	Exchange Rate 95½	$2,030.79
99.	10,095.25 M.	Exchange Rate 96	$2,422.86
100.	316,940.60 M.	Exchange Rate 97 1/16	$76,907.64

---

⁴²Prove by Table XXVI.

BOOK III.

BUYING SPOT COTTON

THE PRINCIPLES GOVERNING, AND
THEIR PRACTICAL, EVERYDAY APPLI-
CATION IN DETAIL.

CHAPTER I.

SECTION I.—THE COTTON BUYER.

STATEMENT.—Buying and selling cotton as a commercial commodity in the South calls into action annually a large number of Dealers.

Operators of large and small means, with and without experience, enter the Trade from Florida to the Rio Grande, expecting a remuneration from their efforts.

Buying and selling cotton carries with it a hallucination hard to throw off when one has once entered the Trade and received experiences mixed with encouragement.

The Dealer who has familiarized himself with the requirements of the Trade in all its particulars possesses advantages necessary to success, so far as those qualifications go.

The requirements include executive ability, good judgment, business experience, financial connections, familiarity with cotton trade transactions, and a knowledge of cotton gradation.

Presuming the student or reader has made himself familiar with *Cotton Grading* as set out in Book I of this series, he is now prepared. to take up the subject, Spot Cotton Buying.[1]

COTTON DEALERS.

For convenience of explanation, the subject may be divided as follows:

LOCAL PRIMARY BUYERS.

INTERMEDIATE BUYERS.

EXPORT OR SPINNER BUYERS.

Local Primary Buyers.—In all the Markets of the South,

---

[1]"Spot Cotton," means the actual bales, not "Futures."

from the village cross road to the large cities, wherever cotton is grown in quantities to justify it, small and large Buyers are found.

They are the ones who first receive the cotton from the Farmer's hands; first to see, sample, examine, buy and pay for it; first to place it in the channels of Trade and start its movement toward destination.

The Intermediate Buyer is a mediator. He may assume the capacity of a Local Buyer, or buy cotton from the Local Buyer, and sell to an Exporter or Mill Buyer. He may take cotton in such quantities as to be in position to assemble it into mill requirements and deliver direct to the mill.

When buying locally, or delivering direct to Mills, his office and function as an Intermediate Buyer ceases, and his position in the Trade is assumed to be that of a Local or Mill Buyer.

The Intermediate Buyer in a local territory is often called a "Scalper," and is designated by the Trade as such. He may buy from Farmers' wagons, or handle in bulk from Local Buyers.

Literally, his position and activities intervene between the two extremes; he buys cotton from the Local Buyer and sells it to the Exporter or Mill man. By reason of his position, he usually occupies a certain territory in which he operates, taking cotton from primary points in this territory, accumulating it in quantities, and offering it to Dealers who can and do buy such lots.

He is termed a Street Buyer when taking cotton at local primary points from the Grower, losing all the functions of a scalper, unless he sells his purchases to another, who in turn delivers to Mill representatives or exports it.

His plan is to operate at some convenient, centrally lolated point, from which he keeps in close touch with both Local and Mill Buyers and the Cotton Exchanges by telephone and telegraph, operating often on a comparatively

SCENE AT AUSTIN, TEXAS.

Buying cotton from the growers. Note how the Buyers examine the cotton in their hands after it has been taken from the bales.

large scale, and through and by such means a large volume of business passes through his hands.

Export or Spinner Buyers.—The Spinner Buyer assumes a different role in the traffic of cotton from any other class of Dealers.

He takes cotton from Local and Intermediary Buyers from many different points in his territory, (in which he is centrally located, or nearly so), in mixed grade lots just as taken by the Local Buyer from the Growers.

He buys in quantities ranging anywhere from ten to a thousand or more bales from each of his representatives in his daily transactions.

His territory may comprise 6, 8, or 10 counties, half a State, parts of two or three States or several States, depending entirely on his prominence in the Trade, financial standing and connections, and the magnitude of operations undertaken.

He may operate alone, or through firm representation. If buying for Export, he keeps in close communication with his correspondents by cable, advising as to amount of cotton bought, where assembled, when shipped, and by what road and vessel it is moving.

These latter statements are also covered in the Documents, when the shipment is made up.

When buying for Mill requirements, the representative looks for and purchases only such cotton as the Mills demand, which usually prescribe specific Grades and even-running.[2]

All Buyers must have a guide for this procedure; this guide is the *Market,* and serves the Trade the world over.

Some one, or several, make the Market, and before going more extensively into the subject of Buying Spot Cotton, it is necessary to know HOW COTTON MARKETS ARE MADE.

---

[2]See Spinnable Values, Book I, page 77.

EXCHANGE COTTON MARKETS.

Daily Transactions.—The New Orleans Cotton Exchange[3] opens its doors at 8 A. M. At that time there are posted on the blackboard reserved for the Liverpool Market the opening prices,[4] then the noon prices and the 2 P. M. quotations, Liverpool being six hours ahead in time. Members begin to congregate soon after doors are opened, but no trading in Futures until 9:05 A. M. At 9 o'clock quotations begin to arrive from New York, which Market opens at 10 A. M., Eastern time, equal to 9 A. M., New Orleans time. At 5 minutes past 9 A. M. the Future business starts for the day by the official call. This is made by the Superintendent[5] of the Exchange stepping upon the rostrum, seizing a wooden gavel and by a blow with it upon the rostrum opening the trading.

He calls out the current month, it being the first trading month, and continues to call the twelve months, beginning with the current month and ending with the twelfth one thereafter, or just "so far as there is a desire to trade."

Each month is called aloud in a way that it can be heard everywhere on the floor, and sufficient time is given for the price for that month to become stationary before the next month is called. Every trade made during the call is repeated aloud by the Superintendent. For instance, say that Smith and Jones sell to Williams and Brown, the Superintendent would call out: "Smith and Jones to Williams and Brown, one January, 12 cents,"—which trade, as well as others, is recorded on the blackboard reserved for New Orleans quotations, and is there visible to everybody.

Besides that, there is one, or, if trading is active, two,

---

[3]The operation of the New York and New Orleans Cotton Exchanges are so nearly similar in their routine transactions as to require no severance in giving a description of them.

[4]First prices made for the day.

[5]Or an appointee of the President or Vice President of the Exchange.

Exchange Officials standing inside the "ring," marking on the board throughout the day, until 2:30 P. M., when trading officially closes. Every trade that is made in Futures— price, by what brokerage house it is sold, and by what brokerage house it is bought, goes on the blackboard and is kept on record in the Exchange office.

A part of the Exchange floor is set aside for this Future business, but is accessible to all of the members without discrimination. In this portion is the so-called Ring or Pit, a circular structure for the purpose of preventing jamming and confusion among the many Brokers who assemble around it to execute their orders.

After the "call" is over, trading across the Ring is done in some or all of the twelve months, instead of only the month called and this character of trading, where the membership call aloud their trades across the ring to each other, is known as "ring-trading" or "ring-trades;"[6] and, as stated, occurs during the intervals between the opening and noon calls, and noon and close calls.

One Broker may call out that he wants to sell a March (Contract) at 12:03, while others may want to buy March at 12.02. Others may, again, cry out that they want to buy May at 12.10; others offer to sell July at 12.18, and so on. If any of these offers to buy and sell are accepted, the trades are closed and the blackboard receives the record. No trading is allowed by private agreement. All trades between Brokers for the account of others must be made by loud outcry across the Ring.

If the Superintendent calls a month during the official calls, and no one offers to trade during the time, the month is called out three times, then he knocks it down as "None."

If some one offers to buy at a certain figure but no one offers to sell, he calls out, say, "Smith and Jones January bid 12 cents," and having called it three times, he knocks it down as "January bid 12 cents," and vice versa; if a

---

[6]See "Rings," "Ring Settlements," p. 325.

Broker offers to sell, say, March at 12.03, the Superintendent making the call, cries out, for instance, "Smith and Brown, March offered at 12.03," and having done so three times, he knocks it down as "March, offered at 12.03."

The call in any position (month) is over when the price does not vary any more after having been called three times, marked each time with a blow from the gavel.

As these calls are made to buy and sell *Cotton Contracts*, the prices at which they are quoted are placed on the board and flashed by wire to all foreign commercial centers the world over, and to every city and hamlet in the cotton belt of the United States at which cotton may be bought.

The Exchange quotations are sent to all the leading cities and towns of importance by telegraph, and from these the telephone gives wider circulation. These quotations are known as "Cotton Exchange Market Quotations," and give to the Trade and Growers their MARKET.

OPERATIONS OF LOCAL PRIMARY BUYERS.

Let it be noted that no class of Buyers operate independently; one class is more or less connected with and dependent on the other.

A Local Buyer must have some outlet for his purchases; the Intermediate Buyer needs a similar connection; the Exporter operates with the Local and Intermediate Buyers in securing supplies for his foreign connections.

The Local Primary Buyer usually arranges with some large Dealer to supply him with the Market during the season, or furnish him with "limits."

To *get the Market,* means to get the cotton quotations as sent out by the Cotton Exchanges daily, and transmit them to the Local Buyer as often as the changes in the quotations justify doing so.

From these quotations, as prices, for *Future* Cotton, the Local Buyer figures his home price, if a definite price is not given by another, to be paid the Farmer, at so many points "on" or "off" a certain Future Month. The number of points on or off are given by the Dealer, and changed when necessary.

Under such conditions, the Local Buyer must finance his own purchases, use his executive ability, business judgment and best interests for himself.

Local Buyers often arrange with some telephone or telegraph company to give them the Cotton Market three or more times a day; Opening, Noon Call and Close of Liverpool, New York and New Orleans Cotton Exchanges, if no more.

Cotton Limits.—Local Buyers often receive certain prices one or more times a day from large Dealers with whom they connect themselves in a business way to handle cotton. These prices are termed *"limits."* It means that it is the best price, or "limit," the Dealer will offer the Local Buyer at the moment for his Cotton. The Local Buyer knows just how much he is to get for his cotton each day, and if he buys, must do so *under* the limit price, to make any profit for himself. This limit is for Middling basis, with stated additions "on" for the Higher Grades, and deductions "off" for the Lower ones.[7]

A Local Buyer may operate on a salary for some firm or large Dealer, and if so, his plan of operation in the local Market is not unlike that of buying independently.

A Buyer operating on a salary, stationed at some local point, gets the opening Market, as other Buyers, about 9:30 A. M. for Texas interior points; for the other Southern States, one hour earlier in Eastern Time territory.

A salaried Buyer may buy direct from the Farmers' wagons, or buy in quantities from Local Buyers, after the Market closes.

Dealers in merchandise often buy cotton direct from the Growers, and many ginners in the South are primary Buyers, also.

---

[7]See Differences, Book I, p. 92.

Cotton may be bought to fill orders accepted; or bought on personal or firm account for speculative purposes. If, bought in fulfillment of orders, such orders are in the form of contracts, usually, either written or verbal.

Local Buyers selling Short or Spot Cotton on hand, confirm the sale by signing "confirmation papers," for the total quantity sold, although the shipment may be made in broken lots at different times. Such papers are generally made in triplicate form signed by both Buyer and Seller.

SECTION II.

A REPRESENTATIVE COTTON FIRM.

NOTE.—To give a better idea of cotton transactions as they actually transpire with Local Primary, Intermediate and Export Buyers in their daily business during a cotton season, and to show the movement of cotton from primary points to places of concentration, or to destination, the following operations of a cotton firm are given.

The Principal offices of this firm are, say, located in New York and Liverpool; the membership composing it are also members of the New York and Liverpool Cotton Exchanges, and all the other principal Cotton Exchanges of the world.

This House (firm) is one of the largest buyers of Spot Cotton in the Trade, and the character of business transacted by it in Spot Cotton is parallel to that carried on by other firms engaged in a large business. It has direct connection with Foreign Markets, through branch offices in Bremen, Germany, Havre, France, and many other commercial centers and cotton spinning districts as distributing points, giving it great advantage in securing a broader outlet for the disposition of its holdings or acquirements.

A firm of such magnitude and exceptional facilities for buying and selling cotton possesses a distinction that can not be had by competitive operators whose representation in the world's Markets are not so broad.

A great percentage of all Dealers handling large invest-
·ments in cotton are directly or indirectly represented in
foreign commercial centers by and through which medium
greater facilities are offered for securing prompt sales.
Such Dealers are almost constantly in the Market.

Many firms operating in the South have representation
on the Cotton Exchanges and abroad, just as the firm
mentioned, with branch houses at Savannah, Atlanta, Memphis, Little Rock, Dallas, Fort Worth, Waco, Galveston and
many other places.

For illustration, let us assume that the representative
firm has a branch office at Waco, Texas, from which it
covers a large part of the territory surrounding it in its
trade relationship.

Contributory Territory.—It may be stated that adjacent
towns handling cotton which finds exit through Waco district office are Oglesby, McGregor, Crawford, Clifton, Valley Mills, Meridian, Morgan, Dublin, DeLeon, Whitney,
Blooming Grove, Corsicana, Hillsboro, West, Hubbard City,
Marlin, Bremond, Lott, Eddy, Lorena, Moody, Temple,
Cameron, Belton, other towns on the Santa Fe Railway
and many other points.

At some of these towns, say at Temple, Hillsboro and
Corsicana, the Waco firm employs salaried or commission
Buyers, who not only buy cotton at these respective places,
but take it from other Buyers at the small villages and
ginneries nearby, and when a quantity of sufficient amount
has been accumulated, it is shipped under instructions from
the Waco House to some designated point for concentration, or assembled at the local compress for compression,
then forwarded, usually in 50 bale lots.

If for Mill delivery, it is put out in even-running Grades;
if to other Buyers or for Export on basis, then it can be
shipped in lots of Mixed Grades.

Buyers operating on limits for this firm at those towns
selling through Waco, figure the values for the Higher and

Lower Grades, as previously stated, or receive instructions designating the differences to apply.

The practice among all classes of Buyers, small and large, is to await the opening Market in the morning before attempting the purchase of cotton. There can be and often are exceptions to this rule, and it is a custom among some large Buyers not to buy until after the "close" in the evening.

A large Dealer who has contracted—say 10,000 bales of cotton in May—for delivery in September, October, November and December following, at 10 cents Middling Basis, with agreed differences, can often operate in the Market independently of Exchange quotations, provided the price of Spot Cotton has declined at delivery time; but in practice such operators generally stay near the quoted values.

Such trades are protected by "Hedging"[8] except in rare instances.

All places mentioned as operating through Waco, are in "common point territory," taking the same Freight Rate to Houston and Galveston.[9]

The Waco House being in close touch with the New York and New Orleans Cotton Exchanges, receives constantly throughout the day the quotations for Futures, conditions and contingencies that affect the Market, and at the close the prices for Spots in the different cotton Markets of the world.[10]

From this data it figures a working basis for its territory, and what applies for a basis for Waco, can be used at the other contributory points. The Waco House may operate on limits from New York.

The New York and New Orleans Cotton Exchanges quote all the twelve months as Future Months, but by customary

---

[8]See Hedging, Book II, p. 109; Book IV, p. 321.

[9]The rate to Galveston is 6 cents per hundred pounds higher than for Houston—Galveston Rate 51 cents; Houston 57 cents.

[10]See "Difference Sheets," Appendix.

usage of the Trade and membership, six of the twelve months are recognized as "active" or "Hedging Months," and from these active or governing months, the prices for Spot Cotton at any point are calculated, and sent out to all correspondents as their basic price for purchase. The six governing months are January, March, May, July, October, and December. August and September are sometimes "active."

In buying and selling Contracts on any of the Cotton Exchanges, (N. Y. or N. O.) some one or more of these six months are the ones dealt in.

Liverpool Cotton Exchange quotes the Future Months coupled—as May-June; June-July; July-August; August-September, etc.; meaning cotton contracted for delivery there can be delivered in either one of them. If May-June is sold, the Seller can deliver in either one of these two months.

Assuming that the season has arrived for the movement of the new crop, *August Futures* being quoted 15 points under *August Spots,* the Waco House calculates its basic price as follows:

Taking Galveston as an exporting point, the interior price, based on New Orleans quotations, will be found.

August Futures[11]		12.35
Plus, Points		.15
		———
N. O. Spot Middling value		12.50
Freight to Galveston	.55	
Brokerage	.03	
Expenses and margin	.12½	
	———	
Points to be deducted		.70½
		———
Middling interior value		11.79½

[11]Future quotations are for Middling, and for illustration here, only. Points are often added to or taken from the Future price, for a Spot base.

This would give an operating base of 11.80 to be used by all Local Buyers, whether on salary or "limit," at their respective points.

The firm having representation through its Waco House may have contracted with Spinners months before at a higher price than that represented as figured here, for large quantities of cotton, but it being customary with large Dealers to follow the ups and downs of the Market at the moment, the price figured here is that obtaining for the August quotations.

Operating in Detail.—To get a starting point, let us assume a Local Buyer representing the Waco House at Gatesville, Texas, buying on "limits," takes cotton direct from the Farmers' wagons.

His limit is 11.80,[12] and he must buy under that figure to make a profit; the greater he makes his Discount from this price, the more profit to accrue to himself.

This Buyer goes to the wagon on which there are one, two or more bales, in the presence of the owner, and often ten, twelve or more Farmers who have cotton for sale. He cuts a slit ten to twenty inches crosswise between two of the bands, from which cut he takes a sample of cotton four to six ounces in weight, examining it carefully for *dirt, stain, trash, gin cuts,* or any foreign substances affecting gradation, and classes it mentally as to Grade. After examining this sample he cuts the other side of the bale similarly, going through the same proceeding as at first in examination of the other samples drawn.

If other Buyers[13] are on this Market, they pull cotton from the same cut, or make other cuts and draw therefrom, and examine the cotton themselves as to its Grade, and on their opinion as to its quality, each makes his bid or offer for it.

---

[12]A pound of cotton at 11 8/10 cents.

[13]Cotton being a cash commodity, the possibility of gaining immediate profits induces many to engage in handling it.

Both sides of the bale rarely show the same quality of cotton.[14] In such instances the Buyers base their purchase price on the side of the bale showing lowest quality, unless it is apparent beyond a doubt that the Low Grade is superficial and not of sufficient amount to affect the whole bale; in such case the cotton is taken at its true grade or best part.

After these examinations of the cotton offered for sale, the buyers begin their bidding.

The Local Buyer[15] having classed, say, three bales on one wagon as averaging Middling, offers 11.70; another Buyer 11.72½; the Local Buyer may raise it to 11.75, and if no other Buyer bids higher, he gets the cotton at that figure, realizing a profit of 5 points, or 25 cents on each bale of five hundred pounds.

If competition is stimulated among the Buyers, the price may be run to the extreme limit of 11.80; in which case no profit results to the Local Buyer who takes it at that price.

If the Market is firm with a tendency to advance, competition becomes very active, but if adverse conditions show reflections against the Market, speculative buying becomes cautious, and close bidding is not so prevalent.

If the Growers accept the prices offered, the cotton is deposited in a cotton yard or warehouse, weighed by a public or some designated weigher, on whose weights the total price of the cotton is calculated, and paid for at once. Payment is usually made by check drawn on some local bank.

In their daily purchases Local Buyers often accumulate variable quantities of cotton, which they usually sell after the Market closes to other Dealers who handle in larger quantities.

Transactions involving large quantities of cotton and immense sums of money are carried on among large Dealers after nightfall.

---

[14]See Bale Formation, Book I, page 14.
[15]Term used to represent the Waco correspondent in this instance.

The plan of operation for taking cotton at primary points as herein described is similar at most places in the South.

In some of the local Markets, Farmers never drive their wagons on a street or market place to sell cotton, but instead, they draw samples from their own bales while they are at the ginnery, or some other convenient point, which drawn samples they exhibit to the Local Buyer, who in turn bids for the cotton as shown by sample.

Growers are desirous at all times to know the state of the Market, and from the Local Buyer, or other Dealers and the newspapers, they keep in close touch with the trend of it.

It is quite common, if the Market is weak, to hear buyers say: "The Market was off 10 to 12 points yesterday. The 'Close' was down that much and the tone of the Market was irregular. I look for a lower Market today, as yesterday's cables reported Liverpool sales only 6,000 bales; Manchester Spinners and other Foreign Buyers were practically out of the Market, and exporters claim they are receiving but few orders for immediate or forward delivery."

The Grower is naturally apprehensive of the Market, and not caring to risk any loss, on hearing such statements, the inducement to sell has all the emphasis needed to cause him to part with his cotton. The sale may be at a loss, yet for fear the loss may be greater, he sells at once to prevent it.

Local Buyers will not often bid on cotton before receipt of the Market, and Growers are told: "The Market has not come in yet, and I prefer not buying until we get it," or "my 'limit' has not been given me for the day."

If the Market is firm with a tendancy to advance, the Buyer who executes all of his cotton transactions with fairness is just as ready to tell the Grower the Market is firm, the demand good, and is equally ready to say: "I look for a better Market today," or "Inquiry for cotton is active and better Premiums are offered for the Higher

Grades," or "Liverpool bought heavily yesterday and the demand for Export Cotton increases."

These statements can be made by all Buyers with impunity, but for any Buyer to attempt to forecast the Market for the future is inflicting upon himself a possible punishment to be received sooner or later.

If he predicts an advance, and it does not come, but a decline follows instead, the Grower who has held cotton upon the advice of the Buyer suffers a loss, and censures the Buyer; when. perhaps, the advice was conscientiously given.

DAILY FLUCTUATIONS.

Spot Buyers at primary points, as well as Intermediary and Export Buyers, follow the advances and declines of the daily Market.

Local Buyers are rarely changed on limit or basic prices, unless variation in price is as much as 1/16 up or down.

Should the Market advance or decline 1/16, and again 1/16, 1/8 or more during the day, the Local Buyer is kept constantly advised.

The character of the business handled by the *Salaried Buyers* is the same in substance as the representative one buying on "limits," except that no Classer (Take-up-man) is necessary to visit their places of business and take up the cotton bought by them, as such Buyers are good Classers themselves. They keep record of their own transactions, reporting often to the parent office, to which they send samples of all cotton taken, and bill out their purchases as instructed. They remain permanently located at their respective points during the season, or may be moved from place to place as circumstances and contingencies may demand.

Quotations are given them often during the day, should the Market fluctuate and require it.

REPORTING COTTON SALES.

When changes of "limits" or basic prices are given, all cotton bought on such prices are reported at once. After the Market closes and on up to 9 o'clock, all buyers for the Waco office report the results of their day's purchases.

After having received the final report from all Buyers, the Waco office knows at once the total purchases made for its account in its territory, and in like manner reports by telegraph or cable the result to the parent office in New York or Liverpool.

All Local and most Intermediate Buyers make primal purchases of a miscellaneous class of cotton, taking any and all Grades offered by the Growers, and arrange the bales in convenient rows at delivery place, by placing them side by side on their edges, in which position they are ready for the Take-up-man,[16] when accumulated in sufficient quantity to demand his visit.

TAKING UP COTTON BY THE INTERMEDIARY BUYER.[17]

As bought stocks accumulate at the different primary points, gathered by Buyers making purchases on quoted limitations, and the cotton being arranged as stated, the Take-up-man makes his rounds over the district, after having previously notified the different Buyers the date he will visit and take up the cotton bought.

This listed cotton to be taken up is sometimes in warehouses, but more often in an open yard, necessitating the Classer's going through the lot in the sunshine or under cloudy conditions, which requires the strictest scrutiny on his part to get the correct gradation.

---

[16]The traveling representative of the Waco office (or any large dealer) who visits the Local Buyers, classes their cotton, takes it up and pays for it. He is a good business man and a good cotton Classer.

[17]He may be and often is an Exporter.

The manner of taking is about as follows: The Take-up-man in company with other Local Buyers cuts the bales on the top side as they are arranged side by side, cutting the bagging in a different place from the original cut, between different bands, cutting deeper and taking a sample of fully eight ounces therefrom. As the bales are sampled and classed, the Classer attaches a tag to each bale, showing its number, and the name of the firm buying it. The bales are numbered consecutively. The tags are printed in duplicate or coupon form.

Into each sample drawn, the coupon tag is placed and securely rolled therein. This coupon tag gives the identical number and name as shown on the remaining tag hanging to the bale.

Sometimes the tag will show the Grade of cotton of the bale and sample.

As the samples are drawn, they are securely and closely rolled, and tightly pressed in a sack prepared for such purposes, and forwarded to the Waco office.

Practically all the cotton bought from Local Buyers is sold "free on board" the cars, or railway platform at loading point.

Before shipment, each bale is numbered consecutively, and some Mark placed upon it for further identification, usually in three letters, as TOM, HON, BEN, WIL, etc., known as the *Shipping Marks.*

Each shipment is generally under a different Mark. If the tag is lost, the Shipping Mark and number identifies the bale. Cotton for Export or destined for Mills often has four letters for identification. The Marks are placed on the bagging with stencil or brush. For some Foreign Markets, they are placed on heavy, white cotton cloth and attached to the bale, secured by or under the bands.[18]

After all the bales are classed, properly tagged and mark-

---

[18]All Marks on Export Cotton must be obliterated except the Export Mark, which B/L must show.

ed, they are weighed, if the original weights are not accepted.

SECTION III.

PAYMENTS FOR LOCAL COTTON.

If the cotton was bought on basis, a calculation is made showing the average Grade and price, the total estimated amount is settled for at once, by check on a local bank, or Exchange (Draft) drawn on some firm or bank at some other place.

Drafts on foreign concerns are not always accepted at once as payments, unless the local bank approves or declares they are good, or the firm on which it is drawn is known to be trustworthy and reliable.

If the cotton is bought at a price "hog round," (so much as it runs without grading) the total weight being ascertained, the sum to be paid for it is easily calculated.

It will be noted that in taking up a list of cotton as described, the Classer cuts only one side of the bale, (a practice quite common in the South in the early part and during fall season) if no weather damage has appeared, but after each rainfall on the fields of open cotton and the damage increases it becomes necessary, not only to examine both sides of the bales, but the ends should be carefully scrutinized, to determine what proportion of bad cotton is mixed with the good.

CONCENTRATION.

After the different Take-up-men have gone over the territory and taken up all the cotton bought, it is localed into Waco[19] for compression.

---

[19]Or, it may be part, or all of it, concentrated at some other designated place for the compress, and Through Billed from there to destination.

Assembling cotton from so many sources, and in such variable quantities, accumulates hundreds, and sometimes thousands of bales, during the busy part of the season.

A large percentage of this cotton has been sold for forward delivery before its arrival at the compress, principally to consumers whose requirements stipulate specific Grades, and to secure these definite Grades necessitates the constant presence at the compress or places of concentration, of expert Classers, who go through these diverse shipments of miscellaneous Grades, assorting them into specific or even-running classes as are required to go out on orders.

As a preferable method when occasion may require, and for convenience, samples sent in by the Take-up-man are laid upon tables in rooms specially prepared for such work at the Waco office, and are passed upon there by the qualified Graders, who keep a list of them properly marked and wrapped, from which list the instructions are given to the compress authorities, notifying them what bales (usually by number and marks), shall go out on certain orders.

Cotton classed out in this way requires no experienced Classer at concentration point. To aid in expediting the work, an assistant is sometimes appointed to help get out the shipments at the compresses.

Shipments are made as required by the orders in hand, and vary throughout in number and quality, ranging from the lowest to highest Grades; each shipment numbered for the purpose of keeping track of it, and the character and quality of cotton for the order is usually specified. For example, No. 23, 250 bales Strict Middling, Fall River, Mass.; No. 24, 300 bales Low Middling, Osaka, Japan; No. 25, 200 bales Good Middling, Providence, R. I.; No. 26, 600 bales Middling, Barcelona, Spain, etc.

As these orders are filled, notation is made of the date of shipment, from what point, the name and the number of the cars transporting the cotton, through what bank the Draft is drawn, its amount, and a copy of the Bill-of-Lading filed in the Waco office, all of which bear record of the transaction up to this point, and when the cotton arrives at destination and notification of its acceptance is given and the Draft paid, the deal is closed.

If, however, when the cotton is received at destination the Grades of it do not come up exactly, or sufficiently near to that ordered or sold, the Draft[20] will be paid in full, when the party shipping is known to be trustworthy and reliable financially; but if the differences seem too broad and can not be settled satisfactorily between the two, the matter is adjusted by arbitration.[21]

"OVERS."

Accumulated "Overs."—Buying all Grades of cotton from various sources, over a broad area of territory, assembling the same at some convenient point suitable for concentration, frequently leaves, after all classified lists have been made up, a mass of odds and ends, termed "Overs." A large percentage of this is often of a nondescript class or possibly high Grade of cotton, the value of which may be, perhaps thousands of dollars, to be carried for indefinite periods, with such added costs as insurance, storage, interest, etc., before satisfactory outlet can be had justifying its sale. This is especially so after excessive and continued rainfall, or near the termination of the cotton season.

In taking cotton at primary points, accepting the same in all Grades, there can be no prevention of accumulation of "overs," when from this accumulation specific classes of cotton must be selected; but as the "overs" are retained, some of them are used in subsequent shipments, a few selected each time, until the end of the season, when final disposition is made in some form of the remnant.

---

[20]Drafts are usually paid before the arrival of the cotton, if not in full, approximately so. If the Sellers are known to be financially reliable they are paid in full; if not, or practically unknown, 70 to 85 per cent of the Draft will be paid.

[21]See Arbitration, Book II, page 102.

DOMESTIC AND FOREIGN SHIPMENT PAYMENTS

Payments made for shipments to American Mills are designated as *Domestic Payments* in contradistinction to those made for Foreign Accounts. The shipments to Fall River and Providence are handled as any local shipment, the usual Documents of which are the Bill-of-Lading, Invoice and Sight Draft, accompanied with instructions to the local bank how the account is to be handled.

Payments on sales destined for Foreign Shipments are made in accordance with the terms of the sale, usually stipulated by the Buyers at time of purchase, the procedure through which the Documents shall pass, as to a certain bank or firm, the character of papers, etc., that must accompany the Draft, which are similar to those required for Domestic Shipments, and like them must be properly indorsed.

New York Banks handling Drafts covering shipments of cotton for Foreign Account handle them at the Rate of Exchange prevailing with the country on which they are drawn.

As the Rates of Exchange on foreign commercial centers vary from time to time, the Dealers must be conversant with these fluctuations in order to be able to determine with accuracy how to calculate for them in making their purchases and sales.

The Rate of Discount, or Premium, changes as the demand for Exchange fluctuates and whether the Draft is drawn payable at 60, 90, 120 or more days, as Drafts in payment for shipments for Foreign Account are always drawn.

Shipments to Barcelona, Spain, are usually paid for with Exchange on London or Paris, while those directed to Japan are adjusted through English reimbursement, with Drafts at 60 or 90 days, ordinarily on London.

Some New York Banks handle Japanese accounts, with proper indorsements, and claims for such accounts can be adjusted through them at the current Rate of Exchange applying.

Foreign Bills-of-Lading, like Domestic ones, usually read to "Shipper's Order," or to the order of some one who must indorse them, thus giving to them the function of a Negotiable Document—an important feature for the bank handling the claim, and a protection to the Shipper.

The Bill-of-Lading is a factor absolutely necessary in all cotton shipments, and a Document that *must* accompany other papers covering the shipment.

THE WACO HOUSE AN EXAMPLE.

The foregoing statement respecting the operation of the Waco House in a Texas territory, is intended to show how and through what channels cotton is received at primary points, accumulated at others, re-divided into separate lists and directed to different ultimate destinations—how it gets from the field to the factory.

Be it remembered, the Waco House is a subsidiary one, representing a large firm operating in all the Markets of the world, and while subsidiary in position, it carries into execution cotton contracts as though an independent organization; although no trades are made by it without the parent firm being advised at all times.

Its manner of purchase, sale and shipment of cotton is made by its own guidance, yet under orders from the New York or London office.

CENTRAL BUYING POINTS.

The description of the operation of the Waco House in a circumscribed Texas territory, prescribes its operation as an Intermediary Buyer, also as an Exporter and Mill Buyer.

Waco being the point or base of operation, may be called

MB—9

a *Central Buying Point*. Of such "points," there are many in the South; and under the present System of handling cotton, their offices are necessary for the expeditious movement of cotton towards consumption.

What is said of the Waco House as a factor in accumulating cotton coming into its control, may be said of all similar concerns operating in the South, having their bases of operation at different places.

There are such Houses at San Antonio, Austin, Galveston, Houston, Fort Worth, Dallas, Texarkana, Pine Bluff, Little Rock, Memphis, Natchez, Vicksburg, New Orleans, Mobile, Montgomery, Macon, Atlanta, Savannah, Augusta, Norfolk, Greenville, and many other cities.

The way these *Central Buying Points* accept cotton from the Growers and receive and distribute it to Consumers, covers in the main, the System of moving the American cotton crops into the Markets of the world.

COTTON GUARANTEES.

Cotton is bought with and without guarantees affecting the transaction. Cotton taken from the Growers needs no guarantee, as the Buyers have the privilege of seeing and examining the bales before purchase, taking it just as their judgment guides them, and just as they find it.

Cotton sold to be delivered as it exists, or in the vernacular of the Trade, "as it runs," requires no guarantee further than the specific number of bales sold. That is, if 100 bales are sold, 100 bales must be delivered.

Cotton bought at one point to be delivered at some other, where the Buyer does not take up the cotton at place of purchase, must be *accompanied by a guarantee* protecting the purchaser as to the quality and weights, unless the Buyer accepts the Seller's weights and Grades.

This feature of handling cotton is an important one, and inflicts no injustice on any Dealer, but protects the purchaser against any designing or fraudulent transactions that may be attempted by unscrupulous Vendors.

The reader should remember that there are two sides to every cotton transaction, and while a Vendor may and does guarantee the cotton he sells, it does not always follow that the purchaser at some distant point where the cotton is received is an honest man, and treats him fairly in grading the cotton received; and if fair gradation is not made, the Seller loses by guaranteeing his sale of cotton to such a person.

Classification can be made on a list of cotton with apparent honesty, yet, while no deception is practiced, the results of such classification, if not correct, may react to the financial loss of the Vendor.[22]

Some Buyers do not recognize the Quarter Grades, accepting every Grade received as clear-cut Middling, Strict Middling, etc., and if it is not such it is reduced to the Half Grades below.

A Vendor taking up a list of cotton and recognizing the Quarter Grades, shipping the same under a guarantee to some other Buyer who does not, will have a loss inflicted upon himself.

SELLING AND BUYING BY SAMPLE.

Growers and beginners who are not familar with Cotton Grading sometimes sell their products or purchases by forwarding samples of their cotton to Buyers, who purchase it on these samples, with the stipulation that the cotton sold must equal in Grade the samples submitted.

If sold on such terms, the gradation is guaranteed by agreement; that is, the Buyer agrees to accept, if the Seller agrees to make good any deficiencies.

Selling by sample is often resorted to in making sales of Low Grade, Tinges, Stains, Sea Island, or any character of

---

[22]See "A Trade in Quarter Grades Exemplified," Appendix.

irregular cottons or staples, the classification of which is considered questionable by the Seller.

If such cotton is sold in this manner, the Seller must guarantee the cotton on delivery to show to be the same in character as that exhibited by the samples.

F. O. B. COTTON TRANSACTIONS.

Cotton sold "free on board" has reference to its delivery. It may be sold F. O. B. at point of purchase, or at point of destination. The stipulations covering these requirements are stated at the time the transactions are made.

Where sale is made F. O. B. at loading point and the purchaser accepts the gradation and weights at such place, no guarantee follows; but if the sale is subject to destination weights and Grades, and payment made before delivery, the shipment must be guaranteed.

Sales of F. O. B. cotton are sometimes made, not only with a guarantee protecting its quality and weight at the Ports, but the same guarantee holds good for delivery at Foreign destination, or at the American Mills.

Cotton sold on F. O. B. terms may be sold by *Sample, Class Marks, Basis, Average* or *Even-running*.

Prices offered for F. O. B. cotton at buying points do not include Freight and Drayage, but if destination terms apply, it is usual to deduct the Freight and Drayage from the Invoice.

The price of F. O. B. cotton compressed in transit is not affected by the expense of compression.

The *time of delivery* of shipments of F. O. B. cotton is an important factor for consideration, a factor coming within the purview of the guarantee as a component part of the Contract.

Stipulations and requirements governing F. O. B. transactions are not the same in all the Southern Markets, but nearly so.

In the main, such transactions are governed by the Cotton Exchanges in the territory in which the Dealers are operating.

Most of the Cotton Exchanges have Rules defining how such transactions shall be conducted, and Dealers who are members are required to conform to them, and in turn, state to others with whom they deal how they care for such form of business.

There is a *general similarity* existing among all of them, however, as to the mode of procedure; that is to say, Dealers handling F. O. B. cotton in Texas, do so practically the same as those operating in Georgia, the Carolinas, Mississippi, Arkansas, or any of the Southern States, barring small differences.

SECTION IV.

MILL BUYING—NORTHERN.

Northern Mills do not require Sellers to Hedge the sales made to them, but instead, rely upon the responsibility of the Sellers to make good their deliveries promised in the sale.

Mills wishing to exercise their own prerogatives may or may not Hedge their transactions. This is a matter of their own business judgment—a proposition separate and apart from that of the customers from whom they purchase cotton.

Mills generally demand even-running Grades, and this requirement is becoming more general in practice. Where deliveries show to be more than one-half in quality below the specified Grade, the whole is subject to rejection; but if less than one-half, that amount "off" in quality will be rejected.

Purchases calling for average Grades, or specific Types, may "contain 5% half a Grade below the lowest Grade spec-

GRADING AND STAPLING COTTON.

The gentleman with the cap on is *grading cotton*, while the other is *pulling for staple* by examining the length and strength of the fibers. Scene in sample room. Courtesy Pacific Mills, Lawrence, Mass.

ified if offset by an equal number of bales half a Grade above the highest Grade specified." This is a narrow range, but it is the Rule, and under it the interpretation is, assuming a Middling purchase to be made, if 5% of Strict Low Middlings are admitted, 5% of Strict Middling will be required to offset them—a 5% loss in "off" Grade must be compensated for in an equal percentage of Premium Grades.

Mill purchases are made from Cotton Brokers who represent any number of Cotton Merchants handling Spot Cotton in the South in large quantities of mixed lots, from which are made separate lists of even-running Grades to go out to the Mills.

It is not unusual for a Cotton Merchant in the South with good lists of cotton on hand to have it listed with several different Eastern Brokers at the same time, who are located in the vicinity of the Mill or Mills.

This condition is not without its faults to the Mills, but may operate advantageously to the owner of the cotton.

Let it be stated that a Mill is in the Market for 1000 bales of cotton of a certain Grade, and a Merchant in the South has this class of cotton listed with, say, a dozen Brokers in Boston or adjacent points. If negotiations are begun by the Mill for this cotton, these Brokers would be telegraphing simultaneously for it, creating in the mind of the Southern Merchant an active *demand,* and a tendency not only to firm the price, but to increase it. This is somewhat overcome by the Mill's buying from the Broker who offers the cheapest price for the lot.

Local Brokers or their representatives are frequent visitors to the Treasurers' offices of Mills seeking purchasers for cotton for their Southern clients, and through personal interviews, Mills have opportunities offered to them for selection of the character of cotton wanted.

As stated, the Mills look to the Broker as the responsible party, and he in turn relies on the owner and Shipper for protection and delivery of the cotton, according to the terms of the sale.

The Mills require from the Broker a straight Sales Note, made on his own behalf and not on that of the Merchant or owner of the cotton.

Owing to the delays and difficulties connected with the purchase of cotton from Shippers at a distance, Northern Manufacturers of cotton have practically abandoned the direct purchase of cotton through any channels save that open to them by local responsible parties.

There are different methods of buying cotton. Purchases are generally under C. & F. (Cost and Freight) terms, and sometimes under C. I. & F. (Cost, Insurance and Freight) stipulations, with Weights, Grades and Staple guaranteed.

"All Short Staple Cotton from Texas, Arkansas and Mississippi, (except the Upland portion) and from New Orleans, Memphis and St. Louis Markets is sold on basis of 53,000 pounds for each 100 bales; that from Oklahoma, North Carolina, South Carolina, Georgia, Alabama, Tennessee and the Upland portion of Mississippi, is sold on basis of 50,000 pounds for each 100 bales, with a variation of 5% either way, in each case."

Long Staple cotton is accepted on basis of 53,000 pounds for each 100 bales, with 5% variation either way.

The allowance for Tare is a specific average of 24 pounds per bale.

All cotton less than 1⅛ inch in length is known as *Short Staple*, while that of 1⅛ inch or more is termed *Long Staple.*

Sellers delivering cotton not up to contract in Weight, Grade or Staple, must "make good" as prescribed by the Rules covering such matters.

Differences between Grades are *fixed* by the Eastern Association on the "third Thursdays of September, November and February" annually, based on the average differences

GRADING COTTON FOR A MILL.

Note the display of rolled samples on the tables, and the gentleman's position and nearness to the light for a better inspection of the Grades. The Mill purchase of cotton is finally determined at the Mill, as shown. Courtesy Pacific Mills, Lawrence, Mass.

in New York, New Orleans, Memphis and Augusta Cotton Exchanges applying at the time.

The United States Government Standards have been adopted and used.[24]

Controversies arising over settlement between Buyer and Seller are settled by agreement between the parties where such can be accomplished, but if not, the subject becomes one of Arbitration, through which medium final adjustment is made.

Sea Island cotton is bought on Type Samples, usually, and disputes on settlements arise when some of the bales delivered show to be "off staple" from the Type Samples submitted at time of purchase.

NOTE.—Beyond the rules of "Buying and Selling American cotton," there is no fixed and hard Rule to govern Northern Mills in every detail of their purchases, which fact gives latitude to them to exercise individual policies in many instances, and while the foregoing statement of Northern Mill Buying expresses in the main their plan of procedure, it should be remembered that variations from it will sometimes confront the Dealer in selling, but not a variation that will conflict with the Rules of the members.

MILL BUYING—SOUTHERN.

NOTE.—The following statements refer to the subject of Mill Buying, looking at the question from the Mill's standpoint.

Nearly all Cotton Mills in the United States operate under associate agreements.

The Southern Mills are members of Southern Associations, while those of the North and East belong to Cotton Manufacturing Associations of their respective districts.

All the Associations have Rules prescribing their manner

---

[24]Mill Buying, Northern, is taken substantially from "New England Terms of Buying and Selling American Cotton," revised and accepted by the Arkwright Club, The New England Cotton Buyers' Association, and The Fall River Cotton Buyers' Association, adopted September 1, 1912.

of buying cotton, and with them as a guide, they secure their raw material.

The Rules for the New England Mills are similar to those of the Southern Associations for purchasing cotton, with some minor differences.

As an illustration, the plans adopted by the Carolina Mills will suffice to show how Mills' supplies are bought in the South under the "Carolina Mill Rules,"[25] and what is said of them will well apply in a general way to the procedure of others.

Mills rarely employ Buyers whose special duties are to buy cotton direct for them.[26] Their custom is to buy from those who are specially engaged in the cotton Trade.

Mills engaged in the manufacture of a certain class of fabrics or yarns do not use the same kind of cotton as those manufacturing a different quality of goods. This calls for the purchase of different Grades, the Mills specifying, when coming into the Market for their raw material, just what they want.

Requirements of Mills call for Specific Grades, and may be *even-running* or *average*. If even-running, "ten percent of the shipment may be one-half Grade below the Grade specified, if offset by an equal number of bales one-half Grade above the Grade specified."

If bought on *average,* "nothing below a Grade specified, there must not be an excess of more than ten percent of the lowest Grade over highest Grade specified."

Mills do not require Sellers of whom they buy to Hedge their sales, as this is left to the discretion of the Dealers

---

[25]Adopted by Cotton Manufacturers' Association of North and South Carolina July 1st, 1910; revised June, 1912.

[26]Some Southern Mills buy mixed Grades, two or more Mills employing one Buyer on salary who buys for all. Notably at Columbus, Ga. Some Mills there are not in an Association. The Texas Mills buy from Local or near-by Dealers, and occasionally, though seldom, from Farmers' wagons. Some Mill Associations have dissolved co-relationship.

themselves. However, it may be stated that Mills will not buy a quantity of cotton to be delivered at some distant date, without the knowledge that the Seller is hedging, or has hedged, unless the Seller be very strong financially, and known to the Trade as one competent to fill his Contracts promptly.

Sometimes Mills will offer a specific price for a specific Grade of cotton and delivery, but such procedure is not the custom.

Mills usually announce to a number of Dealers, whose financial ability is unquestioned, and in whose character they have confidence, that they are in the Market for a certain number of bales of cotton of certain qualities, and seek competitive quotations. The prices sought are for Mill delivery, with a definite time stated for fulfillment; after the receipt of the quotations offered, the Mill decides from whom it will take the cotton and notifies the Vendor at once.

If those transactions are executed by telegram or telephone, the sale must be confirmed by letter, followed subequently by signing a formal Contract.

Under the "Carolina Rules." Weights and Grades are guaranteed by the Seller and no Franchise is allowed.

The time at which Mills buy cotton depends upon conditions, their needs, and the possibilities for a profitable investment.

Ordinarily they buy cotton at the times they make forward sales of their goods.

If the output of the Mill for a six, ten, or twelve months run can be contracted at once, the cotton necessary to produce the quantity will be purchased immediately.

The purchase may stipulate delivery of the cotton, so much each month, for a series of several months; and when so delivered the Seller can deliver any day in the designated month he desires but *must* deliver during any given month the amount contracted for that month.

When Mills contract their products stipulating delivery in the fall, they usually purchase their supplies in the spring. Such conditions warrant the purchase of cotton at once, although much of it may not be needed for several weeks or months afterward.

By such procedure, the Mill is enabled at the time to *know* at what figure it can sell the manufactured goods, because it *knows* the price at which it can buy the basic supplies before selling, and as a business proposition protects, (Hedges), its sales, by contracting with some one financially responsible to carry out the delivery of the cotton.

Parenthetically, it may be stated, Mills seldom buy or sell Contracts on the New York, New Orleans or Liverpool Cotton Exchanges as a Hedge for any of their transactions in cotton purchases, but if the one with whom they contract is not financially strong enough to handle his end of the Contract independently, then they demand that the Seller protect his sale by Hedging on some one of the Cotton Exchanges mentioned, to make the delivery of the cotton certain.

Mill buying is governed by conditions of the Trade, conditions of the Market, Exchange quotations, possibility, or want of it, for an outlet at remunerative prices for manufactured products.

Anything and everything influencing the Market are factors determining Mill investments for basic supplies, until after it has made a Contract for the sale of its products, and protected the same by purchase of the required amount of cotton to manufacture them. It then becomes independent of price fluctuations, yet its custom is to "follow the market" for any additional purchases that might be required. After it has secured by Contract *all* the cotton needed, then it is practically "out of the market" until the completion of its contracts.

Mills do not buy on Middling Basis.

A MILL PURCHASE.

For explanation of Mill transactions, the following imaginary trade is made to elucidate the subject. The Homespun Milling Company, Bigg Falls, South Carolina, is supposed to be in the Market for 1000 bales of cotton, and being acquainted with Dealers at different points who sell for "Mill delivery," communicates with them by telegraph with a view of purchasing.

TELEGRAM.

Big Falls, S. C., May 28, 1913.

To Coate Bros.,
Memphis, Tenn.

Quote us best price FOB here, September, October and November delivery, 1000 bales white cotton even-running Strict Middling, good body, Uplands, ordinary length of staple, from what section you can ship. Carolina Mill Rules and American Standard Classification to govern shipment.

Homespun Milling Co.,
Jno. L. Adams, Pres.

A similar telegram was sent to
W. C. Craig & Co., Memphis, Tenn.
F. M. Crump & Co., Memphis, Tenn.
Stewart Bros. Cotton Co., New Orleans, La.
Inman, Akers & Inman, Atlanta, Ga.
J. G. Siebs & Co., Montgomery, Ala.
W. W. Gordon & Co., Savannah, Ga.
Weld & Neville, New York, N. Y.
Leroy Springs & Co., Lancaster, S. C.
S. N. Cone, Greensboro, S. C.

Telegrams of this purport are not sent over the wires in this form; but instead, inquiries for the sale and purchase of cotton, and private matters connected with the Trade, are sent in *"Cipher Code"*[27] for the sake of economy and secrecy.

When cotton is moving freely, and the season has been good for high Grades, it would be quite easy to secure a list of 1,000 bales from most any large Dealer, and without necessity for sending so large a number of telegrams; but when weather influences have caused a scarcity of the better Grades, an appeal may have to be sent to a large number of correspondents over a great territory to secure the list.

Mills buy directly from the owners of cotton, or indirectly through their Brokers, as conditions require.

The Homespun Mill receiving replies from all the correspondents noted, while not getting the cotton offered by all at the same figure, would probably get equal quotations from two or more of them. Weighing these quotations as to the territory from which the cotton would come, and knowing the section from which it derives its best quality of cotton, it would accept the offer promising best results.

The "American Standard Classification" is used and governs settlements.

Purchases made for delivery in "one, two or more months in the future, the basis of all sales shall be a Mill weight of 50,000 pounds to each 100 bales, with 1% variation each way" allowable.

BUYING FOR EXPORT.

Similarity to Mill Buying.—Dealers purchasing for the Foreign Markets operate similarly to those buying for Domestic Mills.

Trade relationship between the American and Foreign Markets is very close, and those familiar with such business handle cotton for those Markets as easily as for American trade.

---

[27]See Cipher Code under "Terms," Book II, page 104.

Buyers on this side have representation in the principal cotton Markets in Europe and Asia, keeping in close touch by mail and cable.

Cotton bought for Foreign Mills is handled as for Mill delivery here, with the Rules of the Liverpool or Bremen Cotton Exchanges governing the transactions in settlement.

Grades.—Cotton may be sold with respect to Grades, on *Sample, Basis, Average* or *Specified Grade.* If sold "Average" or "Specified," the clause "nothing below" may or may not be inserted in the Contract. "Nothing below" means that none of the cotton shall fall below a certain Grade.

Weights.—Export Cotton is invoiced at gross weight, (meaning no deduction for "Franchise" or Tare), and is guaranteed to weigh at landing, within 1 percent of the Invoice weight. It is paid for upon receipt of the shipping Documents, received usually in advance of the landing of the cotton.* Until landed, and Landing Weights are ascertained, the Invoice Weights are accepted as basis of payment. From this gross Invoice Weight are deducted, first, the Franchise allowance of 1 percent, (explained fully in next paragraph), and, second, the Tare. In the final settlement, after landing, if the Landing Weights are more than 1 percent under the Invoice Weights, claim is made by the Buyer upon the Seller, for such shortage in weight— not the total difference, but the difference in excess of 1 percent. If, on the other hand, the Landing Weight is more than 1 percent *in excess* of Invoice Weight, no payment is made for such excess.

Franchise.—This allowance of 1 per cent referred to is termed a Franchise. Cotton baled in a dry condition will gain weight if exposed to a damp atmosphere, while damp

---

*Payment is made by consignee to the owner of the Documents, usually. Shipper generally sells his Exchange (shipping Documents) to some bank and receives his pay at once.

cotton will lose in weight under reverse conditions. Experience has shown that 1 percent will cover the average variations from such cause. Payment for the cotton being made in advance of ascertainment of the Landing Weight, the Buyer exercises his option under the Franchise, and deducts 1 per cent from the Invoice Weights, then deducts Tare from what remains, and proceeds with the settlement according to the terms of the transaction.

Seller's Protection Under Franchise.—The Seller, being familiar with the provisions of the Franchise, generally takes advantage of it by adding the 1 percent, allowable to his actual shipping weights. If "A" ships 50,000 pounds, gross, actual weight, he invoices it at 50,500 pounds, and guarantees it to weigh at landing 50,000 pounds. The Buyer deducts the Franchise of 1 percent, pays him for 50,000 pounds, (less Tare, of course), and "A" loses nothing. It should not be thought because "A" added the Franchise that he practiced a fraud, for by the terms of the Contract he guarantees the Landing Weights. Had he not added the 1 percent that amount would have been deducted by the Buyer from his Invoice Weight just the same, causing a loss to "A" of 500 pounds of cotton.

Time.—With reference to time, it may be sold "afloat," "prompt," "immediate shipment," "to arrive" or some designated month or months. "Prompt" and "immediate shipments" mean that the clearance or sailing of the vessel "must take place within fourteen days from the date of the Contract."[28]

Quality.—Classification is made in Quarter Grades and based on the Standards[29] of the Liverpool Cotton Association. This governs for cotton delivered in Bremen, Havre and Liverpool.

The Types and qualities of cotton are distinctively recognized as to the territory from which they come; as Texas,

[28]Rules Bremen Cotton Exchange, p. 26, Ed. 1907.
[29]See Standards, Book I, p. 68.

Oklahoma and Arkansas Cottons; Atlantic Cottons; Gulf Cottons.

The Gulf Cottons have reference more particularly to the Uplands,* while the Atlantic Cottons can include the Sea Islands with the Uplands of that district. When Sea Islands are sold they are particularly specified.

Contentions arising over the settlement of shipments of American cotton for damp, "wet packs" or any cotton not coming up to the qualities and weights sold, are adjusted by Arbitration under the Rules of the Foreign Cotton Exchanges.

"C. I. F. AND 6%"

Terms.—Cotton going into the Markets of England, Germany and France is generally sold on the "C. I. F. and 6 per cent." terms.

The Contracts in which such terms are embodied are headed "Cost and Freight Contract for North American Cotton" or "Cost, Freight, and Insurance Contract, American Cotton, Interior Shipment."

The letters C. I. F. are the initials expressing the words "Cost, Insurance and Freight." From the stipulation in the Contract that cotton shall "be invoiced at American actual gross weight less an allowance of 6 per cent.," connected with the initial letters as stated, arises the expression "C. I. F. and 6 per cent.," or abbreviated "cif & 6 terms."

A Contract implying such terms, fully expressed, means that the Seller guarantees *to pay the incidental expenses, cost* of loading the cotton on board ship, to *insure* it against marine disaster, to *pay the freight* from shipping point to destination, and allow a deduction of 6 per cent. from gross or Invoice Weight.

Besides the "C. I. F. and 6 per cent." terms there are

---

*See Uplands, pp. 80, 81.

others known as "Mutual Allowances,"[80] "Friendly Allowances," etc., which, when in effect, sometimes take the place of "cif & 6" provisions.

On the back of each Contract, Rules are printed prescribing the manner in which cotton shall be handled under it, as set out by the Foreign Cotton Exchanges making the governing terms.

Cotton Exchange Contracts state:

100 bales, Texas, Oklahoma and Arkansas Cotton
      shall aggregate   53,000 lbs.
100 bales other Gulf growths, and for cotton
      sold simply as Gulf cotton   51,020 lbs.
100 bales Atlantic Cotton, and for cotton sold as
      American, Upland or Port Cotton   49,261 lbs.[81]

These are the gross weights, from which a net of 5 per cent., covering the Tare and Franchise is reckoned.

---

[80]See "Mutual Allowances," Appendix.
[81]See "Weights," p. 252.

CHAPTER II.

SECTION V.

TARE[32]

Literal Meaning.—The weight of any wrapping, box, barrel, etc., covering and protecting any article for shipment is termed *"Tare."*

Ordinarily, to determine these weights is a matter of little moment, but a broad exception exists with reference to the covering on American cotton bales.

Coarse jute bagging is 44 inches wide and weighs 1½ to 3 pounds per yard. Each band or tie weighs about 1½ pounds. Each bale is bound by 6 ties, making a total of 9 pounds of Tare for ties alone.

Ginners use different weight bagging, and do not always cut the same lengths for similar size bales, causing unequal weights for them.

No controversies arise over the weights of the ties, as they are practically standardized at the weights given. The European Trade accepts them as about 1.3 pounds, being shorter on compressed bales as received by them.

There are two qualities of domestic manufactured bagging, known as Union and York bagging. Union is made from old bagging; York from new jute stock. The former is a poor quality of tightly twisted threads, the latter a fairly good article.

York bagging is not so good as that imported from Calcutta or Dundee, but resembles the Calcutta material.[33] The

---

[32]Recent agreement (1913) between American and Foreign Cotton Exchanges resulted in accepting a 5%, instead of a 6% Tare. See Appendix.

[33]See U. S. Bulletin "Cotton Tare" 1912, pp. 6, 7 and 8.

Dundee, being superior in quality, is used principally in wrapping Sea Island and the long staple cottons of the Yazoo and Mississippi Delta districts.

Customarily, Southern Ginners make a charge of so much per hundred pounds for cotton "ginned and wrapped," practically using 2-pound bagging, but irregular lengths. They have no Rules to govern them in weights of wrapping.

American Mills usually buy all their supplies of raw material *gross weight,* which means they will accept 22 to 24 pounds of Tare for which they will pay as for so much cotton.

Cotton Manufacturing and Cotton Buyers Associations of New England and the Southern States have prescribed Rules governing cotton Tare, allowing weight ranging from 21 to 24 pounds per bale, accepting six yards of 2-pound bagging as minimum weight and 9 pounds of ties.

The American Cotton Exchanges generally conform to the same Rules as to weight allowable for Tare, with the exception of New York, which accepts a maximum of 28 pounds weight.*

Any excess in weights above those adopted subjects the Seller to a Claim for it.

The initial weights of covering put on at the ginneries vary from 19 to 24 pounds, likewise the weights allowable by the Cotton Association and Mills are also variable. Such variations originating from a large number of points, are the causes for controversies, and often litigation.

In practice, Mills generally allow more Tare than the amount placed upon the cotton by the ginneries.

EUROPEAN MILLS BUY NET WEIGHT.

European mills buy all cotton at *net weights.* Fully two-thirds of American cotton finds a Market in foreign lands,

---

*The N. Y. Cot. Exchange recently amended its Tare Rules making 25 pounds the maximum Tare, the Rule to take effect Dec. 1, 1914. Amendment No. 83, p. 114.

approximately 80 per cent. of which goes to England, France and Germany. Rules prescribed by the Cotton Exchanges of Liverpool, Havre and Bremen for handling cotton in those Markets determine in most instances how it shall be handled in other European or Asiatic Markets.

Rules governing the method for getting the net weight on those Markets, dictate an allowance of 6 per cent. from the *gross weight,* to which the American Export Trade conforms, as shown under the "C. I. F. and 6" terms previously stated.

The exactions of the European Trade for Tare are practically the same in all foreign commercial centers, but the manner of making the calculations by the Exchange Rules gives different results. While demanding and exacting 6 per cent. discount from the American *gross weight* as the general practice, the direct application of the Rules in making actual tests occasionally results in showing a greater or lesser amount. The actual tests govern in making the final settlements.

To get the exact Tare, 10 per cent. of the number of bales in the shipment[34] are stripped and the bagging weighed. Ten and sometimes 20 ties are weighed, the weight of which being known, the weight of the whole number on all the bales is determined, by comparison with the weights of the ten. This gets sufficiently near accuracy for all practical purposes, as one tie is about the duplicate of the others in weight.

NOTE.—When cotton is sold with 6 per cent. allowance, the weight per hundred bales of the iron bands shall on an average not exceed 408 Kilos (900 lbs.) and of the canvas 3 9/16 per cent. upon the whole lot. The 3 9/16 per cent. shall be calculated upon the Invoice Weight, less the Franchise and the weights of the bands as ascertained here. Any excess of Tare (iron bands and canvas) to be deducted from the gross landing weight.[35]

It will be noted in getting the exact Tare that 3 9/16 per

[34]Bremen Rules.
[35]Rules Bremen Cotton Exchange, p. 34, Sec. (c) 95.

cent. (less the weight of the ties and Franchise) of the gross weight is supposed to represent the exact weight of the bagging.

What is stated here for Bremen applies equally as well for Havre and Liverpool.

A comparison of the manner of making these computations will make plain the procedure employed in those three Markets for getting the Tare. Bremen calculates the Tare on the *American Invoice weights;* Liverpool and Havre on the *gross landing weights.*

COMPUTATIONS, BREMEN, LIVERPOOL AND HAVRE, COMPARED.[36]

BREMEN.

(100 bales.)

	Pounds[37]
Invoice weight	52,725
Less 1% franchise	527
Leaving	52,198
Less weight of 800 ties	883
Actual Tare on 10 bales 200.7 lbs. On 100 bales	2,007
Allowed by Rules 3 9/16% of 51,315 lbs.	1,828
Excess Tare	179
Less underweight of bands	17
Net excess Tare	162
Bremen Rules allow	900 lbs.
Actual weight 800 bands	883 lbs.
Allowed	17 lbs.

[36]From *"Cotton Tare,"* Dept. Commerce and Labor, 1912.

LIVERPOOL.

(100 bales.)

Landing weight	52,100[37]
800 bands	883
	51,217

Actual Tare 10 bales 200.7 lbs.
Net weight 10 bales 5162 lbs.

Tare on lot 200.7-5162 of 51,217 lbs..............................	1,984
Allowed 3 9/16% of 51,217 lbs...................................	1,824
Excess of Tare	160

HAVRE.

(100 bales)

	Pounds
Landing weight	52,100
800 bands	883
	51,217

Actual Tare 10 bales 200.7 lbs.

On 100 bales	2,007
Allowed 3 9/16% of 51,217 lbs.................................	1,824
Excess Tare	183

The statements show an excess of Tare in the three stated Markets. The Rules applying in all of them allowed 900 pounds for.the bands on each 100 bales, yet by actual test they showed 883 pounds, or 17 less than permitted. The total Tares show by logical conclusion that the excess lay in the wrapping, as the bands were shy in weight.

This shipment was billed out at 52,198 pounds to which 1 per cent. Franchise was added for the German Market, and assumed to be the same weight for Liverpool and Havre, but no Franchise added, as these latter Markets calculate Tare from Landing weights. The differences in results show in the different methods of calculation.

---

[37]Result of actual test.

It should be noted that the 6 per cent clause required by importers from American shippers was lost sight of in the preceding calculations, and in its place the weight of the bands and canvas were ascertained on the basis of 3 9/16 per cent. of the gross weight of the cotton, less weight of the ties, the weight of the ties and canvas constituting the whole Tare.

European Importers pay for nothing but the cotton, to find the weight of which, they must *know* the weight of the covering, which they find under the Rules as described in the foregoing calculations.

Tests made under the Rules for Tare sometimes show it to be less than deducted in the Invoice; if so no credit is allowed for it, but if over-Tared, a Claim is made on the Seller for the amount at the price of the cotton in the shipment.

By agreement, a diminution of weight in Tare is sometimes adjusted under the Mutual or Friendly Allowance clause.

In the mathematical statements shown, Bremen would claim 162, Liverpool 160, and Havre 183 pounds excess Tare. The calculations were made upon the assumption that the weights of the 100-bale shipments were the same, in order to clearly define the results obtained by the operation of the three different methods of calculating *exact* Tare. Liverpool is in harmony with Havre and Bremen in ascertaining the weight of the ties, but to determine the weight of the canvas after the ties are off, "the allowance shall be calculated at the exact relative proportion of the weight of the bales stripped to the total weight of the whole lot."[38]

Discrepancies can arise from *taring* heavy, medium or light-weight bales. It should be remembered that the practice is, after deducting the weight of the bands and Franchise to ascertain 3 9/16 per cent. of the gross weight left,

---

[38]Quotation from Liverpool Rules.

to determine the weight of the bagging, and these two weights added, plus the Franchise, make the total to be deducted from the whole American Invoice weight, according to the Bremen Rules. This procedure is to determine what weight *should be on the cotton,* but to *know* the *actual weight that is on,* 10 bales are stripped and the bagging taken off and weighed, supposedly taken promiscuously from the lot and from the weight of the stripped bagging, the *average* for the whole is made.

If, for illustration, 10 bales averaging 560 pounds are stripped, and the average weight for the whole 100 bales is 510 pounds, it is evident upon its face, that the average of the ten bales is entirely out of proportion to the weight of the whole, and an erroneous deduction follows. Equally illogical would it be to say that the 10 bales tested weighed 510 pounds average, when the average of the whole was 525 pounds.

It is possible, but hardly probable, in selecting 10 bales at random to be tared, to get all of them heavy, or all light weight. In such event, the average found would be faulty.

When American shippers have representation in European Market centers, under the Bremen Rules, in ascertaining actual Tare, "Buyer and Seller representatives shall each select one half of the bales to be tared," which would largely overcome any tendency or effort of the Buyer to practice fraud or deception were he disposed to do so.

Sellers who have no direct representation there usually assign some one as an agency representative to look after the deliveries, said agent being termed a *"Controller,"* whose duties are to receive the cotton at landing, look after its weights, classification, delivery, Tare, and its Arbitration if thrown into controversy.

Tare has a further signification than to represent the actual weight of the covering and bands.

Cotton bought must be sampled under present system of handling, that the Buyer may know its approximate value.

It is not unusual for it to be sampled 3, 4 or more times before getting to final destination. Each time a quantity ranging from 4 ounces to one-half pound or more is withdrawn, the practice being to cut the bagging in a different place as often as samples are taken. Such procedure necessarily reduces the weight of the bale to the extent of the quantity taken.

To offset this lost weight, to cover the sample holes in preparing the cotton at the compress for export shipment, and to take cognizance of the allowable 1 per cent. Franchise, *patches* sufficiently heavy are placed on the bales to make the whole weight fully equal to the 6 per cent. Discount exacted in Foreign Trade.

Actual tests for the weight of Tare have proven the result to be 5.3 to 5.4 per cent., practically $5\frac{3}{8}$, instead of the demanded 6 per cent. That is to say that actual Tare for the wrapping of American cotton is $5\frac{3}{8}$ per cent., nearly, and any excess beyond this is superfluous, yet the policy of Exporters is to place at least this amount of excess[39] on the bale in patches, and allow for it in the original Invoice.

To protect themselves for this difference between $5\frac{3}{8}$ and 6 per cent., Dealers on this side allow for it in making their Export price.

American Sellers can contract with European Buyers to purchase cotton on actual Tares, and upon such terms the weight of covering would be a matter entirely immaterial as to whether light or heavy.

PURPOSES.

Owing to the inequality of the weight of the bagging and ties covering a bale of American cotton and the controversies attendant on its sale over this variable weight, Foreign Trade, to protect itself against loss arising therefrom, in practice, demands a 6% deduction from the Ameri-

---

[39]Difference between 5 3/8 and 6 per cent.

can gross weight, as a direct Discount, to obtain the net weight of the cotton for which only it agrees to pay.

Practically, the Export Trade conforms to this demand, and under the C. I. F. & 6% terms, makes out the Invoices, the theory of the Contract being that a straight deduction of 6% will give the net weight on which final payment is made, obviating the necessity of making a physical test by stripping and weighing a number of bales as described in the foregoing, which is the primary purpose of the 6% Tare; but, as the American bale has grown in weight, approximating 520 pounds average, the direct application of the 6% Tare is excessive. To overcome this the American Trade adds a sufficient weight in patches on the bale to offset the difference between an actual Tare of 21 to 26½ pounds and the 30 or more pounds exacted by reason of the 6% deduction.

Let it be assumed that a bale of cotton of 500 pounds weight has 24 pounds of bagging and ties on it; it is quite evident that a deduction of 6%—30 pounds—would prove excessive, and the Seller is deprived of the value of 6 pounds of cotton; to prevent which, the 6 pounds is made up by patching as stated.

With the intention of gaining a profit on patches, some members of the Trade add an excess, resulting in the European Trade making physical tests for it under the Exchange Rules, as previously stated, and when shown to be over that prescribed by the Rules, Reclamation is made for it on the Seller, virtually destroying the application of the C. I. F. & 6% terms under such proceedings.

The real meaning of such terms is, that the Seller delivers to the Buyer in a Foreign Port, the cotton in the shipment, free from all charges; that is, the Freight is prepaid or deducted from the Invoice, insured for its value plus ten per cent. to cover any cost of advance, with 6% deducted from the gross, to find the net weight.

PRIMARY PRICE TO FARMERS.

Remember that Cotton for American Trade is handled gross weight; that for Foreign Trade, net weight. In both instances the Tare is a requisite consideration in making the price.

A Domestic Dealer in the Export Trade buys cotton *gross weight* and sells it *net weight*, hence he must consider the weight of the bagging and ties in his calculations when buying cotton, whether for Domestic or Foreign Shipments.

American Mills take into consideration the bagging and tie weights when purchasing, as no Mills can spin Tare, and prices given to Growers are made to cover these weights for self-protection, although the supposition is prevalent that the Grower gets the same price for the wrappings on a bale that he does for the cotton wrapped; this is delusive.

For explanation, let us assume a bale of cotton to weigh 500 pounds gross. At 10 cents a pound, the equivalent value net would be as indicated below, with the Tares as shown:

Gross Wt.	Tare	Net Wt.	Price, gross	Price, Net
500	25 lbs.	475 lbs.	10 cts.	10.52 cts.
500	24 lbs.	476 lbs.	10 cts.	10.50 cts.
500	23 lbs.	477 lbs.	10 cts.	10.48 cts.
500	22 lbs.	478 lbs.	10 cts.	10.46 cts.

Based on the above, if a Mill offers, or an Exporter is offered, 10½c net for cotton, the equivalent value would be 10 cents gross weight where a Tare of 24 pounds covered the bale.

The Trade, knowing the approximate weight of bagging and ties placed on cotton in their respective territories, and the price offered for net cotton, can calculate a corresponding price for gross weight.

Prices publicly quoted and those given to Primary and Intermediate Buyers are for *gross Weight* exclusively, and the American Grower knows no other.

The Exporters and the Mills are the ultimate Buyers who must translate net into gross weight when purchasing.

By the usual method for selling Foreign Cotton, under the "CIF&6%" terms, in 100 bale lots, the actual Tare allowable is:

TABLE NO. XXX.

LIVERPOOL.

On 800 ties[40]...900 lbs.
Bagging, less weight ties..3 9/16%
Calculated on *landing weight.*

HAVRE.

On 800 ties...900 lbs.
Bagging, less weight ties..3 9/16%
Calculated on *landing weight.*

BREMEN.

On 800 ties...900 lbs.
Bagging, less weight ties and 1% Franchise................3 9/16%
   And 1% Franchise
Calculated on American Invoice *gross weight.*

MANCHESTER.

On 800 ties...900 lbs.
Bagging, less weight ties..3 9/16%
Calculated on *landing weight.*

HAMBURG.

On 800 ties...900 lbs.
Bagging, less weight ties and 1% Franchise................3 9/16%
Calculated on American Invoice *gross weight.*

---

[40]Eight ties to each compressed bale—all Export Cotton is compressed.

GENOA.

On 800 ties..900 lbs.
Bagging, less weight ties and 1% Franchise.............3 9/16%
Calculated on American Invoice *gross weight*.

BARCELONA.

On 800 ties..900 lbs.
Bagging, less weight ties and 1% Franchise.............3 9/16%
Calculated on American Invoice *gross weight*.

NAPLES.

From American Invoice *gross weight*, 6% deducted.

TRIESTE.

From American Invoice *gross weight*, 6% deducted.

STOCKHOLM.

Cotton is taken at American *gross weight*.

Terms varying from these can be arranged by mutual agreement covering any transaction, or for the season, except those prescribed by the Foreign Cotton Exchanges governing the action of their members.

NOTE.—Were all wrappings for cotton standardized at say 2½ pounds per lineal yard, and all ginners required to cut the same lengths for all bales wrapped, the matter of adjustment for Tare on American cotton would be practically settled, as the weights of the ties or bands are now uniform.

The uneconomic method of repeatedly sampling cotton for purchase will have to be discarded before the subject of Tare will have reached the point beyond controversy.[41]

COTTON WRAPPINGS.

Evidently the primary motive for wrapping the cotton of the South in jute material was from the fact of its use being regarded as economical; the jute being recognized as

---

[41]For a further statement on this subject, see "Tare," Book II, p. 256 et seq.

a cheaper substance than that to be protected, has, from the first, maintained its popularity over all other fabrics for the covering of cotton bales grown in North America, despite the fact of its offering but little protection to the cotton wrapped.

Its loose construction freely admits cotton fibers to protrude through its open meshes, increasing fire risks and raising insurance rates.

This material offers but little protection to the cotton from dirt, soot, smoke, and absolutely none from moisture.

Most jute bagging has been treated with some chemical substance to render it resistant to fire, and were it made absolutely fireproof, the protection desired would not be realized because of its open construction, as just stated.

The application of jute bagging to cotton is directed more especially to its usefulness for covering square bales. Such being large and heavy, can not be handled well without the use of steel hooks, which tear the bagging badly unless it is very strong.

As stated in a preceding section, it will be recalled how Buyers cut the bagging when the cotton is first purchased from the Grower's hands; how subsequent Buyers do the same thing, but cut in different places; and these cuts, often four and five, taken in connection with the mutilations inflicted with the handlers' hooks, virtually destroy the covering, causing it to be very ragged when delivered at compress or destination.

The necessity for the application of patches is now apparent, as they are applied for the purposes designated. (See p. 263, Patches.)

Before patching, all the ties are removed, the expanded loose bale with the old bagging on is placed in the compress, on the bottom of which press a patch is placed, varying in length from 18 inches to the whole length of the bale; on the top of the bale another patch similar in size is placed, the bale compressed and tied out with 8 ties. The original bale had six on it. The compressed bale being greatly reduced in size, the ties are cut shorter. The 8 weigh about the same as the six long ones removed.

"Patch" jute bagging is much heavier than the quality designed for the customary wrapping, and to cover the 6 per cent. weight demanded as Tare, is an easy matter with this heavier material.

It has been contended that the exaction of an even 6% Tare was excessive, and should not apply, because the Foreign Trade makes actual tests for Tare, more directly for the purpose of detecting over-tare than for a knowledge of its exactness, perhaps. If over-tared, a claim is made for the excess; if undertared no allowance is made for it except by mutual concessions.

All cotton to go out on long railway hauls or for ocean steamer, is compressed and patched before shipment.

The usual or average weight of jute wrapping on an American bale of cotton is 12 pounds in comparison with 4 pounds for Egypt, and about 2½ pounds for India.

All countries use jute canvas, but all except the United States use that of light weight and closely woven. The United States uses the heavy, coarse article described.

The United States bale averages about 520 pounds; that of Egypt ranges from 720 to 850 pounds; the East Indian bale 480 to 525 pounds.

Owing to the character of the bagging used in the United States, to the system of sampling cotton, involving repeated cutting of the wrapping, the American cotton bale goes into the Foreign Market in a dilapidated condition.

If the patches practically cover the bale on both sides, its appearance approaches decency; but when it is only partially protected, evidences of negligent handling are plentiful.

Compared to the cotton arriving from India, Egypt, Brazil and Peru, it stands out as a conspicuous monument to carelessness and indifference.

MB—10

The use of coarse, open jute bagging of variable lengths and weights, gave rise to the custom of Foreign Buyers exacting a 6% Tare, as described. Beyond the fact that the American bale has poor protection, its external condition renders it difficult to apply intelligent markings for guidance in shipment. If the patch is closely woven, markings can be made with distinctness, if not blurred with some other mark.

Tearing cotton from the ships hold, when it has been tightly pressed therein, many times obliterates or partially destroys the Shipping Mark, resulting in confusion often in making final deliveries to consignees.

The Mills of Japan require the Shipping Marks to be placed upon white material, usually a heavy grade of cotton cloth, about 2 feet square, placed in position at the time of compression and held by the bands, and it is stated by exporters of cotton to that country that the bales reach their destination with the markings undisturbed.

To continue the use of the coarse open-mesh jute seems without reason, when a better wrapping for all practical purposes can be had in lighter weight, closely woven fabric of similar material, at the same or less primary cost.

BAGGING OF COTTON MATERIAL.

The advocates of the use of this material have been many, who claim for it a better wrapping, lighter weight and less Tare than jute, and point out that its use would bring into requisition a large quantity of low grade cotton that would be well adapted for the manufacture of such material, with primary cost but little increased over that of jute.

Actual tests, however, made in a practical way by the use of such material, has not proven it to be all desired for it. Being open-mesh, it does not protect the cotton any better than the coarse, loosely woven jute, and is more susceptible to danger from fire. Its affinity for moisture is great, and when saturated the fibers contract, causing the mesh to open, and exposure of the cotton follows.

If a "pattern" (two three-yard lengths) be cut out when dry, the same would contract to approximately two and one-half yards when damp, and if placed on a bale in such condition, it would not cover the required surface without intense stretching, which action makes the bagging more "open," and to that extent unfits it for a protective covering.

ROUND BALES.

As an ideal and neat package, the Round Bale can not be excelled.

It was thought that by its introduction into the Cotton Trade the many evils complained of in the square bale would be practically eliminated, and the new bale would be gladly received.

The advantages claimed for it were:

(*a*) A lighter covering and reduced Tare;

(*b*) A lighter bale that could be handled without hooks;

(*c*) The practice of sampling dispensed with;

(*d*) Reduced freight rates for transportation;

(*e*) A closely woven fabric, as 8 or 10-ounce cotton duck for a covering;

(*f*) A completely covered bale, uniform throughout in Grade;

(*g*) All bales practically the same in weight—about 250 pounds each—and compressed to about 30 pounds per cubic foot density, which offered economy in both railroad and ocean transportation space, and,

(*h*) The absence of ties, and a smooth, plain surface for receiving Shipping Marks.

These advantages exist over the badly covered square bales, and their advent into the Trade virtually does away with drawing samples or cutting the bagging, it being the practice of the Round Bale ginneries to buy cotton "in the seed," to throw promiscous purchases into one large room, from which they draw supplies for the small round bales. Cotton blown into one heap, mixes the different grades of seed cotton, and when drawn out for ginning, each bale formed is generally uniform throughout, and guaranteed by the owners of the plant to be a certain Grade. Were samples required, the same would be taken from the cotton going into the bale being formed, and not after completion. Samples could be taken from the bale, as no physical obstruction would prevent.

The bale being compressed to a density of about 30 pounds, excludes the air to such extent that the tendency to loosen or unroll is almost destroyed; and when the covering is applied, fitting snugly to the bale, it easily holds the bale in form without the aid of ties.

The weight and cost of the covering of round bales is the same on each bale, 2½ pounds, at 25 to 27½ cents each bale.[43]

The advantages offered by the round bale are too pronounced to be ignored, and if the great American cotton crops were marketed in this form, the question of *Tare* would be settled.

Public sentiment and Popular prejudice were directed with such force against the universal adoption of the Round Bale, however, that its introduction to the Trade has been retarded.

It is not because of the roundness of the bale, but because of its *definite* and *light weight wrapping* that it offers a possible remedy for Tare controversies. The square bale, compressed to the same density, and as completely covered with a definite weight of light but substantial wrapping, would lead to the absence of contentions in Tare settlements as surely as the Round Bale does.

The absence of metalic bands on the Round Bale is an economic fact worthy of consideration.

The production of the Round Bale at the ginnery, well compressed and delivered in like manner to the Mills without sampling, adds emphasis to the advantage of gin compression and careful wrapping before shipment.

---

[43]See American Round Bale, p. 400.

SECTION VI.—SHORT SELLING.

SHORT SELLING SPOT COTTON.

Short selling any article or commodity carries with it two features, namely; time and quantity—the time for delivery and the quantity specified. It also carries with it the Right of Contract, and implies *futurity*, as to date of settlement.

Two constructions may be placed on the form of Contract, as described in the following comparative statement:

If A, in January, Sells to B 400 bushels of wheat to be delivered in July and August following, the sale is a Contract to which both have agreed, and is recognized as legitimate, although the facts may be developed that A did not have the wheat in his possession at time of contracting it, but did have an acreage sown to wheat which was thought sufficient in area to produce 400 bushels, and on this *probability* of yield the contract was partly based.

This sale was made when both parties to the Contract *knew* the commodity was not in existence, and the time of delivery designated futurity.

The transaction is construed to be legal because the Seller contemplates actual delivery, and the Buyer so recognizes it, by agreeing to receive.

The probability of A's getting the wheat depended on the contingencies of the weather in both growing and harvesting time, and A's ability to deliver it. The possibility of B's not taking the grain at delivery time was not questioned, and is stated here for illustration.

If A sells to B 400 bushels of wheat, and has none sown, nor in his possession, but agrees to deliver to B in July and August that quantity, and C agrees to receive it, this phase of the Contract is parallel to the other, except B has but one source from which to expect the wheat, and that is through A, individually, where in the former case, there were two sources—the land and A's ability.

In the second statement, B may or may not know that A does not have the wheat, yet accepts A's offer at the agreed price and terms. This second Contract is assumed to be clothed with the same features as the first, with the possibility of delivery lessened, as a contrasting difference between the two.

In the sale of wheat, A has *"sold Short"* in both instances. He sold something he did not have, which is the literal interpretation of the phrase.

"Selling Short" for future delivery, as described, does not mean the sale of "Futures" as referred to in Cotton Exchange Contracts.

What is stated with reference to the sale of wheat, applies in the sale of cotton or any commodity.

Short selling is often resorted to for purposes of Speculation, and also often for the contrary purpose of avoiding risks comparable to those of speculation.

If A produces 20 bales of cotton, 12 of which are baled, and 8 yet in the field to be gathered, assuming the price to be 12c a pound, all round, and conceiving this to be a good price, sells the whole 20 bales—12 of "Spot Cotton" and 8 bales of "Short Cotton;" the latter of which are in his possession but in the field, with delivery stated and implied, such sale removes any doubt as to the price of the 8 bales not gathered, and consequently the possibility of any speculation on them.

Suppose that A, operating as a Local Cotton Buyer, and having evidence to lead him to believe that a decline in the price of cotton would soon occur, and to illustrate, say cotton is worth at his point 10c, Basis Middling, sells to his correspondent, (another Buyer operating on a larger scale —an Intermediary Buyer) 100 bales, same basis, at ten days delivery. In making such a sale he is guided by his business judgment—the possibilities of the weather, the daily receipts of cotton and other contingencies. Let it be assumed that he did not have a bale of cotton in existence, nor one growing in the field. He has *Sold Short* 100 bales; sold $5,000 worth of something he did not possess, nor did he know the price of cotton for the ten days future. He reasoned that if cotton declined to 9.80, 9.75, 9.60 or 9.50, he would buy it at the *declined* prices, or some of them, and make his profits on his *purchases,* as he had it sold at a definite 10 cent price. The wider the difference between his purchase price and his sale price, the greater his profit.

In such a sale, he has taken a risk to secure a hoped-for profit. He knew when the sale was made that if the Market declined, a profit resulted; if it advanced, a loss was equally as certain. This method of short selling has all the attributes of speculation, and involves an uncertainty that can not be eliminated, subjecting A to a hazard not unlike gambling. The risk lies in the fact that *declines* do not always come when expected; the reverse is not unusual. A calculated on conditions as he saw them; and possibly encouraged by the advice of other and larger Buyers to "go short," did so. He figured on heavy port receipts, farmers selling freely on all declines, good weather for gathering and an inactive demand for the staple. Such conditions are conducive to declines.

There is always an unknown quantity in the Cotton Market. The Cotton Exchanges of Liverpool, New York and New Orleans stand at the head of the Cotton Markets of the world, and it is beyond the ken of human ingenuity to foretell what its membership may do in manipulating the price of cotton.

Indications as pronounced as those stated may give every evidence of a decline, yet in the face of it, the wires from those institutions may indicate advances.

The Membership are frequently divided on the Future Market. Exclusive of their own manipulations, they are

governed by conditions, as are non-members who buy and
sell. Some members believe the market should go higher,
and buy cotton (Contracts) ; others think it should go lower, and sell. This diversity of ideas induces buying and
selling, and the prices offered and accepted for Contracts
guide the Dealers in Spot Cotton the world over in making
their purchases.

It is argued by some members of the Cotton Exchanges
that the prices for our cotton are founded on *sentiment,*
and that the existence of Exchanges is salutary to the trade.

Short sales can not always be made as described; conditions are factors to be considered. Short sales are made
for 5, 10, 15, 20, 30 or more days. Panicky conditions are
against short selling, and during panics short sales can
not be made for many days ahead, or if so, at only great
risk.

Short selling spot cotton by leading manipulators may
be done with expectation of profits from subsequent purchases at declines, as already stated, or it may be done
for another reason—to-wit, to affect the market adversely,
and establish a basis on which to buy.

Profits on short sales are made on *declines,* and losses
occur on *advances* in the Market.

Evidences of "heavy receipts," "stagnant trade," "glut-
ted market," "labor trouble," "financial disturbances," and
"war rumors," are factors inducing declines. These conditions are inducements to "go short," "or "sell the Market
short," and the Trade is quick to take advantage of it.

While the evidences existing to indicate a decline may
be broadcast and, at their inception, endemic, yet the contagion spreads until the entire buying fraternity, with
scattered exceptions here and there, have "Sold Short,"
more especially if the price be inviting; under this influence
and pressure the Market sags; each and every buyer feels
that the Market should decline; he talks as if there were
no life in the Market; and the very fact of such agitation
conduces to declines, and the Market does decline.

The sentiment to "go short" may be not only statewide, but the contagion may become epidemic and rage over the entire South, even spreading to foreign commercial centers, and when so universal, the power of the great Cotton Exchanges can not, with all their force, revert the tide of sales overwhelming the Market and irresistibly forcing it down.

The first cause for short sales rests with the Cotton Growers. When they intuitively sell at the same time all over the South, the Trade takes advantage of it and helps reduce the declining price, resulting in a loss to the South of many millions of dollars.

When the Markets are flooded with cotton from the Growers faster than the Trade can take it at fair prices, declines absolutely follow, and it is quite an easy matter to make short sales, and such sales are always at the expense of the Grower.

Conditions favorable to short selling are seldom so pronounced as stated in the preceding section, and when not so, the effort to make a profit by bearing[44] the Market with Short Sales is hazardous.

Extensive Short Sales sometimes indirectly cause the Market to advance. This obtains when the prices flashed over the wires show advances, at which time "Shorts" rush into the Market to buy to protect their sales. Such active bidding sustains for a time the increased price and often forces it higher.

Short Selling must not be confused with *contracting* cotton for the Trade, the Mills or Export. The phrase applies more directly to sales made for early delivery, as 5, 10, 20 or 30 days.[45]

Competition between Buyers, when actively practiced, can virtually destroy the effects of any Short Sale if both

---

[44]See Bulls and Bears, pp. 102, 103.

[45]Literally, a forward sale is a "Short Sale," when the article sold is not in possession of the Seller.

"Short" the Market at the same price, but if "Shorted" at different figures, one has an advantage of the other.

If A sells 100 bales Short at 12 cents, and B "Shorts" it at 11.50, A has the advantage of ½ cent a pound over B, or $2.50 a bale; this wide difference is unusual, but explains the idea. Had both "Shorted" at 12 cents, both could offer the same price for cotton.

If A sells at 12, and B 11.50 cents, A can bid to B's limit, or even to 11.60, forcing B out of the market for the time, and yet make $2.00 a bale profit.

Buyers in trying to get this advantage of each other often take desperate risks. If successful, they make money rapidly; if not, they lose it just as fast.

SECTION VII.

COMMISSION SHIPMENTS.

Cotton Growers, and occasionally Buyers, ship cotton to others to be sold for them on a commission basis.

Dealers receiving such shipments are called *Cotton Factors*. They usually accept the cotton to be sold on the terms stated when the shipment is made, or by reason of some previous agreement or advertisement.

The Shipper (consignor) makes up a list of the cotton, showing its weight, number of bales, marks, etc., on the "Notice of Shipment," and the initial and number of the car or cars on the Bill-of-Lading, with total weight, and forwards these Documents to the Factor (consignee) by mail, which are generally received by him many days before the arrival of the cotton.

On receipt of the cotton, samples large enough to show the Class of it are drawn and brought at once to the office, to be held for display when the sale is made.

With instructions to sell, the samples are displayed on the Factor's Tables for inspection of Buyers who generally offer a round price for the entire lot in connection with other cotton offered for sale at the same time.

It is customary for Factors to figure the price of cotton from a basis, and if the offered price is satisfactory as proved by their own calculations, the cotton is sold at once, and the sales reported to the Shipper, showing expense charges in detail, and the net proceeds. A check on a local bank is enclosed with the statement.

The Factor does not guarantee the cotton, but, as the Buyer has a week to take up the cotton, he goes to the bales and compares them with the samples drawn; after comparison, the bales are weighed in his presence, and on these weights final settlement is made.

Some Factors who operate on an extensive scale, do not confine their sales to Local Buyers, but sell direct to the Mill Agents through their representatives in the spinning centers in different parts of the world, either on the basis of Class, or from Samples previously submitted. Such sales are executed by wire.

Factors, if given time to effect sales in this manner, and handling cotton in large volumes, can class it into even-running or specific Grades, and make direct Mill deliveries, and when they do so, they follow the sale with a guarantee covering Weights and Grade, which they protect, with no "fall-back" on the original Shipper.

Factors charge a definite sum on each bale, sufficient in amount to cover Weighing, Drayage, Sampling, Insurance, Storage, Wharfage and a Commission for selling, which are applied for a full month, even though the cotton be sold within a few days after arrival.

Charges are heavier for the first month than for subsequent months.

Shippers consigning cotton to Factors can make a Draft on the Factors at the time of shipment, by prearrangement, and draw a certain amount of money on their cotton, if they so desire, usually at a small rate of interest.

SHIPPING DOCUMENTS.

There are four documents essential to every transaction in connection with cotton shipments. They are:

INVOICE.

DRAFT.

Sight, Time.

BILL OF LADING.

INSURANCE CERTIFICATE.

INVOICE.

The Invoice is a bill, list or statement that describes in detail the Shipment of cotton.

It gives the date of Shipment, number and weight of each bale, and total weight. Often the classification is given and the basis or terms on which sold, and the total value.

Invoices are sometimes made out on sheets showing the number, weight and class on one line, while others are made in form showing bales in consecutive numbers, and in groups of 10 bales.

Invoices usually show the Marks under which the Shipment is made, and sometimes the Gin Marks additional, if Account Sales in return are desired in such Marks. Such returns are not often required.

Some Buyers number the bales in their Shipments consecutively from first to last of the season; others give a number to each shipment, and the numbers of bales are run consecutively on each separate Shipment, usually under a different Mark.

These are matters of detail for the individual Dealer, and are used for the purpose of keeping a perfect and complete record of all business handled.

For Export cotton the Invoice gives the name of the vessel, what Port it leaves, the name of the Shipper and Consignee, number of the Shipment or Contract, the class of cotton and Staple (generally in m/m), the price per pound (sometimes in Pence and Pfennigs), the number of bales in the Shipment, Shipping Marks (usually in 4 letters), total weight less the 6% Tare and Freight, the Freight Rate, the name of the party to whom the Shipment shall be referred if it is arbitrated, and the name of the representative who shall look after any Claims, such as short weight, country damage or difference in Grade, also how the shipment is paid for by reimbursement with a 30, 60 or 90 days Sight Bill of Exchange on some foreign house or bank.

Such a shipment goes out usually under the "C. I. F. & 6% terms."

The following forms of Invoice are sometimes used in shipping cotton to Cotton Factors, to be sold by them for account of the Shipper, or delivery from a Local Buyer to an Intermediary one or, to an Exporter:

NOTICE OF SHIPMENT.[46]

Sherman, Texas, Sep. 10, 1914.

Clark & Co., Galveston, Texas,

Dear Sir: We have this day shipped you from Sherman station 12 Bales Cotton; marks, weights, class and instructions as below. Yours truly,

....P. O.   WRIGHT & SMITH.

MARKS	NUMBER	WEIGHTS	CLASS	REMARKS
TOM	161	520	1	
"	2	536	1	
"	3	498	2	
	4	572	1	
"	5	512	2	
LIT	6	561	3	
"	7	511	2	
"	8	496	1	
"	9	502	1	
	170	525	1	
	1	517	2	
	2	604	1	

Please sell on arrival unless we instruct you otherwise.

[46]This may be used for an Invoice of a direct sale.

INVOICE OF DIRECT SHIPMENT.

The following form is often used in a direct sale shipment:

Our No.........................

No...................   McGregor, Texas, May 8, 1914.

(INVOICE) of 25 Bales Cotton sold to CLARK & ADAMS. Marks TOM. By H. E. Hackney. Date of Sale 5/7. Price B/M 11.50. Difference ¼-½ up, ⅜-1 down. Shipped from McGregor via R₁ R. St. L. S. W. B/L No. 49 to Galveston.

Marks Bales	Grade	Weight.	Price	Amounts	Gross Amt.
TOM 3	Good Mid.	1590	12	$190.80	
2	Strict Mid.	1105	11¾	129.84	
8	Mid.	4160	11½	478.40	
6	Strict Low Mid.	3096	11⅛	344.43	
6	Low Mid.	2985	10½	313.43	
					$1,456.90
			Exch.		3.64
					$1,460.54

E. & O. E.

Received by...

H. E. HACKNEY.

NOTE.—Be sure to fill all blanks at the top.

In the first Invoice the Grades are not given, as the cotton was shipped to be sold "on orders," which might be: "Sell on arrival;" "Will advise you when to offer it;" "Sell by first of next month;" or, "We consign to be sold on your judgment and advice."

In the second Invoice the Shippers sold on their own Class and Weights, and if the cotton was received by the "Take-up--man," the Shipment as shown was final. If the Shippers sold "Weights and Grades guaranteed," then this sale was not final until after re-classed and re-weighed at destination. Should the out-turn show exactly the initial Shipment, the Claim would be paid as stated for the amount in the Invoices; but if any loss in Weights or variation in Class occurs, a *Claim* would be made for them.

Claims are made for *losses*, and *credits* given for *gains* in Class or Weights, in dealings in Spot Cotton for American or Foreign Trade, with certain exceptions.*

---

*See pp. 251, 252 and 257.

Two Shipping Marks are shown in the first Invoice, when in actual practice such small Shipments are usually made under one Mark.

The forms here are not stereotyped. Different Dealers have specified *forms* of their own, devised for their special convenience, which may vary from those shown. These two forms are often used.

DRAFT.

The draft is the *Check* for payment of cotton sold; but to distinguish it from a Check on a local firm or bank, it is called a "Draft" because drawn on a distant firm or banking institution.

It is an *order* from one person or firm to pay to another person or firm a certain sum of money. It gives the date, amount, and time for payment if written to be paid at a designated time.

With reference to time, it is payable "at sight"—that is, when presented; or it may be payable at a certain time in the future, as 30, 60, 90 or more days from date of its order.

Payments made for Domestic or American cotton have Drafts generally written payable "at sight." Those drawn for payment of Foreign Shipments usually read 60 to 90 days, and sometimes 120 days or more.

Time Drafts generally draw Interest, and are bought and sold at a *Premium, Discount* or *Par.*

Many American Banks make a specialty of dealing in Foreign Drafts, referred to as "Buying and Selling Exchange."

An Exporter practically pays for all cotton bought by drawing a Draft on large American or Foreign Banks of unquestioned standing, and the Seller of the cotton who accepts the same sells the Draft for the best price he can get to some local bank. This is called "Selling Exchange."

Banks dealing in such paper handle it on a percentage

basis, and are governed by the demand for it as to the Premium or Discount to be calculated.[47]

Domestic Drafts are passed between Banks at specific rates of Exchange, without Interest consideration, unless it be a Time Draft drawing Interest.

Drafts for Foreign Trade are generally drawn in duplicate form reading, "First of Exchange" and "Second of Exchange," and often in £. s. and d. Stubs for the Bills state the same value as the Bills, the number of bales in the Shipment, name of the vessel, the Insurance Company, and the Bank or House on which drawn, and where located.

BILL OF LADING.

The bill of lading is one of the most important Documents connected with cotton Shipments. It is two-fold in character, having the signification of both a *Receipt* and a *Contract;* virtually, a Receipt from a transportation company, acknowledging the acceptance of something to be shipped. It describes the articles or commodity for transportation, condition, date received, from and to whom shipped, holding the transportation company responsible for delivery at destination, barring certain contingencies, in the order received.

It is a *Contract* by agreement; the Shipper agrees to the terms of the transportation company as specified under "Conditions" on the back of the Bill, and the transportation company accepts the shipment, agreeing to transmit it to destination as per the stipulated terms.

A Shipment under a Bill of Lading may be made "open," as when consigning a list of cotton to a Cotton Factor to be sold on Commission, on whom no Draft is made, with no indorsement of the Shipper on it.

Shipments accompanied by a Draft and Invoice have the Bill of Lading indorsed on the back of it with the Shipper's name, and the words on its face, *"Shipper's Order, Notify."*

---

[47]See Checks and Drafts, Book II, p. 167.

The condition under which the cotton moves is usually stated on the face of the Bill. If desired compressed, the words *"Compress in transit"* should be written on it. Should this not be wanted, then the words, *"Ship Flat," "Flat through to consignee,"* or a phrase of similar import must be written thereon.

Domestic Bills of Lading are those operative in the United States, in contradistinction from those for Foreign Shipments, and are either *intra-* or *inter-*State in character. An *intra-State* Shipment is one *inside* the State; an *inter-*State shipment has reference to the movement of the commodity from one State into another.

Through Bill of Lading.—This form of instrument was devised by the transportation companies to facilitate the handling of cotton from loading point to destination. Under its reading, Shipments are made direct from interior points in the South to Foreign Ports, obviating the necessity of re-billing at the Ports from which exported. The notation, "Shippers Order, Notify" appears on the face of the Bill. It gives the name of Consignor, Consignee, destination, name of vessel, number of bales, gross weight, freight rate divided, as Railroad (Inland), Wharfage and Ocean Rate, Shipping Marks, etc.

Shipments originating at interior American towns, moving on one Through Bill of Lading arriving in several vessels, are treated as "forming one shipment."[48]

Payments for cotton, in connection with its shipment, are safeguarded by the Bill of Lading. The four Documents necessary in its shipment are equally requisite in securing payments for export cotton.

The customary procedure in preparing the papers for a cotton Shipment and payment of same, is: Make up the Invoice, draw a Draft (as one would write a Check), fill out the Bill of Lading by showing the names of the Shipper and the one to whom the Shipment is made, the number

---

[48]Bremen Rules, Cotton Exchange. See "Freights," p. 156.

of bales, their Marks, stating if on the bale or tags, or on both, with total weight. After all data necessary to the Shipment is placed on the Bill of Lading, have the railroad agent sign his name to it, which he does after the cotton is placed on the railway platform or in his possession. Prepare the Insurance Certificate and pin all the papers together.

The Bills-of-Lading are usually made in *triplicate*—one copy, the *original*, for the Shipper; the second or *duplicate* for the office record, and the third for the freight railway conductor if shipment is from a prepay station or "blind siding," otherwise he is guided by the Way-Bill.

The Shipper pins his four papers, Invoice, Draft, Bill of Lading and Insurance Certificate together and presents them to his local bank with instructions how to handle the Shipment.

The Banker writes a letter of instructions to some bank or Banker at or near destination of Shipment. To this *letter of advice* he pins the four papers, and forwards all in one envelope. Upon receipt of the Documents, the receiving bank has full instructions how to proceed. Ordinarily, it presents them to Consignee, collects the money, surrenders all papers to him, and returns the money to the bank at shipping point.

In this way Cotton is often paid for many days before its arrival at destination.[49]

Shippers often send the Invoice direct to the Buyer, reserving the Draft and Bill-of-Lading to go through the bank.

Banks make a small charge to compensate them for their services usually calculated as a percentage on the amount involved, the Rate being determined by the demand for Exchange, or by Rules agreed upon among themselves.

The above applies more particularly to the sale and movement of Domestic Cotton.

---

[49]See Foot Note, Book II, p. 170. Usually three Documents only accompany domestic shipments. S/D, B/L and Invoice.

The same Documents are requisite for Export Cotton, and the Bankers handling them usually buy such "spinners' paper" at certain Rates of Exchange, and give the Shipper a stipulated sum for the Draft covering the sale.

CERTIFICATE OF INSURANCE.

This instrument is attached to the Bill-of-Lading, Sight Draft and Invoice, as an evidence that the cotton to which it has reference is insured.

This Certificate represents and takes the place of the Policy, and conveys all the rights of the Original Policy Holder, (for collecting any loss or Claim), as fully as if the property were covered by a Special Policy.

This Certificate is directed in its application to protecting cotton while in transit from point of origin to destination, whether for Eastern Mills or European Ports.

It specifies every particular embodied in the Original Policy, such as giving the Number, Weight, Marks and Value of the cotton covered; from where and to whom shipped, the time of shipment, by what road and vessel it is moving, and where destined.

OTHER INSURANCE POLICIES.

Specific Policy.—Insurance Policies protecting cotton in yards and warehouses at local points are termed Specific Policies.

Marine Policy.—A Marine Policy covers cotton from the time of its purchase until it is landed at final destination in New England or Europe; the Rate being based on a certain period of time for "shore cover," and without regard to length of time in transit by water.

Blanket Policy.—A Blanket Policy is one which covers the subject insured at various locations, and is intended for use where the value of cotton fluctuates, the purpose being to protect the owner at each location in a State or territory, even though the values are constantly changing.

Cotton in transit by rail can be insured for either the owner or the railroad at a specified Rate per bale without regard to length of time such cotton is moving.

Payment for adjustment of Claims on Export Cotton can be had in many large commercial cities abroad, as well as designated American points.[50]

Cotton Merchants exporting Cotton covered by a Marine Policy, or buying at different Southern points under protection of a Blanket Policy, report daily the number of bales "on hand," number of bales purchased, and number of bales sold or shipped, on special forms furnished by the Insurance Company.

A DOMESTIC PURCHASE AND FOREIGN SHIPMENT.

During the fall season when cotton is moving freely it is not unusual for Export Buyers to buy in lots of 500, 600, 800, 1000 or more bales from other large interior Dealers, and receive from them the whole in several shipments of 50, 100 or more bales at a time, each shipment applying as a credit on the original total sale. Such sales are confirmed by letter.

If the export sale should be one of mixed Grades, the 50- or 100-bale shipments applying on it can be Through Billed from shipping point to destination, otherwise they will be concentrated at some designated point and separated into specific Grades.

In the following domestic purchase and export sale, it will be seen that Messrs. Crespi & Co. bought 800 bales from Mr. Johnson, on which sale Mr. Johnson has made a shipment of 100 B/C.

The following Documents will exhibit in detail the business features covering the movement of this cotton from Hamilton, Texas, to Milan, Italy.

NOTE.—The Bill-of-Lading and Insurance Certificate are omitted because it is not thought advisable to burden this work with them. See B/L and Ins. Cert., pp. 280-288.

---

[50]Insurance data from Messrs. Trezevant & Cochran, Dallas, Texas.

CRESPI & CO.

COTTON

SALES CONFIRMATION.

No. 115

Waco, Texas, October 15th, 1914.

Mr. J. M. Johnson,
    Hamilton, Texas.

Dear Sir:

We beg to confirm our purchase, from you, this day of (800 B/C) Eight Hundred Bales of Cotton, Basis American Middling, good color and staple, free from sand and dust, subject to re-sampling and re-weighing. Grading, Nothing above Gd. Mid. Nothing below St. Gd. Ord. Price 12½c B/Mid. F. O. B. Hamilton Compress. Delivery Prompt.

Grade Differences

Gd. Md.	¼c up
St. M.	⅜c up
Middling 12½c	
St. L. M..............	¼c down
L. M.	⅜c down
St. G. O...............	1½c down

Yours truly,

CRESPI & CO.

(Signed)   By   *L. F. Cowan,*

Sec. & Treas.

Except as otherwise stated herein this contract is understood to be subject to the Rates of The Texas Cotton Association.

SALES CONFIRMATION.

No. 115.

Hamilton, Texas, 10/15, 1914.

Messrs. Crespi & Co.,
    Waco, Texas.

Dear Sirs:

I beg to confirm having this day sold to you the following (800 B C) Bales of Cotton, Basis American Middling, good color and staple, free from sand and dust, subject to re-sampling and re-weighing. Grading, Nothing above Gd. Mid. Nothing below St. Gd. Ord. Price 12½c B/Mid. F. O. B. Hamilton Compress. Delivery Prompt.

Grade Differences

Gd. Md. .... ¼c up
St. M. .... ½c up
Middling 12½c
St. L. M............. ¼c down
L. M. .... ¾c down
St. G. O............... 1½c down

Yours truly,

(Signed)   *J. M. Johnson.*

(PLEASE SIGN AND RETURN.)

Except as otherwise stated herein, this contract is understood to be subject to the Rates of The Texas Cotton Association.

Hamilton, Texas, Oct. 20, 1914.

Messrs. Crespi & Co.,
        Waco, Texas.

Gentlemen:

As per our sale of 800 B/C, made to you on the 15th inst., on basis of 12½c, we have shipped upon your order 100 bales today, as shown by attached Invoice, Numbers, Weights and Grades.

We contemplate moving out 100 or more bales daily until the completion of this contract.

Please accept our thanks for full payment of this shipment.

Yours very truly,

J. M. Johnson.

CRESPI & CO.
>Waco, Texas

Hamilton, Texas, Oct. 20th, 1914.
Invoice of 100 Bales Cotton Bought from J. M. Johnson Against sale of Oct. 15th, 1913, for 800 Bales Cotton @ 12½c B/Mid.

Tag. No.	Class	Wt.	Tag. No.	Class	Wt.	Tag. No.	Class	Wt.
79501	3	470	79541	1	380	79581	2	578
2	1	595	42	4	513	82	1	585
3	4	536	43	3	471	83	5	553
4	2	520	44	2	490	84	4	545
5	3	489	45	1	450	85	3	551
6	5	690	46	3	558	86	1	529
7	4	552	47	1	568	87	5	528
8	2	545	48	2	543	88	2	580
9	4	515	49	3	563	89	6	560
10	3	529	50	5	531	90	3	586
11	6	543	51	2	470	91	4	544
12	1	526	52	2	410	92	1	534
13	2	594	53	1	433	93	3	577
14	3	488	54	4	563	94	5	542
15	5	573	55	2	513	95	4	530
16	4	537	56	4	503	96	3	560
17	2	465	57	3	353	97	1	539
18	1	525	58	4	628	98	4	570
19	4	521	59	6	545	99	3	510
20	3	420	60	3	520	600	2	544
21	1	454	61	1	517			
22	4	540	62	2	473			
23	3	450	63	2	474			
24	2	395	64	3	503			
25	4	430	65	3	483			
26	3	422	66	3	515			
27	5	568	67	4	499			
28	4	526	68	5	515			
29	3	563	69	1	550			
30	1	600	70	4	551			
31	2	534	71	3	517			
32	3	545	72	2	595			
33	4	579	73	4	472			
34	2	540	74	3	556			
35	3	496	75	1	510			
36	1	496	76	2	541			
37	4	561	77	3	534			
38	2	480	78	1	560			
39	3	570	79	3	548			
40	6	601	80	2	598			

1	Good Midd. 18	B/C	
2	St. Midd. 21	"	
3	Middling 28	"	
4	St. L. Midd.....21	"	
5	Low Midd. 8	"	
6	St. Gd. Ord..... 4	"	

Route via St. L. & S. W. Ry.

Average Grade 10 *pts, off.*

· *Total weight* 52,544 *lbs.* @ 12.40

$6515.45

¼% exchange   16.29

———————

$6499.16

Paid for by Draft on Waco office, dated Oct. 20th, 1914.

(Signed) *Classer W. P. Lyles.*

(LETTER OF ADVICE)

PIO CRESPI, PRESIDENT   L. F. COWAN, SECY AND TREAS.

CRESPI & CO.

Cable Address: Cotton
  Crespi

                    Waco, Texas, Nov. 15th 1914.

Messrs. Crespi & Co.,
              Milan, Italy.

Dear Sir:

We take pleasure in confirming our sale made to your good selves of 100 B/C L'pool Middling good colour 28 m/m staple @ 7.40d. c.i.f. & 6% to Genoa, Italy, per s/s Mongibello shipment Liverpool class and arbitration, reimbursement by our 90 days' draft on Banca Commerciale Italiana, Milan, Italy.

This sale is designated as contract No. 76.

          We remain, dear sir,
              Yours very truly,

                    Crespi & Co.,
                    By L. F. Cowan,
                        Secy & Treas.

Invoice No. 76.

INVOICE OF *One hundred* Bales of Cotton

Shipped by CRESPI & CO., from WACO, TEXAS

via *Galveston* per S/S *Mongibello* for *Genoa, Italy.* Insured *with the Standard Marine, L'pool for £1600.=. =.* for account and risk of *Sigg. Crespi & Co., Milan, Italy.* Contract No. *76.* Freight at *107½c per 100 lbs. L'pool Middling gc. 28 m/m staple.*

No claims for short weight, country damage, or difference in grade will be allowed, unless verified by, and samples drawn and sealed in the presence of
Boffito & Pedemonte, Genoa, Italy.

Marks
SLTV 100 Bales Cotton, wg.   52,544 lbs.
CRESPI   Less 6%Tare   3,152

Net weight   49,392
Ins. Cert. No. 526,433
49,392 lbs. at c 7.40d.   £1522 18   4
Less Freight on 52,544 @ 107½c   117 13   6

$564.85 @ 4.80   1405   4 10

REIMBURSEMENT

By our 90 days sight Bill of Exchange, for your account and risk on *Banca Commerciale Italiana, Milan,* favor of Clark & Co.
E. & O. E.
IN CASE THERE SHOULD BE ANY ARBITRATION
PLEASE NOTIFY MR. *W. P. Brown, L'pool.*
WACO, TEXAS, Nov. 15, 1914.
CRESPI & CO.
By *L. F. Cowan,*
Sec. & Treas.

BILLS OF EXCHANGE.—When one is paid the other becomes void. By selling the bill to some bank, Crespi & Co. get the money for their money and the Exchange. By selling the bill to some bank, Crespi & Co. get the money for their cotton at once—the bank cannot collect under 90 days. The bank buys at a price to get interest on their money and the Exchange.

BOOK IV.

COTTON EXCHANGES AND HISTORY OF COTTON

THE ORGANIZED COTTON TRADE OF
THE WORLD, THE DEVELOPMENT OF
COTTON AS A PRODUCT, WITH DATA
AS TO DIFFERENT TYPES.

CHAPTER I.

SECTION I.

COTTON EXCHANGES.

The word "Exchange" means literally to swap, barter one thing for another, give value for value—*exchange* a commodity for its equivalent value in something else—and when so used has a verb signification; but as used in this Chapter, the word denotes a *place* where business is transacted.

To transact a business where commodities of one class are exchanged for another, more especially those pertaining to agriculture, it is quite essential and certainly preferable, that a place be established most convenient to all, where such transactions can be most conveniently conducted at the least expense.

By virtue of an unwritten law in most instances, as well as by municipal legislative enactment in some, every hamlet, town and city in the South has certain streets or parts of them, squares, or places, where the Grower may come with his cotton to Market and offer it for sale; where the Buyer meets the Seller, and where sales are consumated; here the Seller can sell his one bale of cotton on his wagon; sell one to be picked next week, or sell his whole crop, whether few or many bales, by agreement with the Buyer and deliver it in one, two or three days, weeks or months. This the Seller knows to be the place where he is to offer his cotton for sale; here, the Buyers' interests are centered, and here is a legitimate *Exchange* place.

Such an exchange has no rules for its government, further than the sanction of custom. It has no registered membership, and there are no plans nor fees for initiation. The Seller and Buyer are its patrons.

The character, function and purpose of such an Exchange is familiar to every Southern Agriculturist, one with which he is daily thrown in contact, and while to him it is extremely commonplace, nevertheless this fact does not minimize its importance.

While such places are usually without shelter, and are recognized neither by the public nor patrons as *Exchanges*, yet they fulfill the requirements of Cotton Exchanges in all particulars except that of transactions in Future Contracts.

The purposes carried out in these local Market Places aptly fulfill the primary ones of any organized Exchange, the intention of which is to bring together both Buyer and Seller for the execution of the purchase and sale of any commodity offered; but beyond this feature they do not in the least resemble the great Cotton Exchanges of New York or New Orleans, *the only two in America* dealing in Future Contracts.

In these Southern local Market Places, the Vendor can offer directly his own products for sale, or assign his interests to another whom he may elect as his agent or representative to execute his sales or purchases. The right of Contract is neither abrogated, nor abridged, nor is there any limit on the quantity or amount that may be handled through such media.

Any one desiring to enter such a Market Place in the capacity of Buyer or Seller has the sanction of the people and the legitimate business interests of the Country; free to exercise his own business judgment to guide him in his efforts, and the introduction of any amount of capital he may care to invest in his own behalf or that of a co-partnership. There are no restrictions beyond the payment of an occupation tax, or conformity to some minor legal requirement, as may be locally applied in exceptional cases. Barring those limitations, the individual who can classify cotton and calculate the relative Grades, may attempt a cotton business of his own, cognizant of the fact that the results to be attained rest with his individual efforts and business qualifications, subjected to no rules nor regulations beyond that of propriety, integrity of purpose and ultimate hopes and intentions.

There are no preferable places on these local Exchanges for any one to secure a better price than another for his cotton.

There are no negro Buyers, but both White and Black mix and mingle with perfect impunity in offering their cotton for sale, which is usually purchased on a Middling basis, with additions or deductions for the relative Grades above or below Middling.

The fascination of buying cotton is so great for the individual who has made a success at the business, that it creates a desire with the novice to attempt it also, stimulating the uninitiated to enter the field, and through or from such sources, recruits are constantly being added, resulting in keeping in the South such an army of Buyers that competition among them is prevalent almost everywhere.

The present plan of selling cotton to local country Buyers in the South is possible only under a system that will give a Market at all points simultaneously for each and every Grade grown by the Cotton Planter.

This plan has been developed through a series of years, broadening as the South's great cotton industry spread itself from the Atlantic to the Western Texas Plains and the Rio Grande on our extreme Southern boundary, and is still reaching for the Pacific through Arizona and Southern California's fertile soils, fostered by human ingenuity.

As the acreage has widened, the railroads have kept pace with the movement, seeking cotton tonnage, accompanied by the hum of the wire and dot and dash that transmit quotation after quotation, as the price of the fiber varies from local or world-wide causes.

THE FIRST COTTON EXCHANGE.

European Countries having equipment for manufacturing fibrous substances into articles for practical and domestic purposes were the first to accept American Cotton on their looms for the manufacture of cloth. The raw material proving to be well adapted for use in producing various articles suitable for wearing apparel and other purposes, grew in popular favor as its value became known.

The increased interest in the introduction and use of cotton abroad led to investment of capital and an increase in the number of patrons, who vied with each other for its purchase.

As in America, so it was in ·Europe, a necessity was growing daily for the introduction of some *central point* where Buyers could assemble and receive some information relative to the Trade respecting the *purchase*[1] of cotton. As this sentiment increased, it stimulated action, resulting in establishing the LIVERPOOL COTTON ASSOCIATION in 1842, but dealings in Futures were not inaugurated there in until 1870.

Thus was established, for the first time in the history of cotton traffic, an Exchange; not for the purpose of purchase and sale of cotton in America, but for the *purchase* of cotton alone from this country. Members of that Association could buy from and sell to each other, and the presumption is they did so; but the great importance attaching to such an organization was the facility offered Buyers as a place of assembly where they could meet, discuss conditions, demands, or absence of them—any and all things pertaining to the cotton industry. By such conferences face to face, the membership were enabled to agree upon the amount to be paid for American cotton. Being the exclusive Buyers, the privilege of pricing it rested absolutely in their hands, and remained so for years and years.

---

[1]Beyond home use for domestic purposes, Europe was our exclusive *Buyer* of cotton then.

This gave them an advantage in manipulating prices as a prerogative of their own, which could not be overcome by the unorganized American Trade.

Conditions.—At the time of the organization of the Liverpool Cotton Association, and subsequently to it for several years, the knowledge of Future Trading was unknown, or if known, was not practiced.[2]

Transportation across the Atlantic was slow, but after the passage of the *"Savannah,"* a "paddle wheel steamer" that crossed the Atlantic from New York to Liverpool in 1819, the enthusiasm of the Americans stimulated capital to continue its efforts to put into active service steamvessels of better equipment and regular service, but not until 1840 was a regular line established by Cunard to ply between American and European Ports.

The *Savanah* made her initial trip in twenty-six days, quite a feat for that time in a trans-Atlantic voyage; but by 1840 England had introduced her "fast packets," which lowered the record of the first Steamer, and became actively engaged in the transmission of freight and passengers, and cotton constituted a large percentage of the out-going freight.

Railroad Construction was being actively pushed North and South into those districts where cotton lands were being developed, and were exerting efforts for securing cotton cargoes.

The City of New York was rapidly getting into direct touch with the Western Cities and Cotton Mills of her adjacent territory by Railway communication. Facilities for getting shipments through to destination on quicker time were daily improving. Better mail advantages were being offered through this process of commercial evolution, enhancing the cotton industry.

There were no such things as *"Cotton Markets,"*[3] in

---

[2]The author has failed to find any data indicating that Future Trading existed at that time as it is practiced now.

[3]As recognized by the Trade today.

America. The Cotton Mills were the exclusive, primary and ultimate Buyers, through any agency or representation they saw fit to utilize. They were not co-related by Association Rules or guided by co-operative agreements in making purchases. They occupied territory often widely separated. Each bought raw material for its own use at the least prices obtainable, and they competed with each other in seeking purchasers for finished products. Competition was an element that entered into all sales, and had its influence in making prices on primary purchases of raw material.

Dealers who operated for the purchase and sale of cotton were usually men who were merchandizing in other lines, or were men of capital investing their funds in a cotton venture as if speculating in land, horses or cattle.

Mail facilities. The transmission of the mails over the settled portion of the United States from 1800 to 1842 was a subject of great importance , and merited the consideration of our ablest statesmen. During this time the facilities for taking the mails across country gradually increased from the first to the latter date. Wherever the Railroad laid its iron rails, it assumed the function of carrier, and displaced the two-wheel cart and stage coach.

Mails floating by boats on the rivers were slow in distribution, but larger quantities were carried. As Railroad beds were firmed, shorter schedules were put into operation, and mail facilities improved by quicker distribution.

Improvements in the service on the land coincided with equal advantages for mails transported across the waters to foreign consumers of our cotton, yet compared with present up-to-date methods, they were still relatively primitive and slow of movement.

To send a letter across the Atlantic in 1842, and get a reply, often required three and four months, and in some instances, six months. The facilities for service in 1850 were not much better.

Commodities for Export and Import were not so abundant then as now.   Vessels often lay in port for weeks awaiting their cargoes, which necessarily delayed the movement of the mails.

Buyers of cotton on this side who desired some data on which to base a price for the purchase of cotton must perforce seek it through the foreign mails.   If the information proved satisfactory, the Buyer operated on the advice; if not, he would repeat the effort through the same channels for better results.

Data received giving quotations for purchasing cotton were used until changed, and under such a system, a price could be utilized for many days, or lengthened into weeks.

What one Mill or Buyer might offer a customer in Augusta for cotton would be discounted or exceeded by another at the same point, or at some other Port.

Many Cotton Mills of varying capacity had been erected in isolated localities on Southern Streams; the theory of the Southern Manufacturer being that the Mills should be located near the cotton fields for the economic advantage gained by converting the raw material at home into finished products, and by the avoidance of two-way Freight charges.

The Telegraph was not in operation, the Telephone un-. known, and mail communications between Mill and Mill were not regular, and often delayed.

Contracting Mill products at stipulated prices for *future delivery* was not practiced nor attempted.   A Mill selling its product based it on the price paid for the raw material; the purchase of raw material was governed by what the Mill owner *thought* or estimated he could get for the manufactured article.

Prices offered Exporters for cotton were gauged by the amount of speculative risks the Foreign Buyers cared to take, and the competition existing between themselves was a consideration in making American purchases.   This condition was reflected in lack of stimulus for bidding one above another, unless conditions warranted investment purchases promising good results. Foreign and American Mills operated similarly, one fearing to offer an advanced price, reasoning that another might buy for less and undersell it on competition in an open field.

Such conditions were not conducive to expansion of the cotton business, and led to contentions and controversies calling for reformation in the cotton industry, in its production, sale and manufacture.

At different times since Cotton culture began as a commercial commodity, Growers have maintained the position that Buyers, (generally referred to as "Speculators"), were the factors destroying their interests by reducing the price of cotton, and conventions have been held at irregular intervals at various places in the South since 1839, looking to a betterment of conditions from the Farmers' point of view.

Commission Merchants and Spot Buyers, as Speculators located at the Southern Ports and leading interior points, often went to New York to make sales of their purchases, or commitments in their charge for sale. Sales covered Spot Cotton then lying at the Southern Ports or after delivery in New York.

Buyers in New York had offices in different parts of the City, and Sellers desiring to confer with them for the purpose of making sales usually found it necessary to interview a large percentage or all of them, before accepting a price for their cotton.

Circumstances confronted them in New York as had obtained in Liverpool among the Buyers before the organization of the Liverpool Cotton Exchange. While the Buyers' offices were segregated, yet there was no Rule prescribing that they should combine for purposes of eliminating competition. It is not asserted that they did so, but suffice it to say the avenue was open for executing a co-operative purchasing agreement, if desired for mutual benefit.

The Buyer's offices being scattered here and there over the City caused great inconvenience to both Buyers and Sellers, when the latter annually gravitated to New York for executing sales. As Trade increased and Sellers yearly became more numerous on that Market, the necessity for a common meeting point for the consummation of mutual transactions became more and more urgent. The Telegraph made its advent, and became a practical utility in transmission of news and intelligence respecting anything in connection with the Cotton Trade. Railroad lines were continually being extended, and new ones coming into existence. As agencies for moving cotton, they were actively coming into competition with Steamboat lines and fast replacing them in the rapid movement of freight.

The Civil War. The four years of civil strife so affected the Cotton industry as to practically destroy the production of cotton for the time being.

The South, knowing the commercial importance of Cotton, rapidly increased its cultivation after peace terms were declared; and succeeding that serious struggle, the development is well described in the following excerpt:

Mr. Arthur R. Marsh, ex-Vice President of the New York Cotton Exchange, in his speech before the National Association of Cotton Manufacturers at Washington, D. C., on October 4, 1907, said in part:

Before the Civil War the cotton business in New York was simply one form of the old-fashioned commission business, exactly like the business of handling molasses, sugar, hides, wool, country produce, and many other similar agricultural commodities.

*   *   *   *   *   *   *   *   *   *   *   *   *   *

The Civil War completely upset the regular conduct of the cotton business in New York, as just described. While it lasted there were, of course, no regular shipments of cotton to New York from the South, and the only source of supply consisted of lots of cotton which the Government from time to time got hold of through the capture of blockade runners or through confiscation in the South. Naturally, such lots of cotton could not be handled on a commission basis, but had to be bought outright as a speculation. The huge profit made by some of those who bought this Government cotton was the real beginning of general speculation in cotton in this country. And the same thing happened across the water, in Liverpool. The fierce demand and the uncertain and inadequate supply gave opportunity for vast and sudden profits, such as have never been seen before or since in connection with any commodity. And, curiously enough, it was out of this wild speculation of the time of the Civil War that the entire modern method of handling the cotton business was evolved; for, in their eagerness to get hold of cotton, speculators began to buy not only actual cotton on the spot in New York or Liverpool, but "cotton to arrive," when they got wind of a lot of cotton on some ship destined for one or the other of those ports. Here was the beginning of the system of trading in cotton futures, which has gradually revolutionized the whole cotton business in every root and branch, for certain very clever men, whose business was that of cotton merchants and not speculators, saw a way to make use of the extensive trading in contracts for "cotton to arrive" as a protection to themselves in their legitimate buying and selling actual cotton.

It was two or three years after the Civil War that this new conception of the cotton business took shape in the mind of one of the most brilliant cotton merchants the world has ever known, the late Mr. John Rew, of Liverpool, whose firm is still in existence. In 1868 or 1869 Mr. Rew saw that the newly laid Atlantic Cable made it possible for a cotton merchant in Liverpool to ascertain with unheard of quickness the price at which actual cotton could be bought in the Southern States, and the approximate date at which it could be shipped to England. He saw also that if the price that was being bid in Liverpool for "cotton to arrive" was high enough to enable him to buy the cotton in the South and sell contracts for this same "cotton to arrive" in Liverpool, two or three months later, he could enter into the transaction with entire safety, as when his cotton reached Liverpool he could either deliver it to the parties to whom he had sold the Contract, or if some Spinner was willing to pay a higher relative price than the holder of the contracts had agreed to pay, he could back his Contracts and sell the cotton to the Spinner with the larger profit to himself.

The success attained by Mr. Rew in his new departure for buying and selling actual cotton to arrive at some future date connected the "Spot" and "Future" business in such a systematic way as to induce others to enter the field to operate in a similar manner.

In connection with what has been written relative to marketing cotton in the South before the War, in the preceding pages with the operations of Mr. Rew and other able Cotton Merchants following in a like manner, the necessity for the stablishing of the New York and New Orleans Cotton Exchanges became apparent to all leading cotton operators.

After the laying of the Atlantic Cable in 1866 as a successful enterprise, the means of trans-Atlantic communication so facilitated transactions in Spot Cotton for *future delivery*, that by 1868 this form of cotton business constituted a large per cent of the aggregate in Export Cotton.

SECTION II.

NEW YORK COTTON EXCHANGE.[4]

Origin of the New York Cotton Exchange and Its Functions.—The immense volume of business accumulating in the Port of New York constantly increased in the same ratio as cotton production grew in the South, and created an absolute necessity for a *place* and some form of *rules* or regulations where and by which the local Export Trade could be systematically and rapidly handled, which fact led to the organization of the New York Cotton Exchange, briefly stated.

It became an incorporated institution under the laws of New York in April, 1871.

Its purposes were and are, as set out in Sec. 3, of its Charter:

---

[4]The membership is limited to 450 members; applicants "for membership must be of good character and financial standing" and over 21 years of age. Initiation fee $1000. The annual dues are made by the Board of Managers, subject to ratification by the Exchange, and are seemingly not constant.

Membership rights are sold "at the Exchange room" to the highest bidder after being posted on the Exchange bulletin for ten days. Any member may purchase the "right of Membership" from another member. A membership often sells for thousands of dollars.

Rules N. Y. Cotton Exchange, Ed. 1910.

The purposes of said corporation shall be to provide, regulate and maintain a suitable building, room or rooms, for a Cotton Exchange, in the City of New York, to adjust controversies between its members, to establish just and equitable principles in the trade, to maintain uniformity in its rules, regulations and usages, to adopt standards of classification, to acquire, preserve and disseminate useful information connected with the cotton interest throughout all Markets, to decrease the local risks attendant upon the business, and generally to promote the cotton trade of the City of New York, etc.

While the New York Cotton Exchange[5] is a corporation to exercise the broad purposes stated in the preceding, let it be stated it does not buy and sell cotton as a corporate body, but such functions are left to the individuals composing the membership, who exercise this prerogative in their own individual capacity, governed by the Rules of the Exchange in all their transactions. Neither does it deal in Contracts calling for future delivery of cotton, but like those for the purchase and sale of Spots, the *members* only execute such trades.

For the reason previously given and the purposes intended, the primary and one of the greatest functions of this Cotton Exchange was the bringing together of Buyer and Seller, or their representatives. The advantages of this facility alone was an important one.

Membership.—The membership is composed of leading cotton men, among whom are Cotton Manufacturers, Growers, Exporters and Dealers, who buy and sell both Spots and Futures. The records do not seem to bear out the idea that the whole membership ever acted as a unit in *bearing* or *bulling* the Market.

Diversity of opinion exists with them, as with the public, respecting the future course of the Market. A member, or many of them, may entertain the idea that conditions warrant an advance in price; while others, similarly situated, believe it will decline. This diversity of sentiment is a factor inducing declines or a cause for advances.

When by force of numerical strength or an excess in

---

[5]See "The First Cotton Exchange," page 302.

capitalization, the Market is carried this way or that, it is said to be a "manipulated Market."

There is nothing in the Rules to prevent two or more members from operating together, so long as they violate none of the stipulations, and if they operate with sufficient capital and prestige, where conditions are favorable, they can carry the prices up or down as suits their convenience. If they are advanced, the fluctuation is said to be the result of a "bull movement;" if the Market is arbitrarily thrown down, a "bear raid" has taken place.

If illegitimate practices are resorted to, to carry out questionable undertakings, not only the Rules of the Exchange are violated, but the laws of our country as well. The punishment for infracting the Exchange Rules has varying degrees, limited to expulsion as the greatest. That measured by our public laws is governed by the character, nature and extent of the violation.

Among its membership are found leading capitalists and cotton men in many of the largest commercial centers in different parts of the world.

Its wires lead out to all Cotton Exchanges and Boards of Trade and reach all points on the globe where cotton is bought, sold or manufactured. Through such an extensive ramification as a source from which information can be drawn, its facilities for ascertaining data respecting the cotton Trade are unexcelled. Through such a medium, it is enabled at all times to know the demand for cotton or the absence of it; the condition of the growing crop; the daily receipts in all the Southern Markets at gathering time and the number of bales exported; the output of the Mills everywhere; the extent of strikes or political disturbances that affect the cotton interest; in fact, it is enabled momentarily to form an intelligent opinion upon which to base a price commensurate with conditions.

Prices bid and received for cotton on the Exchange are

for those to be embodied in a Contract.[6]   All trades made on the floor of the Exchange are for *Contracts* calling for future delivery of cotton.   The prices for Futures are governed by the demand for them, or may be fictitious if arbitrarily fixed.

Patrons of the Exchange often state to their Brokers what price they are willing to pay for a "May" or "July" or any month they desire to purchase, or will ask that sales be made at stipulated prices.   Where Brokers are not given definite figures at which to buy or sell, they are usually instructed to use their judgment in executing orders, or perhaps, the orders may be transmitted to them with no instructions beyond that of to buy or sell.

Where orders are received extensively or in large volume to buy, the demand is said to be good, and prices go up; conversely the opposite obtains when orders to sell are voluminous.

Since the introduction of the Through Bill-of-Lading enabling Buyers of Spot Cotton to get their requirements at interior Southern points, there no longer exists any necessity for Buyers and Sellers of Spot Cotton meeting personally on the floor of the Exchange for purposes of making direct transactions with each other, as purchases of raw material are bought from Cotton Merchants in the South and shipped direct from them to destination, leaving New York out entirely in the shipments, hence that Exchange does not fill the primary purpose of bringing Buyers and Sellers together as formerly for transactions in Spot Cotton.   Its functions for executing Contracts in Futures for delivery of Spot Cotton on them, Hedging or Speculation, remain undisturbed.

This Exchange has adopted the U. S. Standard of classification.[7]

---

[6]See "Contract" and "Cotton Futures," p. 109.
[7]See Appendix.

NEW ORLEANS COTTON EXCHANGE.[8]

This Exchange operates in a similar manner to the New York Exchange, and for a like purpose. It is the only Exchange in the United States dealing in Future Contracts outside of New York.

Through the wires, it is in close touch with New York, Liverpool, Bremen and Havre, and reaches to every commercial center in the world, where cotton is handled.

Purposes.—Its purposes are so nearly similar to those of the New York Cotton Exchange as to require no specific statement covering them separately.

Being a Southern Market, it comes nearer filling the primary functions of an Exchange than the one located at New York, by bringing together both Buyers and Sellers of Spot Cotton. As a Spot Market, it ranks with the largest in the world, and commands exceptional facilities for handling cotton to the greatest advantage for all interests connected with the Trade.

Its members deal in both Spot and Future Cotton; some in Futures exclusively, and others in Spots only, or handle commitments on Commission.

It is not connected with any other Cotton Exchange in a co-operative way, being controlled solely by its own Rules.

The New York and New Orleans Cotton Exchanges are chartered institutions, entirely independent in their relationship, and trading in Futures on either Exchange is not controlled by any stipulated agreement between them. It was chartered in May 1873.

The prices recorded in New York or Liverpool have a significant influence in determining trade quotations on the New Orleans Cotton Exchange. If Liverpool is higher,

---

[8]"All persons legally of age and of good character and commercial standing" may be elected members of the Association.

The iniation fee is $200; annual dues $100. The number admitted to membership is not stated.

By-Laws and Rules N. O. Cot. Ex. pp. 12 and 13, Ed. 1909.

it reflects a buying power or stimulus there; if New York is lower, it indicates a selling influence is in the ascendency with it, and so on. If New York and Liverpool show higher Markets, buying orders will drift into New Orleans for the purchase of cheaper cotton, but such stimulation soon brings it to parity with the others.

Should New Orleans make an important move, the Trade in the North and abroad is likely to consider it, with reflective emphasis on their own prices.

As a factor influential in bringing the control of the American cotton crops and their prices into the hands of the American Trade, New Orlean's power and prestige can not be questioned, and in connection with New York, they often take the lead, and Liverpool *follows,* in directing Trade.

In the preceding brief description of the purposes and operations of the New York and New Orleans Cotton Exchanges, the author has dealt with what are assumed to be the legitimate functions and purposes of a Cotton Exchange, and the advantages offered by it in the protection of the industry and increased facilities presented for commercializing every bale grown, in the most economical manner.

Cotton Exchanges, as factors beneficial to the Trade, honestly and legitimately managed, are agencies indispensable for successfully handling cotton.

The Exchanges cannot eliminate the human in its membership, it can not weigh the conscience, or measure the integrity of purpose of a single individual. "The trail of the serpent is over them all;" but its Rules are made as a standard of the principles desired to govern. No doubt there are members among them who would not hesitate to utilize any scheme over which they could possibly have influence to direct Trading in a line that would most effectually result to their own personal gain. This assumption is based on the broad idea that there is found in all organizations, whether financial, fraternal or religious, unfit material for membership, and the conclusion is not inappropriately applied to the Cotton Exchanges.

Not all disparities are manipulated ones. Where demand is light in New York, at the same moment good at New Orleans, the feelings respecting Trading on the two Exchanges are quite opposite; concessions might be offered in New York to secure business, while stiffened prices would prevail in New Orleans. The difference in sentiment in the two places would at the time put prices out of harmony, as between the two cities.

What is said concerning the differences of opinion and Market quotations between the two mentioned Exchanges will apply with equal force to Foreign and Domestic Markets.

This Exchange has adopted the United States Government Standard Classification.

OTHER EXCHANGES.

There are Cotton Exchanges in Galveston, Houston, San Antonio, Waco, Dallas, Ft. Worth, Little Rock, Memphis, Vicksburg, St. Louis, Augusta, Savannah, Shreveport, Portsmouth, Norfolk and Mobile, established for the convenience of members and the Cotton Trade, but not for purposes of Future Trading.

The principal Cotton Exchanges abroad, are the Liverpool Cotton Association, the Havre Bourse and the Bremen Cotton Exchange. Liverpool and Bremen are the only two operating in the purchase and sale of Futures extensively, principally for the Hedging features offered. A limited Future business is done in Havre. Until recently, Bremen was precluded from dealing in Futures. Liverpool is the leading Foreign Future Market.

COTTON FUTURES.

Buying and selling "cotton futures" constitutes the prime business of the Cotton Exchanges.   Only the members buy and sell.

New York and New Orleans Cotton Exchanges are the only two in America that deal in "Futures."   Liverpool is the principal "Future" Market of Europe.

Dealing in "Futures," means dealing in *"Future Contracts,"* calling for delivery of cotton on them at some *future time.*

Future Contracts are   executed   for three   specific   purposes, namely:

FOR DELIVERY OF SPOT COTTON ON THEM.

FOR HEDGING.

FOR SPECULATION.

All Future Contracts contemplate actual delivery of Spot Cotton as the following forms state, and amended to conform to the United States Cotton Futures Act, Section 5.

NEW YORK COTTON EXCHANGE.

CONTRACT.

The Contract Form, as thus amended, reads as follows:

"In consideration of one dollar in hand paid, receipt of which is hereby acknowledged, ...have this day Sold to (or Bought from) .... 50,000 lbs. in about 100 square bales of Cotton, growth of the United States, deliverable from licensed warehouse, in the Port of New York, between the first and last days of..........................next, inclusive.   The delivery within such time to be at Seller's option in one warehouse, upon notice to Buyer, as provided by the By-Laws and Rules of the New York Cotton Exchange. The Cotton to be of any grade from Good Ordinary to Middling Fair inclusive, and if Tinged, not below Low Middling Tinged, or if Stained. not below Middling Stained (New York Cotton Exchange inspection and classification, subject to the United Stats Cotton Futures Act,

Section 5) at the price of..................cents per pound for Middling, with additions or deductions for other grades, according to the rates of the New York Cotton Exchange existing on the day previous to the date of the transferable notice of delivery.

"Either party to have the right to call for a margin, as the variations of the Market for like deliveries may warrant, and which margin shall be kept good. This Contract is made in view of, and in all respects subject to the By-Laws, Rules and conditions established by the New York Cotton Exchange, and in full accordance with Sections 113 and 114 of the By-Laws, and subject to the United States Cotton Futures Act, Section 5."[9]

CONTRACT.

New Orleans,...19........

In consideration of one dollar in hand paid, receipt of which is hereby acknowledged...of the City of New Orleans, State of Louisiana, have this day Sold to (or Bought from) ....of the City of New Orleans, State of Louisiana, 50,000 pounds, in about 100 square bales of cotton, growth of the United States, deliverable from approved storage places for cotton in the Port of New Orleans between the first and last days of ....next, inclusive.

The delivery within such time to be at Seller's option in not more than two approved storage places upon notice to the Buyer, as provided by the By-Laws and Rules of the New Orleans Cotton Exchange.

The cotton to be of or within the grades from Good Ordinary to Middling Fair, inclusive, and if Tinged, not below the grade of Low Middling, or, if stained, not below the grade of Middling, New Orleans Cotton Exchange inspection and classification (subject to the United States Cotton Futures Act, Section 5) at the price of...........................cents per pound for Middling, with additions or deductions for other grades, according to the quotations of the New Orleans Cotton Exchange, existing on the sixth business day previous to the day fixed for delivery.

Either party to have the right to call for a margin as the variations of the Market for like deliveries may warrant and which Margin shall be kept good. This Contract[10] is made in view of and in all respects subject to the By-Laws, Rules and Conditions established by the New Orleans Cotton Exchange and in full accordance with Rule 50 of the New Orleans Cotton Exchange.

Signed...

---

[9]N. Y. Cot. Ex. Contract. Amendment No. 6.
[10]N. O. Cot. Ex. Contract, By-Laws 1909, p. 56.

DELIVERY OF SPOT COTTON.

Delivery of Spot Cotton on *Future Contracts* is carried out in all instances under the Rules of the Cotton Exchanges.

Such deliveries are not made except it be to the financial advantage to the holder of the Contract, or under certain conditions otherwise.

The cotton must be delivered at the point stated in the Contract. If bought or sold in New Orleans, it must be delivered there; if in New York, deliveries go there.

Time.—A Contract calls for the delivery of the cotton in a certain month, and the *Seller* has the *whole* month named to make the delivery in, designating any day of the month, and must give to the Buyer a written notice of the specific date on which he will deliver the cotton called for in the Contract. All cotton delivered on Contracts from the three Cotton Exchanges require respectively, in New York three days, in New Orleans five days, and in Liverpool ten days notice, before delivery. These are termed "Notice Days." Liverpool Contracts usually give the Seller *two months* time in which to make deliveries, and he may offer it any time during those months. Contracts are sometimes made restricting the delivery to one month, in which case it must be made in that month.

The least amount contracted for in New York and New Orleans is for the 100 bales, 50,000 pounds *gross weight*, and for Liverpool not less than 48,000 pounds *net weight*.

Price.—The price at which the cotton is bought or sold, is *based on Middling*, with additions and deductions for the Higher or Lower Grades, which are regulated by the *Rules of the Cotton Exchanges* fixing them.

The basis for the Liverpool Contract is also *Middling*, but the Premiums and Discounts for the relative Grades are made by *Arbitration*.

The *Seller* has the option of delivering any Grades prescribed in the Contract which range from Good Ordinary

(White) to Fair, inclusive, and if colored, (in New York), not below Middling Stained or Low Middling Tinged, and nothing below Middling Stained in New Orleans.)

No calculations for "Future" cotton are made in New York or New Orleans for a less decimal than 1 "Point" (One one hundredth —1/100, of a cent) and in Liverpool, for not less than two-one hundredths (2/100) of a penny.

· The time of delivery and the number of Grades being uncertain operates with such force against the Future Contract as to keep it, generally, below the price of Spot Cotton for immediate delivery.

Both parties to a Future Contract can exact a deposit from each other, to be placed in bank for such amounts as the variations of the Market from time to time might warrant, as a "Margin" to protect the Trade.

This "Margin" varies from one to five dollars a bale, governed by the standing and character of the individual and the condition of the Market. When fluctuations are frequent and excessive, the "original margin" may be more than five dollars.

Cotton delivered on Future Contracts in New Orleans and Liverpool is inspected, classed and weighed each time it changes ownership. When cotton has been inspected, classed and weighed under the auspices of the New York Cotton Exchange, this answers for that and all subsequent deliveries for the 12 months following.

Salaried officials classify the cotton delivered, bale by bale, and issue certificates certifying to the Grades, Marks, Lot Numbers, Weights, etc. These certificates are negotiable.

The method of procedure of delivering cotton on future Contracts in New York is as follows: The Seller sends to the Buyer a notice stating the day on which he proposes to deliver the cotton, three or more days before the time. If this buyer has sold to some one else, he endorses the "notice" over to the one to whom he sold, who, to illustrate, accepts the cotton, receiving it on the day named, and pays for it at the price named in the transferrable order, which must be within ¼ cent a pound of the market price of spot cotton quoted by the Cotton Exchange on the day before issuing the order. "He settles for the cotton with the party who issued the order, and if the price is less than his Contract, he pays to the other party to his Contract the difference. If the price he has to pay for the cotton according to the transferrable order is more than the price in his Contract, then the other party to the Contract sends him with the transferable order a check for the difference between the Contract price and the price named in the transferable order."[11]

This is the method of settling Contracts by receiving from, or paying differences to, each other, and shows that they may change hands many times before final delivery of cotton on them.

All Dealers mediating between the party who issues the notice of delivery and the one who receives the cotton, settle with each other the difference between their respective Contracts and the price of the transferable order upon which the cotton is finally received and paid for.

The *optional feature* of the Cotton Exchange Contract is well illustrated in the foregoing. The first party who *bought* the cotton, had the *option* (right) to transfer it to some one else, and he in turn to another, and so on until delivery day, when the last holder of the Contract had to take the cotton, but had the *option* under the Rules to settle with the party delivering, by mutual agreement with him, should he desire it, until after the final hour (3 P. M.) of the last day, when the cotton must be received and paid for, as the Contract is not allowed to circulate any further.

<hr>

[11]From "Cotton Futures" (Shepperson), p. 11.

HEDGING.

A Hedge is a Contract that a Cotton Buyer buys or sells to protect himself from loss by fluctuations in the Market.

For Hedging Spot Cotton, the Future Contract offers facilities not found elsewhere, and to be of full value, the price of "Futures" for the hedge month, should be practically on parity with that of Spot Cotton. The price of the "Future" is for Middling, and to get a comparative value to it the same Grade for Spots should be considered.

Owing to the constant variations in the price of Futures, the parity is never stable at one thing, and the wider the fluctuation, the greater the disparity.

Hedges are impaired by a change in prices of relative Grades. The price of Middling may remain unchanged, but when the Premiums on the Higher or the Discounts on the Lower Grades are altered, the Contract suffers.

When the prices of Middling Futures are moving in unison with that of Spot Middling, the Hedging protection affords an insurance safeguard to the Dealer in Spot Cotton.

Hedges are operative in two ways, designated as *Buying* and *Selling* Hedges, which are conducive to protection from losses under certain conditions, and reflect results in opposite directions.

The Buying Hedge is issued to protect a *sale* of Spot Cotton for *future delivery*.

Let it be assumed that in August a Cotton Merchant has an inquiry from a Mill for 500 bales of cotton for delivery in January. To get a price for this future delivery, the Merchant will add a number of points on the January price to cover expenses of handling and a profit for himself. Say the Exchange quotation for January is 12 cents, and the merchant, estimating that 50 points will pay all expenses for handling and give him the desired profit, offers to deliver to the Mill the 500 bales at 12.50 in January. If the Mill accepts this price, the Merchant at once *buys* 500 bales of January *Futures,* and *protects* his forward *sale* of January Spot Cotton.

The Merchant does not know what the price of cotton will be in January, and does not wish to assume any risk in contracting to deliver it at that time. To obviate this risk, he buys the Contract stated.

If in January Spot Cotton is worth 12 cents for Middling, the Merchant buys it in the open market at that figure, and ships it to the Mill at 12.50 cents, the price called for in the Trade. It should be remembered, Mills buy cotton delivered to them, and the presumption is, in the illustration, the Merchant was not far distant from the Mill, and the 50 points "on" covered the charges for freight, insurance, etc., with his profit included.

After buying the Spot Cotton, he sells his Future Contract, and both transactions, that with the Mill and that with the Cotton Exchange, are closed.

Assuming further, that in January, Spot Cotton is worth 15 cents for Middling, the Merchant must go into the open Market and pay that price for it and deliver to the Mill at 12½ cents. It is obvious he will lose 2½ cents a pound, or $12.50 on each 500-pound bale so contracted. But while he sold his "Spots" at a *loss,* his gain on his *Futures* has equalled the loss on Spots, and if the parity has not been disturbed, the ownership of the *"Futures"*[12] for 500 bales has been a protection, and in this instance, a complete Hedge.

If at delivery time, cotton had dropped to 10 cents a pound, the Merchant would pay that price for it and deliver to the Mill at 12½ cents, as agreed. His *gain* in this purchase would be $12.50 a bale on *Spot Cotton,* and if *futures* had declined in harmony with it, the parity still existing between "Spots" and "Futures," would make the Hedge complete, for the *loss* on the Exchange Contract would balance the *gain* on his Spot Cotton.

---

[12]Contracts calling for delivery of cotton at a future date.

If in January Spots had gone to 13½ cents and Futures bought at 12 cents would decline 2½ cents a pound if Spots had shown the same fluctuation at the moment; but as a fact Spots and Futures do not always move in such harmony, but often to the contrary.

If in January Spots had gone to 12½ cents and Futures to 14, this inequality (disparity) between the two would give an additional profit to the Merchant, as he would buy his Spot Cotton at 13½ cents, deliver it to the Mill at 12½ cents, and lose in the Spot transaction, 1 cent a pound— $5.00 a bale—or a total of $2,500, but as an offset, he would sell his Future at 14 cents, on which he would realize a profit of 2 cents a pound—$10 a bale—or a total gain of $5,000, leaving a net profit of $2,500 on the two deals.

Were the movement in prices to Show January Spots at 12.60 and Futures 11.50, a resulting settlement would show the entire absence of the hedging function, or its protecting influence absolutely destroyed.

The Merchant would be compelled to deliver the cotton to the Mill at 12.50 for which he would pay 12.60, resulting in a loss of 50 cents a bale, and sell his Futures for 11.50, which cost him 12 cents, inflicting another loss of $2.50 a bale or a total loss of $1,500 on both transactions.

A divergence of parities may cause double losses or double gains, or the absence of any gain or loss.

When the price of Futures moves in harmony with Spots, the ownership of a Future Contract gives a protection to the Spot Trade, and gives the Hedge wanted.

A *Selling Hedge* has for its purpose the same consideration as a Buying Hedge, but operates reversely to it in actual practice, being assumed to give protection to *cotton in hand* or that being accumulated.

Let it be stated that a Dealer or Merchant has 500 bales of cotton purchased, or that cotton is being offered to him faster than he can profitably sell it. Knowing the instability of the Market, and fearing a decline may appear at any moment and cause a loss, he seeks protection through the Hedge.

Usually the hedge is not sought unless the Dealer is paying full quotation prices for the cotton and the Market shows some tendency to weaken. If it is firm and advancing, the average Dealer will not sell against it, as the advance protects it so long as it lasts.

A Merchant having in his possession 500 bales of cotton which cost him 10 cents, finding he can not sell it for the purchase price, and thinking the Market will advance in the future, yet not wishing to risk a loss from a decline, *sells*, say in September, 500 bales of January Futures to *protect* his Spot Cotton on hand. Estimating it will require 50 points to cover the expense incidental to this sale, he sells the Contracts for $10\frac{1}{2}$ cents.

If later the price of Spot Cotton advances to 11 cents, and Futures for the same month are on parity with it, the Spot Cotton has received protection wanted, by reason of the Spot advance and the gain of 1 cent on Spots has been offset by a loss of 1 cent advance in Futures.

The Futures were sold for $10\frac{1}{2}$ cents, which will cost $11\frac{1}{2}$ cents to buy them back entailing a loss of $5.00 a bale, but balanced as stated by a gain of equal amount on the Spots.

Had Futures in January declined to $9\frac{1}{2}$ cents and Spots followed to 9 cents, a *loss* of 1 cent on Spots would be offset by a *gain* on Futures. The Future Contract was sold for $10\frac{1}{2}$ cents and can be bought in return, for $9\frac{1}{2}$ cents, leaving a gain of 1 cent on the purchase.

These two statements represent the two transactions as showing in both instances that Spot Middling Cotton has moved in harmony or on parity with Futures.

As described in a Buying Hedge, where Spots and Futures are out of line with each other, losses or gains can follow, and the *hedging function is destroyed when disparity creates a loss.*

The Statements given are based on Middling Spot Cotton harmonizing with futures of the same Grade, with the exception noted. Mills do not buy basic Grades,[13] but Merchants selling to them on specific or even-running Grades, protect their Trade by hedging with *Basic Contracts,* and *risk* the probability of disparities occurring.

Contracts for Speculation may be settled as if bought or sold for actual delivery or receipt of cotton on them or for Hedging.

In its daily business, a majority of the Contracts executed on the Cotton Exchange are settled before the month of their maturity and without actual delivery of cotton on them, and in this manner, a 100-bale contract may change hands many times, the aggregate of which often reaches 3000 bales, and can be settled for by "direct settlements" or "ring settlements."

If a Broker *sells* for a client a Future Contract, and afterwards *buys* for another a similar one, both calling for delivery in the same month, and if both were made with the same member of the Exchange, a direct settlement would be made as between the two members of that institution, for the purchase of the one would offset the sale of the other.

If a Broker sells 100 bales of cotton to A, and A sells it to B, and B sells to C, and C sells to A, all the sales being for the same month, it is obvious the trades have gone from A and returned to him, or have made a "Ring" in their circuit, and all parties to these transactions ascertaining this fact, can very appropriately settle with each other, by each sale offsetting each purchase, each accepting his loss or gain as the exchange of Contracts might indicate.

Such settlements are termed "ring settlements," and frequently a dozen or more members may be directly interested in them.

Each member of a Cotton Exchange buying or selling Contracts for another is morally and legally bound to guar-

---

[13] See Mill Buying, p. 241.

antee the settlement of the Contract according to its terms, but may make "direct" or "ring settlement," if conditions justify it, as prescribed under the Rules.

Rule 8, Sec. A. All Contracts for future delivery of cotton shall be binding upon members, and of full force and effect, until the quantity and qualities of cotton specified in such Contracts shall have been delivered, and the price specified in said Contracts shall have been paid. Nor shall any Contract be entered into with any stipulation or understanding between the parties, at the time of making such Contract, that the terms of such Contract as specified in Section 37 of the By-Laws are not to be fulfilled, and the cotton delivered and received in accordance with said Section.[14]

Should a Merchant send $100 to B, a member of the New York Cotton Exchange, for the purchase of 100 bales of cotton (Contract) in March for July delivery, and he buys it from C, another member, then B, under the Rules, stands as the guarantor to C for the fulfillment of the Contract. In order that B may be protected against loss, he requires the Merchant to pay him the $100 as a *Margin*, and holds the Merchant primarily responsible for the final settlement of the Contract according to its terms; but should the Market decline 17 points, B will settle with C, and close the transaction.

A Speculator operating for the gains he expects to make, and advancing $100 as a margin, is given the *option* to re-margin (pay another $100) should the Market decline 17 points, and should he fail to pay, the Contract is sold. A 20 point decline equals the amount of the Speculator's marginal payment, which is equivalent to a loss of $100.

Charges.—No Contracts are dealt in for less than 100 bales, nor any charge for Margin less than $100. A Customer whose financial rating and moral standing are high, can have transactions on the Exchanges executed without an actual prepayment for margins, but when not so rated, a prepayment must accompany the order.

The Commission is 3 points, 15 cents a bale, equivalent

---

[14]Constitution and By-Laws N. Y. Cot. Ex., Ed. 1910, p. 104.

to $15 on 100 bales, the practice being to charge $7.50 to buy and the same amount to sell a Contract, or $15 for the "round turn."

When the price declines 17 points, it is then within 3 points of exhausting the margin, and if a client is not well rated or does not re-margin, the Contract is closed at this point of decline as stated, with a sufficient reserved amount held to pay the brokerage.[15]

Members buying and selling for each other, under the Rules, can do so on a commission of $7.50 for the "round turn."

The same charges are made for each transfer of Contract from one month to another, as for original purchase or sale.

The payment of a Commission to secure the Contracts, and the Margins to protect them is quite an expense to those engaged in handling Spot Cotton, whether for hedging or for delivery of cotton on them, which fact precludes thousands of small Buyers from connecting a Future Business with that of Spot Cotton in which they deal.

Prices.—There must be something to determine the price of cotton either for Spot or for Future, and to get at the gist of it many things are and can be considered, that have direct and remote bearing on the subject.

A large or reduced acreage; late or early planting; favorable or unfavorable growing season; extended drouths or excessive and continued rainfalls; insect or worm depredation; and exorbitant, moderate, or light demand for raw cotton; financial depressions and disturbances; problematical political confusions in foreign countries; such are among the most prominent factors that may be considered as affecting the price-making feature of the cotton industry.

---

[15]Amended charges on N. Y. Cot. Ex. are $10 per 100 bales, $20 for "round turn" to non-members, and $5.00 for members, or $10 for round transaction.

The primary source from which we get our guidance is the Cotton Exchanges, and Brokers operating on them must consider some of the factors mentioned in determining what prices to make for cotton bought or sold. They are governed in offering to buy or sell Contracts by the prices their customers make for them in many instances, but if no price accompany the orders and they are not restricted as to limitation of them, then the Brokers exercise their own judgment to do the best they can for their customers.

Not only has he to consider the factors mentioned, but he has to consider also the showing of the other Markets, such as New York (if he is a New Orleans Broker), Liverpool, Bremen, etc., the general tendency, speculative feeling, other news at hand that can be construed as guiding factors, in fact, any and every thing that can change or influence trading has its weight, but not to the exclusion of supply and demand for Contracts.

SPECULATION.

A large percentage of the business transacted on the Cotton Exchanges is purely speculative in character, and possesses the features of gambling clearly defined.[16]

This form of speculation in Future Contracts displays the same characteristics as that of a Spot Merchant, who invests haphazard in Spot Cotton, knowing when he buys cotton "for a rise" he gains on the purchase, but if he sells it on a decline, a loss follows.

Those who invest in Cotton Contracts for the specific purpose of making gains in their purchases or sales, know at the time they invest, that if the Market goes up on purchases, they win; if it goes down on sales, they win, but if the opposite takes place in the Market, they lose.

Speculators dealing in Cotton Contracts are privileged

---

[16]See Bucket Shops, p. 321.

with the same options as a Merchant hedging or contemplating delivery or receipt of cotton on them. He can buy or sell at any time; exchange one month for another. If he has a July Contract, he can take up August or December, or any month in place of it if he thinks it will prove profitable.

Added strength is often given to the Market by extensive operations of Speculators therein, or their efforts may impair it. Extensive buying gives stimulus to the Trade, and conversely, large and continued sales weaken it.

The Speculator is governed by conditions affecting Trade similarly to others operating on the Board for different purposes; buying Contracts when the probability for advances seems good, or selling them when declines are indicated. He invests his money with the expectation of winning, knowing there is an attendant risk attached that may involve him in a loss, but deliberates over the fact that there is only *one chance* against him; meaning, there is one chance to win, where an equal probability to lose exists. His speculations are gambling transactions—nothing more, nothing less.

Futures, showing fixed prices for each month, are quoted daily, but these prices for the day usually change in value one way or the other, each succeeding day, and are referred to as "July Contracts," "August Contracts," or in the expression of the Trade, as, "Julys," or "Augusts."

Speculators dealing in Contracts know these fluctuations occur, and buy or sell as indications may warrant a purchase or sale, taking whichever form of contract that seems to show the best indication for a profit.

The Future Contracts admitting the delivery of a variety of Grades on them, and the Buyer not knowing what they will be, is influenced to bid under the Spot Middling price when buying. This naturally causes a Discount from the Spot Quotations, which under normal conditions would range from 15 to 25 points, that is to say, if the price for

Middling Spot Cotton in August is 12 cents, the price of an August Future Contract would be 11 or 11.85 cents. As previously stated, fluctuations often vary widely from these figures, and in exceptional or panicky times, Futures may go to the extreme of 100 or more points above Spots.

An excessive demand for the purchase of Contracts stimulates prices and encourages trading, evidencing also a good demand for Spot Cotton from the Trade and the Mills. Merchants selling to Mills buy Contracts from the Exchanges to protect their sales. Such stimulations are usually backed by orders for Spots, in connection with a desire to purchase.

A light demand for Contracts has its influence on trading, and conduces to lower prices.

A Broker offering to sell Contracts at a stipulated price, if he finds no Buyer, must come down to meet the demand. Conversely, if a Buyer finds no Seller at his bid, he must bid up until he meets the supply or gets an acceptance.

So far as a literal transaction is concerned, there is no difference in the theory of a trade in Future Contracts as a commodity for sale and purchase from that exhibited in the transference of cotton bales from one to another by similar procedure.

Legitimate and Illegitimate Contracts are said to emanate from the Cotton Exchanges, to distinguish between which is at times difficult.

Contracts calling for delivery or receipt of cotton on them, are recognized as *legitimate*. The same conclusion is held by many as applying to Contracts dealt in for hedging purposes, while those bought or sold for *Speculation* are construed as being *illegitimate*.

Merchants familiar with the operations of the Cotton Exchanges and accustomed to handling cotton in large quantities annually, protect a large percentage of their Spot transactions by seeking shelter from fluctuations under the Hedge.

Contingencies occasionally arise resulting in wide disparities between Spots and Futures, as when the cotton fields are visited by heavy storms, destroying and damaging exposed cotton in untold quantities. The disparity may then be such that the Merchants find it highly profitable to sell their Contracts and accept the profits they may show rather than retain the Contracts for hedging purposes.

No one knows the coming of the storm; no one knows the contingencies that may arise, nor how the final disposition of the Contract may be made, although primarily accepted for delivery or receipt of cotton on it, or for a Hedge.

If the Contract be bought or sold for receipt or delivery of cotton on it, or for a Hedge, at the outset, it would seem its legitimate functions are not impaired, but if surrendered for a profit with the original intentions abandoned, such fact would clothe it with the attributes of illegitimacy.

It is a reasonable assumption that all Dealers actively engaged in the Cotton Trade will accept the best financial returns obtainable. If surrendering a Contract at a profit is preferrable to retaining it for a Hedge or receipt or delivery of cotton on it, the Dealer will do so, and what at the beginning would appear as showing legitimate functions, might ultimately be transformed into one giving evidence of illegal bearing, hence the difficulty of drawing the line of demarcation between a legitimate and illegitimate Contract at the time of purchase.

It is quite an easy matter to determine what is an illegitimate Contract at time of accepting it, if it be known it is for speculation pure and simple and the operator an acknowledged Speculator; but if as stated, the owner of the Contract does not know himself at time of purchase what final disposition he will make of it, the problem of deciding its character as to its legal status is involved in doubt, neither can it be determined prior to settlement.

SECTION III.

THE FUTURE CONTRACT IN CONNECTION WITH SPOT COTTON.

Contracts for future delivery can be, and are operative for three distinct purposes as stated in the preceding Section.[17] Of the many uses to which they may be applied as a protection or Insurance against Market Fluctuations, the following are the most important:

(a) A Dealer *buys* 1000 bales of Spot Cotton and ships it to Liverpool. He has paid, say, $50,000 for it, and not wishing to take the risk of a decline, *sells* 1000 bales of Futures against his purchase. Should the Market decline while the cotton is in transit, the loss on the Spots will be offset by an equal gain on his Futures.

Were this Dealer to ship his 1000 bales without connecting the shipment with a Future Contract, and should the Market decline, a loss to him would inevitably follow. Conversely, were the Market to advance, and had the shipment been made to be sold after delivery, a gain would be to his credit.

(b) A large Planter in the South having a fine crop of cotton growing in his fields in August, and being satisfied with December Futures, wires a New York Broker to *sell* 500 bales of cotton deliverable in December. In this way he hedges his crop—he sells it at a definite price, that is, he *knows* in August just what he will get for his cotton in December. Just as in the preceding described under "a," so far as fluctuations are concerned, the Planter knows that a decline in the Market will cause a loss on his Spot Cotton but an equal gain on Futures, and *vice versa.*

(c) A Buyer in the South has 500 bales of cotton on hand which has cost him an average of 10c a pound. He believes the price will ultimately be higher, but indications are

---

[17]Cotton Futures, Book II, p. 107.

pronounced for an immediate decline. He can not sell the cotton for cost, and fearing a further decline, *sells* 500 bales of Futures and protects himself.

(*d*) A Merchant in the South who has supplied his customers throughout the year with both family supplies and money, begins to receive cotton from them rapidly in the fall on their accounts. Not wishing to sell for prices then prevailing, and fearing a decline will continue, he telegraphs to a New York Broker to *sell* a number of bales to cover an amount equivalent to his anticipated purchases, and fortifies himself and customers against any further decline.

(*e*) An Exporter who annually sends large amounts of cotton to Europe, makes sales of Contracts covering the quantity he contemplates buying, *before* he buys the cotton. Knowing approximately the stocks of cotton at the various Southern points where accumulated, the amount afloat, the size and location of stocks in foreign countries, the price for Spots and Futures in domestic and foreign Markets at the time, the Broker is enabled to calculate with some degree of accuracy at what price he can deliver in Manchester, Havre or Bremen, three, four or five months afterwards, and through the Hedge prerogative, takes the risk.

(*f*) It is the present policy of Mills to contract their output weeks and sometimes months ahead. Before doing so, they must *know* at what price it can be done. This is obtained by hedging in two ways: (1) Contracting with Spot Dealers financially strong enough to guarantee the delivery of the actual cotton; (2) Purchasing through some Broker cotton Contracts in sufficient amount to cover the quantity of goods sold.

In the first instance, the Mill is hedged through the financial ability of the Dealer to comply with the terms of the Contract, and the transaction is entirely independent of, and in no way connected with, a Cotton Exchange. In the second, the hedging function rests with the member of the

Exchange who executes the Contract, and is held liable for its final settlement.[18]

In many other ways than those described the Contract for future delivery can be brought into play, giving stability to the price of Spot Cotton.

The Student should remember in studying the theory of a Future Contract in connection with the price of Spot Cotton, that for the Hedge to be effectual in insuring a Spot Price, there must always be a *parity* between the price of Spots and Futures. The moment the two separate or converge, just that moment the hedging function is weakened or strengthened.[19]

In the foregoing let it be stated that the hedging, for the purposes shown, required a settlement of those transactions as if they had been made in a trade in Spot Cotton.

When the Dealer named in *"a"* *sold* his actual cotton, he *bought* his Futures through his Broker, by having him *transfer* the Contract to some one else. If the purchase was made at a higher figure than the original sale price, he lost on his future deal; if bought for less, he made a gain. The expense of executing the trades were charged to *"a."*[20] In like manner *"b," "c," "d," "e"* and *"f"* made settlements for their *Futures* when they closed out their Spots, by either buying or selling as the nature of the Contract required.

USEFULNESS OF THE COTTON EXCHANGE.

Through its extensive facilities for obtaining data covering every phase of the cotton industry, the New York Cotton Exchange is enabled to acquaint every member with these facts immediately upon their receipt, and through the instrumentality of the telegraph and telephone, trans-

---

[18] See "Ring Settlement," p. 325.
[19] See "Hedging," p. 321. .
[20] See "Margins," Book II, p. 111.

mit them to every city, town and hamlet where cotton is grown, bought or sold.

These facilities enable the Grower to obtain a local Market at his home at any and all times for his cotton and to know its value any moment in the day; likewise, any Buyer in the remotest part of the world that is reached by the cable or telegraph knows what his cotton will cost him any time he may desire to purchase.

BUYING AND SELLING FUTURES.

Spot Dealers and Mills desiring to protect their purchases of raw material or sales of manufactured goods, unless they are members of an Exchange, must operate through some member, and when their deals are executed, *do not receive the contract*, but instead, a telegram, or a notation on a printed form, stating that the sale or purchase has been made for them by the Broker.

Buying and selling Futures means that "A" enters into a Contract with some Broker to either receive from, or deliver to, him, not less than 100 B/C, of 50,000 lbs. weight, at some future time. If not a member of the Exchange, "A" must deal through a member, who stands as a guarantor for him. Were cotton 10c a pound, the Broker is "A's" protector in the Contract for $5,000.   ·

"A" does not wish to put up $5,000, neither does the Broker, but if "A" will make an advance payment on it of not less than $100, the Broker will guarantee the fulfillment of the Contract for him. If "A" buys a Contract, every Point advance is a profit on it. Should the Market decline on his purchase, every Point decline is a loss to him to that extent.

"A" may be 500 or 1000 miles from his Broker, who may or may not be personally acquainted with him, or he knows nothing of "A's" financial standing, so, to protect himself from loss on the Contract, he requires a small advance payment (Margin) on it from "A," and should the Market decline to a point where the cotton is not worth so much as when the purchase was made, the Broker will demand another Margin of $100 to protect himself as well as "A's" interest.

The foregoing theory or statement applies on any char-- acter of Future Deal, whether for Hedging or Speculation.

No Market can continuously advance without occasional re-actions.

Advances in price quotations always give gains on purchases, which the Broker must pay to "A" if he demands a settlement. Equally true, "A" must pay his money to the Broker on declines in the Market when he calls for it.

Brokers buy and sell Contracts, the ostensible purpose of which is the receipt and delivery of cotton on them, but as previously stated,[21] shift them from one to another as circumstances suit, in making their own settlements between themselves.

The Broker does not know, nor, indeed, is it material with him for what purpose "A" buys or sells a Contract. If "A" is a Spot cotton Dealer or Manufacturer, and the Broker knows it, it is very natural he will assume "A" is Hedging; but if he is unacquainted with "A" or his business, he may infer that "A" is *Speculating*, and demand $2.50 or $5.00 a bale Margin for protection to him, especially if fluctuations are wide and rapid.

These are moral questions that do not enter into every financial transaction, and the Broker is left to receive or reject any Margins offered that in his judgment do not conform to legitimate rules and regulations.

Brown & Jones, of Macon, Ga., had in September 200 B/C on hand, and at the same time sold 500 bales to a Mill for September and October delivery.[22] The sale price being

---

[21]See "Ring" and "Direct Settlements," p. 325.

[22]Brown & Jones sold 500 bales Short—200 B/C on hand and 300 to be purchased.

satisfactory, but not caring to risk a decline, they sold 500 bales of Decembers as a Hedge. As they delivered the Spot cotton in 50 or 100 bale lots, they bought back 100 bales of Futures at a time, canceling to that extent their Future Contract.

When they completed their deliveries in October, they canceled all their Futures and left their profits in the Spots untouched. In these transactions they neither made nor lost on their Futures.

The cost to Hedge was suppose to be figured into the calculation when making the price to the Mill.

Johnson and Smith at Paris, Texas, *bought* in September, 500 bales of cotton, and at the same time *bought* 500 bales of Futures, for which they paid $500. Their Spots cost them 11½ cents and Futures for December 11 cents. They thought that the Market would go up, and that they would make a double gain, but it declined 20 Points on Futures, in ten days, requiring the payment of another $500 to hold the Contract, which they paid. In 20 days thereafter the Market declined again 18 Points, on which decline they were asked to remit another $500; but they refused to do so, and the Contract with and for them was closed out.

They not only lost on their Futures, but on their Spots also.

It should be noted that they took a double risk in the transaction, by *purchasing* both *Spots* and *Futures,* and at no time did they have any protection as a Hedge. Nothing but an advancing Market could have protected them.

This was a grave error on their part. They should have *sold* Futures when they *bought* Spots, in order to catch the Market either way—going up or down[23]—and no loss could have fallen on them if prices had remained on par one with another.

In practice, it is usual for the Dealer in Spot cotton, who

[23]See Book II, p. 110.

connects it with Futures, to release the Futures as he disposes of the Spots.

Should Johnson and Smith of Paris hedge their 500 bales by selling one hundred of them to some Mill, at the same time they would cancel one hundred bales of Futures, as it would no longer be necessary to carry 500 bales of Futures to protect 400 bales of Spots.

Cotton Exchange Contracts are based on Middling, with additions and deductions for the Higher and Lower relative Grades, as stated.

Mills do not buy Exchange Contracts extensively, as they must of necessity purchase such Grades as their manufactured articles require, and in their purchases usually stipulate some specific Grade or an even-running quality, which can not be obtained directly on an Exchange Contract, by reason of the number of Grades tenderable, many of which would not be acceptable for Mill usage, but for the protection of manufactured goods sold, Mills sometimes hedge.

World-wide distribution of cotton makes a demand for it somewhere at all times, of which the Exchange readily knows through its extensive telegraph and cable system, and in turn is enabled to give a Market for it every business day in the year, and on this data the Trade is made acquainted hourly or oftener through the day.

FUTURE DEALING EXPLAINED.

For the purpose of going more into the details of buying Futures, let us assume that Henry & Watts at Montgomery Ala., have accumulated 500 bales of cotton from collections on farmers' accounts and by cash purchases.

Should the Market be an advancing one, the payment of money to secure a Hedge would be a wilful and unjustifiable expenditure. They could under such circumstances, buy speculatively for a profit in the transaction; and while such action would be attended with little risk, an advancing

Market would offer not only a Hedge, but a continuously increasing one for the Spots on hand.

As stated elsewhere, for illustration, it is assumed the Market has a declining tendency for the moment, but conditions of the growing crop give evidence of higher future prices. So Henry & Watts not being able to place the cotton on the Market for the first cost, and wishing, also, to divide it up into even-running Grades to be sold with other cotton they are daily accumulating, they sell to some Mill or Mills, say, 800 bales of Decembers in September.

To execute the trade, they telegraph to, say, Hayward & Clark, New Orleans, as follows:

TELEGRAM.

Montgomery, Ala., Sept. 5, 1913.

To Hayward & Clark,
        New Orleans, La.
    Sell for our account 800 bales December at 13.05. Check to cover by mail.

HENRY & WATTS.

If Henry & Watts are financially strong, and Hayward & Clark know it, and have formerly done business for them, the order would be executed on the floor of the Exchange as soon after receipt as they could do it.

If 13.05 was the quoted Future Market for December, the sale would be made at that figure at once; but if not, the sale could only be made on a concession, say at 13.03, 13.01 or possibly not over 12.98. Hayward & Clark would not sell below the figure stated in the telegram without conferring further by wire with Henry & Watts, who would confirm at a lower figure, or no sale would be made.

Should the Market have gone to 13.08 or 13.10, by the time of the receipt of the telegram, then Hayward & Clark would be justified in selling for a higher price, getting better results for their customers than they themselves contemplated.

As stated, if Henry & Watts are recognized as "good"

financially, there would be no hesitancy on the part of Hayward & Clark in attempting to execute the sale, but if their credit rating was unknown or doubtful, Henry & Watts would have to deliver to the New Orleans firm a certified check, a bank guarantee, or the cash, before Hayward & Clark would involve themselves in making the sale for their clients.

If in the transaction of this order, Hayward & Clark are allowed to use their judgment, or are given some discretion about selling, they will act at once, but if not, the correspondence would be brought to a conclusion.

Quick action is the rule in the Trade, generally speaking, in business covering both Spots and Futures.

Immediately Hayward & Clark make the sale for their customers, they notify them by wire, as follows:

TELEGRAM.

New Orleans, La., Sept. 5, 1913.

Henry & Watts,
          Montgomery, Ala.
     We have sold at 13.07 for delivery in December, 800 bales for your account.

HAYWARD & Clark.

This sale was made at a figure two Points higher than ordered, and an initial gain of 10c a bale for Henry & Watts. Were the market to show an equivalent decline— the greater the decline the greater the profit on the Future short sale—a further profit of 10c would accrue.

This transaction being executed on New Orleans, is subject to the By-Laws and Rules of the Cotton Exchange there, even if such fact is not expressed in the telegram and the terms stated. The same facts govern for trades executed on the New York Cotton Exchange.

Assuming Henry & Watts to be regular Dealers in Montgomery, and to have a copy of Shepperson or Meyer's Cotton Code, such telegrams as the preceding would go over the wires in Code,[24] not only for the privacy of a personal business, but as economy to the expense account.

Should Henry & Watts accumulate more than 800 bales of Spot Cotton, and wish to carry it longer for a contemplated advance in the Market, they would *sell* Futures to cover the amount additional; but if at the time they have accumulated their 800 bales, they see proper to sell them at once, they would *buy in* their Futures and close that account simultaneously with the sale of their Spots.

In the preceding transactions, Henry & Watts sought shelter under a Selling Hedge[25] for protection to their Spot Cotton.

The expense to protect the Spot Cotton is $7.50 to buy and $7.50 to sell each 100-bale Contract, or $15.00 for the "round transaction." In this instance, the Sellers paid $15.00 for each 100 bales, as they *sold* and *bought in* the Contracts, totaling to them a charge of $120 as an insurance fee to have the price of their cotton at delivery time guaranteed to be the same as at time of sale.

To protect the Brokers who consummated the sale, Henry & Watts paid them a Margin of $800, out of which $120 was deducted for the Commission Charges, leaving $580 to be returned to the Sellers.

Had the Sellers made a profit on their Futures, the amount would have been added to the released Margin of $580; had a loss occurred, its amount would be deducted from that sum.

The preceding statement of the Future transaction is assumed to show neither gain nor loss on it.

Had the Market advanced 20 Points, or even 17 Points, Henry & Watts would be called upon to pay another $800, and were it to advance as much more, $800 would again be demanded. Each time these remittances are made Henry & Watts receive credit for them on their account.

[24]See "Code," Book II, p. 104.
[25]See "Selling Hedge," p. 323.

Had they paid $2400 on a 60-Point advance, this would serve to equalize the price of cotton to that extent with them, and further payments would be required on additional advances, but, should the Market react and regain the 60 Points lost, and the account be closed, the $2400 would be returned to Henry & Watts, less the $120 Commissions.

Note, that if they *sell* cotton in September at 13.07 to be delivered in December, and the price *advances* 20 Points, it will then stand at 13.27, and the Sellers will have to pay 13.27 for cotton to be delivered at 13.07, making a loss to them of $800. Every Point advance is a loss to that extent to them, which they must lose if the Market does not subsequently decline.

On every 20-Point *decline* they will gain $800, less their $120 Commission on only one 20-Point decline. On each 20-Point *advance,* they will lose $800, plus one Commission.

Where repeated Margins are paid to hold a Contract, there are no additional Commissions required, but if at or before the maturity of the Contract, it is canceled and another month is bought or sold in its place, a new Commission must be paid.

Commissions are charged on transferring Contracts from one month to another, as if originally entered into.

BUCKET SHOPS.

For convenience of those who wished to speculate in the rise and fall of prices of agricultural products or those of any branch of industry whose prices are regularly quoted on the Exchanges and Boards of Trade, suitable places in all the busy marts of America for receiving telegraphic advices respecting Market quotations were established, some time after the organization of the large Cotton Exchanges.

To many, especially the uninitiated, the class of business executed in these institutions seems similar in character to that on the organized Exchanges.

Cotton Exchanges do not deal in less than 100 bales as a unit basis for Contracts, while Bucket Shops will take orders for 10 bales or less, up to any amount the individual cares to *risk*.

The quotations on which they based operations were the *quoted prices* for cotton from the Cotton Exchanges.

The individual who staked his money in a Bucket Shop venture did so on the knowledge that there was "only one chance against him." If he bought, and the Market went up, he won; if it went down, he lost.

Trades in Bucket Shops were not based on cotton either directly or indirectly. In fact, they were based on nothing.

In establishing such places of business, the convening of Buyer and Seller for the purpose of executing Contracts with the intentions of delivering or receiving any article dealt in, was not contemplated, but instead, those who entered these places for Speculation, did so with the view of making or losing, as the *Exchange quotations* showed advances or declines; that is, its patrons would place their money on a Bucket Shop Contract as a Dealer at a card game would place his money on a certain card— taking a blind chance to win or lose.

The Contracts were not Contracts in any sense of the word; they were not issued for any definite purpose beyond the creation of something to be given as an evidence that money had been paid as a risk upon an imaginary Speculation on cotton. They were given to show the price at which a March or May had been sold or bought, and while the customer took either side of the proposition he desired, the Bucket Shop took the other.

Bucket Shops secured wire connection through which they obtained Exchange quotations, and these *quotations* constituted the basis upon which they operated.

They were gambling institutions pure and simple, of which the Century Dictionary makes the following statement:

Bucket Shops.—An establishment conducted nominally for the transaction of a Stock Exchange business, or a business of similar character, but really for the registration of bets or wagers, usually for small amounts, on the rise or fall of prices of stocks, grain, oil or cotton, etc., there being no transfer delivery of the stocks or commodities nominally dealt in. Bucket Shop operations are gambling transactions, and should be dealt with accordingly.

CHAPTER II.

HISTORY OF COTTON.

SECTION IV.

The fiber of the Cotton Plant has been known for a long time as a useful substance for the clothing of mankind, but how primitive man first learned that the fibers of this plant could be drawn into threads, and these threads, by dint of infinite labor and barbaric patience, could be woven into a fabric capable of protecting him from winter's storm and the burning beams of summer's suns, or, how the downy luxuriance of its snowy staple would, if massed in sufficient quantity, give rest and comfort to his cheerless sleeping hours, is not known. The memory of past events can not long be preserved in the mind of man, and these speculations, the truth concerning which would no doubt prove interesting, lie enshrouded in the dim, letterless past, seek as we may to call them forth.

From the beginning of cotton culture in the Western Hemisphere as a nucleus, human efforts have energetically carried the industry wherever soil and climate were found suitable for its profitable growth. Seed distribution has been wide, and the development of the industry has drawn the attention of the civilized world to its varied and wonderful qualities.

Nature unfolds and develops man's appreciation and intelligence as his necessities awaken to new needs, and thus it is that the introduction and culture of cotton as a necessary commodity in our daily lives was long received with such reluctance, although scientists for several centuries had pointed out its usefulness as a fabric-producing material, and not only urged its introduction into commercial channels as an active competitor with wool, flax and silk, but predicted that through its universal adoption it would eventually supercede those materials in general usefulness.

From the shadows of the remote past, no definite knowledge has come to us as to who first mentioned cotton.

That the ancients were familiar with its uses before the Christian era is certain, and is stated by nearly all writers on the subject in modern times.

Herodotus, the Greek historian, who lived in the fifth century B. C., makes particular note of this plant in India, referring to the beauty and usefulness of the "fleeces of its fruit" as surpassing those of "lamb's wool," and also as an article of clothing for the people.

Pliny makes mention of it in very definite terms. He does not speak of cotton as cultivated in Lower Egypt, but states: "The Upper part of Egypt, toward Arabia, produces a shrub called by some *gossypium,* and by others, *xylon,* whence the threads which are obtained from it have been named *xylina.*"

"It is small in size, and bears a fruit like a nut, whence is extracted a sort of wool, which for whiteness and softness is beyond compare." He further adds: "The vestments made therefrom are most esteemed by the Egyptian priests."

Pliny does not state how or by what process cotton fibers were manufactured into "vestments" beyond the fact that "threads" were made from it.

Being utilized as a material for priestly robes would seem to indicate that the cultivation of the plant was on a limited scale.

Signor Parlatore, an Italian botanist, in his work on Archaeology, published in 1366, makes mention of Rossellin's opening a tomb in Thebes and finding secured in a sealed vase some cotton seed. Rossellini claims he could not have been the victim of imposition, since he was present and helped to open both the tomb and the vase.

Those seed are now in the museum at Florence. Botanists

have not been able to determine whether they were of the Tree cotton or the cultivated smaller plant.

Statements to the effect that Egyptian mummies were wrapped in cotton fabrics have been disproved, as chemical analysis has shown the materials enveloping them were composed of flax.[26]

Authentic history finally relegated to the pages of mythical lore all the impractical and untrue attributes of this truly wonderful plant, and we find that cotton was grown in India, for the making of clothing, at a very early period, from thence it probably found its way to China, next to Persia and afterwards to other countries; that it was known and cultivated in Egypt at a period almost as early; and that, when the Americas were first explored, the natives were found to be accustomed to the cultivation of cotton and its manufacture into cloth.

Cotton is, therefore, seemingly indigenous to all tropical and semi-tropical regions of the world, though a higher state of development is reached where soil and climatic conditions are most congenial, and where proper tillage fosters its growth.

BOTANICAL CHARACTERISTICS.

Gossypium: The chief botanical types are: 1. *Gos. Barbadense;* 2. *Gos. Herbaceum;* 3. *Gos. Hirsutum;* 4. *Gos. Arboreum;* 5. *Gos. Peruvianum.* (See Encyclopedia Britannica.)

Botanically, cotton is classed in the natural order Malvaceae[27] under the name *Gossypium*—this name (Gossypium) having been given it by Pliny, though his reason for so doing has never been fully understood.

This genus, Gossypium, has caused much perplexity and diversity of opinion among botanists, owing to the fact that

---

[26]Botanic Origin, and Extracts from Prof. A. De Candolle. See Scientific American Supplement, p. 6308, July 28, 1883.

[27]Order of the common Mallows, Hollyhocks and Okra.

the plant is susceptible to changes caused by climatic conditions, soil and cultivation; also, the more eccentric changes known as "sports," which leave the genealogy of the different species still involved in doubt. Linnaeus admitted five species, while subsequent botanists have recognized four or five times as many.

Professor Parlatore, in his description of the cotton he had seen growing in Italy, was led to the conclusion that there were only seven species of cotton, all others being varieties.

While De Candolle, Dr. Royle, Swartz and others, particularizing, admit a different number of original species, it is probable that the cottons of the Old and those of the New World constitute the real typical divisions known to commerce—these are the Eastern and Western, the Indian and American cottons.

The botanical characteristics of the two, while in a degree similar, yet are sufficiently marked so that one can not be mistaken for the other.

The seed of the Eastern plant is never black or naked, while many varieties of the Western plant are conspicuously so. Numerous varieties of each type are to be found constituting distinct races of the same species, which often augumented by the industrious bees and other insects with their pollenizing visits, affords ample scope for the origination of apparently new cottons, the character of which are so pronounced as to good qualities or want of them, that careful experimenters desiring to improve the one or to destroy the other, have ample opportunities along this line of endeavor.

All of the Eastern varieties belong to the species designated by Linnaeus, yet are clearly distinguishable from each other, with one exception, and that is the single purple-blossomed tree cotton, indigenous to the lands bordering the Indian Ocean—the *Gossypium Arboreum* of Linnaeus—the Deo Cotton held sacred by the Hindus. This plant or tree has dark green leaves, red-purple blossoms, and produces a silky fiber, which is used exclusively for making priestly vestments.

Attempts have been made to hybridize this cotton and bring it into general use, but so far without success, and it remains commercially unknown.

SECTION V.

WESTERN OR AMERICAN COTTONS.

In 1519, when Cortez first visited the great Montezuma in his capital city of Mexico, he was presented with a princely gift of immense value, a part of which "consisted of loads of finely wrought cotton," and when the Spaniards were finally received into the royal presence, "attendants strewed the ground with cotton tapestry that his imperial feet might not be contaminated by the rude soil." The cotton hangings in their quarters were the wonder and admiration of these adventurous soldiers. The common people wore cotton shirts and Montezuma's "great square cloak made of finest cotton and sprinkled with Jewels,[28] still lives in the pages of his chroniclers.

From early records, it will be seen that cotton was grown abundantly in Mexico previous to the advent of the Spaniard; that its uses and manufacture were well understood by the Aztecs; that the Indians[29] roaming over the undulating prairies of Texas were blanketed and clad in garments of cotton, and that this plant was also, "found growing wild in Florida and elsewhere in the South." These facts would indicate that it is not assuming too much for America to assert that cotton is indigenous to the tropical and semitropical portions of this continent.

---

[28]See Prescott's American Encyclopedia, page 427.
[29]Watkin's "King Cotton," page 10.

The cottons which have become known to the civilized world since the discovery of America consist of two great divisions. The *G. Barbadense,* a black-seeded variety with its "pure yellow blossoms" and the *G. Hirsutum,* or "hairy cotton" bearing "white or faintly primrose-colored blossoms." The two are not always readily distinguished from each other by the appearance of the seed, as the black-seeded varieties occasionally show seed which have tufts of fiber at one or both ends, and in some instances are completely covered with fuzz, and the fuzzy kind many times show black or naked seed predominating to a more or less extent, and on this account some authorities conclude that the two varieties belong to the same species. Carefully conducted investigations have shown, however, that the variation in the seed may be attributed to the peculiarities of the soil, of climate and cultivation; and that the specific characteristics of the two classes remain distinct after generations and generations.

The cottons in greatest demand and most eagerly sought after by manufacturers of today, are those of the Western Hemisphere, designated as Sea-Island and New Orleans or Uplands, or long and short staple. Two varieties ·not equaled by any other like products of the world.

SEA-ISLAND COTTON.

*G. Barbadense—Sea-Island Cotton—*is said to have sprung from *G. Arboreum*[30] in Persia, and was carried to Barbadoes from India, though the name would seem to imply a Barbadensian origin. It was brought from the island of Anguilla in 1785 to the Bahama Islands, and to the United States in 1786, where it was first grown on St. Simon's Island, which is now a part of Glynn County, Georgia. The culture and improvement of Sea-Island cot-

---

[30]This origin is doubtful; it is more likely from Barbadoes.

ton were greatly aided by the efforts of Kinsey Burden[31] and wife of Colleton County, Georgia, who, by careful selection of the black seed, produced the best varieties now grown in the United States.

The islands lying off the coast of Georgia and a few interior counties, some portions of Florida and South Carolina furnished a home in which the Sea-Island varieties attain their greatest perfection. The cultivation of this cotton in the United States is now principally confined to about sixteen counties in Florida, twenty-nine in Georgia, and four in South Carolina. While these particular counties grow this kind of cotton, not all of their area is given to its culture, but only those parts more particularly adapted to its perfect development; where frost is scarcely known and where it has surpassed all other cottons for length, strength and beauty of its lustrous staple, a single pound of which could be spun into a thread more than 1000 miles in length. This fiber is much in demand by manufacturers whose fabrics require a long staple cotton. However, it is now closely approached by some hybridized varieties of long staple upland cotton originated in Mississippi that are equally in demand.

Farmers who grow Sea-Island cotton in the interior counties necessarily secure new seed, as a means of preserving the identity of the original parental stock, as otherwise the fiber degenerates rapidly into that of short staple upland.

Efforts have been made to grow this cotton in many parts of the Southern States, but results have been so unsatisfactory that experiments in this direction have almost ceased.

---

[31]Cotton production, 1907. Bulletin 95, page 19, Dept. Com. and Labor, B. of C.

"In 1790 the first commercial quantity of this cotton was grown by William Elliott, on the land where Jean Ribault landed his first colonist and claimed the country for France."

Frequent attempts to grow this cotton have been made in Texas. The first effort, in 1878, resulted in 202 bales of fairly good staple being gathered. Annually thereafter some twenty bales were grown, until 1884, when the production shrank to only eleven bales, then ceased until 1895, when seed were again secured from Savannah parties, from which a crop of 991 bales was reported; in 1896, 2,597 bales, in 1897 ten bales, and in 1899 six bales, the last year reported.

The increasing demand for long staple cotton has induced many progressive farmers and others interested in producing long staples, to experiment in many ways with upland varieties, in the effort to produce a better and longer fiber; chief of which is seed selection, better and more scientific cultivation, and proper fertilization.

Sea-Island cotton has been successfully introduced into Queensland, the Fiji Islands, Tahiti and Egypt; but the results accruing therefrom have not been of sufficient magnitude to affect the cotton Trade to any appreciable extent.

LONG STAPLE UPLAND COTTON.

The Bureau of Plant Industry of the United States Department of Agriculture is giving much valuable assistance in directing the Growers' attention to practical and scientific culture of cotton plant with a view more particularly of developing better staple varieties, and improving those now cultivated.

The long staple uplands grow principally in the lower portions of the Mississippi Valley; and by careful seed selection of these fancy varieties and more intelligent cultural methods, satisfactory results have been shown.

As most all the American long staple uplands are ginned by saw gins, the fibres are badly cut and broken, making uneven lengths, neutralizing the Growers' efforts to a great extent, while Sea-Island and Egyptian cottons on the other hand, are treated by roller gins which leave a regular and more uniform fiber.

Stimulated by offerings of fancy prices for long staple cotton, with the assistance of the National and State Agricultural Departments, augmented by individual efforts, no doubt a variety suitable to all climates and soils of the Southern States will be developed to the extent that its growth will become universal; and roller gins will be erected independently, or attached to those now in operation at all points where necessary for the better care of this class of cotton.

From the gratifying success attained on the fertile Mississippi Valley lands, from which upland seed have been distributed to many other points; some even to remote distances, equally as good quality of cotton has resulted from the planting of these seeds.

A different character of cotton from that just described, but seemingly confined to the limits of the State of Arkansas, has staple that is strong, heavy, of good body, frequently pulling full 1⅛ inch, and known as "Bender Cotton" or "Benders," from the fact of its growth apparently being largely confined to the very rich lands of that State bordering the rivers, especially the areas partially enclosed in the river bends; but as to the true history of the origin of this variety of cotton, the efforts of the author to trace it beyond the "river bend" idea have been without success.[82]

SHORT STAPLE WESTERN COTTON.

Of the short staple, or Western varieties of cotton, little is known of its origin, though it is quite probable that it came from Mexico, and of this class we can with certainty recognize two distinct types; one with green seeds and a hardy constitution, the other with white, tawny, or grayish seeds, showing a staple longer and distinctly silky in texture; these two types are the principal production of

---

[82]See Bender Cotton, Book I, p. 54.

the United States, and are known in England and in European Markets as "American Cottons."

While the two classes enumerated constitute the principal ones, there are others so closely allied that it is difficult to clearly distinguish them as separate species, but showing such marked features of the one or the other class as to be more or less akin. Of the grayish-seed varieties, two kinds are found, one with a small seed, while the other is very large, and the same may be said also of the greenish-seeded plant. The fine Venezuelan and West Indian cottons belong to this latter class.

Nankeen is a variety supposed to have orginated in Cuba, which makes, in suitable soil and climate, a fine showy plant, producing a tan or brownish-yellow fiber. The fiber is coarse and short, varying from five-eighths to three-quarters of an inch in length. It is not grown now as a distinct variety, but is frequently found growing spontaneously with other cottons upon the farms of the Southern planter.

BRAZIL'S COTTONS.

Occupying the most considerable part of the area designated as the valley of the Amazon, Brazil is the most important country in South America, and Nature seems to have lavished her best gifts upon Brazil, bestowing upon her a tropical and semi-tropical climate, varying according to altitude, a plentiful supply of moisture wrung by the snow-clad Andes from the north-east and south-east trade winds which come from the sea; a rich alluvial soil, and a long, dry season for gathering the cotton crop; requiring only improved industrial and scientific methods to make this one of the finest cotton growing countries of the world.

Nothing is known definitely of the antiquity of the cotton plant in Brazil, but the earliest historians of the sixteenth century mention the plant and its uses as being well known to the ancient people inhabiting the Valley of the Amazon, and there is abundant evidence that cotton had long been used by the natives at the time of the Spanish invasion of the country in 1500. However, no records exist of the exportation of cotton from this country until late in the eighteenth century, when some mention is made of shipments of cotton to Portugal in 1778, and to England in 1781.

Both herbaceous and tree cottons are grown in Brazil, and there are other indigenous species, attaining a height of from 10 to 15 feet, which yield fair crops for several years in succession. Practically, all the present crop is grown in the valley of the San Francisco River, though a large area of Brazil is adapted to the culture of the cotton plant.

The cultural methods of the country differ widely from those employed by cotton planters in the United States, and in comparison are extremely crude and primitive; but scant preparation of the soil is made for the cultivated species, and the use of the plow is little known. The practice is to "burn off the woods and plant the seed at the proper time," with the simple culture following which consists in the use of the hoe "in chopping out weeds and cutting the sprouts three or four times a year during the growing season."

The roller gin is employed more extensively than any other kind in Brazil, producing a more uniform fiber though little ingenuity is manifested in the manufacture of the presses; hence they are rude, operated by hand principally, making a light bale, averaging about 250 pounds in weight. A large part of the cotton is consumed in that country, the old-fashioned spindle and distaff being used to draw it into threads, while a part of the cotton goes into local Mills, which are annually increasing in number.

In 1904 the Brazilian Mills consumed about 135,000 bales of 500 pounds each. The production had increased in 1906 to 275,000 bales, which increase seems to have made no gain on the requirements of the people, as we have no record of any exportation to Foreign Mills during this time.

COTTON CULTURE IN PERU.

That cotton is indigenous to Peru will scarcely admit of a doubt, for early in the sixteenth century, when the Spanish invaders conquered the country, the natives were found to be accustomed to the culture, spinning and weaving of cotton.

There are two varieties of cotton grown in Peru, which are known in the Market as "smooth Peruvian" and "rough Peruvian." Smooth Peruvian yields itself more readily to the spinner's requirements, is very flexible and easily prepared for spinning. The rough Peruvian possesses characteristics closely resembling wool, is "fairly strong," and is used mixed with wool in the manufacture of woolen goods, for which it is peculiarly suited, being almost as important as wool itself. There is a great demand for Peruvian cotton in England and other Markets supplying woolen manufactures. All efforts to grow it in the United States, have been unsuccessful, owing to climatic influences which limit the life of the plant to one season's growth, instead of a number of years as designed by Nature for its perfect development, which seems to have been found only in the latitude of its native Peru.

Other varieties, including Egyptian, are also grown in Peru to some extent, but they are consumed in local Mills.

The Brazilian methods of culture and handling cotton prevail in Peru, the difference being so slight as to be scarcely noticeable. Often the seeds are planted in a hole in the ground which has been made with no other implement than a pointed stick, and there is little exertion used in either cultivation or fertilization. The manner of baling does not differ materially from that employed in Brazil, and the bales are light, averaging about 200 pounds. In 1885 the total production was about 12,000 bales, while in 1906 it was augmented to 55,000 bales.

COTTON-GROWING IN MEXICO.

Cotton culture in Mexico is older than any known history of the country, and it is evident that centuries ago the natives were acquainted with the uses and cultivation of the plant, and were expert in the manufacture of cotton goods before the advent of the white man.

Geographically, Mexico is splendidly situated, with a climate varying with the varying degrees of elevation from the hot, tropical valleys to cool, delightful, perpetual spring of the immense table-lands, that are eminently suited to the growth and full development of the cotton plant, if improved cultural methods and adequate labor could be employed. The export of cotton from that country could, doubtless, be increased greatly.

The tree cotton and the annual varieties are grown in Mexico, and the fiber is of good length and strength, though thinner and less silky than American cotton, as the plant suffers from insect pests, one of which is the boll weevil. The staple is not so clean.

It is estimated that about 80 per cent of the cotton crop is grown in the district known as "Laguna," which includes "a strip of the State of Coahuila and smaller adjacent portions of Durango and Chihuahua." Irrigation works on the Nazos River supply necessary moisture.

Modern gins are used, each plantation having its own gin and press. The square bale, weighing about 500 to 550 pounds, with five one-inch ties, is used. Statistics of the annual production have not been obtained, but it is estimated at 130,000 bales, all of which is retained by Mills of the Country.

SECTION VI.

COTTON IN BRITISH INDIA.

India is credited with being the birthplace of cotton culture and manufacture, and the mention of the plant by very early historians has led to the conclusion that it originated there, but whether this is a correct view, or whether it was indigenous to some other country and was carried to India centuries ago, may ever remain obscured by the lengthening shadows of the past. It is certain, however, cotton was known to the ancient inhabitants of India, and it is probable that the rude and unwieldly one-thread wheel used by them for spinning the coarsest yarns was copied later in the common domestic spinning wheels long in use in England and America.

The areas from which the commercial cotton of the country is drawn are the Central table lands of the Deccan, the Valley of the Ganges, Western and Southern India, and embraces what is considered the cotton area of India.

The climate is varied according to altitude and uneven distribution of rainfall. A hot, dry season from April to September and six months following with a plentiful distribution of moisture, give the summer and growing period in all the fertile valleys, tablelands, and deltas of the great rivers, ample time to mature her cotton crops and make India one of the cotton growing countries of the world. Within this wide extent of country are areas where the soil is unsuitable to cotton growing, where drought scorches plant life and where a rapidly increasing population demand that the strength of the soil must be given to food production for its people, and with ravages of insect pests in favoring localities, together with the retarding influences of unscientific cultural methods, preclude a probability of any material increase in the production of cotton in India. While production has increased to some extent in recent years, consumption of cotton in that country has increased likewise, making no perceptible change in the quantity for export; it is estimated that besides the amount consumed in local Mills, about 500,000 bales are used in the homes of the people.

Experiments with American cotton in India have proved highly successful, but of the native varieties it can not be said that they are of the finest quality. "The fibers are large in diameter, short in length, irregular in strength and color, and often very dirty."

With the exception of a few districts where improved modern methods are employed in cotton culture, the usual mode of cultivation is but little advanced from that used by the people of India hundreds of years ago. Oxen are used for turning over the soil which covers the last season's cotton stalks, and serves as an inadequate fertilizer for the coming crop. The seed are sown broadcast and the most primitive hand culture is given with hoes and other implements of rudest device.

For some years following 1860 when the South was demoralized by the Civil War the quantity of American cotton was reduced to such an extent that there resulted a great shortage in the world's supply. As a consequence, very high prices ensued, and this in turn stimulated cotton growing in other countries, among them, India.

"The production in 1859 was 1,316,800 bales, and had risen in 1865 to 2,090,400 bales, an increase of nearly 60 per cent.

"In 1905 the total acreage for India was 21,332,000 acres, producing a crop of 2,848,800 bales! an average of about 67 pounds per acre, while in 1906 the total acreage was 22,609,000, producing a crop of 4,038,400 bales; an average of about 89 pounds per acre."

EGYPT AS A COTTON COUNTRY.

The following excerpt from "Consular Report," July, 1894, is interesting and instructive:

"The story of the development of cotton culture in Egypt reads like a romance. In 1821, a French botanist found growing wild in the garden of a Cairo Bey a few plants possessing a long-stapled fiber, which he recognized as cotton of an exceptionally fine quality. The sagacious Mehemet Ali seized upon the discovery and turned it to benefit. Beginning with the vice-regal farms, the raising of cotton became general as soon as it was known that its quality secured for it a quick market at high prices.

"Indigenous varieties were grown centuries ago but the improvement in its character and cultivation did not begin until 1820-21. Sea-Island seed from America and Brazilian varieties were introduced, the former in 1838 while the latter had preceded it in 1820. Both gave promise of favorable growth, but for some reasons which are not given, the Egyptian soon returned to his native seed."

Egyptian cottons have a long, strong, uniform fiber showing equality of growth, and in spinning value rank next to Sea-Island.

Many advantages are offered as the home of the cotton plant here: an equitable climate, long, warm seasons beginning early, with the element of frost entirely eliminated, giving the plant a long time to mature a continuous crop through the growing season. Egypt being practically a rainless region, the growth of cotton is dependent on irrigation. After the Nile has subsided, a rich alluvial deposit from the tropics is left upon the land and while the earliest method of cultivation consisted in sowing the seed broadcast as we sometimes do wheat or oats, but not so thick, little subsequent cultivation was required; and as the crop was never disturbed by storm or rain, there was no loss or damage anticipated from these sources, and a high grade of cotton could be gathered, unless injured by insect depredation.

More modern methods of culture are employed at the present time, and as agricultural lands in the delta of the Nile range in value from $200 to $600 per acre, the Egyptian farmer economizes accordingly.

The cotton is planted on beds from thirty to thirty-six inches apart, which are constructed to receive the water necessary to the perfect development of the plant, nine to ten applications being required before picking begins. The seeds are planted near the top on the sides of the beds, and the plants are often not more than twenty inches apart in the rows; this close planting, inducing shade and dampness, fosters insect life and is calculated to injure the fiber.

The cotton area of Egypt is limited to the extent of land reached by irrigation, for wherever it is possible to carry the vitalizing water of the Nile, the richest vegetation springs luxuriantly. The English have built an immense dam on the Upper Nile at Assouan for the purpose of augmenting the water supply for irrigation, and have reclaimed more of the desert land for increased cotton acreage.

The Valley of the Nile is practically free from insect depredation to the cotton plant, except at the time of nightly fogs that occasionally follow the annual inundations of the lands. The deposits of silt containing an excess of vegetable matter, gives encouragement to rapid growth, stimulated by the deep season in the ground, and the creation of insect life to the detriment of the crop at such periods.

The population of Egypt has been estimated at 10,000,000, and to provide clothing and food for these people, and protect the normal increase, it seems improbable that any great increase will be made in the annual acreage given to cotton.

Cotton growing in Egypt has gradually developed. "In 1850, thirty years after the cultivation began, the crop was only 87,200 bales, and nine years later only 100,800 bales.

By 1865 the production had increased to 439,000 bales. This remarkable increase was due to the scarcity of the staple, caused by the serious check to cotton culture in the United States during the Civil War. By 1890 the production had increased to 789,000 bales.[33]

The annual cotton crops of Egypt range now from 1,-400,000 bales to 1,850,000, grown on nearly 2,000,000 acres.

RUSSIA IN ASIA AND ITS COTTONS.

The cotton growing areas of Asiatic Russia are: Transcaucasia, especially the low, level and fertile lands bordering the Caspian Sea; also, the eastern shore in Turkestan; besides a large area of Turkestan extending from Arabia and Afghanistan on the south, to south of the Kirghia Steppes. It has been shown that much of this great territory is adapted to the growing of cotton; and under governmental encouragement, protection and aid, produces considerable quantities of the fiber. It was not until the American Civil War, owing to the scarcity and high prices experienced at that time that cotton culture in Turkestan received new life and vigor.

Native Cottons and the hardier American Upland varieties are grown in the country; the long staple varieties have been found unsuited to the climate.

In many places the seed are sown broadcast, rude wooden plows and antiquated cultural methods are employed, which minimize the yield; while in the cotton area surrounding Tashkend, there seems to be a decided determination to use the most modern improved implements and scientific cultural methods in growing this useful fiber, which give encouraging results.

The area of Russia devoted to cotton production is subjected to influences that often militate against full yields. Through Central Asia, where the greater abundance is

[33]"Cotton Production," 1906. Bulletin 76.

grown, is a region where frosts sometimes occur late in the spring or early autumn, resulting in heavy losses.

This cotton-producing district yields crops ranging from 600,000 to 700,000 bales annually. It was estimated that the late frost of 1907 destroyed 400,000 bales.

CHINA AS A COTTON COUNTRY.

From the best evidence ascertainable, cotton was cultivated in China for domestic purposes centuries ago, but until recent years no data could be obtained on which to base any information that would be construed as reliable, nor can definite data be secured now by reason of the fact that the Chinese do not know the importance of ascertaining a Nation's agricultural strength or its resources in that line; but from the comparative few who aid the government in securing information respecting the growth of crops, approximations only are given.

As a large per cent. of China's cottons are consumed at home and never enter the Market, no records are kept concerning the total yield for any section or province. Practically all of her productions are consumed by local Mills and are not found among articles of export.

The average annual yield for China is approximately 500,-000 bales. This amount may vary as contingencies affecting the growth of the crop materially increase or lower it.

The herbaceous varieties of cotton are cultivated here and the fiber is of inferior quality, probably owing to the primitive and non-progressive manner of cultivating the plant; where little preparation is given the soil and the seed are sown broadcast, resulting in a stunted, stubby stalk, small bolls and much immature cotton. In some localities better modes of culture are pursued, resulting in better crops.

There are large areas of China adapted to successful cotton growing, but there is a large population making a heavy demand for food products, necessarily reducing the area of tillable land to be planted to cotton, which is grown only in small patches for home consumption and scant exportation.

KOREA.

Korea received her first introduction to cotton culture five hundred years ago from China. The best cotton lands are in the southern part of the peninsula, but there is little probability that much of this territory will be so employed, as the existing circumstances show a great similarity to those of China in exacting food products from the land.

COTTON IN JAPAN.

Though cotton has been known in Japan for some centuries, having been brought from China, it was not until early in the seventeenth century that the culture commenced; but owing to the inferior quality of the fiber grown, the prosecution of the industry made little progress, though Mill construction has increased rapidly. To meet the demands for raw cotton, other countries are relied upon to supply the spinning requirements. The disposition of the people is to buy factory made yarns, and fabrics of foreign manufacture because they are superior to those made from home-grown cotton.

The total production of cotton for Japan ranges from 10,000 to 16,000 bales annually. She buys largely from the United States.

COTTON CULTURE IN OTHER COUNTRIES.

There are other countries producing considerable quantities of cotton, namely:

Turkey, with a production of about 80,000 bales of 500 pounds each; Persia, with a crop of 51,000 bales; Greece, about 20,000 bales; Italy, 10,000 bales; Indo-China, 15,000 bales; Africa other than Egypt, 20,000 bales; Haiti, 15,000 bales; Dutch East Indies, 12,400 bales; Korea, 6,000 bales, and Argentina, about 10,000 bales.[34]

In addition to these, there are still other countries producing some cotton, nearly all of which is consumed in the homes of the people or in the local Mills, rendering it impossible to estimate the exact amount grown.

Cotton consumption is steadily increasing, making larger supplies necessary, and this heavy demand falling largely upon the spinners of Europe, caused them to fear that the supply of upland cotton from the United States would be inadequate to their requirements, so a movement to encourage cotton culture in many European colonies was begun, for the purpose of growing crops of cotton, which, though small as taken separately, in the aggregate, would be sufficient to supplement any possible deficiency in the amount received from the United States to the end that steadiness in annual supply would follow.

The British Cotton Growers' Association, aided by governmental support in their efforts to grow cotton in the Nigerian territory find the best lands for its production lie some distance inland; and to develop these lands into paying properties requires not only competent and skilled labor, but large capital; and to evolve from the primitive forests and virgin soils cotton farms of sufficient magnitude to produce a quantity of cotton that would affect to any appreciable extent the output of the world, will require many years; while the construction of railway transportation facilities to interior points is absolutely necessary to the successful operation of such farms.

The territorial area of Northern Nigeria is estimated at 323,000 square miles covering a region entirely tropical and semi-tropical, a large part of which can be placed to cot-

---

[34]"Cotton Production," 1907, Dept. of Commerce and Labor, Bureau of the Census.

ton culture. An area of 323,000 square miles represents over 200,000,000 acres. The entire "cotton belt" of the Southern States of America contains about 448,000,000 acres, and while vast tracts of forests and waste lands are included in this belt, yet enough remains suitable for the growth of cotton to give acreage sufficient to supply all the world for years to come.

Quoting from "Cotton," a Manchester, England, publication: "Cotton is not only indigenous, but has been culti vated on a comparatively large scale for centuries for native manufactures, which have achieved a reputation throughout West Africa—Kano, the center of the industry, being not inappropriately termed the 'Manchester of West Africa'—the present production of cotton for native use has been estimated at 50,000 bales."

As no railway lines extend into these cotton areas, the production therefrom amounts to naught as a commercial commodity, and by virtue of their inaccessibility, will remain so for an indefinite time.

BRITISH NORTH BORNEO.

Lying between about 110 degrees to 120 degrees east longitude, and crossed by the equator, Borneo is wholly a tropical country; rich, perhaps, in undeveloped fertile soils and agricultural possibilities, but handicapped by its still primitive inhabitants; the enquiry has been raised as to the practicability of awakening the interest in cotton growing among the native population, under the auspices and protection of the British Government, as heretofore efforts in this direction have been meager and tentative. The sample forwarded to the Imperial Institute for examination showed the staple to be short, rough and irregular in length and strength; but it was thought to be, under proper cultivation, capable of material improvement. It is a weary journey from primeval man, forests and wide ocean position, to civilized man, cultivated fields, railway transportation facilities and skilled labor; all of which are essential to the successful production of cotton. When Borneo has reached this stage of advancement, possibly new cotton producing areas may be found there; but not until then will it be of sufficient magnitude to be reckoned as one of the cotton producing countries of the world.

SECTION VII.

COTTON AREA AND PRODUCTION.

The cotton plant reaches the most perfect state of development in the fertile soils of warm countries, and it is between the fortieth parallel north and the twentieth South latitude that the world's supply of the "fleecy staple" is grown. This area "extends from the Mediterranean Sea to the Cape of Good Hope; from Spain to Japan and Australia; and from Norfolk, Va., in the United States, to Buenos Aires, in South America." This whole area, marking the cotton belt of the world, though vast in itself, is circumscribed, as compared to the entire surface of the earth; yet, taking into consideration the corresponding extent occupied by ocean bodies, by lands unavailable, countries in which cotton culture is an unknown factor, and the countries in which it has proved unprofitable, only the southern portion of the United States, British India and Egypt are left as the three principal cotton producing countries of the world, the United States being paramount to all the others combined. This country occupies a position giving it a preponderance sufficient practically to control the Market, and it is self-evident that there is little danger of overproduction of this valuable clothing material for an ever increasing population.

As an index to the future, reliable statistics show the demand of the world for cotton annually increases in a ratio equivalent to, approximately, 400,000 bales; an in-

crease commensurate with the additional acreage; and indications point to an even higher rate of increase.

COTTON AREA OF THE UNITED STATES.

By reference to Map 1—Cotton Producing Area of the
United States, 1907, in "Cotton Production," Bulletin 95,
it will be seen that beginning at Norfolk, in south-eastern
Virginia, a line traced irregularly, avoiding the mountain
regions of North Carolina and Tennessee, including portions of the southwest corner of Kentucky and Missouri,
along or near the northern boundaries of Arkansas and
Oklahoma to the eastern boundary line of New Mexico,
thence south to a point on the boundary line between Mexico and Texas, indicates the limits of the cotton area of the
United States, the greatest cotton producing region of the
world; an expanse of territory 1450 miles in length from
east to west by 500 miles in breadth, comprising a total
area, estimated at 700,000 square miles, or 448,000,000
acres, of which only one-fourteenth, or one acre in fourteen
was given to cotton.

Commenting on the area adapted to the culture of cotton in the Southern States and the amount produced thereon, the following statement from Bulletin 76, Bureau of the
Census, is appropriate and to the point:

"No country in the world possesses the combination of
advantages found in the southern part of the United States
for profitable cotton cultivation. In this section the soil is
naturally adapted to cotton growing, the climate is favorable, the labor better than elsewhere, and the farm man-
agement more intelligent and experienced. Combined with
these favorable internal conditions, are good transportation facilities."

The race for supremacy between production and consumption is a close one. Both have grown and are growing
rapidly. The demands for American cotton have been so
great, with better prices attending them, that the increase

in acreage has been commensurate with the supply wanted.

The extension of the cotton growing area within the last 15 years in the United States has been wonderful.

These increases have been most prominent west of the Mississippi River, with marked increases especially shown in west and Southwest Texas, Arizona, New Mexico, California and Oklahoma.

In the arid and semi-arid regions of New Mexico, Arizona and California, where irrigated lands were accessible and impounded waters sufficient for demonstration purposes, the cotton plant has been introduced.

The Egyptian variety of staple cotton has proven to be well adapted for that territory, but the plan of irrigation as practiced in Egypt was not successful there. The application of water being tested in other ways, has by experience proved satisfactory, thus broadening the area of cotton production in the United States to the Pacific Ocean.

The existing climatic conditions in that territory are not entirely unlike those of Egypt—a long hot, dry season. With water applied as required during the growth of the plant, perfect maturity of the cotton is insured, which ripens a strong, uniform fiber, such seasons being well adapted for the opening of the bolls and ample time for gathering the crop free from injury.

The National Government has given aid and encouragement to the utilization of the arid and thought-to-be waste lands, with the successful results stated.

Irrigation has been practiced with varied results in different parts of Texas, but not so extensively as in the other districts named. Where the water supply is sufficient and adapted to the growth of plant life, good results have followed; but when indiscreetly put upon the land or the water carries mineral substances deleterious to the growth of cotton, the yields following are disappointing .

A large increase in acreage in Oklahoma has added greatly to the world's supply of cotton. Yields from that

State will continue to be large, as the lands are well adapted to the production of cotton. Irrigation is not practiced, and the supply grown is measured by the contingencies, of the weather in connection with the acreage planted.

There were exported from the United States in 1908, 7,401,538 bales; 1909, 8,551,789 bales; 1910, 6,233,492 bales; 1911, 7,807,414 bales, and in 1912, 10,648,573 bales,[65]

The increasing demand for consumption abroad has been met with practically the same rate of increase in production in the United States.

Where 10,000,000 bales supplied consumption five years ago, 15,000,000 bales are eagerly absorbed by the Trade today.

SECTION IX.

EARLY EXPERIMENTS AND PRODUCTION IN THE UNITED STATES.

The knowledge of cotton growing wild in islands of the West Indies, is as old as the history of their discovery by the Spaniards in 1492, though little efforts were made towards its cultivation until 1621. It seems that the time for its introduction as a useful commercial and domestic product was now ripe, and the "Divinity that shapes our ends" kindly took the cotton plant in hand, tendering it for the benefit and civilization of the whole world, and as a late writer expresses it, "Man can not be civilized without clothing"[36] him. Necessity, that rugged teacher, at a very early period, forced upon the first settlers of this country attention to manufacture and a demand for a new clothing material; to which cotton alone was adequate or available. In the ten years following the founding of the Massachusetts Colony, in 1630, a heavy immigration, equal to the whole population was annually added; therefore, the raising of

---

[35]Yearbook U. S., 1912, p. 728.

[36]Watkin's "King Cotton," p. 10.

food products became the most profitable pursuit; and so great was the demand, that the price of cattle went as high as twenty-five pounds sterling; but when in 1640, the Republicans gained the ascendency in the government in England, persecutions for religious non-conformity ceased, emigration to this country fell to almost nothing; and the demand for provisions was so reduced that cattle sold for not over five pounds a head.[37]   The effect was extremely distressing, but it put the intelligent colonists upon new resources, and to help them in this exigency, *"the general court made order for the manufacture of woolen and linen cloth;"* cut off from source of supply in England on the one hand, it remained for benignant Traffic to open a way to supply the deficiency; and trade being opened with the West Indies and Wine Island, where among other goods, much *"cotton wool"* was brought into the colony and the people soon learned a way to supply themselves with cotton linen, by spinning and weaving the new fiber, seemingly the gift of Providence.

The seeds of the cultivated varieties are thought to have been brought from the West Indies, and mention is made of cotton culture in Virginia as early as 1621; in South Carolina in 1733; and in Georgia in 1734.   The most suitable soil for the cultivation of cotton was that of the islands lying along the coast which produced the best varieties, known in France as "Georgia cotton" and in England as "Sea-Island."

In 1822 cotton was reported as "growing to the height of six feet," in Louisiana, though its culture is said to date back to 1722.   In 1822 there were exported from the port of New Orleans, 167,742 bales.   Nevertheless, the evolution of the cotton plant, from a beautiful natural curiosity —a wild weed of the tropics—to a cultivated commercial substance, whose snowy web of a single season's weaving might encircle the globe, was slow; and it was 118 years

---

[37]"Book of the United States," p. 353.

AN ANTEBELLUM GIN.

Showing the old-style wooden screw press, exposed to the weather, capacity of such a ginnery 3 bales per day. Courtesy King Cotton.

A MODERN GIN PLANT AT GATESVILLE, TEXAS.

Interior view, capacity 100 bales a day.   Courtesy of Bob Brown.

after its introduction in Virginia, before a shipment was made to England, a few bags[38] were exported from Charleston, S. C., in 1747, but not until 1770 was it made a staple crop. The record of the shipments to Liverpool are as follows: "Ten bales from Charleston, 3 bales from New York, 4 bags from Virginia and 3 barrels from North Carolina." England looking on, incredulous that such immense (?) quantities of cotton could be grown in the colonies, seized eight of the fourteen of fifteen bales shipped to Liverpool in 1784, impressed with the belief that it had been wrongly entered, and was *not* grown in the American colonies.

MARKETING COTTON IN ANTE-BELLUM DAYS.

Parallel with the settlement and growth of our country is the development of cotton production. As civilization felled the trees and turned the sod, it planted the seed that gave us our increasing cotton crops.

Science, energy, industry and inventive genius have played their parts in contributing to the growth, culture, harvesting, ginning and manufacture of cotton.

The primitive method of gathering cotton from the plants by human hands is the approved one as practiced in every cotton field today.[39] Cupidity led out forefathers to exercise every ingenuity to obtain the most lucrative prices possible under their system of marketing cotton, as do we of today.

Railroads were few, and transported at first but little cotton.

Steamboats were numerous and operated on all our largest Southern streams, constituting the most popular, practical and best means for transportation of both freight and passengers.

---

[38]From "Cotton Production" Bulletins 76 and 95.

[39]Several machines for gathering cotton from the bolls have been invented, patented, and tests for practical service have been made, but none have proved of sufficient commercial importance to merit adoption. Human hands still gather the staple.

The Farmers' cotton was usually received at the gin, and generally not offered for sale until after the entire crop had been made into bales.

A large per cent. of the crop was produced by slave labor, and yields credited to one planter amounted in some instances to hundreds of bales, and in a few to a thousand or more. Planters usually forwarded their entire output by wagons to the nearest boat landing, at which place it was loaded on barges—flat boats—or steamboats, and shipped to Memphis, New Orleans, Mobile, Savannah, or Augusta, from which points it was usually transported by steamer or sailboat to New York.

Cotton arriving at Memphis came in by wagons from West Tennessee, North Mississippi and also by boat from this same territory and Arkansas, where small streams led into the State, on which Steamboats or barges could navigate.

Memphis cotton found its outlet generally in New Orleans, and part of it through New Orleans to New York. A small percentage went up the Mississippi and Ohio Rivers to Louisville, Cincinnati and into Pennsylvania, from whence it was forwarded by Canals to Mills in Pennsylvania and New York, and occasionally to Boston, Mass., by railroad.

Arkansas Cotton drifted down the White, Arkansas, Washita and Red Rivers to New Orleans. That from the Northern part of the State, brought out by the Rivers traversing it, often found a Market in Memphis.

Alabama Cotton sought outlets towit: from North Alabama through the Tennessee River, destined for Memphis; the Chattahoochee carried some to Appalachicola, and borne on the waters of the Tombigbee and Alabama Rivers, some Alabama cotton found a Market in Mobile.

Georgia Cotton, through the numerous water courses of that state, had exceptional advantages for getting out to Sea. The Savannah River transmitted large quantities by way of Augusta to Savannah; the Ocmulgee, Oconee and Altamaha Rivers carried it to Darien and Brunswick on the Atlantic Coast; while that grown in the Western and South Western part of the State moved South on the Flint and Chattahoochee to Appalachicola, on the Gulf of Mexico.

Louisana Cotton was shipped by way of the Mississippi, Washita and Red Rivers to New Orleans.

Mississippi Cotton had numerous outlets on the Mississippi, Big Black, Yazoo and Pearl Rivers, carrying it South to New Orleans or perhaps it went to Memphis, from the Northern part of the State.

North Carolina Cotton concentrated at Raleigh—could move out on the Neuse River when sufficiently high water permitted navigation. The Cape Fear and the Yadkin Rivers· afforded good transportation facilities at certain times of the year, drifting cotton into Wilmington or to some of the Cotton Mills erected on the Stream.

South Carolina Cotton found facilities for its movement into Market for Export on the Pedee, Santee, Charleston or Savannah Rivers.

Texas Cotton was transported from the interior to the Gulf Ports on large wagons, to each of which were attached three to seven yoke of oxen. Sometimes two wagons were connected, the tongue of one secured to the rear axle of the front wagon, to which ten to twelve yoke of oxen were hitched, and in this way large loads of "wagon cotton" were carried to Market. Galveston was the principal Export Market. Houston was the interior Cotton Market.

Primary Movement of cotton at interior points it should be remembered, was first transported by wagons to places of sale or to the boat landings. Large Growers usually consigned it to some Commission Merchant to whom it was intrusted for sale. Practically all cotton was sold by Commission Agencies for Growers or interior Merchants.

Commission Merchants were located in all the American Export Cities in the South, and were the exclusive intermediaries between the Producer and the Importers on the European Markets.

They handled cotton as other articles of commerce, such as Sugar, Molasses, Rice, Tar, Turpentine, Hides, Wool, etc., making itemized Statements of the Sales in similar manner as those Dealers of to-day who operate on a similar basis.

Returns from the Sales often were not received by the Shipper or Owner for months afterward, due to the then prevalent Market conditions and slow movement of Freights and mails.

Market Conditons were very imperfect, owing to the absence of any *central point* from which quotations could be derived giving values, or approximate ones, for cotton, and the Atlantic Cable had not been drawn across the ocean.

New life injected into cotton culture caused increased immigration into the Southern States. Business revived, new industries developed, commerce increased, towns and cities came into existence, and Railroads began to reach out everywhere.

The demand for cotton increased commensurately with its production. Buyers became more numerous as the area widened, and business activity was manifested in all lines of endeavor.

Cotton production jumped from its lethargic condition to one of extreme activity, its votaries full of hope, energy and enthusiasm after the introduction of the "saw gin" into the great industry.

EVOLUTION OF THE COTTON GIN AND COTTON PRESS.

The fingers of man were the principal factors in separating the seed from cotton until the advent of the first machine devised for such a purpose in India many years before the Christian era.

That machine, called a "Churka,"[40] was the forerunner of the present up-to-date Roller Gin, and no doubt from its simple construction of two rollers, a small one of iron above a larger wooden cylinder, gave

---

[40]Scientific American Supplement, Aug. 20, 1908.

the idea for the improved Roller Gin[41] now extensively utilized in ginning Sea-Island and some of the Long Staple Upland cottons.

As described, a crank was attached to a shaft at the end of the large wooden roller, used by one hand to give motive power, while the seed cotton was "fed" to the rollers by the other, and in this way seed separation was effected, producing about three pounds of lint cotton per day. When attached to a foot pedal, horse or water power, the improved Hand Roller Gin, modeled something after the design of the Churka, had an increased capacity of twenty-five to forty pounds of clean cotton per day.

The work accomplished by the Roller Gins was performed on Long Staple cotton, as such Gins were practically inefficient for successful operation on Short Staple varieties, for which reason such cottons were not extensively grown.

The ease and readiness by which cotton could be taken from the seed by hand, held the attention of the Grower to that variety known as Sea-Island, as its fibers were long, and easily removed from the sleek, black seed, which were in sharp contrast to the Uplands or Short Staples, the seed of which held tecnaciously to their fibers and gave no encouragement for the production of this character of cotton; as a result of a day's work by an operator separating the seed from such fibers, gave only about half the quantity of spinnable cotton as that obtained from the Long Staple growths.

Not until a machine had been made that would separate cotton fibers from the seed with greater rapidity than the operation could be performed by hand, did the industry of growing cotton receive much consideration.

Co-equal with the growth and development of the cotton industry in America is that of the introduction and improvement of the *Cotton Gin* and *Cotton Press*. Both have been subjects of much thought upon which the minds of inventors have been engaged with more or less interest at different times, and from the original types of machines first utilized, many improvements of meritorious value have been made.

PRIMITIVE GINS.

Practical efforts at growing cotton in many different places in the South during the latter part of the eighteenth and first years of the nineteenth centuries, had demonstrated the fact that its production was no longer questionable, but the problem of separating the fibers from the seed

---

[41]Roller Gins are made with both single and double rollers, equipped with Gin Breasts, but no self feeders. Rollers are usually covered with leather of walrus hide. Double Roller Gins have a daily capacity of 2000 to 2200 lbs. lint cotton, and may be increased to 2600 to 2800 under favorable circumstances.

on such an economical basis that it could be grown profitably, was a problem awaiting solution, and held cotton culture in abeyance.

Slave labor was comparatively inexpensive; coercive measures were frequently brought into requisition to bring about the greatest results possible by forcing the laborer to detach as much cotton from the seed as fingers and hands could do, yet such industry, often augmented by the aid of women and children around the fireside at night could not obtain cotton in profitable quantifies.

The world was calling for cotton; energy and ingenuity were making continuous efforts to answer it.

Apparently the humble antetype furnished the idea from which inventive genius evolved the first roller gin, as evidently the Indian Churka was the source of that inspira-

CHURKA GIN.

"Churka Gin, the records of which show its usage in India 621 years B. C."—Scientific American Supplement

tion whereby efforts were directed towards the formation of a machine having *rollers* for the purpose of obtaining cotton lint from the seed as performed by that machine.

M. Dubrueill,[42] a French planter, invented a machine in Louisana in 1842 which gave some stimulus to cotton culture. It was evidently framed upon the roller idea, but of this fact history does not speak.

A Mr. Krebs "who planted cotton on the Pascagoula River in Mississippi," invented a Roller Gin, which was used to some extent in that territory. There is evidence that his machine was but a slight modification of its East

---

[42]King Cotton, p. 11.

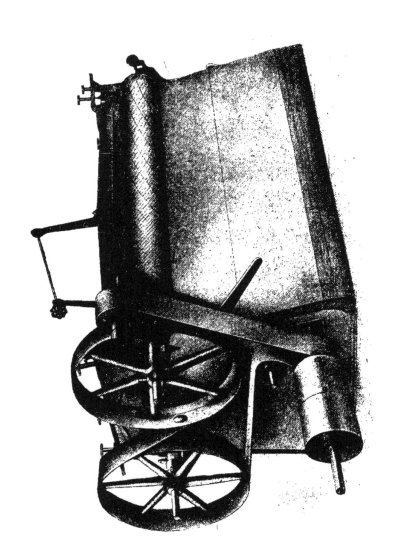

FOSS DOUBLE ROLLER GIN—APRONS UP OR CLOSED.

Showing appearance of gin when in active operation   Courtesy Sea Island Cotton Gin Co., Vidalia, Ga.

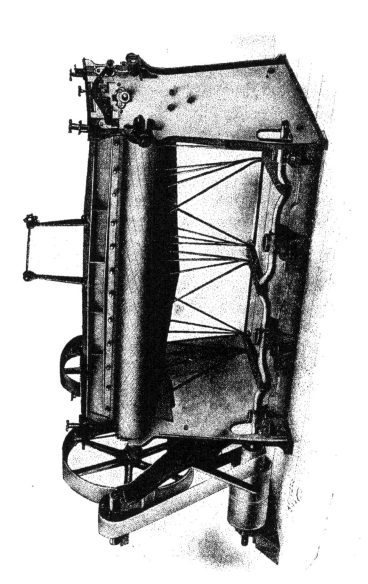

FOSS DOUBLE ROLLER COTTON GIN—APRONS OPEN.

Devised and adapted for ginning long staple cotton; used more especially on the Sea Island varieties. Rollers are covered with best grade of walrus-hide leather. Courtesy Sea Island Cotton Gin Co., Vidalia, Ga.

Indian predecessor. Practical tests were made of it in 1772, but successful results from it are not recorded.

Kinsey Burden, of South Carolina, made a novel and curious Roller Gin of "two old gun barrels fastened on rollers," but the success obtained by it is not mentioned. He introduced it in 1777.

Dr. Joseph Eve of Augusta, Ga., in 1790 introduced a greatly "improved gin," so constructed as to be adapted for either horse or water power.

A Mr. Pottle, also a resident of Georgia, made some improvement on the Roller Gin, and his machine became popular, yet the extent of its usefulness is not known.

Improved Gins of that date gave outputs ranging all the way from twenty-five to seventy pounds of cotton daily, in contrast with one to three pounds secured by hand labor.

WHITNEY'S GIN—A TRANSFORMATION.[43]

One hundred and twenty years ago, in 1793, Eli Whitney gave an impetus to the cotton industry of the South that has moved by leaps and bounds ever since.

Prior to that time the lint was taken from the seed by hand, or Roller Gins, the amount of a day's work by hand equaling one pound of clean cotton. Crude and primitive forms of machines began to appear, the best of which constituted a pair of rollers operated by hand, through or between which the fibers were drawn, and upon the best constructed machines, 60 to 70 pounds of lint cotton could be produced for a day's labor for one hand.

The importance and value of the fiber as a material for making wearing apparel and other useful articles was well ──-──wn, yet to secure it in sufficient quantities to justify its introduction as an article of general use, was a problem to

---

[43]See Appendix. The credit given to Whitney as being the originator of the Gin bearing his name has been disallowed by some, alleging one Miller as being a co-inventor with him. See also, "Saw Gin."

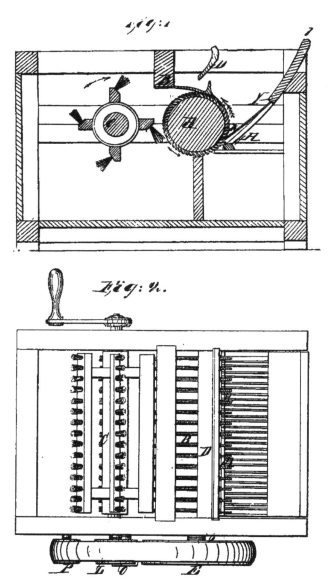

E. Whitney,

Cotton Gin.

Patent granted to Eli Whitney, March 14, 1794, it being the first patent ever issued for a gin, and was signed by George Washington, President, Edmund Randolph, Secretary of State, and Wm. Bradford, Attorney General of the United States.

solve, due to the fact of the heavy expense attached to its production in sufficient quantity.

The primitive method of obtaining a sufficient amount of clean cotton, practically precluded its general usefulness, during which time, its culture was not extensively fostered, until the Roller Gin made its advent, after which a little life and stimulus was given to the industry.

The announcement that a machine had been invented by Whitney that would take from the seed 600 to 900 pounds of lint cotton in one day, while wished and hoped for, was thought to be incredible, but a confirmation of the fact was joyously hailed as a beneficent innovation.

The original Gin, as devised and patented by Eli Whitney, March 14th, 1794, consisted of a roller into which short, sharp, metalic hooks or teeth were fastened in longitudinal rows, and also in direct lines following each other around it; in this way forming a cylinder almost covered with small, regularly arranged, crooked teeth. On another shaft, lying parallel with it, carrying cross arms, to the ends of which, stiff bristles were attached, so arranged in a suitable frame as to revolve while in action in opposite direction to the roller carrying the crooked teeth; yet the line of travel of the circumference of the brush was with that of the movement of the receding bent spikes on the roller.

In the frame between the roller and brush, metal wires or strips intervened, separated from each other by sufficient width to allow the free passage of the hooks on the roller, but not wide enough to permit the passage of cotton seed.

Above the spiked roller was arranged a longitudinal hopper into which seed cotton was placed for seed separation. The operation of the machine consisted in turning the roller shaft by a hand crank, the shaft being connected by a belt to a pulley on the end of the brush which was revolved at a greater speed, causing the bristles to brush away the cotton fibers from the bent teeth as they constantly brought more cotton from the hopper.

The movement of the roller in Whitney's Gin caused the seed cotton to turn over in a reverse direction, producing a "Roll" as may be seen today in all "Gin Stands" of the saw type.

What was termed a "Hopper" in Whitney's Gin, is now recognized as a "Gin Breast."

The mechanical construction of the "saw" as devised by Whitney in its application to cotton for separating the lint from the seed, has remained practically as he devised it. From the day of its introduction to the world to this time, "gin saws" have continued to pull, break and tear from the seed practically 99 per cent of the world's crop of cotton.

At the time of the advent of the saw gin, the production of the United States, was in round numbers, about 35,000 bales, of 225 pounds weight to the bale.

The condition of the South then in trying to develop the culture of the cotton plant, may be well expressed in an opinion given by Judge Johnson, of South Carolina, in a "Suit brought by Whitney and Miller to recover from the State $50,000 appropriated by the Legislature for the purchase of the right to use the gin in the State." In giving his opinion, he said in part: "The whole interior of the Southern States was languishing, and its inhabitants emigrating for want of some object to engage their attention and employ their industry, when the invention of his machine at once opened views to them, which set the whole country in motion. From childhood to age it has presented to us a lucrative employment. Individuals who were depressed with poverty and sunk in idleness have suddenly risen in wealth and respectibility. Our debts have been paid, our capital has increased, and our lands have trebled in value. We can not express the weight of obligation which the country owes to this invention; the extent of it can not be seen."[44]

What that Judge·said then, is applicable now; "The extent can not be seen." From an annual crop of 35,000 bales then to that of 15,000,000 for the United States now, states the immense increase in 120 years that has resulted from Whitney's invention.

From a commodity practically unknown as of financial importance 120 years ago, cotton has now reached to that point in commercialism which gives to it the immense value of ONE BILLION DOLLARS ANNUALLY, with an influence felt around the globe, touching with more or less emphasis all the leading industries.

ORIGINAL SAW GIN.[45]

One Mr. Hodgen, (or Ogden) Holmes[46] of Augusta, Ga., received a patent for a Gin bearing date of May 12th, 1796, about three years after Whitney's patent, bearing like Whitney's the signature of George Washington.

Holmes' invention consisted of small circular saws arranged on a shaft, the teeth engaging the cotton with which they came in contact, and tearing the lint from the seed, upon the same principle as the spikes or wire teeth devised by Whitney; otherwise, the mechanical construction of Holmes' invention was very similar to that of Whitney's.

The principle involved for ginning cotton by Holmes' method being recognized by Whitney as the same utilized in his own invention, became the basis for an action in the courts resulting in much litigation, that was finally decided in Whitney's favor. This prohibited Holmes from further manufacture and sale of his "Saw Gin," but a court's decree did not stop the manufacture and sale of Saw Gins by Whitney, and others to whom he might assign the right

---

44From "King Cotton," p. 12.
45See Brook's "Story of Cotton," p. 97, and "Saw Gin," p. 363.
46"King Cotton," pp. 96 and 97.

of so doing. Like Banquo's Ghost, it would not down; and today, wherever cotton is grown, the whir and hum of the Gin Saw is heard.

Inventors both North and South have exercised their wits to devise a better Gin than exhibited by the *circular saw*, but let it be said to the credit of that piece of mechanism, it is still in the ascendency and its utility remains supreme.

Let it be stated that up to the time of Whitney's invention all Cotton Gins were of the Roller type, and with but few exceptions, were operated by hand, but almost simultaneously with the appearance of Whitney's Gin, two others came upon the Market, one devised as stated by Holmes, the other by a Mr. Joseph Watkins.[47]   The former utilized the principle of the circular saw while the latter used a wooden cylinder into which metallic hooked spikes were fastened similar to Whitney's idea.

Principle.—As previously stated, the principle elucidated and put into practical operation by the use of the "Saw" and "Brush" for separating fibers from seed cotton as set out by Whitney in 1794, remains about the same today in the best and latest improved Saw and Brush Gins.

While it may never be known who originally invented the *Saw Gin,* universal credit rests with Whitney, and the world bows to him as a benefactor.

If "The man who causes two blades of grass to grow where only one formerly grew" is a benefactor to his race, how much more are we indebted to the man who causes thirty-six million acres of land to be grown to cotton where *ten* were formally planted?   This Whitney has done for the South, and what has the South done for him and his posterity?   Where does his monument stand and what is the epitaph thereon?

_____

[47]"King Cotton," p. 96.

MODERN GINS.

Whitney's idea of seed separation by means of circular saws, is the basis for construction of all modern Gins operating upon Short Staple or Upland cottons.

Improvements have been directed toward better material for Saws,. specially designed Ribs, Breasts, Mote Boards, Brushes, Bearings and general finish.

Saws.—Gin Saws are usually made in two sizes—ten and twelve inches in diameter, with the teeth so formed as to offer the least *cutting* to the fibers in order that they may be drawn from the seed with greatest length obtainable.

All leading manufacturers practically make the same form of Saw. All Gin Saws break more or less fibers.

Ribs.—Gin Ribs in the best improved Gins perform the same office designed for that purpose by Whitney in his original model. Each manufacturer of Gins makes a Rib of his own devising, which when arranged in phalanx form in the machine makes a series of narrow slots through which the Gin Saws pass freely, taking through the accumulated lint caught upon them while the openings are not sufficiently wide to admit the passage of matured seed.

In Huller Gins, devised for taking out broken bolls, hulls, sticks, trash, etc., a double row of Ribs are arranged with one row in front of the other so as to execute well the work required of them, which is a decided improvement over the Single Breast Gin, raising the quality of cotton one or two grades when Bolly, badly picked and trashy cotton are passed through.

Gin Breasts.—The gin breast is the receptacle first receiving the cotton and admitting it directly to the Gin Saws, and was designated by Whitney as a necessary "Hopper" for applying the cotton directly to the saws underneath.

Gin breasts are so arranged for opening or closing, that cotton can be held and more thoroughly ginned. Closing the Breast holds the seed longer upon the saws; opening it al-

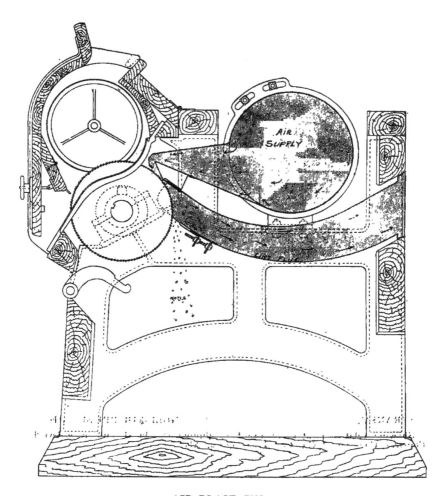

AIR BLAST GIN.

Transverse sectional view, showing relative position of Breast
and Gin Saws, and the direct application of the air forcibly
applied for cleaning the saws.   Courtesy Lummus Cotton Gin
Co., Columbus, Ga.

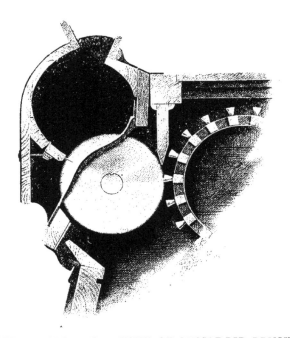

TRANSVERSE SECTIONAL VIEW OF SINGLE-RIB BRUSH GIN.

Showing relative position of roll box, ginning rib, brush and mote board
Courtesy Continental Gin Co, Birmingham, Ala

lows the seed to pass through imperfectly cleaned. To clean the seed well is an important consideration in the construction of good machinery, desired by both the manufacturer and the ginner who operates it.

Mote Boards.—These are specially designed parts of the Gin Stand and placed under the Gin Saws and Brush, operate for the purpose of throwing out motes, broken seed, leaf particles, dirt etc.

Gin Brushes.—As component parts of that character of Gins utilizing Brushes, they are devices for performing two distinct offices, namely: Cleaning the Saws of fibers by direct contact of the Brushes with the teeth of the Saws, and generating rapid air currents which not only aid the removal of the cotton from the Saws, but operate to carry the cotton to the Condensers.

AIR BLAST GINS.

Modernized ginning is constantly under the eyes of all leading Gin manufacturers, and in their active competition for business, nothing is offered by them to the Trade that does not have the stamp of actual test back of it.   A physical demonstration of every new device offered receives their attention first, and if practical experience shows it to be meritorious it is offered to the public.

Actual tests made with the Gin Brush demonstrated the fact that the air currents generated by it cleaned the Saws of their accumulated cotton to some extent when the bristles did not touch them.   Following this discovery, the Air Blast Gin was constructed.

In this Gin no Brush is used, but instead, through a specially designed frame, air currents of great force are so applied as to be directed in line with the receding Saw teeth taking the lint from them and carrying it by a continuous flow to the Condenser.

The merits claimed for it are that lighter draft is necessary to run the Gin and a better sample of cotton is made.

GIN ACCESSORIES.

Connected with modern ginneries, some or all of the following accessories are found: Elevators, Cleaners, Distributers, Feeders and Condensers, each performing a specific work for a special purpose, as an economical measure for handling the seed cotton from the wagon to the bale.

Elevators.—In the construction and introduction of modern labor saving machinery, none has met with a greater welcome from the Southern Cotton Growers than the present pneumatic elevator system installed for taking cotton from their wagons rapidly and delivering it to the Gin Stands, with strong air currents.

Pneumatic Elevators, usually constructed of heavy sheet metal in tubular form, from ten to twelve inches in diameter, are so arranged and connected as to allow a telescopic part to hang from outside of the building, which part may be raised or lowered as desired.

Further necessary connections deliver the cotton to the Cleaners, Distributers, or to any stall or place arranged to receive it.

Properly connected Fans or Blowers supply the suction for drawing the air through the Elevators.

Cleaners.—Specially devised machinery for stirring or agitating the cotton while being relieved of a large percentage of foreign substances. After cleaning, it is usually deliverd directly to the Distributer. For handling dirty, trashy or Bolly cotton, they are indispensible for obtaining the best Grade that can be secured from it.

Not all ginneries are equipped with Cleaners, or Separators, as they are sometimes called.

Distributers.—Receptacles into which the cotton is first drawn on its passage from the wagon or storage bin to the Gin Stands. Through their operation cotton is distributed to all Gin Stands with accuracy and in quantities to accommodate the capacity of each.

Feeders.—Above, and attached to each Gin Stand, the

Feeders perform their work. They receive the cotton directly from the Distributers and "feed" it regularly to each Gin Stand.

Condensers.—As a component part of present day methods for better ginning, the installation of Condensers, which dispense with the old-time "lint room," is an innovation in the line of improvement. Ginned cotton escaping from the Gin Stands, passing through specially devised shutes or large zinc pipes, passes on to the Condenser, which is composed of one or two large drums of wire net construction, through whose meshes the air passes freely, but the cotton, not being able to go through, is forced between them by the turning of the drums, coming out in "bats" of more or less thickness and falling directly into the Press.

Bales so formed can be sampled with greater ease than those made by one or two men tramping cotton into the Press box, as formerly practiced in the early days of ginning.

General Remarks.—The tendency to increase Gin capacities to secure a greater output at local points has induced the erection of ginneries containing from four to ten Gin Stands each, usually arranged in batteries of two to five Gin Stands on opposite sides of the same room suitably arranged or constructed to receive them. All modern accessories for better and more rapid ginning, and all conveniences the public might demand, are introduced by many of the largest Southern ginners.

In comparison of the results obtained from ginning cotton on a Roller and Saw Gin, evidence shows that both break fibers in the same proportion, but cotton from a Roller Gin shows the fibers are more curled and twisted, which has a tendency to cause the formation of "naps," especially noticeable when this cotton is put in the Carding Machines.

Cleaner cotton is credited to the Saw Gins, because they

are specially devised with other apparatus connected with their operation for taking out the excess trash.

A curved saw tooth round and smooth, so made as to strike the fibers at right angles, will not injure dry cotton if the saws are not run at too great speed.

Most cotton ginned in America is passed through "custom ginneries" whose owners usually charge so much per bale for cotton "ginned and wrapped," and whose personal gains are determined by the number of bales ginned, thus gauging their revenue; and it too frequently happens, especially during the rush of the ginning season, that gin saws are run at too great a speed; resulting in a comparative loss on the cotton ginned, by reason of unduly breaking the fibers. During such times a Roller Gin would be equally hurried, and the results obtained would be just as bad.

COTTON PRESSES—BALING.

The problem of marketing cotton, after its merits became known as an excellent substance for the manufacture of wearing apparel and other articles, was a hard one to solve by the agriculturist.

Cotton production was comparatively new. Two factors had to be considered in any effort to find a solution of the situation that would give profitable returns to the Grower.

First, owing to the nature of cotton, some form of receptacle or package was needed for its safe transportation; second, the South had to look for a Market in foreign countries, from which she was separated by a great ocean with transportation facilities for crossing meagre and slow.

In the first efforts at transportation, cotton was sent to England for a "trial market," in sacks of 200 to 300 pounds weight, and for a series of years from 1790 to 1810, the entire amount of American cotton transported was shipped in that form. The demand by the maritime vessels for a smaller package of greater density, for the economy of space, gave cause for the creation of some form of *Press* that would put a greater quantity of cotton in a smaller package than could be packed into a sack by the weight of a man tramping it therein.

The Wooden Screw Press.—Practical tests based upon repeated trials for a series of years, had demonstrated the fact that the buoyancy of cotton was hard to overcome when confined in bulk and any Press that might be made to confine it in a dense and compact form would have to be constructed of strong material, and believing the power for doing this to be obtained through the mechanical principle of the screw as the proper one, so the Wooden Screw Press was devised. It was built of heavy hewn timbers, four of which stood upright on appropriate base sills of other equally as heavy material. Between the four uprights, a large box was built and attached, sufficient in size to hold a 500-pound bale of lint cotton, tramped as tightly as two men could pack it by their weight. Two long arms of 40 or 50 feet in length, of hewn or round timbers, serving as levers, were attached to the top of the large wooden screw and spread as an inverted V towards the ground. The large screw was carried up or down through heavy bolted timbers, confined between four uprights, as if working through an immovable nut, which bolted timbers were bored and threaded to suit the threads on the wooden screw.*

To the ends of the levers near the ground, mules were hitched for finally forcing the screw down to the point of bale completion.

At time of beginning the pressure for a bale, gravity acting on the massive screw with its lever attachments, often reduced the bale to half completion without the necessity for the application of any other force, and here it was thought that both time and money were saved by the exertion of such a latent force doing half the work, and devoid of any expense beyond the wear upon the machinery,

---

*See cut, page 1.

but subsequent inventions of better and more economical Presses have proven the falsity of such conclusions.

This form of Press made a square bale, pressed to a density of about 8 pounds per cubic foot, which was covered with jute or hemp bagging and bound with ropes.

In order to avoid the initial expense of erecting a Wooden Screw Press, different mechanical devices involving the principles of the lever, the pulley and the wedge, have engaged the attention of inventors at different times, and Presses of various types have resulted, some possessing degrees of merit, and many put into practical operation, all of which have finally given away to the Screw, Hydraulic and Steam power.

About the year 1870 the metallic screw was utilized, and soon displaced the heavy, clumsy wooden one for actual service, in connection with a better devised press box.

The advent of the small metallic Screw, (5 to 7 inches in diameter), as a convenient and cheap means of applying the requisite power for making a bale of cotton gave a new impetus to cotton culture.

Contemporaneously with it appeared the Hydraulic Press, each of which formed a bale pressed to a density of approximately 12 pounds to the cubic foot.

The metallic Screw, Hydraulic Power, and the energy of Steam are the agencies now employed for reducing cotton lint to cotton bales. The Screw and Hydraulic Presses are most in use at the present time.

For the "man in the Press," the *Steam Packer* has been substituted, to the advantage of both the cotton and the Ginner. By its use, the cotton is packed just as evenly as the bats of cotton from the Condenser fall into the Press.

Modern Presses are made in both single and double-box styles, usually equipped or built as self-packers. The Double Box Press is attached to a metallic central upright, about which it revolves. Such Presses are installed to accommodate a double battery of Gins, or several Gins in one building. In a ginnery so arranged, no necessity arises to stop the movement of any of the machinery, as a completed bale is "tied out" of one box, while cotton continues to flow uninterruptedly into the other.

COTTON COMPRESSES.

Continued requests for smaller packages of greater density by vessel owners transporting cotton to foreign Ports stimulated inventive genius for many years in efforts to perfect such a package to the last degree.

Tramping cotton in sacks of 200 to 300 pounds weight for export compressed it to 5 pounds per cubic foot; the Wood Screw Press condensed it to 8 pounds; the metallic Screw or Hydraulic Presses of today press it to a density of 12 pounds in the original bale at the ginneries. The powerful Compresses not unusually exert a pressure of 50 to 60 pounds while the bale is under the Press, but when released and re-expanded, a density of about 22½ pounds per cubic foot is registered. The records show that but few bales "dock" at Liverpool with a greater density than 20 pounds per cubic foot, owing to expansion of the bale when released from the Press and the inability of the ties to maintain its density.

In 1832 a Compress was built in New Orleans, known as the "Levee Cotton Compress," the erection of which cost a half million dollars with capacity of 200,000 bales per annum. The Orleans Cotton Compress, with an annual capacity of 150,000 bales, erected at a cost of $754,000, with warehouse facilities for storing 25,000 bales, was completed in 1835.

The Tyler Hydraulic Compress was introduced in 1845. In 1851, ten Tyler and two Duval Compresses were in operation in Savannah, Ga., the capacity of all aggregating 7,000 bales per day, or 168,000 per month. At the same time there were "42 warehouses, covering 40 acres of ground and capable of storing 310,000 bales of cotton."

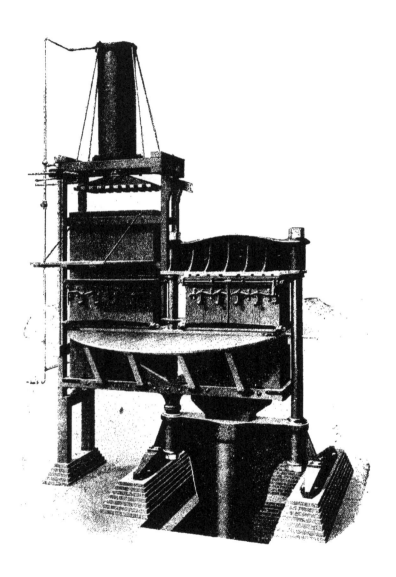

MUNGER'S GINNER'S COMPRESS.

Devised to be installed at ginneries.   (See p. 400.)

DOUBLE BOX SCREW PRESS

Devised to accommodate two batteries of Gin Stands (See p 396)

The compression of cotton at a comparatively early date of its culture went far towards answering the demand for a condensed package. The immense outlay to erect such plants narrowed their contruction to the efforts of a limited few who, practically having a monopoly of the industry, were reaping the exclusive revenue arising from them. This led to other thoughts, and a different line of endeavor. Inventive genius being again called into action, directed its ingenuity toward perfecting a Press that would condense or compress a bale of cotton to the necessary density required by the transportation companies and perfect and install it at the ginneries, which has resulted in the creation of the Munger Ginners Compress, the American Round Bale, and the Lowry Round Bale Presses.

Munger's Ginners Compress.—This Compress is of the revolving double-box press type, constructed sufficiently strong to withstand the strain required of it, and produces a compressed bale at the ginnery having a density of something more than 30 pounds of cotton per cubic foot. Only eight ties are required to retain the integrity of this bale.

The bale is made of several layers of cotton, and is finally completed by direct action of the hydraulic ram slowly compressing it to the density required.

Slow compression allows the gradual escapement of air, which finally being expelled and the fibers brought into rigid contact with each other, completes the bale.

It is claimed no injury results to the cotton fibers subjected to this heavy pressure.

The American Round Bale.[48]—The theory of making a round bale for preparing cotton for Market is quite an old one. Patents were issued to Mead in 1847, and to North in 1848, for machines to make this type of bale; but not until the improvements made by Bessonette (of Temple, Texas) in 1893 in his machine, was any progress made toward introducing such a Press into practical operation. With some

[48]See Round Bale, Book III, p. 252.

improvements on this style of machine, it is the present form of Press now manufactured, sold and used by the American Cotton Company.

The bale is made by winding the cotton on a central core for a beginning, after which the bat is gradually wound around in one continuous manner until the bale is completed to 25 or more inches in diameter.

The bale is formed between rollers that constantly press against the cotton, and excludes the air from the cotton as the bale gradually increases in diameter, virtually eliminating any tendency for the cotton to expand after the bale is made, which obviates the necessity for the use of any ties to hold it in its original form.

After completion, the bale is wrapped with a hemp or duck material, and end pieces sewed on, which makes a complete covering and protects the cotton well from gin to factory, as this covering is never cut for the purpose of sampling the bale.

American Round Bales are usually compressed to an average of 33 pounds per cubic foot.

The absence of ties and the use of a light weight covering[49] subjects the bale to a tare of only one per cent.

Samples are drawn from the bale when half completed, and are relied upon to represent the cotton after completion of the bale intended in this way to give the true quality of the cotton. Each sample bears the same number and registration as that given the bale from which it is taken.

Lowry Round Bale.—As a Round Bale of different construction, the Lowry Bale soon followed the Bessonette into public notice. This bale was formed inside a metallic cylinder, built up so to speak, in spiral layers from the bottom.

---

[49]The covering on the American Round Bale weighs 2½ lbs., costing about 20 to 25 cents. Two Round Bales weigh 500 lbs., wrapped with a covering of 5 lbs., worth 40 to 50 cents. The American Square Bale has 27 to 30 lbs. on it after leaving the compress. Exclusive of the Patch, the original cost is practically $1.00 a bale for bagging and ties.

The metallic cylinder prevented lateral expansion while compression was given perpendicularly as the bale was formed. As this bale is practically out of use and almost obsolete, further description of it is unnecessary. It was generally reduced to a density of about 50 pounds to the cubic foot, while in some instances in making demonstration tests, 86 pounds were recorded. An idea of such a density may be understood when it is stated that oak possesses a density of 54 pounds.

Shipment of Compressed Cotton.—The advantages to be gained by shipment of compressed cotton may be well illustrated by comparison.

The modern bale as it comes from the ginnery is of such a size that 25 of them fill an average size box car, while two and a half times as many bales from the ordinary compress can be stowed in the same space.

The Munger Gin compressed bale is so uniform and is reduced to such a density, that 140 to 170 are placed in the same size car.

The American Round Bale being approximately the same in density as that from the Munger Compress, can be stowed in the same place, that is to say 150 to 175 of them can be placed in a. car that would accommodate only 25 uncompressed bales.

The percentage of loss in space for transporting round and compressed square bales is slight, although it is alleged by some that the loss is greater with the round bale.

REVIEW QUESTIONS

REVIEW QUESTIONS

What are the causes for changes in the appearance of open cotton in the field?

Do these changes create different qualities of cotton?

What are these qualities called?

Why the necessity for naming these different qualities?

How are the discolored cottons designated?

What terms are used for this purpose?

What are the tri-foliate "forms" called that envelope a boll of cotton?

Do parts of these "forms" ever become mixed with the seed cotton when it is gathered?

Do they affect gradation?

Into how many parts are cotton bolls divided?

How many seed are usually found in each section or "lock" of cotton?

Do these locks ever become mixed with dry, dead leaves or "squares?"

Do they ever fall from the bolls, lodge on the limbs of the plant, or drop to the ground?

What is the result of such action on the appearance of the cotton, and what does it cause?

What result is shown on cotton if ginned damp or wet?

In what other way may "gin cut" cotton be produced?

Can wet cotton be as well cleaned as dry cotton?

Why not?

Do fibers of damp cotton adhere more closely to trash and dirt than dry ones?

If too much dampness occurs, what result is shown on the ginned cotton?

Do "naps" affect gradation?

What are the causes for, and what produces, "gin falls?"

To what extent do they affect gradation?

REVIEW QUESTIONS.

Into how many parts are the names of the qualities divided?

What are the three parts called?

How many Full Grades?

How many Half Grades?

How many Quarter Grades?

Can the Full Grades be clearly defined?

Why are the terms "Strict, "Fully" and "Barely" used?

What is Fully and Barely Middling?

What is the difference between Tinge and Stain?

Which of the two is lightest in shade of color?

Can the line of distinction between them be clearly defined?

Are other colors ever imparted to cotton besides the reddish colorings distinguishing them as Tinges or Stains?

How many Grades and subdivisions of cotton are recognized by the New York Cotton Exchange as white cotton?

How many Tinges and Stains?

What Grades of cotton accepted by the Trade not recognized by the Cotton Exchanges?

What are the highest and lowest Grades of Tinges and Stains?

REVIEW QUESTIONS.

At what season of the year are the best or Higher Grades of cotton generally found?

What are the influences affecting the physical qualities of cotton?

Is there any definite mechanical rule by which cotton can be graded or classed mathematically correct?

What guides a Classer in his capacity to technically determine a Grade of cotton?

Do all Classers have a matured idea of what constitutes a Grade of cotton?

What are the causes for different opinions among Classers respecting the Grades of cotton?

When two Grades of cotton approach each other in all respects closely, how are they Graded?

In the main, is there a general agreement between Classers as to what constitutes a Grade of cotton?

Can Classers familiar with Texas cottons, easily Grade the cottons of the Carolinas or Georgia? Why not?

What is the specific duty of a Classer?

Do Classers always agree with each other in taking up a list of cotton, or with themselves in a second classification?

Why is it their opinions do not always coincide?

What are the substances affecting gradation, or for what must the Classer look to determine a Grade?

Why should cotton not be gathered damp, or if damp, why the necessity for drying it before ginning?

What sometimes causes damp or "wet pack" bales, when dry cotton has passed through the gin stands?

What are some of the causes for "two-sided" bales of cotton?

How should a bale of cotton be cut and a sample drawn to get the best results respecting the true character of the cotton in the bale?

REVIEW QUESTIONS.

How many grades in the Government's Official List?

Should a full list of the Commercial Grades be had to classify all of them?

Should the student have an opportunity to hold the samples, and gain some knowledge of them by the touch, in connection with their visual appearance?

Can written or printed description teach the art of cotton grading successfully without a physical examination of the cotton?

Is a knowledge of both necessary to the operation of a successful cotton business?

Why are the Types of cotton repeatedly used, called the "Working Types?"

Is there any definite rule for displaying samples for gradation work? (No.)

How should a sample be handled to show the character of the cotton to best advantage?

Should a sample be torn in two in an attempt to grade it?

In what form are samples best preserved?

For what purpose should a sample of cotton be torn in two?

Should reference be had to the Government's types, and why, in the study of gradation work?

What is one of the most important factors in determining the Grade of a sample of cotton?

How should side, or over-head lights be regulated?

How should the Classer stand in a side-light to get best results in classing a sample?

How should classification be performed in the open air or in the sun light?

Can anyone class well in the open air who is accustomed to performing such work in a room with side, or over-head lights?

In active, practical work, does a Classer stop to think each time he examines a sample, how much of this or that substance affects it to make it a "Grade?"

What is generally the result of the first impression made by a Classer in passing upon a sample?

With what rapidity does an experienced Classer grade cotton?

REVIEW QUESTIONS.

Could a Low Grade of cotton be brought to a Higher one by taking out the foreign substances, if the fiber is not faulty nor other imperfections appear?

In the Table, under the heading "Look For," why do the Grades become lower in quality as the scale of the Table descends?

What can you say of Inferior cotton?

Define Low Ordinary, Ordinary, Strict Ordinary, Good Ordinary, Strict Good Ordinary, Low Middling, Strict Low Middling, Middling, Strict Middling, Good Middling, Strict Good Middling, Middling Fair, Strict Middling Fair, Fair.

How are the Tinges and Stains classified?

What are the differences in grading Tinges, Stains and white cotton?

Can anyone class Tinges and Stains without a knowledge of the gradation of white cotton?

Are the Premiums and Discounts for the Higher and Lower Grades constant?

Why do they vary at different times?

What valuation is given to the Good Middling Tinged Grade by the New York Cotton Exchange?

What is meant by the terms "Fully" and "Barely" with reference to cotton Grades, and what other names are sometimes given to them?

What is meant by the words "*shy*" and "*full*" in connection with cotton grading?.

What is the policy of cotton Buyers or Mills with reference to classing the shy and full style Grades of cotton?

What is Bolly Cotton, where did it originate, how is it secured, and what are the peculiar features causing it to differ from other cotton?

Are its fibers always matured, if not is its value impaired?

What can you say about all Bolly Cotton being Tinged or Stained?

Can it be delivered on any Contract made on the New York or New Orleans Cotton Exchange?

How is the valuation placed upon this cotton?

What is Sea-Island cotton?

Can you define some of its qualities and tell how it is graded?

How is Sea-Island cotton generally sold to the Trade?

As a Staple what other varieties supercede it?

Define Bender cotton and give some of its features as compared with Uplands, Gulf Types, Texas, Oklahoma and Sea-Island varieties.

Where does it grow principally and in what State did it originate?

As a staple cotton, what is the prevailing length of it?

What are Linters and from what source do we get them?

Are Linters graded as our standard Types of cotton?

How many pounds of Linters are usually obtained from a ton of cotton seed?

Can Linters be delivered on any of the Cotton Exchange Contracts?

What are cotton fibers?

Are cotton fibers given greater tensile strength if stored with seed cotton in a suitable place for some weeks before ginning?

Does protracted dry weather affect cotton fibers while the plant is growing? Answer: (Yes.)

REVIEW QUESTIONS.

What is necessary to be used to guide the student in cotton classification?

How many Full and Half Grades constitute the Government's Official List? Name those Grades.

What was conceived by the Government in establishing these nine Grades?

How many samples of each Grade are in one box?

Of what is each sample a representative, in the box?

Why were twelve samples placed in each box?

Why are instructions given that these samples be not touched or handled?

Under what guidance do our cotton crops pass into the channels of Trade?

Do the Standard Types of cotton adopted by the Cotton Exchanges harmonize in all particulars with those of the United States Government?

What are these lists called?

What do Official Lists represent?

Is every crop of cotton grown always an exact counterpart of all the crops that have preceded it?

Can you tell why the peculiar characteristics of one crop is "creamy," and other "white," another "dingy" or faintly "smoky," yet sufficiently defined as white cotton of "good color?"

Do these peculiarities change gradation?

How many samples of each Grade do the Cotton Exchanges put in their sample boxes?

What is the approximate weight of each of those samples?

Do all the Cotton Exchanges have the same Standards?

What is the cause of this difference among them?

Is Middling in Augusta, Savannah, New Orleans, Memphis and New York the same in quality?

What can you say of the Standards in New York and New Orleans respecting their differences?

What is the difference in Standards in Houston and Galveston?

How do the Standards of Liverpool, Bremen and Havre compare?

How do the cottons of the Carolinas, Georgia and Mississippi compare?

Are the cottons east of the Mississippi River, known as Uplands, the same as the Short Staple varieties in Oklahoma and Texas?

What can you cay of Private Standards, how, and why are they used?

What are Class Marks?

How do the Government Standards compare with those of Liverpool?

REVIEW QUESTIONS.

How are commercial values of cotton measured?

How are Grades determined?

What are known as Grade Values, and what do they fully represent?

What is meant by Stapling cotton?

What is the Staple of cotton?

What is meant by Staple Values of cotton, and is the length and strength of the fibers necessary to be known to get at these values?

Do Staple Values modify Grade Values, and *vica versa?*

Do Grade Values show the same Premiums as Differences as exhibited in Higher Grade Staples?

Are Staple Values affected by contingencies of the Market similar to Grade Values?

How is Staple cotton classed?

Do all Mills use the same character of cotton both as to Grade and Staple?

What are the requisites necessary to supply a Mill with its needs?

What is meant by selling cotton on its Merit?

How can a Merit Value be two-fold?

What is the average Grade and Staple used by the American Mills?

Are the Premiums for the High Grade Staple different from those of High Grade Short Staple Cotton?

What is meant by a weak or perished Staple?

Why do Classers sometimes differ as to what constitutes a "weak" or "good" Staple?

Where the fibers possess unmistakable evidence of good length and strength, is there any cause for controversy over such fact?

What is meant by a "good body" of cotton and how can you determine it?

Are the Staple cottons grown in the lower Mississippi Valley the same as Sea-Islands in all their qualities?

What are the highest types of Staple cotton grown and where principally found?

What is meant by "pulling for staple?"

How should a beginner in classing cotton determine the length of the fibers?

How should one draw fibers to determine the Staple of the cotton?

Why should guess work not be tolerated?

What is the final destination of all cotton?

Are the Mills restrictive in their demands for raw material?

Can a Mill equipped for the manufacture of a specific line of goods use any Grade or Staple of cotton?

What is "Even-running" cotton, and why do Mills specify such cotton when purchasing?

Will Mills accept a shade of variation from a specific Grade demanded?

What do they usually specify when in the Market to purchase cotton?

What is meant by Spinnable Values, and how are they measured?

What is meant by averaging Grades and Values?

Is an average list an even-running one?

Is an average list always the same, or can there be an average list of High Grades or Low ones?

Why is it advantageous sometimes to average a list of cotton?

What is meant by so many Points "on" or "off" Middling?

How do operators generally deal with each other in handling large lists of cotton?

What is meant by a sale "hog round?"

Do Dealers requiring High Grade cottons accept average lists without specifying "nothing below" a certain Grade?

REVIEW QUESTIONS

What is meant by the expressions, "differences in Grades," and "differences in value?"

Is it necessary to know the relative value of the Higher and Lower Grades in figuring an average list of cotton?

Define the meaning of Table XII.

Do the Differences established by the Cotton Exchanges always conform to those accepted by the Trade?

How are Grades of cotton distinguished with reference to their value?

Can these Grades or Difference Values be determined by the Mill?

Are Spinnable Values always in line with the Differences established by the Trade?

How are the Premiums and penalties prescribed by the Trade and Cotton Exchanges determined?

How are these arbitrary Differences made?

What are the results of practical tests made by the Mills and the technical colleges in their textile departments, as to the percentage of waste in any specific class of cotton?

If the percentage of waste is heavy or light, what does it indicate?

Is the amount of waste in any Grade of cotton always constant?

What is the approximate waste in percentage of a Middling bale of cotton?

Are the Spinnable and Trade Differences the same in percentage?

What would you consider the cause for these Differences?

If the Spinnable Differences should ultimately apply, would there be the same need for such an extensive variety of Grades as are handled by the Trade today?

REVIEW QUESTIONS.

For what purpose are abbreviations and terms used in the Trade?

For what purpose are Arbitrators necessary in adjusting differences in cotton transactions?

What course may a Dealer pursue if dissatisfied with the result of an Arbitration?

Are controversies ever settled without the use of Arbitration or legal procedure?

What is meant by "Bear" or "Bears?"

On which side of the Market do Bears operate?

What is meant by the terms "Broker" or "Brokerage?"

Where do we find, and who are those who operate as Brokers?

What are the charges per 100 bales for buying and selling an Exchange Contract?

On what class of business do these charges apply?

Do Brokers charge the same Commission for handling the business of other Brokers as they charge for non-members?

On what is the Brokerage reckoned?

Do Brokers deal exclusively in Future Contracts, or can they handle both Spot and Future business?

Can they operate through Agents?

What is meant by the terms "Bull" and "Bulls?"

What is the difference between the operations of a "Bull" and a "Bear?"

Which desires the Market to go up and which wants it to go down?

When may a Bull become a Bear or a Bear operate as a Bull?

Are all fluctuations in the Market caused by manipulation?

How can the Market fluctuate without manipulation?

What is meant by a Code or Cipher Code?

For what purpose is it used, how does it safeguard business, and why is its usage economical?

How are Codes arranged for practical usage in every day transactions?

What are the principal Codes generally used?

What latitude of information in the Cotton Trade is covered by the Code?

In brief terms, what is the Commercial News Department Code called?

For what purpose is it principally used in the Trade, from and to whom are "C. N. D's." generally transmitted?

Is this Code different from the ordinary Cotton Code?

What are the three principal reports from the Cotton Exchanges transmitted to the Trade everywhere?

What are the principal Reports transmitted after the "close" for the day?

Can the Code be used in the transmission of cablegrams as well as telegrams for domestic Markets?

What do you understand to be the meaning and purport of a Contract issued from the Cotton Exchanges?

Are Contracts ever made between Dealers in the Trade outside of the jurisdiction of the Cotton Exchanges?

Tell what is meant by the term Discounts and how it may be applied in different ways?

What are Cotton Factors, what character of business is executed by them, and where do they generally operate?

What is meant by "Flat Cotton?"

If cotton is to be "shipped Flat" what notation should be made on the Bill-of-Lading?

What is meant by "Future Sales" as applied to Cotton Exchanges?

Can Future Sales be made between Dealers without buying or selling a Contract on the Exchange?

What do you understand by the term "Futures?"

Are members of the Exchanges forced under the Rules to deliver to, or receive from, one another Spot Cotton on their Contracts, or can they settle with each other by transferring the Contracts and paying for the differences in value?

What is meant by a "Hedge"?

If a Dealer is Hedged in one month, can he transfer this Hedge to some other month?

What does it cost to Hedge a Contract?

What is an "Invoice" and why its necessity in a shipment of cotton?

What is meant by "Long Cotton"?

What is the difference between Long and "Spot Cotton"?

What do you understand to be the meaning of "Margin" or "Margins"?

Can you give an illustration and tell how to use it?

What do you understand by the expression, "Market Opens," "Market Closes"?

What is meant by "Parity"?

What do you understand to be the meaning of, and how are "Premiums" used?

What do you understand to be the meaning of "Premium" and "Discount Grades"?

Can you tell what is meant by "Reclamations"?

Define what is meant by a "Scalper" and how he operates?

Define "Spot Cotton" and "Spots."

Why the necessity on a Domestic or Export Bill-of-Lading for the notation, "Shippers Order, Notify"?

Is it customary for Cotton Buyers to give Cotton Shippers full credit for the face value of the Draft on the cotton?

Describe when it may or may not be done.

What are "Splits"?

What do you understand to be the meaning of "Straddles" or "Spreads"?

REVIEW QUESTIONS.

How are Cotton Quotations for Spot Cotton generally given in the public press?

How are the Futures quoted with reference to their Fractional denominations?

What Decimal Fraction is the limit in making cotton calculations, established by the Cotton Exchanges?

What is meant by, and the value of, a Point?

For convenience, how are Points generally expressed?

Where Cents are connected with Points how are the quotations divided to show the value of each?

How would you express and read 10 Cents and 2 Points, 12 Cents and 20 Points, 18 Cents and 75 Points, 8 Cents and 50 Points?

What is the difference between 1/4 of a Cent and 25 Points, 3/8 of a Cent and 37½ Points?

What is the value of 1 Cent, 1/2, 1/4, 1/8, 1/16 and 1/32 of a Cent in Points?

In working any of the given Problems where Common Fractions are connected with the price, can you convert these Common Fractions to Decimals and perform the operation of solving the Problem by that means?

How would you express 8 Cents and 25 Points as a Decimal of a Dollar?

Express 10⅜ Cents, 6¼ Cents, 12½ Cents, 15¾ Cents, 9 1/16 Cents 2½ Cents, 8 3/32 Cents as Decimals of a Dollar.

How would you find the sum of $161 3/8, $102 1/8, $252 3/8?

How far must every Decimal be carried, or how many must be pointed off, where the use of the Point is involved?

How many Points are there in 12½c, 8¾c, 6¼c, 3½c?

Find the difference in Points between 10 Cents and 12½ Cents; between 5 Cents and 15 Cents, 7½ Cents and 9 Cents.

What is the difference between 1/32 of a Cent and 3⅛ Points?

What part of a Cent is 7/16 of it expressed in Points?

Express in Points 5/16, 3/8, 1/2, 11/16, 3/4 and 7/8 of a Cent.

REVIEW QUESTIONS.

Can cotton calculations for ascertaining the value of cotton, be made by starting from a certain point, and figure up or down from it?

What is this point called from which the reckoning is made?

Can calculations be made correctly by starting from a certain point as a *Base?*

What are such forms of calculations called?

Do Basic cotton calculations shorten the operation for making them?

Is it material to know the number of Grades in making Basic cotton calculations?

Why is it convenient in making such calculations to use numbers or letters to represent the Grades?

Do members of the Trade use the same symbols for indicating the Grades?

In working from a Base, how are the Premiums and Discounts represented?

Are Premium Values worth more, and those bearing a Discount worth less than the Basic Value?

What Grade of Cotton is generally used as a Base?

Do some Dealers use a different Grade from Middling on which to base their calculations? (See "Difference Sheets," Appendix p. —)

Is there always a definite amount to be discounted for Tinges and Stains, beyond what may be arbitrarily applied?

What Grade of Tinge has a Premium over Middling?

Do you remember what value is placed on Good Middling Tinged?

What Grade is used everywhere as a Basic Grade?

In making a calculation for getting the value of any quantity of cotton, is it necessary that the Differences up and down be the same?

Why is it convenient sometimes to get the average price, before attempting to get the total value?

Can you tell how to find the average price under Rule 2, First Process?

Is the average price found under this Process absolutely correct?

Is this Process often used by the Trade?

What is the difference in finding the average price under Second Process to that found under First Process?

Why is the result obtained in the Second Process not absolutely correct?

Are the averages found under this Process sufficiently close for practical purposes?

Why is it that Cotton Buyers sometimes find their classification at time of sale to be different from that when the cotton was purchased?

If several Buyers have the same Basis price but different Premiums and Discounts for the relative Grades, will that make a difference in figuring their cotton?

What is meant by the statement that B "had a quarter basis, five-eights, or one-half basis" in giving a price for cotton?

What is meant by the word "*Discretion*" as a term applied in cotton transactions?

What is meant by the sixteenth or 6¼ Point Process?

Is this Process often used in the Trade? Tell how to use it?

Why is it so often used?

Can the average be found in Points without the use of the 6¼ Point?

, Explain why Buyers sometimes speak of the Grades as "Goods," "Stricts," "Strict Lows," "Lows;" or as "ones," "twos," "threes" and "fours"?

Do these same formalities obtain all over the South?

What is one of the most important factors to be considered in determining a price to be paid for cotton?

What are Domestic Freight Rates?

What are those Freight Rates called that apply exclusively in a State?

What are those called applying between States or from one State to another?

What organization or body generally controls Intra- and Inter-State Freight Rates?

Do railroads have the right to establish their own Freight Rates?

Can they utilize their self-made Rates without the surveillance of the Railroad Commissions having jurisdiction over them?

What do you understand to be Ocean or Maritime Freight Rates?

Does any Commission or Organization have any jurisdiction over or supervise the Freight Rates made by Maritime transportation companies?

How are they sometimes governed in certain instances?

Are Maritime Freight Rates constant in application or are they subject to fluctuations?

Does competition enter as a factor in directing the Freight Rates to be applied?

What effect is sometimes had on the schedule of charges where Maritime transportation companies bid against each other for traffic?

Do Maritime transportation companies ever contract with Shippers for the transportation of Freight in one part of the year to be transported at some subsequent time?

Does the privilege of contracting the transportation of Freight open an avenue for speculation on the same?

Are the Rates exhibited in the circulars or bulletins of the Maritime companies exactly the same as those made by private agreement?

If an Exporter secures the minimum Freight Rates, and finds at the time of the exportation of his cotton that the Freight Rates are much higher, what is his course to pursue to realize a profit therefrom?

Can or may this profit be sometimes destroyed by active competition?

REVIEW QUESTIONS.

What is a Check or Draft?

What is the material difference between the two and how do they apply?

With reference to time how are Drafts made?

What is a Draft sometimes called?

What is meant by a Draft selling for Par, Premium or Discount?

What do you understand to be the meaning of one person *drawing* on another?

If a Draft is not paid when presented how may it be protected without being protested?

What do Drafts usually show?

How many parties are connected in a Draft transaction?

What is a Domestic Draft, a Foreign Draft?

How are Domestic Drafts paid with reference to time?

Are Drafts for Foreign accounts made payable "at sight"?

What is Buying and Selling Drafts called?

Who usually deal in Drafts as commodities to be bought and sold?

How do banks charge or what Rate do they usually make for Buying and Selling Drafts?

What do you understand to be the "Course of Exchange"?

What are the advantages to be had in the use of Drafts in the settlement of cotton transactions?

Do they eliminate the risk of sending money?

How may a Drawer of a Draft in Memphis, Tenn., for $1,000, have paid to himself this same amount of money in New York?

What are "Reserve Agents" or "Correspondents of a Bank"?

How do banks distribute their deposits for safekeeping?

For what purpose are these deposits placed in the hands of other banks?

Can individuals arrange for Exchange accounts similar to banks?

Can Exchange sometimes be cheapened by transmitting the Draft through two or more commercial centres?

Who determines the basis for money transactions between the United States and Foreign countries?

When does a Draft on any Foreign country sell for Par and what is this kind of Exchange called?

Why is Intrinsic Par of Exchange different from Commercial Par of Exchange?

What character of Exchange for Foreign countries, is dealt in by our banks?

How is Exchange computed for England, Ireland and Scotland, and through what Foreign city are the Drafts usually drawn?

How are Drafts generally drawn for payment of cotton shipped to France?

Are they sometimes drawn payable through London?

Through what point are Drafts generally drawn for payment of cotton destined to Germany?

What five Foreign countries have the same Monetary Unit value?

What three have the same Monetary Unit value, but different from the five preceding ones?

What countries have their Monetary Unit coinage divided into 100 parts as subdivisions?

What character of Drafts are used for the payment of Foreign cotton, and for what length of time do they usually read?

What are the standards of weights used throughout Foreign countries?

In what denomination of those measurements are cotton fibers measured?

REVIEW QUESTIONS.

Over what extent of territory do Cotton Buyers in the South operate?

Why do so many people attempt to buy and sell cotton?

With what must a Dealer familiarize himself to buy and sell cotton successfully?

What three classes of Buyers operate in the Market?

What must a Dealer know before he begins a day's business buying cotton?

Define a Local Primary Buyer, an Intermediate Buyer, an Exporter or Spinner Buyer.

Can you tell how cotton Markets are made, and from what source do we get our quotations on which to buy or sell?

At what time of the day does the New Orleans Cotton Exchange begin its business?

What is the nature of the first business transacted thereon?

How many "Calls" are made during the day, and what are they?

What is the character of the business transacted on the Exchange?

Are trades ever made in private on the Exchange and no records kept of them?

What do you understand to be "Ring Trades" or "Ring Trading"?

For what purpose was the circular enclosure on the floor of the Exchange made?

How are the quotations sent out from the Exchange, and to whom are they sent?

Describe the operations of a Local Primary Buyer, an Intermediary Buyer, an Exporter or Mill Buyer.

What are "Cotton Limits"?

Do all Local Buyers operate independently, or on salary, or on commission?

Describe a representative cotton firm.

Do most large Dealers in cotton possess a membership in some of the Cotton Exchanges?

When, and how can a large Dealer operate in the Market independent of Exchange quotations?

How do large Dealers figure out a "working basis"?

How many months do the Exchanges quote as Future Months?

Why are they quoted as "active" or "Hedging Months"?

What months are generally recognized as the Hedging Months?

How does Liverpool quote her Hedging Months?

Describe how a Local Buyer takes cotton from Farmers' wagons at primary points.

On which side of the bale of cotton is the basis made for purchase?

Are the Growers paid for their cotton at once, if so, state how it is generally done?

At what time of the day is a large percentage of the cotton business in the South done by large Dealers?

What is the plan of exhibiting samples of cotton for the sale of it at some places?

Do Buyers sometimes talk in a way to induce holders of cotton to sell it?

Is it a good policy for a Buyer to attempt to forecast the Market for a Grower?

Do Buyers generally follow the fluctuations of the Market?

When do Buyers usually report their cotton sales?

Describe the functions and purposes of the "Take-up-man."

How many Marks generally accompany a shipment of cotton locally?

REVIEW QUESTIONS.

How are payments for local cotton usually made?

Are Drafts in payment for Foreign cotton accepted without some knowledge of the party on whom they are drawn?

What is meant by buying cotton "hog round"?

How are the bales usually cut for sampling where a list of cotton is taken up?

When should the bales be closely scrutinized for a more rigid examination?

What do you understand by "concentration of cotton," and why the necessity for it?

Where is cotton usually concentrated, and what often results after shipping lists are made up in fulfillment of orders?

What becomes of the "overs" after all shipping lists are completed?

What papers as official documents usually accompany Domestic Shipments?

How are Domestic Shipments paid for?

What banks handle the largest percentage of Exchange for payment of Foreign cotton?

What guides the banks in determining what Rate of Exchange to apply on such payments?

Through what Foreign Commercial Centers are Drafts principally drawn for settlements for cotton destined for England, Spain, Holland, Belgium, Denmark, Sweden and Italy?

Through what points for shipments of cotton to France, Germany etc.?

How are B/L's worded to protect both the Shipper and Banker in their shipments of cotton?

What do you understand to mean a "Waco House," as stated in this Section?

What authority has this House for executing its own transactions and under whose jurisdiction does it operate?

Define what you consider a "Central Buying Point."

Are there many similar "points" in the South, and are they essential to the successful operation of the present System of handling Spot Cotton?

What are "Cotton Guarantees," how do they apply, and when are they required for the protection of both Seller and Buyer?

How is cotton sold "by sample," who sell it that way, and what kind of cotton is often submitted?

What is meant by F. O. B. cotton?

If a Purchaser accepts cotton at loading point, F. O. B., is a Guarantee necessary?

How far and how long do Guarantees sometimes follow cotton?

Can cotton be sold on F. O. B. terms, by sample, Class Marks, Basis, Average or Even-running?

Are Freight, Drayage and other incidental Expenses attached to cotton bought F. O. B. at loading point?

Are the charges for compression taxed against the price of cotton purchased either F. O. B. point of origin or destination?

Is *time of delivery* for shipments of F. O. B. cotton a factor to be considered when purchasing?

What institutions, in the main, govern in F. O. B. transactions both North and South?

Do similar Rules prevail over the South governing transactions in F. O. B. cotton?

REVIEW QUESTIONS.

Do *Northern Mills* require Sellers to Hedge their sales to them?

How may a Mill Hedge its purchase without resorting to an Exchange Contract?

Do Mills ever Hedge their sales of manufactured articles, where Contracts call for delivery in the future?

What character of cotton do Mills generally buy?

What variation or latitude do they allow from a specific Type of cotton?

From whom do Mills usually buy their raw material?

Whom do the Vendors represent and how do they make sales of the cotton committed to them?

Do Mills offer a specific price for a definite class of cotton, or do they seek competitive offerings when in the Market?

To whom do Mills look for protection in their purchases?

Why have Northern Mills changed their former policy and assumed their present plan of buying?

What are their usual methods of present-day buying?

On what basis are the Uplands, Short Staple Western and Long Staple cotton sold to the Mills?

What is their allowance for Tare?

What Rules govern in the sale and purchase of their basic materials?

How and when are the Differences in Grades established?

What Standards are still utilized by them?

How are controversies settled?

How do they buy Sea-Island cotton?

In a general way, how do *Southern Mills* operate in buying cotton?

Are the Southern Mills in the Eastern districts governed by associate agreement?

Are their Rules similar to the Association Rules of the Northern Mills?

By what Rules are the Southern Mills guided?

What character of cotton do they usually prescribe for their use?

Do Southern Mills require that Vendors Hedge the cotton sold to them on Contract?

Do they offer a specific price for a specific Grade?

How do they finally execute a purchase, after notifying the Trade they are in the Market?

Through what medium do they generally operate?

Do Southern Mills buy for Mill delivery, Weights and Grades guaranteed?

At what time are the Mills generally in the Market?

Do Mills contract their cotton for delivery in future months?

What advantage have the Mills by contracting their output for months ahead, and how do they protect themselves against fluctuations in the cotton Market?

As a general practice, do Mills protect their purchases of raw material and sales of manufactured fabrics, by hedging on the Cotton Exchanges?

How and when can a Mill make itself independent of the Market?

Do Mills buy on Middling basis?

Describe a Southern Mill purchase.

What Standard is used by the Associated Southern Mills?

How do non-associated Mills in Georgia and Texas buy cotton?

What is the difference between purchasing for Domestic Markets and for Export?

Is the relationship between American and Foreign Markets very close?

Through whom do Buyers on this side principally conduct their business for Foreign Trade?

How can cotton be sold abroad with reference to Grades, Samples, etc.?

With reference to time, what do you understand to be the meaning of the terms, "afloat," "prompt," "immediate shipment" or "to arrive" as designated for some month?

How is Foreign Cotton generally sold with reference to net or gross weight?

What is the maximum or minimum weights for tenderable cotton in the Foreign Markets?

What is the limit of gradation allowable and what Standards or what Association govern?

How are settlements for contentions over the delivery of Foreign Cotton made?

Under what terms are Foreign Cotton shipments usually made?

What do you understand to be the full meaning and purpose of the "C. I. F. & 6%" terms?

Explain what you consider to be a Franchise.

Explain a shipment of cotton under "C. I. F. & 6%" terms.

What are the weights that apply, per 100 bales, for the different Types of American Cotton?

REVIEW QUESTIONS.

What do you understand to be the meaning of "Tare" as used in connection with cotton transactions?

How do American Mills buy their cotton with reference to Tare?

What is the policy of Foreign Mills with reference to Tare?

Can you define the difference between Bremen, Liverpool and Havre with respect to their plan of computation in ascertaining Tare?

What is the general policy on the part of European Buyers in taking American Cotton?

Why do they exact a 6% Tare, and yet will strip some of the bales of their wrapping, weigh those wrappings, to determine an exact Tare?

What is the real purpose of the Tare?

Can you make a statement showing a shipment of Export Cotton, with a direct application of the 6% Tare?

Distinguish the difference between buying Domestic and Foreign Cotton respecting the weight of the Tare?

If the Tare on a 500-pound bale of cotton is 22 pounds, and Foreign Importers exact a 6% Tare, how does the American Exporter protect himself against a loss in weight equal to the difference between 22 pounds and 30 pounds?

When an American Farmer is paid a certain price gross weight for his cotton, does he really get pay for the bagging and ties on it?

Can you show that he does not?

How is actual Tare computed for cotton delivered in Liverpool, Havre, Bremen, Manchester, Hamburg, Genoa, Barcelona, Naples, Trieste and Stockholm?

As a general practice, how, and with what materials are American cotton bales wrapped?

Why is the jute bagging not a good wrapping for the safe protection of the cotton?

What is the difference between the character of wrapping used for cotton in the United States compared with India, Egypt, Brazil and Peru?

What is about the average weight for the American, Egyptian and East Indian bale of cotton?

Do you think a wrapping composed of cotton material will make a good covering for the protection of cotton?

Describe the advantages claimed for the Round Bale.

Why has not the Round Bale been universally adopted if it possesses all the merits claimed for it as an economic package?

REVIEW QUESTIONS.

What two essential factors are considered in connection with selling cotton for future delivery?

Describe two imaginary transactions in which these two factors have expression.

What is "Short Selling"?

Can a sale be made "Short" and be legitimate?

When would a Short Sale be construed as being illegitimate?

Does Short Selling in every instance signify that the sale of "Futures" has reference to an Exchange Contract?

Can Short Sales be made of any commodity, such as wheat, corn, oats, stocks, bonds, etc., the same as cotton?

What is the difference between the sale of Spot and Future cotton?

Why do Dealers ever "sell Short" or "Short the Market"?

As an unknown quantity, what may be considered as a factor in the Cotton Market that sometimes reflects against the success of a Short Sale?

Do the membership of the Cotton Exchange ever act as a unit in putting the Market up or down?

Why is it they do not?

As a practice, do Farmers ever sell Short?

What would you consider some of the conditions that would induce you to sell cotton Short?

Would you consider Short Selling Spot Cotton the same as contracting cotton for the Trade, the Mills or Export?

How can competition between Buyers virtually destroy the effect of the Short Sale?

Do Buyers ever attempt to take advantage of each other as regards Short Sales?

Who sometimes send cotton to Commission Merchants for sale?

What are Commission Merchants called who handle cotton consigned to them?

Describe how a Shipper makes up his shipments for consignment?

What is the first thing a Factor does after receiving the cotton?

When he receives instructions to sell, how does he proceed, and in what way does he make returns and how does he generally pay for such shipments?

What advantages have Cotton Factors for the sale of cotton who operate on an extensive scale?

What further advantages have they if given more time to make a sale?

How are Factors paid for their services in making sales of their customers' cotton?

How can Shippers consigning cotton to Factors receive money on the cotton before the Factors get it and sell it?

What are the four necessary Documents connected with transactions for the sale of Export Cotton?

Define the purport, meaning and use of the Invoice.

What important information is covered in the Invoice, both for Domestic and Export cotton?

Is the Invoice for consignments of cotton to Factors the same as that made up for a straight sale to a Domestic Buyer or for Export?

Define the difference between the three different forms of Invoices.

In a shipment of cotton why is the Draft necessary, and why does a Draft sometimes call for payment at a future date?

If a Shipper desires cash on his Draft what are the usual proceedings he undertakes?

Sometimes he can get the face value of the Draft, sometimes less and sometimes more; why is this?

What class of people deal in Drafts and pay cash for them?

Why is it that Drafts sometimes do, or do not draw Interest?

What kind of money is generally specified for Drafts issued in payment of Export Cotton?

Are Drafts for Export Cotton drawn in single, duplicate or triplicate form?

Why are stubs sometimes attached to those Drafts or Bills of Exchange?

What does the Draft show with reference to the shipment, as compared to the data in the Invoice?

What is the Bill-of-Lading and for what is it issued?

What do you understand to be an "open" Bill-of-Lading?

Why are the words "Shipper's Order, Notify," noted on a Bill-of-Lading?

Is the Bill-of-Lading absolutely necessary in the shipment?

Why is the Certificate of Insurance a necessary Document to a shipment of foreign cotton, and what data does it specify?

Define the data and meaning of a "Specific," "Marine" and "Blanket" Policy.

REVIEW QUESTIONS.

Can you give the cause for establishing the New York Cotton Exchange?

Its membership is limited to how many members?

What are the requisites an individual must possess to be entitled to a membership in this Exchange?

What is the initiation fee, and what are the annual dues?

How may an individual secure a "right of membership"?

Can you outline briefly what are the purposes of this Corporation?

Does this institution buy and sell cotton as a corporate body? If not, how is it bought and sold?

What is the principal character of business executed on the floors of this Exchange?

What was one of the original primary functions of it?

From among what class of business men are members found?

Do members of this Exchange deal exclusively in Spots or Futures?

How do you understand that members may operate as a unit factor to "manipulate the Market"?

Do the Rules allow the membership to operate together with a view of executing trades to their pecuniary interests?

Is the membership of the New York Exchange confined to resident individuals only?

How does this Exchange prove itself valuable to the Trade as a factor in securing and distributing information relative to the cotton Market?

When prices are bid or received for cotton does that mean for Spot Cotton or for Cotton Contracts?

What are members of the Exchanges called?

How does a Broker operate for a client in buying or selling a "Future," when the client makes no price for the sale or purchase of the Contract?

How may the prices of Futures be increased or decreased by legitimate action on the part of the public?

What would you consider to be the cause for an advance in the price of cotton?

As one of the primary functions of the New York Cotton Exchange was for the purpose of bringing together both Buyer and Seller face to face, and as such function now exists only in a limited degree, what do you consider to be the cause for it?

Compared to New York, how does the New Orleans Cotton Exchange operate?

How long has it been in existence?

Why is it a better Spot Market than New York?

Is it connected with any other Cotton Exchange, or is it an independent institution operating under its own Rules?

Does it have wire connection with important cities of the United States and Foreign Commerical Centers?

Do you think this Exchange has been instrumental in helping to bring the control of the price of American Cotton in the hands of American people?

Do you think Cotton Exchanges are advantageous to the Trade, if their transactions are legitimate?

What Cotton Standards have been adopted by this Exchange?

What Exchanges outside of New York and New Orleans, sell Futures?

Define a "Bucket Shop" and its purposes. [See page 342.]

REVIEW QUESTIONS.

What constitutes the principal business of those Cotton Exchanges dealing in Futures?

What do you understand to be the meaning of the word "Future" as applied to the Trade?

Under what three heads may Future dealing be divided?

Do all Future Contracts contemplate the actual delivery of cotton?

What is the least number of bales embodied in a New York or New Orleans Cotton Contract?

What are the essential differences between a New York and New Orleans Cotton Contract?

What rules govern the delivery of cotton on Contracts?

All Contracts call for delivery of cotton in certain months, in what part of the month may the delivery be made?

On the delivery of Cotton on a Contract who has the right to say on which day of the month it shall be delivered, and what class of cotton will be delivered?

How many days has the Seller to notify the Buyer in New York, New Orleans or Liverpool when the cotton will be delivered?

What are these days called?

On what Grade of cotton is the price of Cotton Contracts based?

If Contract Cotton is based on Middling, how are the values for the Higher and Lower Grades determined?

Can each party to a Contract exact a deposit from the other as a "Margin" for protection?

How many times is cotton inspected, classed and weighed in New Orleans, New York and Liverpool each time it changes ownership?

Who classifies the cotton delivered on Contracts on any of these Exchanges?

Describe how a delivery of Spot Cotton is made on a Future Contract.

What do you understand to be the optional features of a Contract?

What is the meaning of a "Hedge"?

Define what is meant by a Buying Hedge.

When may a Hedge absolutely protect Spot Cotton?

Describe in detail, by illustration, how a Buying Hedge will give absolute protection; will give a gain or a loss.

Why does a disparity between Spots and Futures affect the purpose of the Hedge?

Can you tell how a divergence of parities may cause double losses or double gains, or the absence of any gain or loss?

Define a Selling Hedge and tell how and in what way it will give protection to a Dealer in Spot Cotton or a loss to him.

Of what does a large percentage of the business transacted on the Cotton Exchange consist?

Do Speculators in Contracts have the same rights in dealing in them as those who operate for Hedging?

Tell how speculations in Contracts resemble gambling transactions.

Describe transactions that may be settled by "direct settlement," or "ring settlement."

How does a member protect a Contract he has bought or sold for a client, and what is required on the part of the client to protect the Broker?

What are the brokerage charges and the minimum amount paid for Margins on each Contract dealt in?

What are the factors considered by Brokers and Dealers in aiding them to determine a price for cotton?

Ordinarily, if Futures fluctuate, what effect does this have upon Spot Cotton?

What is considered a legitimate or illegitimate Contract?

In how many ways can a Future Contract be operative?

Define how Future Contracts can be connected with Spot transactions as defined by *a, b, c, d, e,* and *f.*

What must be the condition between Spots and Futures in order to make the Hedge effectual?

If A sells a Future Contract to protect his Spot cotton, what does he do with his Contract when he sells his Spot cotton?

Tell how A can hedge by buying Futures, and under what condition will it protect Spots?

Can you tell some of the ways Cotton Exchanges can be useful to their members, the Trade and the public?

How may Spot Dealers operate, who are not members of the Exchange if they seek protection under a Hedge?

If a Dealer buys or sells a Contract, does he receive the Contract after the deal is consummated?

What does buying and selling Futures mean?

Why does a Broker demand a Margin to protect himself when he buys or sells a Contract on the Exchange, for a client?

What is the ostensible purpose of every Contract, and are they always adjusted according to those purposes?

Describe how a Cotton Firm may enter the Spot Market, connect that business with Future Contracts and inflict a loss upon itself.

If a Dealer has a quantity of Spot cotton on hand at a time the Market shows a tendency to decline, would it be advisable to *sell* Futures?

Would it be advisable under such conditions to *buy* Futures?

If a Dealer has a large quantity of Spot cotton hedged and sells some of this cotton at different times, how does he make disposition of his Futures?

Do Mills as a general practice resort extensively to the Exchanges for Contracts for protection?

Tell how one must operate to buy or sell Futures.

If a Dealer is not known to be of high financial standing, what will a Broker require from him as a safe-guard to himself?

If a Dealer is known to be financially strong and responsible, are his purchases or sales executed with promptness, without an immediate remittance?

Are trades upon the Exchanges, all things being satisfactory, always executed with promptness and dispatch?

Is the Cotton Code employed extensively between Brokers and Dealers, in their immediate transactions?

Can you tell how many Points advance on a Future will equal the value of the Margin paid, or how many Points decline will consume the amount of Margin paid?

If a Dealer pays $100 on a Contract, how many Points decline must occur before the Broker will call for another Margin or sell out the Contract?

Does a Broker charge additional Brokerage for transferring a Contract of a client from one month to another month?

REVIEW QUESTIONS.

What do you understand to be the meaning of the word "Exchange," as applied to any transaction?

In what respects do the different market places for the sale of cotton in the South resemble Exchanges?

Do these market places have a listed membership and Rules and Regulations to govern them?

Who were the first people to begin the manufacture of cotton for practical and domestic purposes as a commercial commodity?

As the manufacturing business grew, why did the idea become emphasized that it was necessary to have some *central point* at which Buyers could assemble for the purchase of cotton, or to give and receive information?

As this idea grew, what was the result of it and when was the first Cotton Exchange in the world established, and when did dealings in Futures on that Exchange begin?

After the establishment of that Exchange, who were the controllers of the cotton traffic of the world and the exclusive price-makers for American Cotton?

Describe the conditions that confronted the American people in the early days of cotton culture.

Were there any such things as "Cotton Markets" in those days as we know them now?

What can you say of their means of communication by mail, courier and telegraph or telephone?

Who were the principal Sellers of American Cotton in those days after it left the Farmers' hands?

Why was it that for a period of nearly 100 years after the introduction of cotton as an agricultural product, that its culture received but little stimulation?

When was the first Gin invented of any practical importance and why did Whitney's invention give such great stimulation to the cotton industry?

What kind of gin was in use before Whitney's invention, and what was said to be the daily output from such a Gin?

What constituted the total weight of lint cotton taken from the seed by one hand as result of a day's labor?

Describe how the cotton of the Southern States found a Market in ante-bellum days?

How was cotton handled then as a commercial article compared to Sugar, Molasses, Rice, Tar, Turpentine, etc.?

MB-15

· If a Grower sold cotton through a Commission Merchant, did he receive prompt pay for it immediately upon its receipt by the Consignee?

What character of labor was generally employed in the production of cotton before the Civil War?

What were the principal means of transportation in getting cotton to Foreign Markets after leaving the Farmer's hands?

Describe the conditions that confronted the Southern Cotton Grower and handicapped him in the sale of his cotton by reason of the absence of a source from which he could get some idea of the value of it.

APPENDIX

APPENDIX.

QUARTER GRADES.

A Trade in Quarter Grades Exemplified.—Let it be stated that A sells a list of 100 bales of cotton to B, which consists of a wide range of Grades, say from St. Good Ordinary to Good Middling, inclusive, and in the list are several bales of "good style" of Middling, and many bales of "shy" Middling.

The "good style" of Middling is known as Fully Middling by the Cotton Exchanges, and the "shy" Middling as Barely Middling.

If B in this sale accepts the "full" Type of Middling for Middling, he should accept also the "shy" Middling for Middling, because the good qualities of the first should offset the deficiencies of the last, and enable A to get whole value for his cotton.

Further illustrating: Suppose B says to A, "Your 'good style' Middling is not good enough for Strict Middling; I shall cut it *down* to Middling, and your 'shy' Middling is not equal to a Midddling; I shall mark it *down to a Strict Low Middling.*"

Now, if the Fully Middling is worth 12 Points[1] more than Middling, equal to 60c on a bale of 500 lbs., and Barely Middling is worth 17 Points[2] less than Middling, or 85c on a similar weight bale, B has gained by such action $1.45 by reducing the gradation on both bales.

It should be stated that the recognition of the Quarter Grades by the Cotton Exchanges and the Trade redounds to the interest of the Producer; for without their position in the classification list, it is evident, as in the case just stated, all Grades not showing clear Types of any particular Grade would be reduced to the Half Grade Type *below*, at the expense of the Seller or Grower.

Present Trade conditions and Mill Rules warrant the raising of one Grade to its Half position above, at the same time demands the reduction of a Quarter Grade to the Half Grade position below, thus giving and taking value for value, as elsewhere stated.

Trade Recognition of Quarter Grades.—It may be argued that the intrinsic value between a Fully and a Barely Grade of cotton is so slight as to merit no distinction for spinnable purposes, by reason of the very small percentage of foreign substances contained in them in excess or diminution of their proximate Grades; but the fact remains that these Quarter Grades have been arbitrarily established by the Cotton Exchanges, recognized by the Trade to which

---

[1]Cents per hundred, on and off, for Fully and Barely Middling.
[2]Cotton, made by the New York Cot. Ex., Sept. 11, 1912.

it has become accustomed, and any system of gradation eliminating them from the list will operate financially against the Grower, unless all cotton could be delivered "even-running;" for under such conditions, it is evident that for every "barely" Grade delivered the same should be offset by one "fully" in Type, and no loss could result were the Differences in Premiums and Discounts the same and no excess of weights preponderate either way; but as the Differences applying on the Lower Grades are wider than those on the Higher Grades, to accept the same number of Fully or Barely cotton would operate against the interest of Purchaser, if many Quarter Grades were offered.

The United States Department of Agriculture did not see fit to establish Grades of cotton for those recognized as "Quarter grades," because of the fact that the law directing the establishment of them inhibited the Secretary of Agriculture from doing so, it being alleged that the *Spinnable Differences* between Quarter and Half Grades were too slight to admit of the difference in distinction, and that it was an uneconomic proposition.

In fairness to the Cotton Grower and the Trade, it would seem a matter of justice for the Department of Agriculture to widen its range of Grades to include at least the Tinges and Stains.

Narrowing the official list made by the Department, if finally adopted by all the Cotton Exchanges, will go far towards effectually eliminating confusion in the Trade, and will result unfavorably to no one, as every "shy" is compensated for with a "full," and each accepted at the same price as the Full Grade it represents.

Should *spinnable differences*[3] ever govern in directing the purchase of cotton, the above statement would no longer hold good.

MIDDLING.

The different Cotton Exchanges, in establishing their Standards, have held to similar names in making up their official lists, but their *grade names* do not signify the same character of cotton.

The Middling Uplands of Texas and Oklahoma are distinctly different to that character of cotton called Middling Uplands grown in the red lands east of the Mississippi River, and by reason of the fact that the U. S. Department of Agriculture has not assumed the prerogative to classify them separately, the New York Cotton Exchange has not adopted the Government Standards as its official list of Contract Cottons, preferring tohold to its own Standards, adopted by all the Cotton Exchanges at a convention held in 1874.

The Department of Agriculture, in making its Standards, claims to classify them without regard to the source from which the type samples came, and in this manner standardizing *all* the Uplands

[3]See "Spinnable Value," Book 1, p. 70.

grown, assuming such procedure should produce a set of Types which "would be representative of white American cotton as a whole."[4]

U. S. GOVERNMENT STANDARDS.

By reason of a want of harmony existing among the Cotton Exchanges as to their Standards, and the resulting confusion that often occurred because of the members of one Exchange operating with those of another, the efforts and influence of the producers and manufacturers of cotton were brought to the attention of the United States Congress, urging the enactment of a law standardizing American cotton for the American Trade.

Mr. A. S. Burleson, Congressman from Texas, succeeded in getting a bill passed standardizing American cotton, which Standards have been adopted by nearly all the principal Cotton Exchanges of the country.

The Act making appropriations for the Department of Agriculture for standardizing cotton becomes effective June 30, 1909.

In establishing the Grades of cotton, the Secretary of Agriculture (James Wilson at that time), was further authorized "to prepare in practical form the Standard of said Grades, and furnish the same upon request by any person, the cost thereof to be paid, when delivered, by the person requesting the same, and certified under the signature of the said Secretary and the seal of his Department."

"Carrying out the provisions of this Act, the Secretary of Agriculture convened in the city of Washington in February, 1909, a committee of cotton experts including, besides the Department experts, representatives of the different interests of the trade. This committe consisted of Mr. Joseph A. Airey, of John M. Parker & Co., New Orleans, La.; Mr. James Akers, of Inman, Akers & Inman, Atlanta, Ga.; Mr. F. M. Crump, of F. M. Crump & Co., Memphis, Tenn.; Mr. C. P. Baker, of the Lawrence Manufacturing Company, Boston, Mass.; Mr. Lewis W. Parker, of the Olympia Mills, Greenville, S. C.; Mr. John Martin, Paris, Texas; Mr. Nathaniel Thayer, of Barry, Thayer & Co., Boston, Mass.; Mr. Geo. W. Neville, of Weld & Neville, New York City; Mr. Charles A. Vedder, of John D. Rogers & Co., Galveston, Texas; and Dr. N. A. Cobb and Mr. R. L. Bennett of the Department of Agriculture. The committee was assisted by the following expert classifiers: Mr. W. P. Barbot, of the Classification Committee, New York Cotton Exchange; Mr. Jules Mazerat, Chairman Classification Committee, New Orleans Cotton Exchange, and Mr. J. R. Taylor, with the firm of Wolf & Company, Dallas, Texas.

"The Department furnished the committee every facility for its work, having on hand types of cotton from the different exchanges

---

[4]Substance of a letter to the author from Dr. N. A. Cobb, Technologist of the Department of Agriculture, dated Jan. 8, 1913.

and markets, and materials for making up the grades as provided by law."[5]

In preserving the Types for future reference, that the indicated ones may not become deteriorated, the Department has placed 50 sets in vacuum storage for use as working duplicates, believing by this means to preserve them indefinitely as exact Standards as originally adopted.[6]

While this plan of preservation of the type sample is unique and untried, the result will be watched with much interest by the Trade, as nothing of which the author has any knowledge has been attempted by any of the Cotton Exchanges or members of the Trade to keep them intact indefinitely under such form of equipment.

TEXAS COTTON.

A curious fact may be stated here, to-wit, that men who have been connected with the Trade for many years in Texas state that no thought of *selecting* staple cotton north of Bryan, on the H. & T. C. R. R., up to Dallas, and north of that line east of Dallas, was had many years ago, but now that whole territory has to be gone over carefully to get any commercial 1 1-8. Formerly it was the custom to ship it out classed as 1 1-8 without question.

This reduction of the length of Staple over Central Texas territory is attributed to the improved methods of soil preparation, seed selection and cultivation; the efforts in growing cotton being directed more to the production of *early* varieties than to improvement of the Staple, and this has had a tendency to bring down the price of Texas cotton.

The black lands north and northeast of Dallas still continue to produce 1 1-8 cotton of good "body," but when the sandy or clayey lands east of this district are reached, 5-8, 3-4 and 7-8 cottons are found.[7]

BOLLY COTTON.

There appeared on the Texas Market in the fall of 1913, cotton from the Bolly Cotton area of West Texas, exhibiting all the characteristics peculiar to Low Grade white cotton. It was shipped and received as Bolly Cotton, but devoid of the tinge or stain that usually characterizes Bolly Cotton.

This fact is attributed to two circumstances: First, the cotton had matured and opened before it was tinged with frost; second, excessive and continued rains soon following, accompanied by the custom-

---

[5]From Circular Letter of Dr. N. A. Cobb to the author.
[6]Year book U. S. Department of Agriculture, 1911, p. 65.
[7]Mr. Geo. W. Neville, in letter to author Dec. 31st, 1912.

ary winds of that region which blew some of it to the ground, reduced its Grade. The excess rain caused the open bolls to become more or less rotten, and in attempting to gather such cotton from the stalk part or all of the rotted bolls became mixed with the seed cotton. The customary term of Bolly Cotton was applied to it.

The fiber of that cotton was good, but the gradation was reduced to Good Ordinary and Strict Good Ordinary.[8]

GRADE PRICES LOWERED.

Buyers taking up cotton are often confronted with conditions that require lowering the price of the Grade, as when Gin Cuts, Naps, Spots and Off-color appear. If the Grade of a bale shows to be M., but Gin Cuts, Off-color or any of the imperfections noted appear, its value will be reduced to S. L. M. The same results would follow on any of the Grades. The cotton under such conditions would be quoted as M., Strict Low value; G. M., Strict M. value, etc.

TRADE DIFFERENCES.

The Differences "on" and "off" for the Grades above and below Middling as made by large Dealers do not always, in fact rarely, coincide with those made by the Exchanges, nor do those made by one Dealer always conform to those made by another.

A Dealer may change his own Differences one or more times during the cotton buying season.

In putting out his notices of change, he refers to them as *"Difference Sheets."*

The Differences are sometimes based on Good Middling, but generally on the Middling Grade.

It should be remembered that Differences have no bearing on what the Middling price shall be, but only affect it in a relative way. The Differences can apply just the same on Middling cotton at 6, 8, 10 or 12 Cents a pound, as at 5 or 15 Cents.

If cotton is 7 Cents a pound, Strict Middling may be 3-16 Cents "on;" if it is 12 Cents, "Stricts may still be 3-16 Cents "on."

Let's look at the following *Difference Sheets* put out recently by a large Dealer, with instructions, and based on *Good Middling*:

DIFFERENCE SHEET.

Please note the following grade differences to govern our purchases from September 16, 191.... (Liverpool class):

F. G. M., 3:16c on G. M., G. M. pass; F. M., 3-16c off G. M.; M.,

---

[8]This cotton was shown to the author in the office of the McFadden Agency at Waco, Texas, in October, 1913.

7–16c off G. M.; F. L. M., 15-16c off G. M.; L. M., 1 7-16c off G. M.; F. G. O., 2 1-8c off G. M.; G. O., 3 1-8c off G. M.; tinges, F. M. and above, 1-4c off white; tinges, M. and below, 1-2c off white; stains, F. M. and above, 1-2c off white; stains M., 3-4c off white; stains. F. L. M. and below, 1c off white.

On basis orders we allow no premiums for cotton above F. G. M. and any M. F. and B. M. F. cotton on such orders has to be invoiced at F. G. M. prices.

We will thank you to please acknowledge receipt of this letter.

Yours truly,

This firm gave the following change in its Difference Sheet, with no explanation why such changes were made:

Please note the following new grade differences to govern our basis purchase, on and from Monday, October 14, 191.... (Liverpool class).

F. G. M., 3-16c on G. M.; G. M. pass; F. M., 3-16c off G. M.; M., 7-16c off G. M.; F. L. M., 7-8c off G. M.; L. M., 1 3-8c off·G. M.; F. G. O., 2 1-16c off G. M.; G. O., 3 1-8c off G. M.; tinges, F. M. and above, 5-16c off white; tinges M. and below, 5-8c off white; stains, F. M. and below, 1 1-4c off white.

On basis orders we allow no premium for cotton above F. G. M., and any M. F. and B. M. F. cotton on such orders has to be invoiced at F. G. M. prices.

We will thank you to please acknowledge receipt of this letter.

Yours truly,

The fixing of these Differences is made by this firm itself, and any subsequent ones are established the same way.

The cause for so doing may be the Mill buying from this large firm, or it may be a purely arbitrary matter with the firm itself.

These Differences were not in harmony with those of the Cotton Exchanges at the time, and evidently ignored the work of the Revision Committees of those institutions in establishing gradation Differences.

Instead of giving the full list of Grade names Dealers often give advice respecting those Grades on which the changed Differences apply only; that is to say if a Premium of 1-16 and 1-8 are added to S. M. and G. M., the instructions usually read: "Until further advised, increase the Premium on S. M. 1-16, on G. M. 1-8: reduce the Discount on L. M. 1-4, on S. G. O. 3-8."

The Differences applying on similar Grades are not always the

same with different Dealers, which fact finds reflection with the Local
Buyer. One Buyer may have a basis or limit exactly the same as
another, but the *Differences* not being similar, gives one Buyer tem-
porarily the advantage over the other.

HISTORY OF 6 PER CENT TARE.

Cotton has been grown in America for 123 years as a commercial
commodity. At the beginning it was put up in 225 pound packages.
These original average weights have gradually increased from 1790
to the present time, being now about 520 pounds.

When the weight had reached 380 to 400 pounds, with the weight of
the covering known to be approximately 23 or 24 pounds, European custom established the practice of deducting 6 per cent of the *gross weight*
to cover the weight of the bagging and ties, which practice at the
time met with no objection, but since the average weight in more
recent years has risen to about 500 pounds, to deduct 6 per cent of
it would necessarily take 30 pounds from the gross weight. So if
the covering on a bale weighed 24 pounds and the 6 per cent applied
deducted 30 pounds, a loss of 6 pounds of cotton would fall to the
Seller, for if the bale weighed 500 pounds, with an actual Tare of
24 pounds on it, the net amount of cotton left would be 476 pounds;
but if 30 pouds were deducted, 470 pounds would stand to the credit
of the Seller.

Since the advent of the 500-pound bale on the Foreign Market,
with demands from that source of Trade for a continuation of the
application of the 6 per cent Rule, controversies and contentions
have followed.

ORIGIN OF BUCKET SHOPS.

Man's cupidity leads him into investments which perhaps no other
influence would induce him to assume the risk or undertaking. This
natural propensity or gambling instinct was no doubt the primary
motive that led to the establishment of these *places for "Trade,"*
as they were termed by those operating them for the benefit (?) of
customers or patrons who cared to take risks on the rise and fall
of any commodity regularly quoted on any Stock, Cotton or Produce
Exchange or Board of Trade.

The New York and New Orleans Cotton Exchanges dealing in no
less than 100 bales of cotton for future delivery; the Chicago Board
of Trade in no less than 1000 bushels of wheat, 5000 bushels of corn
or oats, 250 barrels of pork, 250 tierces of lard and 50,000 pounds of
ribs, made the initial purchase of any of these commodities beyond
the reach of many, and to get that class of investors or speculators

who wanted or would take a risk on a *small amount*, the Bucket Shop was established.

From a few, establishing themselves at first near the great Exchanges and Boards of Trade, others followed in city and town until the number had grown to approximately 25,000 before the strong arm of the law was evoked for their destruction.

The term "Bucket Shop" originated in Chicago, according to historical data furnished by members of the Board of Trade. Occasionally when trade was dull some member would call out, "I'll send down to the shop and get a bucket full,"[9] meaning, in a spirit of levity, that he would patronize one of these "Shops" for a "bucket full of Trade," and thus stimulate the market. Designating such places as "Shops" and patronizing them by the "bucket," led to the expression, "Bucket Shop." The name still remains, and has reference to those establishments where *small amounts* can be dealt in as represented by trades in Stocks, Grain, Cotton, etc., in contradistinction to those made on an organized Exchange.

It is argued by members of the Exchange that legitimate transactions in any commodity maintain and stimulate prices for that commodity, whether the transactions apply to deals in the actual article or for future delivery, they being based on the judgment and practical experience of the best business men; while, on the other hand, where *wagers* are posted as to a rise or fall in the price of any article, no amount of reasoning can substantiate the claim that any benefit can accrue to the price of the article so dealt in.

To deal in an article—real estate, live stock or any kind of investment, contributes to the stability of prices; but to *bet* the prices will be up or down tomorrow, next day, or some other time in the future, adds nothing in support of valuation.

Contracts bought or sold on a Cotton Exchange for *speculative* purposes solely, are identical in character to those handled through a Bucket Shop.

Where such Contracts are entered into without the purpose of Hedging, or without the purpose of receiving or delivering cotton on them; where they are bought or sold with the intention of making or losing as the Market responds to their wishes or against them; where they enter a field of investment of this kind knowing that an equal chance exists for their losing or winning; where money is placed on a Contract with an expectation to win, cognizant of the fact that a loss may follow, and with no other considerations contemplated, such transactions are nothing more nor less than gambling, and just as reprehensible as any ever executed in a Bucket Shop.

———

[9]"Grain Trade Talks," No. 4, p. 2, Ware & Leland, Chicago.

It has been argued that an excessive demand for the purchase of Futures stimulates the price of Spots, while a weak demand reflects against them. If this stimulation is caused by speculative investments and no other, or the absence of such investments causes declines, then, logically, the inference is that the price for actual cotton is governed by gambling transactions when dominant in the Trade[10], and on this point, State and National legislation has been invited to outlaw Bucket Shops, and the *gambling* features practiced on the Cotton Exchanges.

Bucket Shops have been legally destroyed in most every State in the Union, and their nefarious effects on legitimate trade no longer exist, but National laws to control or destroy the baneful practices of illegitimate trading on the Cotton Exchanges are still subjects of Federal consideration and investigation.

COTTON TIPS.

Members of the Exchanges and large Dealers who are in close touch with the Market often give out information to their customers, and many times to Dealers generally, purported to safeguard the parties advised, in preventing their going into the Market to buy or sell Futures or Spots.

This advice may be wholesome and beneficial to the receiver, or an ulterior motive may be concealed in the message.

If a Broker or Dealer desires to help a friend by transmitting to him a knowledge of the advantages to be gained by a contemplated advance in the Market under some co-operative manipulation soon to be executed, the friend receives the benefit of the advance by going into the Market and buying either Spots or Futures, and selling when advised by another "tip," "to get out of the Market," "unload," etc.

Usually the recipient of a message to "buy cotton" or "go short," is left to his own interpretation of it as to whether he shall or shall not, if not a personal warm friend of the adviser.

Operators desiring the Market to advance may send large numbers of telegrams and letters of advice to Dealers and Growers, urging a withholding of their cotton from the Market as an inducement for a better price to ultimately follow (as a logical sequence to the advice offered), or advise diametrically opposite to this, by gratuitously urging the sale of cotton, to avoid the loss that will result from a contemplated decline, which, from the character of the action advised, will be sure to follow.

In addition to private wires, and a cover of the mail, the columns

---

[10]See "Speculation," Book III. pp. 316-328.

of the press are often invaded with data to influence the public to buy or sell cotton, or to urge Spot holders to cling to their cotton or sell it. Cotton tips are not always sure guides to success.

"BORROWING COTTON."

Large Dealers will sometimes take cotton from smaller ones under peculiar conditions of purchase, more particularly when the Market is depressed or declining.

For instance: Evans & Taylor, who buy cotton from the Growers at primary points, have accumulated, say 300 B/C, and the Market has declined since their purchase. They want to hold this cotton longer, but wishing to avoid the expense of carrying it or not be subjected to any loss by reason of "country damage" or further decline that may occur, find a way of sale as follows: A large Dealer will offer to take their cotton, say in November, at a certain number of Points off of New York March, and pay within $5, $8 or $10 of the value of a bale at the price of cotton at that time, as an advance payment on the cotton, and carry this cotton at his own expense until a certain day in March, April or May, at which date Evans & Taylor can make settlement with him. If the Market has advanced at time of settlement, Evans & Taylor will be allowed the profit; if it is lower, they will not be subjected to any loss because they were guaranteed against any loss by the large Dealer.

The resemblance to "borrowing" the cotton appears in this way: Let it be stated the large Dealer has sold a large quantity of cotton "short," and finding difficulty in getting the cotton in a way that would prove profitable in filling his commitments, guarantees the small Dealer against any subsequent decline up to the time of settlement, and if any profit accrues, the small Dealer gets it.

These advantages are offered to the small Dealer to induce him to surrender the cotton into the hands of the large one. In this way the large Dealer is enabled to fulfill his contract, and perhaps secure the right to handle the cotton without payment of full value for it at the time of its receipt; or probably no payment on it at all until final sale, if the large Dealer has a reputable character and is financially strong, and the small Dealer does not need the money.

This plan of selling is creditable to the small Dealer, as he has "all to gain and nothing to lose," but it is not often practiced, and when it is resorted to, it is usually under *confidential* terms. The large Dealer hedges his side of the transaction.

STANDARD NEW YORK EXCHANGE AS AMENDED.

At a meeting held by the New York Cotton Exchange in the latter part of the year 1913, resolutions were passed adopting the U. S. Government Standards for classing Texas and Gulf Cotton, and making Standards of Upland Cotton to match the Government Standards for Texas and Gulf Cottons, unless the Agricultural Department in the meantime should standardize Uplands.

The Exchange expressed a preference for the Liverpool Standards, which was practically agreed upon in the summer previous at a conference held in Europe between American Cotton Exchanges, European Cotton Exchanges and European Spinners, but finally adopted the U. S. Standards, as above stated.

From its Official List it eliminated Fair, Strict Middling Fair, Good Ordinary White, and Low Middling Tinged. These changes in Standards and elimination of Grades went into effect November, 1914, when Monthly Revisions were established, instead of revisions three times a year, as previously.

It made the Tare on square bales 25 pounds, to conform to a recent revision of European Tare from 6 per cent to 5 per cent.[11]

LIVERPOOL DUE "UP" OR "DOWN."

One often hears among the talent, the expression that, "Liverpool is due to come in 3 points up tomorrow," or "Liverpool is due to come in 5 points down on tomorrow's opening," or similar expressions, indicating that something exists by or from which a reckoning may be made to forecast the "opening Market" for Liverpool on the following day.

In determining this matter the Future Markets of both New York and Liverpool are compared and brought into the calculation to ascertain what is due, up or down, by utilizing the difference in parity relationship.

Let us assume say Jan. 19, 1914, that March-April Liverpool *closed* at 6.90 (Pence), equalling 13.80 (Cents) in New York.

The Liverpool close at 4 o'clock p. m. equals 11 o'clock a. m. New York time. March, New York, say at 11 o'clock is 12.69, the difference then at the moment for the two Markets is 1.11 American Points, that is to say, Liverpool and New York are running within 1.11 Points of each other on the Market Option.

---

[11]From a letter to the author from Mr. Geo. W. Neville, ex-President New York Cotton Exchange. Since the above resolutions were passed, the N. Y. Cotton Exchange has adopted the U. S. Standard types, effective April 1, 1915. Letters to the author from Mr. Wm. V. King, Supt. N. Y. Cot. Ex.

Let us say that New York closes at 12.65, or 4 Points down from the 11 o'clock quotation. Adding 1.11 Points to the American close gives 13.76 as a parity value between New York and Liverpool, which, reduced to Pence, equals 6.88 as the figure at which Liverpool March-April will open on the morning of Jan. 20th.

The closing on the 19th being 6.90 as compared to a calculated opening of 6.88 on the 20th, shows a difference of 2 Points that Liverpool is due to come in *down*. Reasoning on the same line, were New York to close higher, then Liverpool would be due to come in *up*.

Contingencies that may cause the American or Foreign Markets to vary widely at times, have their reflections against relative or parity values, and Liverpool may, and sometimes does, come in *up*, when due to come in *down*, or vice versa.

The calculations for the opening in Liverpool may be figured with accuracy, but the behavior of the Market can upset the indicated opening.

AVERAGE MONTHLY OCEAN FREIGHT RATES ON COTTON PER 100 POUNDS, AS QUOTED BY STEAMSHIP AGENTS.

(The averages are computed from weekly quotations; the quotations themselves represent merely what rates were asked by transportation men.)

From Report, Department of Agriculture, Washington, D. C.

Route and Year.		Dec.
To Liverpool From:		
Galveston—		
1912		
1913		
New Orleans—		
1912		
1913		
Savannah—		
1912		
1913		
New York—		
1912		
1913		
To Bremen From:		
Galveston—		
1912		42.5
1913		54.0
New Orleans—		57.0
1912		61.5
1913		
To Havre From:		
Galveston—		
1912	47.0	65.2
1913	51.9	50.0
New Orleans—		
1912	56.5	55.0
1913	47.9	62.0
New York—		
1912	42.0	
1913	49.0	
Savannah—		
1912	42.5	
1913	47.0	
To Barcelona From:		
Galveston—		
1913	43.8	45.0
New Orleans—		
1912		
1913		
New York —		80.0

REVISION COMMITTEE.

Quotations made by both the N. O. and N. Y. Cotton Exchanges are for M. cotton, with additions and deductions for the Higher and Lower relative Grades. To establish the values of these relative Grades, falls within the province of the Revision Committee, which for New York consists of seventeen members, ten of whom shall constitute a quorum. This Committee meets on the second Wednesday of September, the third Wednesday of November, and the first Wednesday of February, "to consider the state of the Market, also suggestions and opinions that may be presented by members, * * * and shall establish the differences in values of all grades, on or off, as related to Middling cotton, which shall constitute the rates at which grades other than Middling may be delivered on contract."[12]

The offices and functions of the Revision Committee of the N. O. Cotton Exchange are very similar to those of New York. The N. O. Committee is composed of the Committee on Spot Quotations and the Appeal Committee on Classification acting jointly. Three members of the former and four of the latter Committee constitute a quorum, "whose duty it shall be to furnish, as hereinafter provided, quotations of all grades of cotton enumerated in the rules of the Exchange."

This Committee meets "monthly, at 11 a. m., on the second Wednesday of each month," and shall also meet at any time when called to do so by a "request signed by fifteen (15) members of the Exchange."[13]

The quotations for the different Grades are based on the Standards of their respective Markets.

The fact that the Revision Committees of the two Exchanges have had delegated to them the authority to establish relative values for the different Grades has been the cause of much censure and criticism, followed with subsequent legislative and Congressional investigations, such being instituted to ascertain the facts existing and to deprive the Committees of the right to establish values for the Higher and Lower Grades, except under certain restrictions that might be allowed, either by law or by the modification of their own Exchange Rules.

It is conceded that some factor or agency should make the relative Grade values. Whether based on the average price for

---

[12]Charter, By-Laws, and Rules N. Y. Cotton Exchange, p. 22, Edition 1910. Since New York has adopted U. S. Government Standards, revisions will probably be made monthly hereafter as in New Orleans.

[13]Amended By-Laws New Orleans Cotton Exchange, Nov. 4, 1912, p. 23, Edition 1909.

such Grades in a number of Southern Markets, on spinnable values, or both, the result of such action should merit no censure, if the valuations are fair and equitable to all interests concerned, which is a desideratum sought.

"On each business day the Committee shall establish and announce the difference between grades in the manner and under the conditions described in the United States Cotton Futures Act, Section 6, and in compliance with such rules and regulations as the Secretary of Agriculture may from time to time promulgate."—Part Amendment No. 76, N. Y. Revis. Com., stating how often the Revision Committee shall meet to establish Differences.

WAREHOUSES.

Connected with every cotton manufacturing concern of any magnitude, is found a Warehouse of a greater or less capacity, as a factor necessary for the protection of the raw material purchased.

Many large Commission Houses, Exporters and Importers, both in America and foreign countries, provide suitable warehouse facilities, deeming them necessary adjuncts for properly caring for and protecting the cotton bought, sold, or committed to them for handling.

Warehouses serve a good purpose, namely: To protect cotton from the destructive influences of the weather, to prevent the occurrence of fire, offer better facilities for sale, and as places for concentration.

They are usually of one story, in America, ranging in style from a light frame structure, covered with corrugated sheet iron, to heavy brick, cement or rock walls.

The South contains a large number of lightly constructed warehouses of the first mentioned class, found at many primary points in all the Southern States.

At all the Southern Ports, and connected with Southern and Eastern Mills, brick Warehouses are universally in evidence.

The Mills, as a rule, own Warehouses, but in some exceptional cases, independent Warehouses in proximity to the Mills care for the Mills' cotton.

The cotton Warehouses of Manchester and Liverpool, England, are usually built of brick or stone, and often rise to the height of six and seven stories, the cotton being hoisted or lowered by means of properly constructed block and tackle, operated by steam, gasoline or electric motors.

Outside of Warehouses under the direct ownership of the Mills, private parties are the possessors of many in Liverpool, also many are owned by the Liverpool Dock Board, a Government institution.

All Warehouses formerly built in Bremen rose to the height of one story only, while some of those of latter day construction are built of brick, 4 floors; the foundations made of cement; the floors of double wood, separated by asbestos, and the double roofs of concrete.

The Warehouses have separate apartments divided by fire-proof walls.   The pillars supporting the superstructures are of reinforced concrete, covered with brick.

Such structures, often spoken of as "Cotton Safes," are practically, if not absolutely, fire-proof.   Should fire occur within their walls, combustion would be prevented when the doors were closed, as no air could enter to aid it, for the roofs, like the walls, cut off the entrance of air.

At the front of the new Warehouses, sprinklers are attached, ready in any emergency to do duty in not only protecting the cotton inside, but as a provision against the spread of fire to any adjacent buildings.

The Warehouses at Havre are of one-story construction, strongly built, usually of brick, with suitable division walls of fireproof material, equipped with such apparatus for fire protection as local conditions demand.   The occurrence of fire in the Warehouses at Havre is very rare.

WAREHOUSE CAPACITY.

LIVERPOOL.—The capacity for maximum storage in Liverpool Warehouses reaches a total of 1,800,000 bales, principally handled by the Liverpool Salvage Association, who have 500 Warehouses and sheds certified by it for cotton storage.

Ninety-five per cent of the Warehouses are more than a quarter of a century old.

MANCHESTER.—While cotton represents only a fraction of the storage capacity of the Manchester Warehouses, she can, through the Manchester Ship Canal Co., protect 125,000 to 150,000 bales.

BREMEN.—There are a number of old-style, one-story Warehouses at Bremen of an average capacity of 3,000 bales each, while the new buildings protect about 15,000 bales.

HAVRE.—The author has no data on the Warehouse facilities of this important port.

WAREHOUSE CHARGES.

LIVERPOOL.—One penny (2c) per bale per week, as a rental or storage charge.   Insurance varies, a cheaper rate being extended as the time lengthens; that is, a rate applying for one month would be proportionately less were the Insurance extended to six or twelve months.   It is usually based on the $100 valuation.

MANCHESTER.—The rate is 1 1-2c per bale per week, with Insurance about the same as Liverpool.

HAVRE.—Storage is 1 Franc per month for 1000 Kilos, equal to 19.3 cents for 4535 lbs., or about 20c for 9 bales per month, slightly more than 2c a bale a month, which it will be noted is much cheaper than Liverpool or Manchester.

The rate of Insurance is $2 per $1000 valuation.[14]

The reader's attention is drawn to the fact that all Mills and Buyers of cotton in large quantities, at exporting points, carefully pro-

APPENDIX

tect their purchases, by shelter under the Warehouse, and no matter when, where or at what time a Mill purchase is made, the item for Warehouse storage must be considered, and charged against the price made to the Grower, and he should know that if his cotton is not warehoused at home, he pays the price to have some one else warehouse it for him.

MUTUAL ALLOWANCES.

By arrangement between Buyer and Seller, tariff exactions are sometimes modified by conceding to each other certain allowances to be deducted from or added to the Invoice Weights. The Invoice Weight is not only guaranteed, but should any gain accrue, the Seller is accorded that amount as a credit on the shipment, whereas, if any loss is found, the Buyer is reimbursed.

Such "allowances" are termed "mutual." In their application the 1 per cent Franchise may be recognized or disregarded, or recognized as covering the weights only, as the terms of the contract may prescribe.

To prevent the origination of foreign Claims on export shipments many Exporters enter into arrangements with their foreign correspondents or Buyers of cotton, stipulating the terms of delivery respecting the Tare on shipments as set out in Mutual or Friendly Allowances.

FRIENDLY ALLOWANCES.

Not infrequently in the early part of the season indefinite quantities of cotton reach the foreign Buyer through the medium of "Friendly Allowances," which in its literal interpretation means allowances agreed upon as mutually satisfactory.

This custom is evident at a time when Spinners are short of raw material and offer no exactions as to Tare, but rather than be thrown to any delay in getting the cotton they offer to accept a certain allowance and make no test for Tare.

The foreign representative of the Shipper willingly accepts the proposition as the latitude is allowed for securing gains by escaping the direct application of the 6%, or any rate Tare in such mutual agreements. The Spinner knows that he must concede something to allow the free moevment of the cotton to his mill, therefore proposes to accept a certain allowance for Tare at something less than the 6% Rate.

Friendly Allowances should not be confused with Mutual Allowances.

[14]The data respecting Warehouses were obtained in May, 1912, from Mr. Geo. W. Neville, New York; Mr. J. I. Briggs, Liverpool; Mr. C Albrecht, of Albrecht, Weld & Co., Bremen; and Mr. Etienne Dennis, Havre, through Mr. Neville

AMENDMENTS TO THE UNITED STATES COTTON FUTURES ACT.

As re-enacted August 11, 1916, the following most important changes have been made.

"In the seventh subdivision of Sec. 5, authority is conferred upon the Secretary of Agriculture, in case of disputes referred to him, to include in his findings a complete classification of the cotton for the purposes of delivery on future contracts. Under the act of August 18, 1914, his findings were confined to the specific question of grade, quality, or length of the staple in dispute. For example, if the dispute involved grade only and the cotton was found to be less than seven-eighths of an inch in length of staple, the Secretary had no authority to include in his findings a statement as to length of staple.

"A new section, known as section 6A, is inserted, which provides an optional contract under which parties may, without being subject to tax, agree that, under certain specified conditions, the buyer may demand delivery of the basis grade named in the contract."*

The amendment of the law by enacting Sec. 6A clause, seems to have given satisfaction to both members of the Cotton Exchanges and the Trade.

The list of Official Cotton Standard has been broadened to include Tinges, Stains and Blues.

The entire official list as made and adopted, is:

Middling Fair	Strict Low Middling
Strict Good Middling	Low Middling
Strict Middling	Strict Good Ordinary
Good Middling	Good Ordinary
Middling	

Yellow Good Middling Tinged
Yellow Strict Middling Tinged
Yellow Middling Tinged
Yellow Strict Low Middling Tinged
Yellow Low Middling Tinged
Yellow Good Middling Stained
Yellow Strict Middling Stained
Yellow Middling Stained
Blue Good Middling Stained
Blue Strict Middling Stained
Blue Middling Stained

This list is known as the "Official Cotton Standards of the United States," and can be purchased directly from the Secretary of Agriculture, Washington, D. C. Those who desire to purchase should request application blanks from Mr. Charles J. Brand, Chief, Office of Markets and Rural Organization, Washington, D. C., upon which blanks, application should be made for the whole list of Official Grades, for the list of white cotton or for one or more boxes of any Grade.

*Service and Regulatory Announcements, U. S Dept. of Ag., No. 10, Sept. 1, 1916.

The list of white cottons cost $20; the list of colored cottons, $25, and any one box samples, $2.50 each, in Washington. The charges for transportation are additional.

Those possessing a set of the old Standard types, may box and express them to Washington, charges collect, and receive a credit allowance of $5.00 for them as part payment for a set of revised types.

The following Cotton Exchanges and Cotton Associations have adopted the Official Cotton Standards, on which they base their daily quotations:

New York Cotton Exchange
New Orleans Cotton Exchange
Montgomery Cotton Exchange
Selma Cotton Exchange
Little Rock Board of Trade
Mobile Cotton Exchange
Augusta Cotton Exchange
Savannah Cotton Exchange
St. Louis Cotton Exchange
Vicksburg Cotton Exchange
Charleston Cotton Exchange
Memphis Cotton Exchange
Norfolk & Portsmouth Cotton Exchange, Norfolk
Galveston Cotton Exchange
Waco Cotton Exchange
Houston Cotton Exchange

Dallas Cotton Exchange
Paris Cotton Exchange
San Antonio Cotton Exchange
Ft. Worth Grain & Cotton Exchange
New England Cotton Buyers' Association, Boston
Fall River Cotton Buyers' Association
Oklahoma State Cotton Exchange, Oklahoma City
Cotton Manufacturers' Association of South Carolina
Texas Cotton Buyers' Association, Waco
Cotton Manufacturers' Association of North Carolina

"In addition, most of the largest cotton mills, factories, etc., are using the Official Cotton Standards in the conduct of their business," evidencing the fact that the Government's efforts to put out standard types of cotton acceptable to the Trade is meeting with success.

Under the Cotton Futures Act, the Secretary of Agriculture being the referee in disputes arising over Grade, Staple or Quality of Cotton delivered on Contracts, has established certain Rules and Regulations governing his actions in matters of controversy, and in defining what shall not be delivered on Contracts, specifies the following:

GIN-CUT COTTON.

Gin-cut cotton is cotton that shows damage in ginning, through cutting of the saws, to an extent that reduces its value more than two grades, said grades being of the official cotton standards of the United States.

Gin cutting of a less extent than that mentioned above which reduces the cotton below the value of Good Ordinary would render the cotton untenderable though the extent of injury were less than that described, as the fifth subdivision of section 5 states specifically that cotton the value of which is reduced below that of Good Ordinary shall not be delivered on, under, or in settlement of a contract.

REGINNED COTTON.

Reginned cotton is such as has passed through the ginning process more than once; also such cotton as, after having been ginned, is subjected to a cleaning process and then baled.

REPACKED COTTON.

Repacked cotton will be deemed to mean factors', brokers', and all other samples; also "loose" or miscellaneous lots collected together and rebaled.

FALSE PACKED COTTON.

Cotton bales will be deemed false packed whenever containing substances entirely foreign to cotton, or containing damaged cotton in the interior with or without any indication of such damage upon the exterior; also when plated (that is, composed of good cotton upon the exterior and decidedly inferior cotton in the interior) in a manner not to be detected by customary examination; also when containing pickings or linters worked into them.

MIXED PACKED COTTON.

Mixed packed cotton shall be deemed to mean such bales as show a difference of more than two grades between samples drawn from the heads, top, and bottom sides of the bale, or when such samples show a difference in color exceeding two grades in value, said grades being of the official cotton standards of the United States.

WATER PACKED COTTON.

Water packed cotton shall be deemed to mean such bales as have been penetrated by water during the bailing process, causing damage to the fiber, or bales that through exposure to the weather or by other means, while apparently dry on the exterior, have been damaged by water in the interior.

COTTON OF PERISHED STAPLE.

Cotton of perished staple is such as has had the strength of fiber as ordinarily found in cotton destroyed or unduly reduced through exposure, either to the weather before picking or after baling, or to heating by fire, or on account of water packing, or through other causes.

COTTON OF IMMATURE STAPLE.

Cotton of immature staple is such as has been picked and baled before the fiber has reached a normal state of maturity, resulting in

COTTON OF SEVEN-EIGHTHS INCH STAPLE.

After investigation it is likely that a standard for cotton seven-eighths of an inch in length of staple will be issued. In the meantime, the examiners authorized to hear disputes will pull the cotton so that the ends will be squared off fairly well without unduly reducing the bulk of the drawn sample. When the measure is applied a fair quantity of the cotton must remain in order to show that the sample has not been pulled too fine before measuring. When thus pulled and measured as cotton experts are accustomed to do its fair average length shall be not less than seven-eighths of an inch, in order that the cotton be tenderable under a contract made in compliance with section 5 of the act.

BIBLIOGRAPHY.

Helpful sources from which material information has been drawn were found in the following books, bulletins, reports:

AGRICULTURAL DEPARTMENT:
    Census Bulletins
    Consular Reports
    Crop Reporters
    Reports of the Commissioner of Corporations and Cotton Exchanges
    Yearbooks.

"BOOK OF THE UNITED STATES." Edition 1838.

BROOKS: "The Story of Cotton."

COTTON EXCHANGES:
    Constitution and By-Laws of
        Bremen
        New Orleans
        New York

    Rules of
        Galveston
        Little Rock
        Memphis
        Savannah

DISPENSATORY, UNITED STATES: Edition 1890.

"ENCYCLOPEDIA BRITANNICA."

MAURY: Geographies.

MILLS:
    Dallas Cotton Mills, Dallas, Texas.
    Eagle & Phoenix Cotton Mills, Columbus, Georgia.
    Pacific Mills, Lawrence, Massachusetts.

PEREIRA: "Materia Medica," Edition 1854

PRESCOTT: "American Encyclopedia."

WATKINS· "King Cotton."
Scientific American Supplement.

The Author is indebted to the following gentlemen for their valuable assistance in compiling this work and desires to express to them his profound thanks for this service:

CRESPI & CO., Milan, Italy, and Waco, Texas. Cotton Buyers and Exporters.

DODSON, GEORGE B. & CO., Galveston, Texas, Ocean Freight Brokers and Freight Contractors for Export Cotton.

EIERMANN & LUCUS, Hamburg, Germany Publishers.

GORDON, W. W. & CO., Savannah, Georgia Mill Buyers and Exporters of Sea Island Cotton.

GUENTER, ANTON, Bremen, Germany. Cotton Controller and Adjuster.

HESTER, HENRY G., Sec. New Orleans Cotton Exchange.

LOEB, HERMANN, Shreveport, Louisiana. Cotton Buyer and Exporter

MAYFIELD, E. B, Austin, Texas Railroad Commissioner.

NEAL, W. J., Waco, Texas, Agent Geo H. McFadden & Bros. Agency.

NEVILLE, GEO. W., New York. President N. Y. Cotton Exchange, Mill Buyer and Exporter.

PARKER, LEWIS W., Greenville, S. C., Ex-President American Cotton Manufacturers' Association.

TREZEVANT & COCHRAN, Gen. Ins. Agts., Dallas, Texas

WOODBURY, C. J. H., Boston Massachusetts. Sec National Association of Cotton Manufacturers.

INDEX.

Lightning Source UK Ltd.
Milton Keynes UK
UKHW02f2054230818
327721UK00010B/570/P